Contents

	Acknowledgements	5
	Author's Note	6
	List of Abbreviations	7
	Foreword by Nigel West	10
	Preface	13
	Prologue	17
Chapter 1	By Interceptions Which They Know Not Of	20
Chapter 2	Treachery, the Practice of Fools	23
Chapter 3	Double Cross	32
Chapter 4	A Most Unlikely Enemy Agent	36
Chapter 5	Mission Impossible	43
Chapter 6	Escape	54
Chapter 7	The Radio Oranje Episode	70
Chapter 8	Who Was 'Doctor Schneider'?	74
Chapter 9	'Playing With the Souls of Innocent Men'	90
Chapter 10	Mulder's Story	94
Chapter 11	Mulder's Later Activities	100
Chapter 12	The Further Adventures of Mulder	105
Chapter 13	The Case of Mulder and de Langen	111
Chapter 14	Mulder's Future	117
Chapter 15	'As Sordid a Tale as Any We Have Had'	123
Chapter 16	The Trial, Day One	131

Chapter 17	The Trial, Day Two	139
Chapter 18	The Trial, Day Three	158
Chapter 19	The End of the Affair?	162
Chapter 20	Judgement Day	167
Chapter 21	The Death of a Spy	172
Chapter 22	Fall-out and the Media	179
Chapter 23	'The Kent Spies', 1940	186
Chapter 24	'The Kent Spies' on Trial	192
Chapter 25	The Self-Confessed Agent	207
Chapter 26	Three Men in a Boat	220
Chapter 27	'The Greatest Living Expert on Security'	226
	Postscript	234
Appendix 1	Directory of Key Personnel Mentioned in Official Documents	249
Appendix 2	The Role of the Intelligence Services	255
Appendix 3	Dronkers' Instructions on How to Use Secret Ink	260
Appendix 4	Abwehr Structure: *Ast* Hamburg Spring 1939	263
Appendix 5	German Ranks Mentioned in the Text	265
Appendix 6	Definitions of a Spy	266
Appendix 7	Inventory from Joppe and Dronkers' Personal Possessions	268
Appendix 8	Mulder's Organisation	273
Appendix 9	Intelligence Obtained from Mulder	276
Appendix 10	Genealogies of Seignette and Dronkers Families	279
	Bibliography	281
	Notes	284
	Index	307

Acknowledgements

The author would like to express his thanks to all those who have provided information or assistance. I am especially indebted to intelligence historian Nigel West for his support and encouragement, and for having faith in me in agreeing to write the Foreword. Also, a special thank you to Clare Owen, my editor at Amberley, for showing an interest in my proposal after I was shortlisted for their History Prize, and guiding me through the publication process as well as Aaron Meek and Louis Archard for taking over the project. I would also like to thank Peter Miebies in the Netherlands, second cousin of de Langen, whose blog I stumbled upon by chance and who steered me through the minefield of genealogy and became a sort of unofficial personal researcher for all things Dutch. Thanks also to Alan 'Fred' Judge, senior researcher, and Joyce Hutton, archivist/assistant curator of the Intelligence Corps Museum, Chicksands, for allowing me to include information on 123 Field Security Section and Major Reginald de Vries. Alice Orton, of I.B. Tauris for permission to quote from *The Secret World*. All those in the Harwich region: Aileen Farnell of the Harwich Society; Ray Plummer, honorary archivist, and Anne Kemp-Luck, honorary assistant archivist, Guildhall, Harwich; Bryans Knights, former Harwich river pilot and nephew of the late Clifford Cannon; Gavin Bleakley, Peter Goodwin, and Julian Foynes for their photographic contributions and assistance in tracking down the location of *Fairhaven*. My erstwhile friend Dr Peter Magirr for his invaluable help in decyphering a redacted secret ink recipe; David B. Harris, barrister and former Canadian intelligence officer; William Fischetti, Assistant Director of the State Historical Society of Missouri; and the staff of the National Archives at Kew. Finally, my wife, Evelyn, for her initial edit of the manuscript, and our two cats, Wilfred and Sprinkles, for trying to sabotage the whole thing by walking over the keyboard and wrecking my typing.

Author's Note

Unless otherwise specified in the Notes, all quotes and extracts have been taken from files in the National Archives at Kew (TNA). When quoting from these files some minor formatting changes have occasionally been made to ensure the text flows better; otherwise, no changes have been made to the original punctuation or spelling. In these files many MI5 documents use the term 'German S.S'. In this context it is generally meant as a generic name for the German Secret Service rather than *Schutzstaffel*, the Nazi Party's security service. Likewise, the terms 'MI6' and 'SIS' are used interchangeably to mean the overseas branch of the British Intelligence Service.

The author and publisher would like to thank the following for permission to use copyright material in this book:

All files in the National Archives are © Crown Copyright and are reproduced with permission under the terms of the Open Government Licence.

Quotes from *Hansard* contain Parliamentary information licensed under the Open Parliament Licence v3.0.

Foreword © Nigel West 2015

Extracts from *The Secret World. Behind the Curtain of British Intelligence in World War Two and the Cold War* reproduced with the permission of the publisher, I.B. Tauris: © Edward Harrison and © the Literary Estate of Lord Dacre of Glanton (Hugh Trevor-Roper).

The Intelligence Corps Museum, Chicksands, for allowing me to include (unpublished) information on 123 Field Security Section and Major Reginald de Vries.

Every attempt has been made to seek permission for copyright material used in this book. However, if we have inadvertently used copyright material without permission/acknowledgements we apologise and we will make the necessary correction at the first opportunity.

Every effort has been made to verify the information in this book. Any mistakes are of my own doing and will be rectified in any subsequent editions that are produced.

List of Abbreviations

ADB1	Assistant Director, B1, Espionage (MI5)
ADE	Assistant Director, E Branch (MI5)
AWS	Aliens War Service
B	B Branch, Espionage (MI5)
B1a	Espionage: Special Agents (MI5)
B1b	Espionage, Special Sources section (MI5)
B1c	Sabotage and Espionage, Inventions and Technical (MI5)
B1d	Special Examiners (MI5)
B1e	Latchmere House (Camp 020) (MI5)
B2b	Counter-espionage: Agents (MI5)
B3d	Communications: Liaison with Censorship (MI5)
B4	Espionage: Country Section (MI5)
BAOR	British Army of the Rhine (post-Second World War)
BNV	Bureau Nationale Veiligheid or Office of National Security (post-war Dutch intelligence service)
C4a	Security Branch (MI5), post-war
CIA	Central Intelligence Agency
CID	Centrale Inlichten Dienst (Second World War Dutch intelligence service)
CSDIC	Combined Services Detailed Interrogation Centre (also known as the London Cage); (*q.v.* MI19)
CSS	Chief, Secret Intelligence Service
CX	Reports prepared by MI6 (SIS)
D4	Security and Travel Control: Officer in charge, Security Control at Sea and Air Ports (MI5)
DAD	Duty Assistant Director, Press Censorship
DB	Director, B Branch (MI5)
DDG	Deputy Director-General (MI5)
DG	Director-General (MI5)
DMI	Director (or Directorate) of Military Intelligence

DNI	Director (or Directorate) of Naval Intelligence
DPP	Director of Public Prosecutions
DPW	Directorate of Prisoners of War; also Director of Political Warfare
E1b	Alien Control: Seamen (MI5)
FBI	Federal Bureau of Investigation
FOIC	Flag Officer-in-Charge (Royal Navy)
FSS	Field Security Section, Intelligence Corps
GC&CS	Government Code & Cypher School
GHQ	General Headquarters
HD(S)E	Home Defence (Security) Executive
HPSS	Home Port Security Section, Intelligence Corps
IB or I(B)	MI5 Security Branch; also General Post Office Investigation Branch
IRB	Inter-services Research Bureau (cover name for SOE)
ISK	Intelligence Service Knox/Intelligence Section Knox/Illicit Services Knox
ISOS	Intelligence Service Oliver Strachey/Illicit Services Oliver Strachey
ISSB	Inter-Services Security Board
KMar	Koninklijke Marechaussee, or Royal Military Constabulary in the Netherlands.
KNSM	Koninklijke Nederlandsche Stoomboot Maatschappij (Royal Netherlands Steamship Company)
LRC	London Reception Centre (*q.v.* Royal Victoria Patriotic School)
MI5	British Security Service
MI6	British Secret Service (*q.v.* SIS)
MI8c	Communications branch of the War Office (*q.v.* RSS, Radio Security Service)
MI19	Directorate of Military Intelligence (War Office): branch responsible for obtaining information from Prisoners of War (*q.v.* Combined Services Detailed Interrogation Centre (CSDIC))
MOK	Naval Chief Command Baltic, Kreigsmarine (German Navy)
MTB	Motor Torpedo Boat
NID	Naval Intelligence Division, Royal Navy
NSB	National Socialist Movement (Netherlands); Dutch Nazi Party
OC	Officer Commanding
OKM	Oberkommando de Marine (German Naval High Command)
OKW	Oberkommando der Wehrmacht (German Army High Command)
PCO	Passport Control Office
PTT	Dutch Post & Telegraph Service
PWR	Police War Reserve
RHSA	Reichssicherheitshauptampt (Reich Main Security Office)

RN	Royal Navy
RNR	Royal Navy Reserve
RNVR	Royal Navy Volunteer Reserve
RPS	Royal Patriotic School (*q.v.* RVPS)
RSS	Radio Security Service (*q.v.* MI8c)
RVPS	Royal Victoria Patriotic School (*q.v.* London Reception Centre; RPS)
SCO	Security Control Officer (MI5)
SD	Sicherheitsdienst, the intelligence arm of the SS
SIC	Security Intelligence Centre, Home Defence (Security) Executive
Sipo	Sicherheitspolizei, or Security Police (Germany)
SIS	Secret Intelligence Service (*q.v.* MI6)
SLB	Legal section (MI5)
SMS	Seiner Majestät Schiff (German Kreigsmarine: His Majesty's Ship, First World War)
SOE	Special Operations Executive (*q.v.* Inter-services Research Bureau)
SO (I)	Staff Officer (Intelligence), Royal Navy
SS	Schutzstaffel (Security Service of the Nazi Party); also German Secret Service
W/Board	Wireless Board
WRC1	War Room Registry (MI5). WRC was the Assessments Section; WRC1 dealt with officers and agents of the old Abwehr I and III
WRC5	War Room Registry (MI5) – function unknown
XX	Double-Cross Committee (or Twenty Committee)

Abwehr abbreviations

Abt	Abteilung (Abwehr branch)
Ast	Abwehrstelle (Abwehr station)
Branch I	Espionage
H	Heer (Army)
L	Luft (Air)
M	Marine (Navy)
Wi	Wirtschaft (Economics)
I	Communications
G	False documents, secret inks
Branch II	Sabotage
Branch III	Counter-espionage
KO	Kriegsorganisation (War Organisation), Abwehr in Allied and neutral countries

Foreword

With the passage of more than three-quarters of a century it might be thought that the task of reconstructing wartime espionage missions would present some difficult challenges. How can we imagine what conditions were really like at a time when Great Britain stood virtually alone against the Axis powers, in constant danger of invasion? What sense of insecurity lay in the minds of a population that had witnessed the Nazi blitzkrieg occupy much of western Europe? The Molotov–Ribbentrop Pact of 1939 had ensured that most of the Continent was in the grip of ruthless, totalitarian dictators who were determined to enslave the surviving democracies.

This was the political and economic backdrop to the events that unfolded in 1942 when the Abwehr infiltrated agents into southern England on a variety of missions. Some were sent to check on the credentials and continuing reliability of other, well-established networks; others undertook specific assignments, such as the collection and transmission of meteorological data for the Luftwaffe, or the sabotage of strategically important industrial sites.

Paradoxically, given the length of the intervening period, we now know more about the secret counter-intelligence operations conducted during those hostilities than at any time since, courtesy of MI5's declassification policy instituted by the former Director-General Sir Stephen Lander. A Cambridge history graduate, Lander became convinced that the famed Security Service registry contained a wealth of historically significant material that could be released safely to the Public Record Office at Kew without danger of compromising current operations which, in an era preoccupied by terrorism and political extremism, were often reliant on the support and co-operation not just of Whitehall, but of the general public. Convinced that a degree of transparency, especially in relation to wartime activities in the distant past, would enhance the organisation's reputation and status, Lander embarked on an ambitious programme to open thousands of hitherto secret files to public scrutiny. The impact has been transformational, and we can now learn of the complex manoeuvring that lay concealed behind the investigation of each case of German espionage.

The picture that emerges is multi-dimensional. Signals intelligence, in the form of intercepted enemy communications, often alerted the British authorities to an imminent attempt to infiltrate a spy along a particular route. So, well prepared, the relevant port security personnel, immigration and regional liaison officers would be on the look-out for the tell-tale clues that might betray the unsuspecting culprit. Having been identified, the spy would be skillfully interviewed by well-briefed interrogators who had access to dossiers on the individual's past, their companions on training courses, and even the true names of their Abwehr handlers. Confronted with such overwhelming evidence, and under considerable psychological pressure from specialists at Latchmere House (Camp 020) who knew just how to manipulate their prisoners, even the most recalcitrant inevitably succumbed to their captors. The only question that remained was, having established an advantage over the Abwehr, how should the situation be exploited to maximum effect?

Just one part of the counter-espionage spectrum was disclosed in 1972 when J. C. Masterman eventually received the government's permission to publish a slightly edited version of *The Double Cross System of the War of 1939–1945*, his post-hostilities internal account of MI5's double-agent operations, a copy of which he had retained with MI5's reluctant consent, thereby revealing MI5's role in the recruitment and management of controlled enemy agents, and its participation in Allied strategic deception campaigns. Before its release, Masterman's final manuscript was excised of all clues to the true identities of individual agents, and purged of references to 'Most Secret Sources', Whitehall's euphemism for ISK and ISOS, the cryptographic products that had served to compromise the enemy's activities. The Abwehr's fragmented, decentralised structure, its tendency for micro-management and its reliance on wireless channels supposedly protected by hand or machine cyphers ensured a huge volume of traffic exchanged between headquarters, the military districts in which the various Abstellen were located, the Kriegsorganisations, often in foreign countries, and the lowest-echelon representatives abroad, which provided plenty of work for Allied cryptanalysts. The result was a rich daily harvest of encrypted intercepts which were read, often contemporaneously, by the codebreakers based at Barnet and then Bletchley Park. Their reports, circulated to a strictly limited number of indoctrinated counter-intelligence officers, provided the solid foundations on which investigations could be mounted. The degree to which the Abwehr's future operations were compromised remains one of the greatest triumphs in the history of espionage. Quite literally, British personnel were being briefed on their adversary's structure, personalities, future plans, funding and training. The detail, accumulated sometimes months before an agent embarked on a mission, was truly breathtaking, and more than enough to fill a damning dossier developed for an impending interrogation.

Some spies who emerged from detention at 020, such as TATE and MUTT, were selected for a future directed by the XX Committee and survived the war, while almost a dozen others, including Johannes Dronkers, faced a very different fate. What made him different from other, similar examples of German agents infiltrated into the country masquerading as refugees? Why was he selected for prosecution and, ultimately, execution? Close scrutiny of Dronkers' experience, pieced together by patient research in the original files, and a successful attempt to trace his family in the Netherlands, reveals some uncomfortable aspects to MI5's investigation, and raises the suspicion of high-level political interference. Under pressure to demonstrate to the British public that the authorities were fully committed to confronting the threat of enemy espionage, and efficient in detecting those demonstrating disloyalty to the Allied cause, MI5's management at the very least acquiesced to Cabinet demands for Nazi spies to be led to the scaffold. Dronkers' own, very remarkable story began to emerge in 1981, but it is only now that the whole case can be examined in detail.

Nigel West
www.nigelwest.com

Preface

During the Second World War, MI5, the British Security Service, prided itself on the fact that all foreign agents who arrived in Britain were swiftly captured, many of them 'turned' as double agents, and those who demurred were interned or despatched by the noose. The only agent not captured (Jan Willem Ter Braak, alias Engelbertus Fukken) was found to have committed suicide in 1941 in an air-raid shelter in Cambridge. The exploits of double agents such as SNOW (Arthur Owens), TRICYCLE (Dušan Popov), TATE (Wulf Schmidt), ZIGZAG (Eddie Chapman) and GARBO (Juan Pujol Garcia) are all well known and have been well documented over the past two decades. As more official documents are released, we learn a lot more about the contributions they and others made to the war effort. Although he was not a double agent, Dronkers' story was a strange one which has remained obscure. Indeed, the episode has received very little mention in the intelligence literature of the Second World War, despite key Security Service (MI5) case files being declassified and released into the public domain by the National Archives at Kew in 1999.[1] As intelligence historian Nigel West has written in his Foreword, this programme of releases began in 1997 under the auspices of Sir Stephen Lander, Director-General of MI5 from 1996 to 2002, because he believed that while they are 'necessary to ensure the effectiveness of current work … those records must in due course speak for themselves'.[2]

A bowdlerised version of the Dronkers case was first published in 1953 by former Dutch intelligence officer Lieutenant Colonel Oreste Pinto,[3] whom General Eisenhower once described as 'the greatest living authority on security'.[4] However, not all shared his opinion. Wartime MI5 Director of Counter-espionage Guy Liddell begged to differ, recording in his diary that, according to Superintendent Len Burt who was on secondment to MI5 from Special Branch, Pinto had a 'thoroughly bad record' when he had applied for naturalisation in the UK in 1930.[5] When Pinto wrote his account he would have been constrained by the Official Secrets Acts (1911, 1920 and

1939), and would not, therefore, have had access to all the documents. His version of events verges on self-aggrandisement as he boasts how he, and he alone, cracked the case seemingly without the involvement of the myriad of other MI5 officers or related intelligence organisations. Yet, as we shall see in Chapter 27, the official record repeatedly contradicts Pinto, revealing his account to be implausible in general and inaccurate in certain material specifics.

I first became aware of Dronkers in 1981 when a brief entry about him appeared in the first detailed unofficial history of MI5's early years by intelligence historian Nigel West.[6] That an enemy agent had been captured and taken ashore at my birthplace, Harwich, came as no real surprise. This is, after all, a major port on the east coast of England which had seen action during the Second World War.

Granted its charter in 1238, Harwich has had a long and colourful maritime history, with well-established connections to the Royal Navy and the Dutch. Once called 'a pretty town' by Elizabeth I, having sent three ships to help defeat the Spanish Armada, it was at one time the home of Captain Christopher Jones, master of the *Mayflower*, who had set sail from there prior to leaving Plymouth on his voyage to the New World in 1620. In 1652 a Royal Navy dockyard was established; in 1679 Samuel Pepys was elected Member of Parliament for Harwich, and also served as Secretary to the Admiralty. On 11 November 1688 it became the target of an invasion by William of Orange, but strong winds forced him to land at Torbay instead. During the First World War it was home to the Harwich Force of naval warships and a submarine force under (Sir) Roger Keyes. In 1916, Captain Charles Algernon Fryatt was executed by the Germans having tried to ram a U-boat in 1915 which had attempted to sink his ship, the SS *Brussels*, belonging to the Great Eastern Railway Company, then operating out of Harwich.

During the Second World War, the town had close ties to the Royal Navy, had troops garrisoned there and was in close proximity to the occupied Low Countries. Many Italian prisoners of war were held there at No. 670b Shatesbury Camp and No. 680 Shaftsbury Camp in Dovercourt.[7] Harwich would also feature later in GARBO's stable of notional agents (Agent DORICK was supposedly based there). On 21 November 1939, only a few months after war with Germany had been declared, HMS *Gipsy* was sunk by a magnetic mine in Harwich harbour while heading out on patrol in the North Sea. More recently, it became a victim of a huge flood which hit the east coast of England from the Humber to the Thames estuary, and the Dutch coast on 31 January 1953, causing the deaths of 307 people, and the evacuation of 30,000 others (including the author and his family). It is probably best known for its ferry link between Parkeston Quay and the Hook of Holland.

A slightly longer account of Dronkers' story appeared in 2000 in Lieutenant Colonel Robin 'Tin-Eye' Stephens' declassified history of Camp 020 on Ham Common, London.[8] Stephens was the camp's former commandant. However, the story had merited only brief mention in Guy Liddell's war diaries in the entry for 16 June 1942.[9]

Given the dearth of published information and growing questions about Dronkers, it became necessary to delve into MI5's official files, now available from the National Archives at Kew, most notably including those covering its intelligence aspect and the subsequent trial, as well as other sources. The problem with studying official files is that one always has to bear in mind that they may have been 'weeded' prior to release, and there is evidence that this has in part been the case here.

As I pored over the documents, the process of wartime spy-handling unfolded before me, and I was able to piece together what I believe to be the most complete profile of Dronkers available to date. Still, some uncertainty unavoidably remains, because as we shall see from the record of his once-secret interrogations, not all of the pieces of the puzzle agreed; some of them were contradictory. What at first appeared to be a straightforward open-and-shut spy case, if there is ever such a thing, became increasingly intriguing as the story unfolded. This gave rise to many more questions, some of which still remain unanswered. However, using what is commonly known in information circles as the 'mosaic effect', information missing or redacted in one document can sometimes be found in another seemingly innocuous place, often overlooked by the censor because no connection has been made. By consulting other files about other agents or German intelligence officers which often contained useful fragments of information, I was able to make a few discoveries which I hope may shed more light on this intriguing case and make the jigsaw puzzle a little more complete, although I should point out that some of these discoveries are still far from conclusive.

It was also interesting to read the language of the courtroom during the trial, originally held in camera but now open for all to see. I was struck by the peculiar way in which the court drama unfolded. Was Dronkers really a spy? Was he really guilty of the charges of which he was accused? Did British authorities go too far in this particular case, or were they justified in their actions? In the modern counter-terrorism context, these are questions of the sort that are also being asked today with regard to torture, extraordinary rendition and legislation aimed at the international terror threat. The war years were difficult times, it is true. Desperate measures needed to be introduced to curb the Nazi threat of world domination, but measures enacted by the British authorities then seem as barbaric and, at times, as unjust, as they do today. And what led the Second World War British authorities to want to secure a capital conviction against Dronkers, rather than simply to 'turn' him, as they had done – and would continue to do – with many others? Was there perhaps some sort of political connivance on the part of the government of the day to ensure a conviction? Finally, did the climate of war-torn Britain predetermine Dronkers' fate, and amount to a miscarriage of justice being committed? This book is my attempt to answer at least some of these questions.

I have frequently quoted verbatim from MI5's files and court transcripts so that readers can know exactly what was said, rather than having to speculate broadly about the factual basis of Dronkers' situation. This is important, because, while I have my own opinion about the outcome of the story, it is for readers to make up their own minds.

David Tremain
Ottawa, 2016

Prologue

Early in the morning of 18 May 1942 the auxiliary yacht *Joppe*, a sail-powered yacht with an auxiliary motor, flying the Dutch flag and carrying a crew of three Dutchmen, limped out of the morning mist into view of a Royal Navy convoy in the North Sea just nine miles off the coast of Harwich, Essex. The yacht was boarded by members of His Majesty's Trawler *Corena* and taken into tow to Parkeston Quay, Harwich. Like many similar vessels, the *Corena* was an MS trawler sold to the Admiralty in August 1939 for £9,500.[1] Its only armament was a 12-pounder anti-aircraft gun, although it is assumed that the crew would have been issued with small arms, such as Lee-Enfield .303-calibre rifles, Lanchester 9 mm sub-machine guns or Webley .455-calibre revolvers. The captain was Temporary Lieutenant Clifford Kennard Cannon, RNR, who had joined the pilot service on the River Thames in 1936 or 1937.[2] Cannon and his ship were based at Harwich, a sub-area of Nore Command, as part of Minesweeping and Patrol Group 4 in the Royal Navy's Home Waters Fleet.

The headquarters for the Harwich sub-area was HMS *Badger*, a 'stone frigate' in Hamilton House, a former Georgian Customs house at Parkeston Quay, under the command of Flag Officer-in-Charge (FOIC) Harwich, Rear Admiral Hugh Hext Rogers, MVO, OBE. He had retired in 1935, only to be brought back into service in the Royal Naval Reserve in 1939, first as a Commodore then as a Rear Admiral.[3]

The three Dutch seamen captured by the crew of the *Corena* gave their names as Johannes Marinus Dronkers, Jan Bruno de Langen and John Alphonsus Mulder. Mulder was born in Solo, in the Dutch East Indies (now Java), on 24 September 1915 to Johan Alphonsus Mulder and Lucia Geertruida Jansje Martherus; de Langen was born in The Hague on 21 April 1921 to Bruno Jan de Langen and Marie Margaret van Gorcom. At Harwich the trio was refused permission to land in the United Kingdom by immigration officer Reginald Charles Smith, arrested by the Intelligence Corps and taken first for interrogation at the 123 Field Security Section (FSS) headquarters at

'Fairhaven', a requisitioned Edwardian villa on Marine Parade, Dovercourt.[4] After the initial questioning, they were taken by train to London under escort by police officers from the local constabulary and placed into custody at the London Reception Centre (LRC), also known as the Royal Victoria Patriotic School (RVPS), in Wandsworth. Later they would be transferred to Latchmere House (Camp 020) on Ham Common. The incident was to be yet another episode in the cat-and-mouse game played by MI5 in thwarting efforts by the Abwehr to land enemy agents on the shores of Great Britain.

Unbeknown to Dronkers, MI5 already knew about his imminent arrival, as it was undoubtedly a decrypted message from the Abwehr which led to his discovery. Minutes in his MI5 file from Reginald Gibbs to H. L. A. (Herbert) Hart, and another to Major Ronald Haylor from Hart, both dated 10 May 1942, and another from the Chief Officer, IRB,[5] dated 12 May, refer to 'Karel Van Dongen', the cover name assigned to Dronkers. Not only that, but B4's Registry had a Secret Cross Reference file on 'Karel Van Dongen' dated 8 May 1942.[6] A Minute Sheet dated 10 May 1942 written by Hart[7] of MI5's B1b Espionage, Special Sources section, to Gibbs of B1b marked MOST SECRET states:

> Special sources shew that the Germans are sending and may have already sent a spy to the U.K., probably a Dutchman, certainly a seaman, who is to write letters to a Spanish cover address, and to sign them Karel VAN DONGEN. He may write either in Dutch or English. Nothing else is known.
>
> Can an urgent direction be given to the Censorship (I.B. possibly)* [Post Office Investigating Branch] to look for letters so signed, and directed? What are the chances of their being spotted?[8]

The 'Special Sources' referred to by Herbert Hart was likely this message intercepted by Bletchley Park:

> 8.5.42 7649
> Berlin – Madrid. Ref. Your 946 (ISK 7520). In our 1412/42 Most Secret of 10/4/42 a cover address for an agent of AST KAESEREI[9] who is to be put to work in GOLFPLATZ (ENGLAND) was requested. The agent is a seaman and writes Dutch and English; which language is preferred? The letters will be signed KAREL VAN DONGEN. Please give address immediately, as start is to take place in the next few days.[10]

A report prepared by MI5 and given to Arthur Thurston, the FBI's first Legal Attaché ('Legat') at the US Embassy in London, on 11 March 1943 would confirm that:

> ... the alias given to him by the Germans for signing his secret writing letters, shewed him to be identical with an agent of Ast The Hague, whose arrival had been forecast by information from Special Source.[11]

On the same day as Hart's message to Gibbs (10 May), a similar note from Hart to Major Haylor of B1d[12] added,

> It is not known from where this man will be coming, or if he will come as a seaman or escapee. He probably may not use the name given except for writing his letters.[13]

A further message from Alan Grogan of MI5's B3d, Liaison with Censorship, to the Chief Officer, IRB stated,

> With reference to my conversation with Miss Macdonald I write to confirm that we have information that a foreign seaman, certainly a Dutchman, is employed by the Germans to work in the U.K. as an agent, and that he is or will be communicating in secret ink through a cover address in Spain.
>
> I should be glad therefore if arrangements can be made with the Iberian Section – and also with Naval Section in view of the man's calling – to submit to I.R.B. (Miss Macdonald) all letters addressed to Spain where the writer can be identified by his use of the Dutch language, by his name or from any other evidence as being Dutch.
>
> As arranged with Miss Macdonald the letters submitted as a result of this request would be examined by her, and Miss Macdonald would refer to me any letters which appeared to her to be of particular interest to M.I.5. The balance of the submissions would be sent to Testing Department for examination.[14]

On the day of Dronkers' arrest, 18 May, another minute was written by Hart to Gibbs with the following:

> Reference my previous minute about the Dutch seaman who is to write to Sapin [*sic*] from England signing himself Karel VAN DONGEN, we now learn that he will write to the following cover address, in English:
>
> Amalarico Pero Sanz
> Alemeda de Recalde No.29, VI Derecha
> BILBAO, Spain[15]
>
> If not already on, will you put on the I.B. List and modify the previous instructions about language.

Bilbao was one of the Abwehr's *Nebenstelle,* or outstations, in Spain, along with Huelva, San Sebastian, Mellila and Tetuan.[16] A collective sigh must have been heard around the offices of MI5's 'B' Division as yet another potential spy case reared its ugly head, following in the wake of the recently captured Pieter Jan Schipper, a ship's master, and his two crew, David Davids and Arthur Pay, at Margate in Kent on 24 April 1942.[17] Their case will be discussed later in Chapter 26.

By Interceptions Which They Know Not Of

The King hath note of all that they intend, By interceptions which they know not of.

Shakespeare, *King Henry V*

The intercept referred to in the Prologue which had piqued MI5's interest came about because of the success of the Government Code & Cypher School (GC&CS) at Bletchley Park in breaking the Abwehr (German military intelligence) Enigma hand cyphers. This meant that British Intelligence now had the upper hand in knowing the enemy's intentions and who might be sent to spy on them. The seeds of this had actually been sown in 1940 but would reach fruition in late 1941 when historian and Junior Fellow of Merton College, Oxford, Hugh Trevor-Roper (later Lord Dacre), and E. W. B. Gill, Bursar of Merton, were working in the Radio Security Service (RSS), otherwise known as MI8c, the communications section of the War Office.[1] Their job was to monitor German radio traffic and possible German radio operators working in Britain. By this time, Agent SNOW (Arthur Owens) was already working for MI5 and the Abwehr as a double agent and had informed 'Tar' Robertson, his MI5 case officer, of the type of message Abwehr agents would transmit and to which station in Germany they would report.

With this in mind, Trevor-Roper and Ernest Gill, who Trevor-Roper described somewhat uncharitably as a 'genial philistine with very little respect for red tape', took it upon themselves to monitor and intercept messages sent by the Abwehr and forward them to the Government Code & Cypher School. As Trevor-Roper described it:

However, in this indiscriminate flood of material we did ultimately discover some mysterious signals which, from the accompanying operators' chat, we knew to be German, and this we dutifully sent to the cryptographers of the Government Code & Cypher School, or GC&CS, recently installed at Bletchley Park ... At the time we were given to understand that our stuff was not wanted; it had been identified as harmless, and could be ignored ... Gill was not satisfied with this rebuff, and so we decided to prove our point by working on the material ourselves ... When we read the messages, we found that we had stumbled on a great treasure, the radio transmissions of the German Secret Service, or Abwehr, in particular its stations in Madrid and Hamburg, the former conversing with its substations in Spain and Spanish Morocco, the latter with its agents on the Baltic and North Sea coasts, some of whom were preparing to land, by boat or parachute, in Britain.[2]

Trevor-Roper had originally cracked the Abwehr cypher in early 1940 and reported his and Gill's findings to their Commanding Officer, Colonel J. P. G. Worlledge. However, Worlledge was rebuffed by Major Felix Cowgill, head of the Secret Intelligence Service's Section V, Counter-espionage, to whom RSS reported, and the findings were ignored. The head of Bletchley Park, Alastair Denniston, was also not amused at having Trevor-Roper and Gill encroach on his territory, dismissing them as amateurs and saying that Abwehr traffic was unimportant. Colonel D. A. Butler, the head of MI8, also instructed the RSS not to concern themselves with code-breaking. It seems that Broadway, the headquarters of MI6, were concerned that if the pair persisted there was likely to be a leak as the amount of British cryptographic activity broadened, particularly when Trevor-Roper's circulation list of North African Abwehr traffic included the Post Office wireless section.[3] Undeterred,

Gill and Trevor-Roper, stubborn and mischievous men both, persisted nonetheless; they were soon reading much of the Abwehr's traffic with its out-stations. To the dons' glee, even when Bletchley established its own cell to monitor the same Canaris links, it was RSS and not GC&CS which broke the next four hand-cyphers.[4]

When the RSS was taken over by SIS in May 1941 Worlledge was sidelined and replaced with Lieutenant Colonel E. F. 'Ted' Maltby of the Royal Signals as Controller, RSS. At that time, RSS was based at Arkley View, a large country house near Barnet, in Hertfordshire, although Section V was located at nearby St Albans.

Trevor-Roper's initial intelligence work focussed on ISOS messages decrypted from Abwehr hand-cyphers. But the significance of his role would increase greatly after the breaking on Christmas Day 1941 of the Enigma machine code used for the majority of Abwehr wireless signals.[5]

Cowgill had instructed that the raw intercepts were to be sent to Oliver Strachey, brother of the author Lytton Strachey, at Bletchley Park.[6] On

28 October 1941 work began on breaking Abwehr hand cyphers. Because Dillwyn 'Dilly' Knox was at that point terminally ill with cancer, his work on them was assisted by Mavis Lever (later Batey and author of his biography), and Margaret Rock. By 8 December 1941 Knox and Strachey had succeeded and the first decrypt was issued on 25 December 1941. These became known as ISK and ISOS respectively, which stood for Intelligence Services Knox and Intelligence Services Oliver Strachey, otherwise referred to as 'Most Secret Sources'.

> During 1941 information from ISOS was solely responsible for the capture of five of the 23 agents the German secret service sent to Britain. The material was also of great importance in running six of MI5's double agents. By the end of 1942 ISOS would enable the capture of 20 enemy agents out of the grand total of 87 taken prisoner.[7]

Interestingly, Anthony Blunt, working in B1b as Guy Liddell's personal assistant, would betray ISOS material to Soviet Intelligence in April 1942.[8] Blunt, who had been recruited by Soviet talent-spotter Arnold Deutsch in 1937 as a Communist agent, would later go on to become Surveyor of the Queen's Pictures and receive a knighthood. On 15 November 1979, Prime Minister Margaret Thatcher announced in the House of Commons that he was the 'Fourth Man', who had been associated with Guy Burgess, Donald Maclean and Kim Philby.

It was against this and two other factors that Dronkers' potential career as a spy had to compete, and a combination of other circumstances came into play in the Netherlands which motivated him to become involved in espionage. He was to claim later that he had never intended to carry out his spying mission, but to renege on the deal struck with the Abwehr and seek asylum in the UK.

Treachery, the Practice of Fools

Tricks and treachery are the practice of fools, that don't have brains enough to be honest.

Benjamin Franklin

When war with Nazi Germany was declared in Britain on 3 September 1939, the British government assessed the country's security-related legal infrastructure as inadequate. Anticipating threats from spies and saboteurs, as there had been during the First World War, Parliament would quickly answer the legislative call to duty. Already in place was the Emergency Powers (Defence) Act (1939); the Emergency Powers (Defence) Act (1940)[1] would follow the fall of France on 10 May 1940. This latter legislation included Defence Regulations which provided for conscription, as well as the famous Defence Regulation 18B which provided for the internment of suspicious individuals. In June, when Italy declared war, with thousands of Italians living in Britain and a steady influx of refugees, the new Prime Minister Winston Churchill had ordered authorities to 'Collar the lot!' It was therefore assumed that spies and serious saboteurs would be charged with treason. However, unless the agent was a resident of the United Kingdom, it was questionable as to whether an enemy agent recently infiltrated into the country would qualify under the laws of treason, which applied only to those who owed allegiance to the Crown. As Sir Edward Coke was quoted as saying in an 1817 edition about the laws of treason:

An enemy coming in open hostility into England, and taken, shall be either executed by marshall law, or ransomed; for he cannot be indicted for treason, for that he was never within the protection or legiance of the king, and the indictment of treason saith *centra ligeantium suam debitam*.[2]

Dame Rebecca West in *The New Meaning of Treason* quoting from *Hale's History of the Pleas of the Crown* adds that:

> ... if an alien enemy come into this kingdom hostilely to invade it, if he be taken, he should be dealt with as an enemy, but not as a traitor, because he violates no trust nor allegiance.[3]

In contrast, William Joyce, known during the Second World War as 'Lord Haw-Haw', was convicted of treason on a technicality in that he owed allegiance to the Crown even though he was an alien (originally an American citizen) because he had been the holder of a British passport that was valid until July 1940. Since he began broadcasting his propaganda on 18 September 1939, the authorities were able to charge him with three counts of high treason when he was caught in 1945, and execute him following his trial in 1946. In any treason trial the two key points which the prosecution must prove beyond a reasonable doubt are:

1. Did the person do the acts alleged in the charge?
2. Does the person have a duty of allegiance to the head of state (e.g. the Crown)?[4]

A legal precedent had been set with the trial by court martial of Carl Hans Lody (alias Charles Inglis), a lieutenant in the 2nd German Naval Reserve (Seewehr) who had arrived in Newcastle on 27 August 1914 and was arrested as a spy shortly thereafter. He was convicted of war treason[5] and shot by firing squad in the Tower of London on 6 November 1914.[6]

At a meeting at the War Office on 1 December 1939, MI5 representatives Sir Eric B. Holt-Wilson, Deputy Director (1917–1940), and Brigadier O. A. 'Jasper' Harker, his deputy and subsequently Deputy Director (1940–1947), were in favour of all alleged spies being tried by courts martial. But Sir Alexander Maxwell, Permanent Under-Secretary at the Home Office, objected on the grounds that trying British subjects by courts martial would be politically unacceptable; therefore, more draconian means were needed. A compromise was reached on 22 February 1940 when it was agreed that enemy aliens could be tried by courts martial but only with the consent of the Attorney-General. This was to become the Treachery Act (1940), a draconian piece of legislation designed *pour encourager les autres* (to encourage others, as a deterrent) and key to our story as it was to have a significant influence on the outcome of the case against Dronkers. If convicted, a spy would face certain death:

> Spies, when taken, are punishable by death since, as Vattel observes, 'there is scarcely any other means of guarding against the mischief they do.'[7]

The Bill was introduced into Parliament in May 1940, sponsored by Sir John Anderson, Home Secretary and Minister for Home Security, and Viscount Simon, Lord Chancellor in Churchill's government, although not a member of the War Cabinet. Anderson stated that under current legislation there was no provision for the death penalty for acts of treason. Earlier legislation had made it difficult to prosecute offenders unless there were two witnesses to the same offence.[8] In order to better understand the British government's position it is useful to quote from the *Hansard* notes on the bill extensively:

> The main provision in this Bill is contained in Clause 1, which provides that the extreme penalty of death may be exacted in certain grave cases of espionage and sabotage. Under this Clause, it is an offence for any person, with intent to help the enemy, to do or attempt or conspire with any other person to do any act which is designed or likely to give assistance to the naval, military or air operations of the enemy, to impede such operations of His Majesty, or to endanger life...In each case, be it noted, the act must have been done with intent to help the enemy.
>
> When the Emergency Powers (Defence) Bill was introduced in Parliament at the outbreak of this war, it contained no provision for the death penalty to be imposed for acts done with intent to assist the enemy, as it was thought at that time that the most serious types of offence for which the death penalty would be appropriate could best be dealt with under the Treason Acts. As a result, however, of further consideration, the conclusion has been reached that the Treason Acts, although, as I have said, they probably cover all the actions made punishable by Clause 1 of the Bill, cannot safely be relied upon as extending to all the classes of persons by whom such offences might be committed.
>
> In the third place, legislation is necessary because it has been thought desirable to make provision enabling enemy aliens to be tried in suitable cases by court-martial. Section 1, Sub-section (5) of the Emergency Powers (Defence) Act provides that Defence Regulations shall not authorise the trial by courts-martial of persons who are not subject to the Naval Discipline Act, to military law or to the Air Force Act. It was the intention of Parliament, when that Act was passed that all civilians charged with offences against Defence Regulations should be tried by civil courts.[9]

Lord Simon expressed doubt as to whether

> ... under the existing law of treason you could proceed against an alien who has come here suddenly, surreptitiously by air or otherwise, for the purpose of wreaking clandestine destruction or doing other acts against the safety of the realm.[10]

The key here seems to lie in the phrase, 'the act must have been done with *intent to help the enemy*' [my italics]. Therein lies the difficulty: How does one prove intent?

Under the Treachery Act (1940) it was not necessary to prove treason, but only, as in Clause 1 of the Act, that the accused had either *committed or intended to commit* [my italics] an act which would endanger life or endanger the forces of the Crown, or had *conspire[d] with any other person* [my italics]. The need to prove intent was exemplified in an article published in *Modern Law Review* in 1941,[11] by David Seaborne Davies who expressed doubt as to whether in fact the required *mens rea* [a guilty mind or criminal intent; the knowledge that the act to be committed is a criminal one] 'with intent to help the enemy' was clear and that the onus of the defence was to prove intent; there being no such intent, then there could be no treachery as proscribed under the Act.[12] Davies then went on to argue that the Act covered any person regardless of nationality, and that the clause '...which is designed or likely to give assistance ... to impede' would require that the prosecution prove that committing such an act would raise a prima facie [Burden of proof; enough evidence for a case to be made] presumption of the existence of the required *mens rea* and would shift the burden to the defence either to disprove or raise a reasonable doubt about its existence. However, as we shall see, whether Dronkers actually *intended* to help the Germans once he was in Britain, whether the Crown had a prima facie case against him and whether there was reasonable doubt are all debatable. Indeed, the whole concept of reasonable doubt may even be a misnomer. Such was the hostility to this contentious Bill that it is worth examining the reaction of some MPs, because in their opinion and that of others, the Bill was seriously flawed. The MPs all raise points about 'intent to help the enemy' and the death penalty, both of which would have a direct bearing on the later trial of Dronkers. All quotes are from *Hansard*.[13]

Sir John Anderson stated that 'the extreme penalty of death may be exacted in certain grave cases of espionage and sabotage' and 'must have been done with intent to help the enemy', which prompted Eleanor Rathbone, an independent MP for the Combined English Universities, to question

> ... what would happen if the court were convinced of the guilt of the prisoner where the offence was not so serious and there might be hesitation to apply the death penalty and where another penalty was deserved?

Anderson attempted to clarify what was meant by Clause 1 of the Bill and how it related to 'grievous cases of sabotage' by saying that 'an act of treachery can be made the subject of a charge under Clause 1 but the charge must be of a grievous description'. He referred to the fact that

... under the Defence Regulations as they now stand there is provision ... in Regulations 2A and 2B for dealing with acts done with intent to assist the enemy and with acts of sabotage ...[14]

However, Anderson neglected to explain what was meant by 'grievous cases of sabotage'. (This was somewhat clarified by the Lord Chancellor in the House of Lords' debate when he said that it was the 'blowing up of a building, blocking a road or something of that kind'.) Anderson also cited Clause 3, whereby there could be a 'joinder of charges':

Notwithstanding any rule of law or practice, charges for any offences, except treason, may be joined with a charge for any offence against this Act in the same indictment or charge-sheet, if those charges are founded on the same facts, or form, or are part of, a series of offences of the same or a similar character. [Treachery Act (1940), Clause 3]

George Benson, the Labour MP for Chesterfield, stated that it was not on the 'contemptibility of treachery' to which he took issue with the Home Secretary, but the death penalty which he found 'morally repugnant',

... and I do not feel I can allow the Bill to go through without making a protest ... I am not concerned with the fate of the individual but what I am passionately concerned with is the attitude of the community to him ... I feel passionately that the death penalty is beneath the honour and dignity of a great and civilised community ... and rests on an old fallacy which has been disproved innumerable times. If you increase severity beyond a certain point that does not increase its deterrent effect ... [T]he whole of our history shows that the severity of punishment does not, beyond a certain point, increase the deterrent effect. I conclude by saying that to rely upon a savage penalty is to rely on a method which has invariably failed. The only method of putting down crime is the increased efficiency of your police force, not the severity but the certainty of the penalty.

Sir Ralph Glyn, Bt, the Conservative MP for Abingdon, acknowledged the deep feelings Benson had on the matter when he added that,

The Home Secretary emphasised the fact that this is only for grave acts. One rather wonders whether more definition will be given as to what constitutes a grave act. In questions of treachery and plotting against the safety of the State, we have never yet in this country had to confront a situation of actual invasion, and one of the most difficult things for the Government, and for all those in positions of responsibility, is to give to people in every part of the country a feeling of confidence that this situation is well in hand. There is, I am afraid, a rather widespread feeling to-day that we have been somewhat lenient and that there are possibly people in our midst who are not all they would wish to appear. I believe that to be a fact, and if that fact is known, and there are rumours about such people, it seems to me to be all the more essential that Parliament should pass a Measure of this sort which will give a sense of confidence to the country that the new situation will be met, and met with firmness and courage by those who have to act.

Thomas Edmund Harvey, another MP for Combined English Universities, also expressed his opposition to capital punishment and asked the House of Commons to

… consider not merely the question of principle, but the question of expediency. We have reason to know from history the grievous results that have followed from the execution, even under proper military law, of those who were technically guilty of espionage.

He suggested that execution may cause ill feeling at a later date, citing past executions during the American War of Independence and those of leaders of the 1916 Easter Rebellion in Ireland as examples. He was possibly thinking of the likes of Nathan Hale in the former and Roger Casement in the latter, to name just two. He also questioned the death penalty because of its irrevocability:

How is any court to make a perfect judgment as to intention? In most cases it can be only by inferring it by a process of reasoning deduced from acts. In any case there may be mistakes which afterwards may come to light, and if the death penalty is inflicted, there is no possibility of redress. I do not ask that the Government should deal leniently with this terrible offence. It is urgently necessary in present circumstances that severe measures should be taken. However, I hope that in the Committee stage it may be possible to move to the Clause which inflicts the death penalty an Amendment allowing to the court the alternative of a very long sentence of imprisonment.

There were many others: the Revd James Barr, Labour MP for Coatbridge, who had chaired the Select Committee on Capital Punishment in 1930, stated that capital punishment was not a deterrent. Samuel Sydney Silverman, Labour MP for Nelson and Colne, also opposed the death penalty and took exception to the wording 'with intent to help the enemy':

I agree that that is the first thing which the prosecution would have to prove. The onus of proving that would lie upon the prosecution. I see the importance of that fact, but is there not a legal rule that the court may infer an intention? If you prove that the consequence of an act is to do these things defined in the Clause, and if it is a presumption of law that every man intends the reasonable consequences of his act, then the prosecution might escape by saying, 'I cannot prove any actual intention positively, but I can and I do prove that it is a reasonable consequence of this act that it will have this effect; as every man is presumed to intend reasonable consequences I have proved reasonable consequences, and I have therefore proved the intent.' I am certain that that is not what the Government had in mind or what they desired, but is there not possibly a danger there? If so, could it not be removed in some way?

However, Sir Donald Somervell, the Attorney-General, dismissed the suggestion of danger, saying,

The words are quite plain. We are dealing with a case of a most serious character — a capital charge — where the burden on the prosecution has to be fulfilled to the last scintilla, if one may use that expression, and although, of course, the circumstances may build up evidence from which a jury may draw an intent — after all, the last arbiters are the jury ...

The debate lasted from 5.25 p.m. until sometime after 8.43 p.m.; at 8.21 p.m. while the House sat in Committee Thomas Harvey moved for an Amendment 'in page 1, line 12 at the end to add "or imprisonment for a period not exceeding 20 years"', which was supported by Cecil Wilson, Labour MP for Sheffield Attercliffe, and George Muff, Labour MP for Hull, East. Harvey emphasised that his Amendment

... does not remove the death penalty from the Bill, but enlarges the power of the court by enabling it, wherever it thinks fit, to impose, in place of the death penalty, a very serious penalty of imprisonment. No one can say that a period of imprisonment not exceeding 20 years is a light penalty; it is a terribly heavy penalty. No one can feel that this grave offence which is being dealt with under the Bill would be lightly dealt with if it were punished by a sentence of that kind; but as has been pointed out, there will almost certainly be cases where, if the court had the power to inflict a penalty other than death, it would prefer to do so. As the Bill is drafted at present, the court would have no power to do so unless there was a subsidiary charge conjoined with the major charge which, under Clause 3 of the Bill, would enable the court to dismiss the major charge and convict on the minor charge. Unless two charges were brought at the same time the court would have no option, if the prisoner were found guilty, but to pronounce sentence of death.

Osbert Peake, Parliamentary Under-Secretary of State for the Home Office, advised against the adoption of the Amendment saying that

I cannot advise the Committee to accept the Amendment moved by the hon. Member for the English Universities (Mr Harvey). I would remind hon. Members that this Bill is designed to deal only with the most serious cases of the base crime of treachery. Less serious cases either of sabotage or espionage, or of acts done with intent to assist the enemy, can be dealt with under Defence Regulations 2 (a) and 2 (b). This Bill is intended to deal only with cases of the most serious character. Unless there is the clearest possible evidence of all the most serious elements in the charge, undoubtedly the prosecution will exercise the right under Clause 3 to join with the more serious charge other charges under the Defence Regulations to which I have referred. Of course that will always be done if there is a doubt in the mind of the prosecutor as to whether a conviction for the more serious charge is likely to be obtained.

The real argument against accepting the Amendment is that it would be contrary to British judicial procedure and to our tradition to give any alternative to the death penalty, and to place upon a Judge the intolerable burden of deciding which of those alternatives to choose.

One cannot help but note that most of the MPs opposing the Bill were from the Labour Party and the Combined Universities, which begs the question, was the opposition to the Bill really based on moral grounds, or was it partisan?

The Bill finally passed its Third Reading in the House of Commons at lightning speed on 22 May 1940; it was sent to the House of Lords the following day, and received royal assent that same evening. Few pieces of legislation, short of those brought in by Britain, the United States and Canada post-9/11, have been rushed through Parliament or Congress as speedily.[15] The Act remained in effect until 1946 when it was suspended on 28 February under the Treachery Act (End of Emergency) Order;[16] then it was repealed for England and Wales under the Criminal Justice Act 1967, and for the rest of the United Kingdom in 1973.[17] Interestingly, beheading was only abolished as a method of execution for treason in 1973. However, hanging remained available until 1998 when, under a House of Lords amendment to the Crime and Disorder Act 1998 proposed by Lord Archer of Sandwell, the death penalty was abolished for treason and piracy with violence, replaced by a discretionary maximum sentence of life imprisonment. These were the last civilian offences punishable by death.[18] The last death sentences passed, on Edgar Black (1963), Patrick McCarron (1964), David Chapman (1965) and Liam Holden (1973), were all reprieved or had their sentences quashed on appeal.

On 20 May 1998 the House of Commons voted to ratify the 6th Protocol of the European Convention on Human Rights prohibiting capital punishment except 'in time of war or imminent threat of war'. The last remaining provisions for the death penalty under military jurisdiction (including in wartime) were removed when section 21(5) of the Human Rights Act 1998 came into force on 9 November 1998. On 10 October 2003, effective from 1 February 2004, the UK acceded to the 13th Protocol, which prohibits the death penalty under all circumstances.[19]

During the Second World War a total of seventeen individuals were executed under the Treachery Act.[20] They had either outlived their usefulness, or had proved to be of no use to British authorities in the first place. Of those prosecuted and found guilty under the Act, all but Josef Jakobs would be hanged; Jakobs was shot by firing squad in the Tower of London on 15 August 1941. This was because Jakobs was a serving sergeant in the Wehrmacht and was tried by court-martial. Dorothy O'Grady, the only woman to be tried and found guilty under the Treachery Act on 18 December 1940, made a successful appeal to have her case commuted to fourteen years' penal servitude.[21]

Only one trial under the Act in November 1940 failed to secure such a guilty conviction, that of Sjoerd Pons, a twenty-eight-year-old Dutch 'refugee' arrested at Hythe on the Kent coast a short distance from the Grand Redoubt, Dymchurch, on 3 September 1940 – one of the so-called 'Invasion spies' or 'Kent spies'. This was the first trial to be conducted since the Act had been passed and would be a test case for others to follow. Another case, that of Dutchman Pieter Jan Schipper, who had arrived at Margate in Kent on 24 April 1942, together with David Davids and Arthur Pay, a West Indian, resulted in Schipper being interned for the duration of the war under a Home Office Detention Order without a trial. Both these cases are significant because they have a bearing on the subsequent trial of Dronkers and will be discussed later.

3

Double Cross

It is essential to seek out enemy agents who have come to conduct espionage against you and to bribe them to serve you. Give them instructions and care for them. Thus doubled agents are recruited and used.

Sun Tzu, *The Art of War*

While Dronkers was in British custody the issue of what to do with him would be carefully considered by MI5. One of the options open to them was to 'turn' him into a double agent as part of the Double-Cross System, which had come into being on 2 January 1941 and was run by the Twenty Committee, otherwise known as the Double-Cross Committee (from the Roman numerals XX). The committee was chaired by the Christ Church, Oxford don John Cecil Masterman (later Sir John), then working for MI5, with Thomas Argyll Robertson (better known as 'Tar' from his initials) of MI5's B1a in charge of running these double agents, and John Marriott as Secretary. As John Curry, the author of the first official history of the Security Service, explained:

The Twenty Committee was technically a sub-committee of the W Board, which originally consisted of the three Directors of Intelligence, CSS and Captain Liddell as representative of the Security Service. To these were added Sir Findlater Stewart of the Home Defence Executive and Colonel Bevan of the London Controlling Section (operational cover plans). The W Board was created to co-ordinate the dissemination of false information, but in practice it undertook the responsibility for the control of double agents, exercising that responsibility through the Twenty Committee. The Twenty Committee in turn acted as a clearing ground for information about the agents, approved traffic for them, discussed the policy adopted by B1a in individual cases, passed on intelligence information gained from double agents to the proper quarters and indicated how the agents could best be used for the benefit of the departments concerned.[1]

The Directors of Intelligence were the Director of Military Intelligence (DMI), Director of Naval Intelligence (DNI) and Director of Air Intelligence (D of I).

Masterman's account of the Double-Cross System first started life as an internal report for MI5 written in 1945 and was not published until 1972 in the United States of America, amid controversy in the UK. It is frequently mentioned in other accounts of MI5 or of individual double agents, such as those mentioned earlier. The committee's creed as outlined in Masterman's book was:

1. To control the enemy system, or as much of it as we could get our hands on
2. To catch fresh spies when they appeared
3. To gain knowledge of the personalities and methods of the German Secret Service
4. To obtain information about the code and cypher work of the German Service
5. To get evidence of enemy plans and intentions from the questions asked by them
6. To influence enemy plans by the answers sent to the enemy
7. To deceive the enemy about our plans and intentions[2]

More specifically,

(1) <u>To control the German intelligence system in this country</u>. This was an end in itself because we felt that if we provided a reasonably satisfactory reporting system from this country the Germans would be satisfied and would not make excessive efforts to establish other agents. Naturally it was better for us to know what was being reported from this country than not to know. Even if a good deal of true information had to be given, we did at least know what information the Germans had and what they had not. Furthermore, we could not enjoy the other benefits on the deception side unless we had a fairly complete control of the German intelligence system.

(2) <u>For the apprehending of other spies</u>. This was a primary object of the system, but it became less and less important because, while ISOS, the SCOs, the LRC and Camp 020 were uncovering new agents as they arrived, the Abwehr showed signs of being satisfied with the intelligence they were receiving from those agents under our control.

(3) <u>Code and cypher work</u>. Apart from the original "break" through the use of SNOW's traffic already mentioned, the traffic of some of our later agents was found to be of great assistance to GC&CS in reading messages over an important part of the widespread Abwehr network. GC&CS said on one occasion that GARBO's new cypher had saved them nearly six months' work, and some agents were kept going, e.g. TREASURE,[3] merely to act as a crib to GC&CS, after their value as agents had otherwise ceased.

(4) <u>Assistance to Censorship</u>. Information provided by letter-writing double agents in the form of cover addresses in neutral countries and types of secret ink used by enemy agents were communicated to Censorship, thus enabling them to keep in touch with German secret ink technique and developments, to discover the best re-agents and to put on the Watch Lists all over the world the addresses thus obtained. One important indirect consequence of this was to enable the USA authorities to obtain an insight into and watch over the activities of enemy agents in the Western Hemisphere.

(5) <u>To gain evidence of enemy intentions</u>. The questionnaires and individual questions given to agents gradually built up a very complete picture of what the Germans wanted to know and therefore what their operational intentions were. For example, when their questions about this country shifted from anti-invasion defence in South-East England to the location of food dumps and kindred subjects, we were able to suggest to appropriate authorities that German strategy no longer envisaged an invasion but was busy with the thoughts of a more long drawn-out war of attrition based on a submarine warfare and an attack on our supply lines.

(6) <u>To gain knowledge of the personalities and methods of the German Intelligence Services, particularly of the Abwehr</u>. This was self-explanatory.

(7) <u>To prevent enemy sabotage by controlling their saboteurs and thus securing knowledge of their methods and equipment</u>. One of the most remarkable aspects of the generally low standard of efficiency in the Abwehr during the war was the ineffectiveness, broadly speaking, of their sabotage in this country (the work of Abwehrabteilung II). We were satisfied that apart from the sabotage carried out under our control the Abwehr achieved practically nothing, certainly nothing of any importance. The most important incidents were three which were effected through MUTT and JEFF (which were duly publicised in the press) and a fourth by ZIGZAG, which was important as it supplied us with knowledge which made it possible to take precautions against other attempts on the same lines, i.e. by placing explosives contained in a piece of coal aboard a ship (in this case the s.s. "City of Lancaster"). The Germans dropped special sabotage equipment for the purposes of these incidents staged under our control and the fact that most of it proved to be captured SOE material indicated that they regarded it as superior to their own at that time.

(8) <u>To give misinformation to the enemy; in other words to take part in deception</u>. Further details on this subject are given below.[4]

Controversy had arisen over the fact that between September and November 1940 a total of twenty-one German agents had arrived in Britain, all but one of whom had been arrested. Dick White, then Assistant Director of MI5's B Division – who would later become Director-General of MI5 (1953–56) and Chief of the Secret

Intelligence Service (1956–68) – was incensed that five spies (including Josef Jakobs and Karel Richter) had already been executed on the orders of Winston Churchill, who had been demanding blood. White was adamant that 'Intelligence should have precedence over blood-letting',[5] believing that it was far better to successfully 'turn' and run agents, forcing them to transmit disinformation to their German masters rather than to suffer death if they did not co-operate. MI5 had already done this with SUMMER (Goesta Caroli), part of the so-called 'Welsh Ring', who had been interned in September 1940. It therefore became necessary to determine whether MI5 should run captured spies and saboteurs as double agents if they were not going to be tried in court, or what other course of action was needed. The thorny issue of a spy maintaining his freedom in exchange for co-operation with the authorities had first arisen at a meeting at the Security Intelligence Centre (SIC)[6] on 10 September 1940. Lord Swinton,[7] Chairman of the Home Defence (Security) Executive, outlined to representatives from the Home Office, the Armed Services, GHQ Home Forces, MI5 and MI6 a procedure to which Sir Edward Tindal Atkinson, the Director of Public Prosecutions, had also agreed: an alleged spy could make a statement under caution to the police or be interrogated by MI5. If the spy chose the latter course of action, then at a later date he would be asked to make another statement, again under caution, which would then be used as evidence for the prosecution. MI5 would later learn on 7 October 1940 that no deals regarding a spy's life could be made without the explicit authority of Lord Swinton. A memorandum in March 1941 stated that 'the Prime Minister has laid it down as a matter of policy that in all suitable cases spies should be brought to trial'.[8] On 17 June 1941, Swinton added:

> I have given my undertaking that any spy or enemy agent whom we no longer require … for intelligence purposes shall be brought to justice if the case against him will lie. The right man to decide any case can be brought is the DPP, and we should have the insurance of his opinion and advice in every case.[9]

In November 1941 agreement was reached after discussions between Lord Swinton, MI5, the Director of Public Prosecutions (DPP) and Sir Donald Somervell, the Attorney-General, that there would be no prosecution if MI5 had already used a spy as a double agent or made any promises to him. The fact that such information could be revealed in open court could not be entertained under any circumstances. There were two conditions set: first, that MI5 could approach the DPP about whether it would be possible to offer some sort of inducement to the agent if prosecution would compromise security; second, MI5 would not consult the DPP if there was no prima facie case. The DPP also ruled that 'no action could be taken against non-British subjects in respect of acts committed outside the territorial jurisdiction of British courts'.[10]

A total of eighty double agents are listed in the most recent edition of Masterman's book (although there may have been more), of which all but six were run by MI5, the others being run by SIS.[11] However, Dronkers did not become one of these agents, the reasons for which will be explained later.

4

A Most Unlikely
Enemy Agent

Dronkers was just over six feet tall, with grey hair and brown eyes. He was born in Nigtevecht near Utrecht on 3 April 1896 to Marinus Dronkers, a retired Water Board officer born in 1874, who worked on the canals as a bridge keeper and died in 1938, and Jannetje Moor, also born in 1874. The registration of his birth was witnessed by Gerrit Smink, also a bridge keeper, probably a colleague of Marinus, and Jan Winter, a carpenter. He had three sisters: Johanna Jacoba, who married Hendrik(us) Jan Morren, a carpenter contractor of Ymuiden (Ijmuiden); Elisabeth Cornelia, who married Pieter Cornelis Pieterse of Arnhem and lived to the ripe old age of 100 years, dying on 5 November 1995; and Maria Martina, born in 1898 and who died the following year. Dronkers gave his permanent address as Aert van der Goestraat, 23, The Hague.[1]

Educated at the elementary school in Ymuiden and secondary school in Zaandam, the young Dronkers left school at the age of sixteen and went to sea as a mate's apprentice on the KNSM[2] cargo ship SS *Hector*,[3] a ship of 3,438 tons, until 1913 when he left the sea because of a serious lung problem. During the First World War he worked as a bookkeeper at the Artillerie Inrichigen (Royal Artillery Ordnance Establishment Works) at Hembrug near Zaandam until he was dismissed during an office reorganisation. In 1918 he returned to work for the same shipping line as a mate's assistant on the SS *Medea*,[4] a ship of 1,311 tons, making several trips to the Mediterranean. However, in 1919 he was declared physically unfit for navigation on account of his eyesight and found work in various offices, first as a builder's clerk with the Ryke Waterstaat (State Water Board) in Ymuiden.

After being laid off yet again due to lack of work, he found a job at the press bureau of Arnold Vas Diaz in Amsterdam, described as 'a bouncy, bearded Hollander'.[5] Not long after this the company sent him to London to set up an office in the City,[6] at 20, Copthal Street, mainly to transmit daily market reports and rates of exchange. To do this Dronkers employed the assistance of a certain Arthur Scott. According to Dronkers his spell in London would have been sometime in April 1924 and lasted for five or six months. Business relations were with the firm of Kleinwort & Son, and the Equitable Trust Company of New York. At that time he was living c/o a Mrs Nelly Basey (or Baisey) at 1, Maley Avenue, Tulse Hill, London SE 27, now considered West Norwood.[7] In spite of the fact that during his stay in England he had never reported to the Dutch consular authorities, the Home Office had renewed his permit for a further three months.

One morning he received a telegram stating that his services were no longer required since there was no more money to pay him. The following day Vas Diaz came over in person and instructed him to return to Amsterdam. His return was delayed for a week owing to illness but two months later Dronkers found himself back in London working for a Mr Cohen in Swan Chambers in the City, which was another branch of Vas Diaz. He was to remain there for another two months, again staying at Mrs Basey's in Tulse Hill. At that time he was being paid £250 per annum, with the occasional bonus. But after two months he was again obliged to return to the Netherlands, there being no further work for him.

In Velsen, on Thursday 10 June 1926, he married Elise Antoinette Eleonora Seignette, a Dutch woman from a fairly well-to-do family of French origin, whose parents were Benjamin Egbertus Cornelius Seignette and Elisabeth Koorn.[8] It is unknown how they met. The wedding certificate gave his occupation as 'clerk'. The ceremony in the town hall was witnessed by Dronkers' father, at that time unemployed, and Auke Hendrik Jansen, a municipality messenger living in Velsen.[9]

Elise, who was born in Helder (now Den Helder) on 16 January 1893, but was then living in Heemstede, came from a large family of ten siblings. Confusingly, she was not the only girl in the Seignette family to have been called Elise or Eleonora – there was another sister with the same names, Elise Antoinette Eleonora, who had been born in 1891 but died the following year, and another, Eleonora, born around 1895 who had married Gerard Jozeph Marie Moussault (born 1893) on 21 September 1920.

A Trace Summary from the SIS Registry lists Dronkers as having a brother-in-law, J. C. Klever (some of the files say C. J.), who worked for the Official Censor Service of the PTT[10] and whose name appeared in a Suspect List of October 1940. It was Elise's sister Hermine Louise, born around 1896, who had married Cornelis Johannes Klever (born in Benschop, 12 September 1894) on 26 May 1932 in Rotterdam. To compound things further, Cornelis Johannes had a brother Cornelis, born 17 May 1890.[11]

To date, no further details of Klever's background have come to light, other than that he was an unfrocked theological student whose life was on a slippery slope downwards and had a police record. Major Sampson's interrogation report of 23 June 1942 quotes Dronkers as saying that Klever had married his wife's sister Hermine Louise in 1931 or 1932, that he was a

Stock Exchange broker, and that in spite of the fact that he had seemed fairly wealthy he wore cheap clothes. He was aged 49, thickset, about 1.65 m tall, 140 pounds (Dutch, equivalent to 154 pounds), with dark blond hair which was balding in the middle and going grey; he had blue eyes and wore glasses, was clean-shaven, had good teeth, a straight nose and round chin. He had a tenor voice and spoke Dutch and German, also a little French. He had also been working trying to get advertisements for newspapers, such as the *Deutsche Zeitung in die Niederlanden*. There was also a Cornelis Klever who was a friar in a Carmelite monastery in Boxmeer, who may actually have been the brother of Cornelis Johannes and the unfrocked theological student, not Cornelis Johannes. Further details of the genealogy of the Dronkers-Seignette families can be found in Appendix 10.

Having opened what was described as a share-broker's office but was in fact a 'bucket shop' in The Hague or Rotterdam, Cornelis Johannes Klever became involved with Willem van Baalen,[12] 'who has also a very shady reputation in Holland', although the files do not elaborate on this. Dronkers described van Baalen as also being a Stock Exchange broker, aged about 55–57, about 1.70 m tall, about 160–170 pounds (Dutch), with red-brown hair, going grey, a round, red face, well dressed, an almost whispering voice, who always seemed to be in a hurry.

Dronkers had gone to work for his brother-in-law as a clerk for about six months in 1935 or 1936, receiving a weekly wage of 25 guilders. The condition of his employment was that his wife's inheritance of 14,000 or 16,000 guilders be part of the deal, but his dealings with Klever had resulted in disaster – he had lost almost all of it, apart from 500 or 600 guilders, and also had to pawn Elise's jewellery. His work had involved collecting money from people who wanted to speculate with small sums of money and share the profits from these transactions.

Throughout his life Dronkers had had to scrape a living. He next found work with Tieleman and Dros, a manufacturer of preserves and tinned goods in Leiden established in 1877, but again lost his job as a result of reorganisation. The couple lived a peripatetic existence: in 1931 he decided to relocate to The Hague where they lived, first at Van Slinglelandtstraat, 156, but then moved to Valeriusstraat, 55, before finally ending up at Aert van der Goestraat, 23.[13] While there, he worked periodically at the Labour Exchange since he could find no other employment. The couple had no children, possibly because of the penurious state in which they constantly found themselves.

In 1938 things in Dronkers' life were about to take a sinister turn. According to Helenus 'Buster' Milmo, Assistant Director of B1, in a letter to Mrs K. G. Lee of the Home Office Aliens Department on 19 June 1942, 'It has also been ascertained that Dronkers was in contact with the German Secret Service as far back as 1938,'[14] reputedly while he was in England.

At the beginning of 1938 van Baalen and Klever had been in touch with a certain Dr Hampkus, a member of the German Intelligence Service living in Cologne. The three met at van Baalen's office at Laan van Meerdevoort, 85 in The Hague, known as the longest avenue in the Netherlands. Between them they concocted a scheme to obtain secret information about military matters in England from an alleged friend living there. But since neither van Baalen nor Klever could write English and the information was supposed to have been written in that language, they decided to bring in Dronkers to impersonate their non-existent 'friend' to translate the false information they intended to send Dr Hampkus in order to swindle him. Except Dronkers had only pretended to be in England and was actually sending the information from the Netherlands. He even travelled to Cologne with Klever who introduced him to Dr Hampkus.

> The method of transmitting the fictitious reports was ingenious. The trio wrote letters to English boarding houses asking [*illegible*] terms and enclosing envelopes addressed to Van Baalen in Dronkers' handwriting. [*illegible*] envelopes, which were returned with an English stamp and an English postmark, were [*illegible*] as proof that the reports had come from Dronkers in England. In fact, only one [*illegible*] was sent in on the British attitude towards German aggression in Czecho-Slovakia [*sic*] [*illegible*] was composed by Klever and copied by Dronkers. Other envelopes were used for l[etters] from Dronkers asking for money and stating that he was obliged to return to Holland [as] he had no funds. He maintains that he received nothing but the first payment o[f] 85 guilders. He suspected that Van Baalen received further sums from the Germans [but] has no proof of this.[15]

That Hampkus was connected to the Abwehr in Cologne is confirmed in a redacted letter to someone in MI6 from 'Buster' Milmo on 15 November 1942, referring to a redacted CX report of 30 October 1942. The letter mentions the double agent BRUTUS (Roman Garby-Czerniawski) and 'a certain Hamkens' who is likely the same person as Hampkus:

> One small point which occurred to me the other day a propos of BRUTUS's knowledge of the Cologne Stelle is this. You will remember that BRUTUS refers to a certain Hamkens connected with the Cologne Stelle who instructed him at the beginning of 1939 in the matters on which he would be required to report as a spy from Belgium. Dronkers, on whose case you have of course received all reports, also makes reference to a certain Dr. Hamkens who, at the end of 1938 instructed him in the mission he was to undertake on behalf of the Cologne Stelle against this country. It seems probable to me that these two men are identical, but it is unfortunately not possible to establish from descriptions as Dronkers is unable to describe Hamkens.[16]

According to F. Jackson of the Royal Victoria Patriotic School the whole operation had lasted three months, with Dronkers receiving 85 guilders for his first translation, 200 guilders (€1,829 in today's money) on his first visit to Cologne and a further 200 guilders a month later. Unfortunately, there is no mention of Hamkens/Hampkus in the heavily redacted BRUTUS files available from the National Archives at Kew.[17]

The true identity of Hamkens/Hampkus still remains a mystery. However, research has revealed that four men with the name Hamkens can be ruled out as serious contenders or having any connection to Cologne or the Abwehr:

1. Otto Hamkens (1887–1969) who was Regierungspräsident of Schleswig (Head of an Administrative District);
2. His brother Carl Wilhelm Hugo Hamkens (1883–1962).[18] Both were members of the Nazi Party, although there appears to be no connection with Cologne or the Abwehr;
3. Wilhelm Hamkens (1896–1965), farmer and political activist, who with Claus Heim was responsible for stirring up anti-Semitism in Schleswig-Holstein;[19]
4. Ernst Hamkens (1869–1945), farmer and politician who was a member of the German People's Party (DVP) and a deputy in the Reichstag (1924–1930) representing Schleswig.

MEISSTEUFFEN[20] mentions a Dr Ernst Bornheim, a lawyer, working for *Nest* Cologne, whom he met for the first time on 24 April 1941 at the Hotel Baur au Lac in Zurich. Referring to a later meeting he had with SCHUCHMANN[21] he added, 'The name of the man from Cologne is Dr Bornheim, as he is a Colognian, he even in Secret Service goes under his real name, a lawyer in private life [*sic*].'

Bornheim may be a possible contender for Hamkens/Hampkus (probably a *nom de guerre*) as he appears to be an important member of the sub-station and features prominently in MEISSTEUFFEN's recruitment and operation. *Nest* Cologne was primarily concerned with economic intelligence and its *Nestleiter* was Oberstleutnant (Lieutenant Colonel) Albrecht Focke, Referat VI Wi of the RSHA.[22] Bornheim is mentioned in a telegram dated 14 April 1942 to the Superintendent of Police in Bathurst, Gambia, from B1b as specialising in economic intelligence who 'trains, equips and distributes agents all over the world'. In 'Précis of a telegram received from Bathurst dated 13/4/42' it mentions MEISSTEUFFEN admitting to knowing a Dr Bornhurd, a lawyer in Cologne, and that it is his real name.[23] This telegram can also be found in the file of Berend Schuchmann, sometimes referred to as Schuckmann.[24] Bornheim is also referred to as 'Bornhurd' in a telegram in the MEISSTEUFFEN files from H. A. R. 'Kim' Philby to MI5, dated 15 April 1942: 'He knows Doctor Bornhurd and Kapitan-Leutnant Schuchmann.'

One of MEISSTEUFFEN's files mentions a Dr Falkner, most likely No. 1 in the 'Institut fuer [sic] Wirtschaftsforschung' (i.e. economic intelligence), as well as a Dr Becker as No. 2 in *Nest* Cologne. However, this Becker does not appear to be the same SS-Obersturmbahnnführer August Becker (1900–1967) responsible for designing the vans with the gas chamber fitted at the back. Instead, it is more likely to be Dr Carl Hermann Nicolaus Bensman (alias Dr Becker, Dr Bender, Bens[...], Nick, Nico), described as 'one of the most active Abwehr officials directing espionage activities against the Western Hemisphere' who was assigned to *Nest* Bremen in 1938.[25] He also 'belonged to the best society in Bremen'.

Bornheim is described as being the same rank as Becker (unspecified), but 'certainly one of the more important men of the Institut fuer [sic] Wirtschaftsforschung'. A full description of Bornheim by MEISSTEUFFEN gives the following:

Alias: None
Age: About 37 or 38
Build: Medium sized, on the verge of getting not actually fat but beefy.
Height: About 1.74 m or 5'6"
Weight: About 76 kg
Hair: Brown hair, always a little oiled, therefore it looks darker than it really is. It's getting thin, in front as well as on top. His freckled forehead and skull gives the hair something of a reddish tint to it.
Eyes: Darkish grey-green.
Spectacles: Never wears glasses in the street, only occasionally when reading or writing.
Face: [no shape given]
Complexion: healthy complexion, well eating and drinking and an 'out-of-door' tint to it.
Nose: [see Chin]
Chin: Nothing particular about either nose, chin or teeth.
Teeth: [see Chin]
Cleanshaven: Yes.
Appearance: Seen from behind, he has very broad hips for a man, which gives his walk something feminine. In fact his 'chassis' or 'undercarriage' seems a little too small for his upper part.
Clothes: Rather well dressed. In April 1941 he bought a light yellow raincoat in Switzerland which he probably still uses.
Voice: Speaks German with the broadish Cologne touch to it, and a trifle 'with a cold in the nose'.
Peculiarities: Smokes only cigars, no cigarettes. Fond of shooting, has about 25 miles outside of Cologne a small property and has rented the shooting rights of a decent sized area around it. His wife and children are living out there; he drives out as often as possibl[e].

Languages: German, and very very few words of French, pronounced with a strong German accent.

Nationality: German.

Places where seen: Seen at Cologne, Zurich, le Havre, Biarritz, etc.

In what capacity employed: He is certainly one of the more important men of the Institut fuer [*sic*] Wirtschaftsforschung.[26]

Whether Dr Bornheim and Hamkens/Hampkus are indeed one and the same remains still a matter of conjecture and requires positive identification.

On 17 May 1939, Dronkers managed to get a job in the Post & Telegraph Service (PTT) through the recommendation of a Mrs Munter, a friend of Elise, who in turn was a friend of Mrs Van Damme, wife of the director-general.[27] He was not required to pass any sort of test or entrance exam and was given a job as a temporary clerk; at the end of each short term his contract was renewed. His work was not in the actual Post Office building but in an administration section where the telephone directory was compiled at 12 Kortenaer Kade. The building, which was the former headquarters of the central administration, is now a national monument.

At the Post Office Dronkers' net salary of 107 guilders per month (approximately €970 in today's money) was insufficient to make ends meet so he began dealing on the black market. At that time, according to F. Jackson of the Royal Victoria Patriotic School, at least 50 per cent of the Dutch population was dealing in alcohol, coffee and cigars. Dronkers claimed to have been dealing in coffee, tea, salad oil, cocoa and condensed milk. Later, before he left the Netherlands, he had made a good living out of silk stockings and socks. Indeed, his profits on a dozen pairs of stockings was 70 guilders, where a pair normally sold for 65 cents, and tobacco at 3½ guilders per half ounce.[28] His principal contacts were in the Café Prinses in The Hague and also another café at Prinsestraat, 99.[29] He also mentioned the firm of NAP at Geldersche Kade in Amsterdam[30] which was buying up large quantities of copper wire, but they (unsure who 'they' were, but presumably employees) were caught and the head of the firm arrested.[31] So why, Jackson wondered, would Dronkers give up such a profitable existence and leave his wife, and to what end? He had

> ... succeeded so well that he not only made an ample living but could even put a considerable amount of money aside, proved by the fact that he gave JAN 500 guilders [slightly over €3,219 in today's money] and was, moreover, still in a position to leave his wife behind well provided with money. In other words, since the invasion of Holland this man has gone through a period of prosperity such as he never enjoyed before.[32]

We shall come to the identity of 'Jan' later as the story unfolds.

5

Mission Impossible

'Will you walk into my parlor?' said the spider to the fly; 'Tis the prettiest
little parlor that ever you did spy.'

Mary Howitt (1799–1888), 'The Spider and the Fly'

On 10 May 1940, in spite of Dutch neutrality, the Germans invaded the
Netherlands, Belgium and Luxemburg, without any warning or formal
declaration of war. This was followed on 14 May by the bombing of
Rotterdam, which killed 800–900 civilians and destroyed 25,000 homes.
Unable to defend themselves adequately, on 15 May the Dutch surrendered.
The Dutch government escaped to Britain; in its place the Netherlands were
ruled by a Reichscommissar, the Austrian Nazi Arthur Seyss-Inquart. The
Germans introduced forced labour for all males between the ages of eighteen
and forty-five, along with rationing, and persecution of the Jews. By the
winter of 1944/45, there was famine, the *Hongerwinter*, and the Dutch were
starving, with 4.5 million people affected. It was only alleviated by the Allied
liberation in 1945.

Because of all the food shortages and German blockade from farm areas,
many Dutch became involved in dealing on the black market. This was to be
the reason Dronkers gave his captors as to what motivated him to become
a willing recruit as a spy. He claimed that he was scared of being found out
about his dealings on the black market, which had caused him to think about
escaping, yet for patriotic reasons he was loath to do so. A few months before
his 'escape' he claimed he had been warned repeatedly by friends that many
people involved in the black market had been arrested and heavily punished,
some condemned to death (although most prosecutions meant a maximum of
two to three months' imprisonment). That being said, the Germans tended to
turn a blind eye to it, so long as those involved were not Jewish.

One of those persons who had tipped him off was a 'Mr Van der Vechter',
a notorious member of the NSB (National Socialist Movement in the

Netherlands) who, according to P. Van Dyck's report of 11 June, was now Postmaster General. This must have been Willem van der Vegte, a Dutch National Socialist who, from January 1942, was Director General of the Dutch PTT.[1] In 1949 van der Vegte was tried by the Dutch Supreme Court for deliberately providing assistance to the enemy in wartime and received a four-year sentence, which was commuted because of his disability (he was missing a leg from a car accident).

For Dronkers this tip-off was pivotal and undoubtedly changed his mind about escaping. It frightened him so much that his 'whole nervous system went wrong ... he lost three stone in weight in a couple of months and he felt that to save his life he had to get away at all costs'. Indeed, Jackson describes him as,

> A mental case ... a dithering fool, old before his time, a bundle of shaking nerves, maudlin and sentimental, who nearly weeps when the talk comes to Holland or the House of Orange, unintelligent, a typical piece of flotsam, with no special qualifications whatsoever, utterly useless and worthless as an agent ... Of all the persons that have passed through this establishment, this man is most unlikely as an Enemy Agent.[2]

Colonel Stephens at Camp 020 described him as a 'feckless individual'.[3] With such disparaging comments as these, it is easy to see at this early stage that the die had already been cast and why perhaps MI5 considered he was not important or reliable enough to become part of the Double-Cross System.

Another reason Dronkers gave for not escaping was that he feared all Post Office workers were going to have to join the NSB, or else resign. It is known that before the war he had been a member of the Christian Historical Party (Right) and a member of their union.[4] But Jackson found his story disingenuous and hard to believe that having to join the NSB was that much of a hassle – Dronkers' escape was 100 per cent more dangerous than dealing on the black market. He therefore concluded that there must have been an ulterior motive. J. A. Riddell of B1d at the Royal Victoria Patriotic School in his report of 9 June 1942 was strongly of the opinion that Dronkers might have been caught out in his black market activities and that after threats of reprisals to his family he was obliged to accept work for the Germans.

In a statement made at the RVPS on 16 June 1942, Dronkers admitted that in April 1941 he had been approached by his brother-in-law, Klever, who asked whether in principle he would be prepared to go to England as an agent of the German Secret Service. Dronkers told him that providing there was sufficient financial inducement he would do it.

The factors influencing a person's decision to commit espionage or treason are often referred to by the acronym MICE: Money, Ideology, Coercion (or Compromise) and Ego (or Excitement). Ronnie Haylor offered his own suggestions why Dronkers was recruited in a report dated 16 June 1942:

He is the type of man who might be chosen since he speaks English and has been in England. He was also at one time a seaman and must be presumed to have some knowledge of ships and ports which might be useful for observation purposes. He has also on his own admission been involved in black market activities which might have brought him to the notice of the German authorities and given them a lever with which to coerce him.[5]

From this it can be inferred that Dronkers' motivation for spying was both *money* and *coercion* on account of his black market activities, even though as Jackson has noted, the importance of these dealings was less than Dronkers claimed.

A few months before his departure for England Dronkers had gone to Rotterdam to see if he could get in touch with any merchant seamen. It is not known whether he was acting on his own initiative or was already under instructions from Klever. On his third visit to the Café Atlanta at Aert van Nesstraat, 4, he met 'Jan', the watchman of the *Joppe*, who Jackson described as a 'congenital idiot'. However, P. Van Dyck of the RVPS, who wrote the sixth interrogation report on 10 June, pointed out that the Café Atlanta

> ... is usually frequented by good middle class people. Seafaring people are not its usual clientele and it seems to me an extraordinary coincident [*sic*] that the one man he should have picked out happened to be a sailor and what is more a sailor who could provide him with a boat for which he had been looking apparently for weeks.[6]

A couple of days after the approach Dronkers was taken to a café in The Hague to meet a Mr Alexander Verkuyl.[7] Dronkers described him as aged about 35–37, about 1.65–1.70 m tall, with blond hair and blue eyes, clean shaven and well dressed. He worked as a stockbroker and also had dealings on the black market. They also met at Verkuyl's house at Waalsdorperweg, 307, The Hague, and at cafés.

At their first meeting Verkuyl asked Dronkers whether he would be prepared to go to England as an agent of the German Secret Service, to which Dronkers repeated what he had told his brother-in-law: provided the money was enough he would do so. He said he did not hear anything more from Verkuyl until the beginning of February 1942 when Verkuyl asked him to meet him in the same café in The Hague as before. Ten days later they met again, this time at the Café de la Paix, where he was introduced to a 'Dr Schneider' who had recently arrived from Germany (probably from the Hamburg Abwehr *Abstelle*). As was pointed out in a 'Provisional Report on Yacht "Joppe"' prepared by MI5:

> Dr. Schneider knew about Dronkers' connection with the German Secret Service in 1938 and was also aware that he had only pretended to go to

Rough Justice

England at that time. Dr. Schneider also seemed satisfied with his excuse that he could not live in England and keep his wife in Holland for 200 Guilders a month. A link is thus established between his connection with the Germans in September 1938, and his appointment as an agent in February 1942. He nevertheless maintains that he had no dealings with them between these dates, even after the invasion of Holland in May 1940.[8]

Thus the Germans had some leverage over Dronkers, so when 'Dr Schneider' asked him whether he would be prepared to work for them, he made a Faustian pact by saying 'yes'.

It was agreed that Dronkers would receive 100 guilders a month while he was still in the Netherlands and that he would be given instruction as to his mission in England. While there, his wife Elise would be paid 50 guilders a month and an unspecified lump sum would be paid into a bank account in his name. Further payments would also be made, the amount and frequency of which would depend on the services he provided. When Dronkers returned to the Netherlands, he would be given a permanent position 'in the administration of some official section' at a salary of at least 300 guilders per month. Another meeting was arranged for the following Saturday to confirm this agreement. To the impoverished Dronkers all this seemed too good to be true.

It also emerged from a 'trace' in the SIS Registry sent to MI5 on 21 May that ' A Dronkers of the Hague (brother-in-law of J.G. Klever) Official Censor Service PTT figures in Suspect List dated 10/40'.[9] A communication was sent back to SIS requesting further information, although this does not appear to have been forthcoming, causing some irritation within MI5 about SIS being uncooperative. A register of known Dutch Nazi sympathisers (members of the NSB) prepared by the Bureau of Political Investigation in Zaandam in 1945 also lists a Johannes Dronkers, born 14 January 1914. Information such as this, if available to SIS in 1942, may have led to confusion about the real identity and background of the Johannes Marinus Dronkers in MI5 custody.[10]

After his initial meeting with 'Dr Schneider' Dronkers was instructed to call at Vondelstraat, 11, in The Hague at 7.00 p.m. on the following Monday. This address, in a statement made by Colonel Hinchley-Cooke at New Scotland Yard (undated, but likely 20 June, and later read out in court at the Old Bailey), was 'known to me as the headquarters of the German espionage organisation operating against this country'.[11]

When questioned by MI5, Dronkers was unable to remember exactly when he started his instruction, but thought it was on 16 March 1942 and took the form of twice-weekly sessions. His mission was to find out about the nature and location of anti-tank guns and their units, and where large so-called 'Crusher' tanks were being built. Dronkers probably misheard as this was most likely the Mk II Crusader tank, known as a 'cruiser tank'. Crusader tanks had already been in use against the Germans during the North African Campaign in 1941, so this was most likely in order to target the Nuffield factories in Birmingham and Coventry where they were being built.

He was also expected to find out about American and Canadian troops stationed in the UK and how they were equipped, whether they brought with them their own equipment or whether they were equipped on arrival. This shows how little the Germans apparently knew of the economic situation in Britain at the time and the 'Lend-Lease' agreement with the United States which was actually equipping Britain with military matériel, not the other way round.

The Germans apparently knew about a new aero engine that was being developed but not details of what it was called or where it was being built. No further particulars are available, but this might have been the Rolls-Royce Griffon engine, which had gone into production in the early 1940s, having been developed in 1938. It could also have been a reference to the Power Jets W.1 turbo-jet engine built by British Thomson-Houston for the Gloster E28/39 already under development by Frank Whittle, and colloquially known as the 'Gloster Whittle'. The Germans had developed the Messerschmitt Me 262 jet aircraft which had its first flight in April 1941, albeit with piston engines, and in July 1942 with jet engines. It did not become fully operational until 1944. The Germans also wanted to know about where the Vengeance aircraft – the Vultee A-35 Vengeance dive bomber – was being made. Dronkers said he thought 'Schneider' had told him it was at Brough on Humberside in the East Riding of Yorkshire (the home of Blackburn Aircraft Limited).

In fact, the RAF had ordered 200 such Vultee A-35 Vengeance aircraft on 3 July 1940, a further 100 in December and more in June 1941 under the Lend-Lease scheme. However, when it did go into service with the RAF in October 1942 with 82 and 110 squadrons in India, the Vengeance was almost obsolete and so was used either as a target tug or on operations during the Burma Campaign. It does not appear to have been built in Britain, but by Northrop (Mark I) or Vultee (Mark II) in the USA, so the operative word here is 'assembled' in Britain from parts shipped over from the United States. A note sent on 26 August from Milmo to B1a, with Flight Lieutenant Charles Cholmondeley's name on it, observes:

I have the impression, possibly quite erroneously, that the question about the new aeroplane engine and the manufacture of the 'Vengeance' aeroplane in England are of some importance.[12]

For the Germans to be asking for this kind of information suggests that there must have been another spy who was already supplying them, otherwise how would they have known anything about it in the first place? One possible source is Dr Karl-Heinz Krämer, codenamed HEKTOR by the Germans. Born in 1916, he was tall, good-looking, and worked for Abwehr 1L (1 Luft) under Nikolaus Ritter as the counter-intelligence and trade attaché in Stockholm. Krämer was supplying the Germans with monthly production summaries from the Society of British Aircraft Constructors and from other contacts in Sweden. One of these contacts was codenamed JOSEFINE (which was actually a number of sources in the Swedish government, but also thought to be Count Johann Gabriel Oxenstierna, the Swedish naval attaché in London).[13] A third possibility is one of Ritter's agents, known only as *Der Kleine*, who is mentioned in the MI5 file on Herbert Wichmann (see Chapter 8) as furnishing information on the state of the aircraft industry. This agent was SNOW's accomplice Walter Dicketts (Agent CELERY) whom James Hayward describes as being 'an incorrigible rogue with an unfortunate knack for getting caught'.[14] The MI5 file on Major Julius Boeckel also reports that both SNOW and TATE were supplying the Germans with information on the British aircraft industry and the RAF.[15]

Another item on the Germans' shopping list was information about a new type of ammunition for 25-pounder anti-tank guns. This could have been a shaped charge under development in Canada or a more potent version of the 20 lb solid armour-piercing (AP) shot. Transport was another area of interest: Were there any new harbours on the west coast, or old ones which had hitherto been regarded as unimportant but were now being developed for transport? That being the case, how many ships were there and how much traffic was there? This is most likely because there were German U-boat bases in Brittany which had already wrought havoc and destruction attacking convoys in the North Atlantic. Or was it because of the Allied invasion the Germans still expected? They were particularly interested in stores being built near these ports and whether any stores were being transported by land. Dronkers was to find out about factories too: Where were the important ones located? What were they making, and how many people were employed there?

It is something of a mystery, not least to Dronkers himself, as to how 'Dr Schneider' expected him to obtain all this intelligence, and his MI5 files do not offer any further information. Once he had arrived in England and been cleared by the British authorities, Dronkers' instructions were to find a job as a clerk with the Dutch government-in-exile. It required a leap of faith on the part of the Germans that he would have been accepted by the Dutch government-in-exile – which was not a foregone conclusion, given MI5's reaction. Dronkers protested to 'Dr Schneider' that in such a lowly position he was hardly likely to be of much use. In order to be able to collect the kind of information that 'Dr Schneider' required, Dronkers would have had to develop a network of agents working in those areas, something he is unlikely to have achieved, given his apparent mental state. His job would likely have been in London, making it difficult to travel to, say, Portsmouth ('Dr Schneider' had requested information about a floating dock) or Southampton, a journey of about three hours by steam train in those days, on a limited salary and with regular disruptions of trains by air raids and so forth. After completing his mission, he had been instructed to try to return if possible:

> If at any time I should then see any possibility of returning to Holland, I was to do so. For instance, I could try to get a job as a sailor on a ship bound for Portugal and desert there.[16]

During his meetings with 'Dr Schneider' Dronkers was given instruction in the preparation of secret inks (outlined in Appendix 3) which he was to use in communications. He explained how he had been instructed to write letters using invisible ink. He gave a description of the young man, aged around 30, who instructed him in secret inks: height 1.85 metres, blonde hair, blue eyes, a straight nose and round chin, clean shaven and very well dressed, with a deep bass voice who only spoke German to 'Dr Schneider'. The description given by Jacobus Johannes Grobben of his secret writing instructor, 'Dr Korell', puts his age as being about 35; tall and slim but strong; about 180 cm tall; about 80 kg in weight; light blond curly hair with a parting on the right side; a long face with a pointed nose, smooth chin, with teeth in good sound condition; his voice was described as normal; he was dressed in light trousers and a sports jacket.[17] The description given by the Erasmus brothers of their instructor concurs with Dronkers': aged 30, tall (1.85–1.90 m), weight (90 kg), blond hair, blue eyes, slightly crooked nose (not mentioned by the others), similarly dressed in jacket and trousers. One difference is that no one else had mentioned he smoked. However, another description given by the Erasmus brothers of a man they knew as Hiller was different: he was older (45–50), shorter (1.65 m), lighter (65 kg), dark hair and going bald, rounded chin and had a gasping manner of speech. One description even gives him a Hitler moustache![18]

There are a few similarities in terms of age (30–35), height (180–185 cm) and colour of hair (blond). While Dronkers described his nose as pointed and Grobben as straight, it could be one and the same – straight but pointed. Grobben does not mention the colour of his eyes, except that he is slightly cross-eyed but this is not mentioned by Dronkers; being blond, the eyes were most likely blue. Schipper also noted that he recognised Grobben's description of 'Dr Korell' although he did not think it was his real name. It is therefore likely that Dronkers, Schipper and Grobben, as well as possibly the Erasmus brothers, were trained by the same instructor, in addition to the other older man (Hiller). Grobben's case, and that of the Erasmus brothers, will be dealt with in the Postscript.

Whoever the instructor was, he probably worked under Werner von Raffay in IG of *Abt* I, an Abwehr captain in the reserve whose birthday is listed in the diary of Herbert Wichmann for 1945 as 12 January.[19] In Appendix C of a report of *Ast* Hamburg up to 1944 von Raffay is described as being aged 50, 1.78 metres, dark, severely wounded in the First World War and 'a little queer in the head'.[20] The same document reports that after 1943 agents were forbidden to use secret inks in Britain as Berlin suspected that the British had discovered their secret.

Dronkers noted down the addresses to whom his communications were to be sent in a Dutch–English dictionary. He revealed these addresses to his MI5 interrogators on 16 June when he identified the pin pricks he had made:

Fernando Laurero, Rua Sousa Martin 5.30, Lisboa (Lisbon), and
Froeken [Miss] Eva Yschale, Grevmagnigaten 13V (?), Stockholm
… the first one starting with the letter 'F' and underlining one letter on each following page until the full name and address were spelt out, after which I marked the street number at the bottom of the next page. The second address I marked in the same way, starting with the letter 'S'.

Any news I obtained, I was to write primarily to the Portuguese address, but if by any chance I should have several communications to make within a very short space of time, I was to write one or two of these to the Swedish address. I was instructed however to use the Swedish address as little as possible.

After arrival in the United Kingdom and after having passed the Authorities, I was to write an innocent letter to the first address stating that I had arrived safely. I was to write in Dutch. I was to sign my letters C. Van Dongen.

I was further informed that after the month of September 1942 they would no longer be interested in any news from me and my activities would cease.[21]

The former is probably Laureiro, which is also listed as a contact for Hans von Meiss-Teuffen in one of his MI5 files (KV2/742).

Portugal was a neutral country during the Second World War and Lisbon was a hotbed of spies from both the Allied and the Axis powers. The MI6 station was in the British Passport Control Office on the Rua Emenda, while the Abwehr operated out of the German legation in the Rua de Buenos Aires, with the aristocrat Albrecht von Auenrode as its head.[22] He was assisted by Fritz Kramer, alias Cramer. The SD was represented by Erich Emil Schroeder.[23]

It is curious that the Germans had set September as the cut-off date, after which Dronkers was told not to bother sending any more information. Why stop there? Assuming they had a successful agent in place, why would they have not wanted him to remain there to collect further intelligence – unless, of course, they expected him to fail? What was going on during this period which was so important to the Germans, but not later on?

* * *

In 1942 various campaigns were underway – the North African Campaign, Operation Barbarossa, the German invasion on the Eastern Front which commenced on 22 June 1941, and the Dieppe Raid (Operation Jubilee) which would take place on 19 August. Had the Germans already got wind that the Dieppe Raid was in the offing? Or were they expecting that the major invasion on the French coast, which was to come later with Operation Overlord (D-Day) on 6 June 1944, was going to happen during the summer of 1942?

Operation Jubilee was originally conceived as Operation Rutter in April 1942 by Combined Operations Headquarters (COHQ) and approved by Lord Mountbatten, Chief of Combined Operations, on 4 April, although some sources disagree on whether Mountbatten actually signed off on it. By the time Dronkers arrived in England in May, training of Canadian troops and British Royal Marine Commandos was already underway on the Isle of Wight. This may be why the Germans needed to know about troop dispositions. Several sources have suggested that intelligence leaks might have occurred:

> There were plenty of comments just after the event like Robert Bruce Lockhart's, to the effect that the Germans had known about the operation except perhaps for the actual date. For months MI5 and the ISSB were kept busy investigating possible leaks and indiscretions. 'Responsible authorities in the UK,' wrote [C.P.] Stacey in 1946 (without identifying them), 'had thought it decidedly probable that some information might have reached the Germans concerning Operation Rutter.' Before the end of March 1943, there had already been two major investigations into Jubilee's security at the request of the Joint Intelligence Committee.[24]

It was also suggested that German intelligence had been forewarned on four occasions but had not bothered to warn those defending Dieppe. Two of these warnings had apparently come from agents under the Double-Cross System.[25] Austrian author Gunther Peis quotes two Abwehr officials saying,

> 'In mid-August 1942', the former head of the Hamburg Abwehr station, Kapitan zur See Herbert Wichmann, told me, 'a radio agent in England told us about preparations for a landing in the Fécamp area. Fécamp is only about fifty kilometres west of Dieppe.'[26]

Peis alleged that German agent 3725 had warned the Abwehr 'about a landing operation that was to take place near Dieppe'. That agent was codenamed TATE by MI5. He further alleged that freelance agent OSTRO, working out of Lisbon, had also warned them. OSTRO's real name was Paul Georg Fidrmuc, a Sudeten Czech who, intelligence historian Nigel West tells us, actually correctly identified Dieppe as the likely target, mainly from guesswork as opposed to actual intelligence. West devotes a whole chapter to the leak theory in his book *Unreliable Witness*[27] in which he discusses and ultimately debunks the myths surrounding it.

As West points out, Luftwaffe reconnaissance flights had identified a build-up of landing craft and other ships along the south coast of Britain, particularly around the Isle of Wight. The Germans had also succeeded in breaking low-grade Royal Naval cyphers which would have allowed them to keep track of British shipping in the area. Therefore, they knew that an operation was imminent, but not the exact location. It might explain why Major General Konrad Haase, commander of the 302nd Division of LXXXI Corps and known as *Der Kleine Haase* (Little Haase) to distinguish him from Lieutenant General Curt Haase (*Der Grosse Haase* – Big Haase), had ordered the Dieppe garrison to be at a state of readiness. It would also help to discount to some extent the idea that the Germans had been forewarned of the raid by agents, as a recent account of the Canadian forces during the Second World War illustrates:

> The defenders knew that an attack was most likely to be launched in the period when the moon and tide were favourable, as they were on August 19, and long-standing orders had put the coastal garrisons on alert. The Germans did not need forewarning: their defences were in place. They simply responded efficiently when the attack came.[28]

That being said, Robin Neillands states that the 302nd Division was,

> Charged with defending some 80km of coast and was, allegedly, not a first-class formation, being ill-equipped, undertrained and largely composed of non-German soldiers, mostly Poles and ethnic Germans from the newly occupied territories in the East. Finally, the 302nd was said to be under strength.[29]

Other theories came from Stanley Lovell and Arthur Bonsall. Lovell, who had been Director of the Office of Strategic Service's (OSS) Research and Development Branch, alleged in his memoirs[30] that SIS had inadvertently tipped off the Germans by allowing one of their double agents to send a message to the Abwehr in advance of the landings at Dieppe. Bonsall, who worked in the German Air Section of Bletchley Park, and later became Director of GCHQ (1973–1978), which succeeded GC&CS, stated:

When told to be ready for the impending raid on Dieppe in 1942, we hoped that a code that only changed at regular intervals of several weeks would yield advance information about the movements of German fighter aircraft in Northern France. But it made an unscheduled change early on the day of the raid, providing some confirmation of subsequent German claims that they had known about the raid in advance.[31]

If there were other agents supplying intelligence, it makes no sense for the Germans to have thought that someone as unstable as Dronkers could have been relied upon to provide any useful intelligence. Why bother to send someone else when all they had to do was contact their other trusted agents already in place in England (who, unbeknown to them, were double agents)? Unless, of course, the Germans already suspected them of being double agents and wanted confirmation from an alternative source, namely Dronkers, although this seems unlikely and there is no evidence to corroborate it.

***

A report from Helenus Milmo of B1b addressed to Colonel 'Tin-Eye' Stephens and dated 18 June stated that in early May Berlin had asked Madrid to supply a cover address for an agent 'controlled by the Dutch Branch of the Abwehr'.[32] He goes on to say that Dronkers was not actually given the Bilbao address but only those in Lisbon and Stockholm. The Lisbon address had also been given to two other agents, codenamed FATHER[33] and MEISSTEUFFEN, but the Stockholm address was unknown to MI5.[34]

In marked contrast to that of Pons, Kieboom, Meier and Waldberg, who, in addition to receiving instruction in secret writing, were also trained in radio procedures and Morse code transmissions, Dronkers did not receive anything like that amount of training. The former were equipped with two radio sets, and Waldberg even carried a pistol. Given the possibility of imminent German invasion of Britain in September 1940, the Abwehr must have felt it more urgent to have instant communication.

During his interrogations by MI5 Dronkers claimed the *Joppe* belonged to a certain Mr Nygh, a lawyer and President of the Fisheries Office in Rotterdam or Ymuiden, who had been entrusted with issuing petrol to various fishing vessels in Hellevoetsluis. Yet in a statement made on 16 June he contradicted himself by saying that the boat belonged to 'Dr Schneider'. An MI5 file reference states that as of a report of 1939 Nygh (or Nijgh) was thought to be Hendricus Nijgh, a journalist and director of Nijgh and Van Ditmar, an advertising agency in Rotterdam.[35] MI5 would later claim that Nijgh was a prominent Nazi who was 'on friendly terms with a famous agent'[36], although the name of this agent was never mentioned.

6

Escape

Grant me the shelter of your house a while, and you will not regret your friendship.

Richard Wagner, *Der fliegender Holländer* (*The Flying Dutchman*)

In order for Dronkers to fulfill his role as an Abwehr spy it was necessary for him to 'escape' to England. But each time he was interrogated the circumstances of his escape varied somewhat, largely depending on when he was being interrogated, who was interrogating him, or whether he or one of his compatriots was telling the story. The first account of Dronkers' escape appeared in a report marked 'Secret' on 18 May 1942 by Major Reginald 'Rex' de Vries, the Security Control Officer (SCO) for Harwich, to Lieutenant Colonel John Adam who was the MI5 officer in charge of D4, Port control at sea ports and airports, and de Vries's immediate superior. It reads as follows:

SECRET
From: Major R.F. De Vries, Horley, Crane Hill, London Road, Ipswich
To: Lt.Col. J.H. Adam, C.I.E., C.B.E., Box No.500, Oxford.
<u>Dronkers, Johannes Marinus</u>
(As accompanying WS Form 4b)
Dutch IC Number 084291 issued The Hague 2.9.41
The above is the organiser of a party of three Dutch refugees who arrived at Harwich today – short reports on the other two are attached.

By occupation he is a clerk and since 17.5.39 has been engaged in this capacity at the G.P.O. Hague. He says that several German high administrative officers are now installed at the G.P.O. The story of his escape is as follows:-

He got to know the watchman aboard the "Joppe" which was lying in the Voornsche Canal at Hellevoetsluis – his name is John, surname unknown. The owner of the yacht was [*illegible*] Nygh a lawyer living at The Hague and by way of being a Quisling. Nygh was appointed by the Germans as the local Fishing Board President and the caretaker John was given the job of handing out petrol and permits to the local fishermen.

John is a loyalist although he did not wish to leave his family and arranged details of the escape and supplied Dronkers with 170 litres of benzine for the aux. "Fiat" engine on the launch. Dronkers paid John about 500 guilders in all to arrange for the escape. It should be noted that Nygh had no knowledge of what was going on.

The means that Dronkers and his two friends employed in getting past the Dutch Quisling police into the coastal prohibited area is interesting. Passes are examined on a bridge over the canal and about six weeks ago a friend of John's stole three from the police office while the police were busy checking them outside. These passes were already made out to their legitimate holders and signed so the original typed names were erased and the names of these three men were typed over. The alterations are quite plainly visible and it does not say much for the vigilance of the police that these erasions were not noticed [*sic*].

Of the other two men – de Langen also worked in the G.P.O. and was known to Dronkers for 2 years or more. Mulder was a stranger to them and had been introduced through two friends of Dronkers.

These two men were also supplied with faked passes and arrived at Heenvliet by steam (?) tram from Rotterdam at about 21.00 hours on Friday the 15th of May. Dronkers hid them in the fore peak all night. At about 7.00 hours on Saturday the 16th the yacht left Heenvliet through the Nieuwe Sluis with John still aboard. He was dropped just outside Hellevoetsluis while the other two remained hidden. The tide was at half ebb and Dronkers purposely ran the yacht on a sand bank a little further west. Under the eyes of the German guard he made frantic efforts to get off but as the tide was ebbing his position seemed quite safe as far as the sentries were concerned and they paid no more attention to him.

At about 17.00 hours he got under away and an hour later was off Ribben. Just north of this spot there is a German guard ship and he ran between this ship and the coast heading north. A little later he turned west and made for Harwich. After ten hours the engine gave out and the rest of the journey was made under sail.

Wind was at the turn S.S.E. Force 4. Visibility good. No surface craft of any sort was seen during the trip. An R.A.F. Bomber sighted them and dived low but no response was made to their signals.[1]

According to Dronkers the wind was N.W. when he left the Dutch coast.

No German naval craft are in Hellevoetsluis – only a few watch ships. On Thursday the 14th inst. about 200 iron barges that had been lying there for 18 months were towed to Rotterdam for what reason is unknown. These barges had been equipped for taking on tanks and had about a 6 inch concrete floor put in. Apparently it was considered by all the locals that in any sort of sea these craft would break up. [Possibly they had been part of the original invasion fleet for Operation Sea Lion.]

Dronkers was told that R.A.F. raids on Flushing between 21st and 29th of April did considerable damage to the harbour and caused a great number of casualties.[2]

Dronkers was at sea until 1926. He seems a reasonably educated man, speaks fair English and appears a loyal subject who is very anxious to take up any work he can. He is able to supply accurate information as to the position of the "Flacks" at Hellevoetsluis.

He was refused leave to land and is being sent to LRC under Police escort.[3]

De Vries refers to 'Jan' as 'John' (the anglicized version), but in other documents he is always referred to as 'Jan'. A 'Quisling' was a term coined during the Second World War to mean someone who collaborates with the enemy. It was derived from the Norwegian leader Vidkun Quisling (1887–1945) who established a Nazi collaborationist regime in Norway. He was executed by firing squad on 24 October 1945.

Approximate details of the *Joppe* were given as follows in a separate report from de Vries to Major H. V. Haylor of the London Reception Centre, Wandsworth Common, SW18:

SECRET
From: Major R.F. De Vries, Horley, Crane Hill, London Road, Ipswich
To: Major H.V. Haylor, London Reception Centre, Wandsworth Common SW18
Details of yacht "Joppe"
Carrying Dutch escapees, Dronkers, Mulder and de Langen
Length: 30 feet
Beam: 11 feet
Draught: 4'6"
Fiat 4 cylinder engine, built 1936–37.
4 gallons of petrol remaining.
The yacht will lie at Harwich under constant Police supervision.
It has not been possible yet to complete a full rummage.[4]

De Vries states that 'these are not exact as the yacht is still afloat and Dronkers did not know the exact measurements'. Unfortunately, no photograph or other record of the boat exists in the MI5 files, other than later documents discussing what to do with it, but its ultimate fate is unknown. Indeed, the condition of the boat was creating some cause for concern. In a report to Major Haylor dated 20 May, de Vries notes, 'Experts opine that it is possible this yacht had been beached for some time before this trip as she is taking water rather badly and some of the seams have sprung.'[5] This is also corroborated in a signal sent to the Director of Naval Intelligence (DNI), Vice Admiral John Godfrey, from Rear Admiral Hugh Hext Rogers, Flag Officer-in-Charge (FOIC) Harwich, on 22 May, stating that

> ... she is now making water very rapidly and it is suspected that she must have been hauled up a long time before this trip, as it is clear the seams opened on contact with the water. This bears out the view that Dronkers' account of the method of escape is open to suspicion.[6]

Dronkers gave a more detailed account of the escape to F. Jackson of the Royal Victoria Patriotic School on 20 May 1942, in which he states that he went a couple of times to Rotterdam to see if he could get in touch with some sea-going people. In March, he met in the Café Atlanta in Rotterdam a certain 'Jan', but never heard his real name. 'Jan' was the caretaker of a boat called *Joppe*, a small sailing yacht with a Fiat auxiliary motor, which was lying in Hellevoetsluis, the property of Mr Nygh, a lawyer and President of the Fisheries Office. Nygh had been entrusted with the distribution of petrol to the various fishing vessels, and consequently the tank of the *Joppe* was always full.

'Jan' had a permit to sail the *Joppe*, as he frequently had to take Nygh out to inspect some fishing vessels. He took Dronkers out with him on a couple of trips when Nygh was not there, first to show him the boat, and second, to have him seen aboard in Hellevoetsluis, so that Dronkers' presence on the *Joppe* at the time of escape would not cause suspicion. According to Dronkers, 'Jan' was violently anti-Nazi, but he thought that he was strongly influenced by money because he gave him, in all, about 500 guilders.

Since Dronkers could not sail the boat alone, he therefore looked for a couple of helpers. The first of these was Jan Bruno de Langen, a colleague in the Post Office, whom he had known ever since he became a civil servant, and who he knew was anxious to get away. John Alphonsus Mulder only entered into the plan about a week before the escape, recommended to Dronkers by a mutual friend, Mr Verkuyl. Mulder, as we shall see later, was wanted by the Gestapo and had to get away as soon as possible.

According to Dronkers, on Friday 15 May, the three escapees went to Nieuwesluis on the Voornsche Canal, where the boat had been taken. 'Jan' supplied them with false travelling passes, which were examined on their way to Nieuwesluis by the Dutch authorities. He also gave Dronkers the keys to the *Joppe*. At about 7.30 p.m. they went aboard. De Langen and Mulder hid themselves in the fore-peak while Dronkers returned to the shore and spent the night at the Café Meyer. The 'fore-peak', sometimes referred to in the documents as the 'fore-hold', is 'the extreme forward lower compartment or tank usually used for trimming or storage in a ship' (*Merriam-Webster*).

The next morning Dronkers returned aboard at about 5.45 a.m., while 'Jan' came aboard at about 6.30 a.m. They left at once for Hellevoetsluis, passing through the lock, and a little further on 'Jan' was dropped off. They could not go out into the open in daylight so at about 9.15 a.m. at low tide they ran purposely, or so it appeared, onto a sandbank, possibly the Plaat van Scheelhoek, a bare triangular sandbar and now a bird sanctuary. Somehow they had to stay there until evening. At about 5.00 p.m. they floated free and steered against the tide in the direction of Stellendam. What is puzzling is why they did not proceed with their journey on the night of 15 May under cover of darkness.

At 6.00 p.m. they passed a German guard-ship but saw nobody aboard. Once they were out of sight of this ship, they changed course and sailed due west. On Sunday morning they had to stop the engine in order to cool it, but then could not get it to restart. The rest of the journey continued under sail. On Sunday evening they passed a buoy, the sea became rough and the boat shipped water. On Monday 18 May at about 5.00 a.m. they saw a convoy, and steered directly for it. The HMT *Corena* took them aboard and towed them into Harwich.

Jackson's report of 30 May adds to their story. Since his first interrogation Dronkers appeared to have undergone a remarkable change. During this second interrogation Jackson observed,

> His nervousness has disappeared; he looks better and younger and now replies quite normally and reasonably to any questions put to him. It would seem as if at the time of the first interrogation, he were really still much upset by what he had just gone through, that is to say, the events during his escape and had not yet been able to collect his thoughts in coming to a normal state of mind. He now acts like a man of mediocre intelligence but quite normal and with powers of reasoning.[7]

Dronkers said that he had met 'Jan' on his third visit to Rotterdam, the first two having been without success. He considered 'Jan' quite a normal individual, glad to make some extra money but also a keen patriot and loyal Dutchman, and quite shrewd. Jackson pointed out to him that he could not understand how 'Jan' could have failed to see that by helping him and the others to escape and then remaining in Holland himself, it would bring him into a position of the utmost danger.

Regarding the passes, Dronkers said that 'Jan' had obtained the *ausweis* for him three weeks before he left; the one for de Langen came from Verkuyl, who had obtained it from 'Jan' one week before leaving; Mulder's pass also came from Verkuyl via 'Jan' three days before leaving. A friend of 'Jan' had changed the names: the same man who had procured the passes and stolen them from the office in which he was working. Dronkers destroyed his pass after passing the guard-ship, instructing the others to do the same, but de Langen and Mulder did not do so. Mulder, however, destroyed a call-up for medical examination which he had received from the Germans after having volunteered for service on the Eastern Front.

Dronkers thought that there must have been a misunderstanding due to his nervousness about the position of the guard-ship and the sandbank – they were several miles apart and there was a promontory between them, so that it was impossible to see the sandbank from the guard-ship. The sandbank, however, was only about 200 yards away from the shore, and during all the time that the *Joppe* was on the sandbank it was well within view of the anti-aircraft guards on shore, who apparently took no notice of it at all. When they passed the guard-ship, he could see nobody either on the bridge or on deck.

According to a later statement on 31 May, Dronkers and Mulder said they were introduced to each other by Verkuyl at his house at noon on or about Sunday 10 May. It was agreed Elise Dronkers would be taken care of by the provision of about 2,000 guilders which Mulder would receive for a financial transaction of which more will be outlined later. Beginning on Monday, Dronkers would go on a week's leave to Heenvliet. While there he would go out several times with the boat in order to prepare the escape and to keep attention from being drawn to him; at the same time he would make arrangements for the pass to be handed to Mulder through Verkuyl, who would also let Mulder know at what time on Friday he should take the train to The Hague. The sailing time of the boat from the *pribbe* (sandbank) was arranged for about 11.00 p.m. on Saturday 16 May. But as the statement shows, everything went very differently.

Mulder was instructed that after 11 May he should remain in touch every hour of the day with Verkuyl. Dronkers would await Mulder and de Langen at Heenvliet Station where the two would officially meet, even though they would both be traveling on the same train from The Hague. Verkuyl had had to go to Rotterdam to receive Mulder's pass from 'Jan' and on the afternoon of Wednesday 13 May Mulder went to Verkuyl's house to collect it. On the morning of Friday 15 May, he received a telephone call from Verkuyl saying that the departure hour from The Hague was arranged for 4.42 p.m. and that he should take the 6.05 p.m. tram from Rotterdam in the direction of Heenvliet. Verkuyl brought de Langen and Mulder to Rotterdam as arranged; they all got out at Heenvliet and Dronkers came to meet them at about 7.30 p.m. Together they walked to Nieuwesluis where the boat was moored. De Langen and Mulder immediately climbed into the fore-peak and Dronkers let down the cover at about 8.30 p.m. At about 11.00 p.m. Dronkers came back aboard with writing paper and let Mulder and de Langen come out into the cabin where they could sleep. He then spent the night at the Café Mayer.

At 5.30 on the morning of 16 May, Dronkers came back aboard the boat, instructing de Langen and Mulder to go back into the fore-peak before 'Jan' came aboard about half an hour later. At about 7.00 a.m. they cast off and began their journey to Hellevoetsluis. Dronkers put 'Jan' ashore onto a coal barge near the lock, after which he steered the boat on his own towards the Heringvliet. About 10.00 a.m. de Langen and Mulder were roused by the noise of Dronkers knocking and shouting that they could come out. They crept through the opening into the cabin and at the same time felt the boat grounding and stopping immediately afterwards.

Through the ebb tide they could see that they had run aground onto a sandbank right under the coast. They remained in the cabin, as they could easily see Hellevoetsluis and also the German *kazematten* (casemated fortifications). They thought that running aground on the sandbank had happened by accident, but Dronkers had purposely remained there, not wishing to get off. He thought it better to remain there than to anchor on the sandbank and then to leave at 10.30 a.m., in spite of Mulder and de Langen trying to urge him to get off it. Where the story differs from the original account is when they stated that the tide began to come in at 2.00 p.m. and that at about 5.00 p.m. they weighed anchor and began their journey.

De Langen and Mulder remained continually in the cabin but as they had still to pass the German 'watch-ship', they crept back into the fore-peak in case there was an actual visit by the Germans. At about 8.00 a.m., on receiving shouts and knocking by Dronkers, they came out again. They could see through the portholes that the 'watch-ship' was now behind them. However, they did not dare come out on deck, but stayed below until about dusk when they could no longer see land. Without binoculars, they kept a constant look-out through the portholes on their surroundings and for any eventual danger. After they had passed the watch-ship they changed course and sailed due west in the direction of Harwich.

At about 11.00 a.m. the engine started to overheat, so they stopped it. Fifteen minutes later when they attempted to restart it the engine would not budge. By then Mulder was at the wheel. They obviously must have eventually succeeded as they sailed at full speed until about 2.00 a.m. when Mulder handed over the helm to Dronkers. Mulder and de Langen were about to go below to sleep when all the lights, including that for the compass, went out. Fortunately, they had some Christmas candles and placed one on top of the compass, with Mulder and de Langen keeping an eye on it so that it did not burn out.

By the morning of 17 May the wind had risen and there was a high sea running. Suddenly the engine stopped again. This time, all attempts to restart it failed when they discovered the batteries were empty. The wind had dropped, but the sea was still running high so they hoisted the sails, floating and drifting around in a northerly direction. At about noon they sailed in a south-westerly direction, with no maps and only a compass to guide them. At 5.00 p.m. Dronkers announced that there was a buoy ahead which they should make for, moor up to it, and wait for the morning since they had no lights. However, they only reached the buoy at 11.30 p.m. and could not see enough to moor up to it. During the morning and afternoon they heard distant rumbling, which could have been the air raid on Flushing. They saw two floating mines, and at about 11.00 a.m. an aircraft flew overhead with its navigation lights on. They signalled to it with a lantern, but it did not appear to notice. After darkness had fallen again they saw seven lights to the left of them and three to the right. The sky was full of aircraft and seachlights, and in the darkness they nearly ran into a buoy at 1.00 a.m.

At 4.30 on Monday morning dawn was breaking but there was still no land in sight. A storm had arisen and the boat started to fill up with water. It was then that they decided to steer a course due east in the direction of the lights they had seen earlier. Suddenly at around 5.00 or 6.00 a.m. they saw a convoy of ships and sent SOS signals on the horn. One of the trawlers guarding the convoy, HMT *Corena*, responded and steered directly for it, taking them aboard around 6.30 a.m. and towing the *Joppe* into Harwich. Lieutenant Cannon's statement, taken on 25 June by de Vries for Dronkers' trial, takes up the story:

On the night of 17/18th May 1942 I was on patrol at 51 Buoy and at 4.40 a.m. proceeded to B.8 Buoy to sweep the channel. On arriving back at 51 Buoy I observed a yacht flying the Dutch flag in the vicinity of the Sunk Float. I proceeded towards her, flashing with my Aldus lamp [*sic*]. One of the occupants of the yacht commenced waving a coat and made towards me under sail. As they got alongside me the eldest of the party came aboard exclaiming 'We've escaped from the bloody Germans'. A brief description of this man is:- tall, drawn-in face, aged about 50. The spot where I picked up the yacht was approximately 9 miles E.S.E. of Harwich and the time was approximately 5.45.

The three men were taken straight to the Ward Room and did not leave until the Security Control Officer arrived ... Several times he remarked 'My poor darling wife is left behind.'[8]

Once aboard, Dronkers reportedly jumped up and down and did a little dance. According to Mulder and another, 'His joy was so great that he burst into the song "Tipperary" in excellent English.'[9]

In his statement (undated) made at Scotland Yard, Major de Vries, the Security Control Officer (SCO) for the Port of Harwich, stated:

On May 18th 1942 at about 7 am I received information from the Operations Room Harwich Naval Base that three Dutchmen had been picked up by HMS M/S *Corena* and were being brought into Parkeston Quay Harwich. I therefore went to Parkeston Quay and at about 9.30 am I saw the M/S *Corena* berth alongside Parkeston Quay, having in tow the yacht *Joppe*.

I went aboard accompanied by Sergeant Speirs, Intelligence Corps (Field Security Wing). I went to the saloon where I saw three Dutchmen, Dronkers, Mulder and de Langen. I said to them: 'Good morning, I am the Security Officer.' The three men all stood up and Dronkers and Mulder replied in English, 'Good morning.' Having ascertained that their luggage was ready I had them taken with it onto the Quay by Sergeant Speirs. I then drove them in my car to my office.

On arrival at my office the three men were searched; their clothing was not removed. I then questioned each man separately.

I dealt with Dronkers first and asked him to give me information about himself and about the circumstances in which he had left Holland in the yacht *Joppe*.[10]

Dronkers gave his name and current address in The Hague, the name of his wife, confirmed that the details of his identity card were accurate, that the *Joppe* was the property of Mr Nygh, how he had come to meet 'Jan', and the circumstances of his escape. He claimed that he wanted to obtain clerical work in Britain but at this point did not mention anything about his espionage mission. Also present at the debrief were Sergeant Herrewyn of the Intelligence Corps (Field Security Wing), who spoke Dutch and who explained the meaning of one or two English words to Dronkers, and Lieutenant Sir Lionel Smith-Gordon, Bt, RNVR, Staff Officer Intelligence at the Harwich naval base. Rear Admiral Rogers (FOIC Harwich) also added in a signal to the Director of Naval Intelligence (DNI) on 22 May:

> Referring to my 1544B/19/5, the Dutch auxilliary yacht 'Joppe' was picked up by HMT 'Corena' early in the morning of May 18th and brought into Harwich with three Dutch refugees aboard. The boat and refugees were taken in charge by Security Control Officer and the boat was subsequently handed to the Customs Authorities. After preliminary interrogation by Security Control Officer, at which Staff Officer (Intelligence) Harwich was present, the refugees were handed over to police to escort them to Combined Interrogation Centre in London ... Staff Officer Intelligence at Harwich has nothing to add to these reports except to express the opinion that the bona fides of the refugees seem to him to be more than doubtful.[11]

The three Dutchmen were taken by train to Liverpool Street station and then by car to the Royal Victoria Patriotic School in Wandsworth, London. The RVPS was a Gothic monstrosity built in 1859 in the Scottish Baronial and Chateau-esque style as an asylum for girls orphaned during the Crimean War. During the First World War it was used as a hospital. In 1939, after the girls had been evacuated to Wales, it was taken over by MI5 to house prisoners and immigrants to the UK. In 1941 it became known as the London Reception Centre (LRC).

Jackson confessed to being completely nonplussed by the whole affair. He found it strange how Dronkers should walk into a café and immediately find someone ('Jan') who was the caretaker of a yacht owned by a prominent Nazi (Nygh). Dronkers then confided in Nygh who, for a small consideration, agreed to help him. 'Jan' was the only person who could take the yacht through the lock on the Voornsche Canal because he had an official pass, which he agreed to do, and this later being dropped ashore a bit further away while Dronkers and his companions escaped to England. The obvious question which Jackson asked was, how would 'Jan' explain away the disappearance of the yacht, and what would happen to him, given that he helped take them through the lock? Dronkers replied, 'Do you know, we neither of us ever thought of this.' In Jackson's 30 May report it appears that at that point he believed Dronkers was telling the truth:

> My personal opinion is that Dronkers is <u>not an Agent</u>. To me, he appears to be sincere and too stupid to decieve us successfully [*sic*]. If the whole case should be a plan to get an Agent into this country, I feel that Dronkers is not that Agent. I think that the version he gives of the escape is the one he believes to be true.[12]

Such were the contradictions in the various accounts that on 31 May, Jackson and his colleague R. S. Sands suggested Dronkers and Mulder put their heads together and come up with a story they could agree upon. MI5 would also approach SOE (the Special Operations Executive) to try to learn more about Mr Nygh and determine what happened to 'Jan'. Ronnie Haylor sent a letter on 13 June to Commander John Senter of the Naval Intelligence Division, attached to SOE (and later Head of Security at SOE), asking him to look into the matter. Jackson and Sands wrote in their report:

> After the interrogation of Mulder today, it was explained to him and Dronkers that there were discrepancies between their stories; that it would be impossible to come to a conclusion of their case until we had a uniform story, and that therefore the best thing they could do would be to sit together and compile in writing, the exact story of their escape. They were given the necessary writing materials and left alone. This report is in the file. Examiner Sands and myself were unseen witnesses to the ensuing conversation of 2½ hours between them and the result of this test is completely negative.
>
> The only thing this proves is that they are not both wrong. If either of them is wrong, the other one does not know about it. It does not, therefore, interfere with my theory that whereas Dronkers, who is somewhat of a fool, is genuine, Mulder is not.
>
> There are two possibilities:-
>
> (1) The whole escape story is a 'plant'; Dronkers was carefully contacted by a German Agent in the Café and afterwards Mulder was planted on him, the escape of Dronkers and De Langen therefore, being entirely genuine as far as they know themselves, or
> (2) The whole escape story being genuine, with Mulder, a subversive element, coming into it by coincidence.

As I am still loath to accept the theory that if this were a German 'plant', they would have considered us stupid enough to swallow the story of 'Jan' staying behind, I hesitate in giving a definite opinion and can only make one definite suggestion, to the effect that the help of SOE be called in, in order to find out in Holland, what happened to the watchman of the little yacht of Mr Nygh.

If this man has been arrested and executed, I am willing to accept their story. If this man is still a free agent in Holland [I] think it would go a long way to proving that the whole thing was a 'plant'.

De Langen, I consider entirely innocent, quite independent from whatever the story of the escape may prove to be and I recommend his release.

It is my considered opinion that Dronkers, also, is innocent, also independent from the boat story, because if the whole matter had been arranged, I think he has been the innocent victim.

Personally, I have no objection to this release but I feel that on this point there will be considerable opposition. Mulder, should be held under any circumstances.[13]

Further judgement was passed on Mulder on 5 June in the Radio Oranje report (see Chapter 7) when Sands stated that Mulder was a 'born actor'. This was based on the fact that Rudy Burgwal[14] claimed that he had only met Mulder once and was introduced to him by Frederick Stumpff,[15] but Mulder stated that he met Burgwal through Henk Klatt who then introduced him to Stumpff (see Chapter 11). As Lt Col Robin 'Tin Eye' Stephens expressed in his account of Camp 020:

Mulder attracted some interest by contradicting himself at every opportunity; but it was Dronkers whose story rang the least true.[16]

Dronkers' declaration was naive, to say the least. Had the Germans not been aware of the escape plan, as an accomplice 'Jan' would almost certainly have been arrested and severely punished, if not killed. Therefore, whoever owned the yacht, whether it was Nygh or 'Dr Schneider', had intended its use as part of the plan. It would also seem that German watch-ships or guard-ships would have been closely monitoring all sea-going traffic. The fact that no one appeared to be aboard (or rather, visible on deck) indicates that they had been forewarned and told to let it go without a challenge. There were also anti-aircraft batteries on the coast, but they were obviously preoccupied by the air raid going on, for as Dronkers noted, 'The sky was full of planes and searchlights.'

Jackson concluded that Dronkers must be a 'mental case' and conceded that it was quite possible that he had not thought about the consequences of the missing yacht. However, he wondered whether 'Jan' was also a mental case too, or that he had planned to commit suicide afterwards, 'because that is what his conduct amounts to if the story is true'. He goes on to say that:

> If Dronkers were any other than he appears to be, I would unhesitatingly reject the story as an utter impossibility and brand this so called escape as a plant ... Of all the persons that have passed through this establishment, this man is probably the most unlikely as an Enemy Agent. On the other hand, nothing on earth will make me accept at its face value, the story that is told us.[17]

However, he conceded that de Langen and Mulder were 'genuine escapees, in good faith'.

Dronkers attempted to explain away the discrepancies in his and Mulder's accounts of their escape in a letter (dated probably 18 June) which he addressed to Mulder and de Langen, referring to them as 'friends' and claiming,

> The two facts which you pointed out to me yesterday concerning the non agreement of our statements and which are the reason for our long delay here I myself also regret very much; the more so as it is my fault and you have become the victims. However it can't be helped and it is difficult for me personally to tell you the reason, but as you have a right to know I am writing to you, at the risk of being thought to be childish or cowardly.
>
> During the last four months that I was in Holland I was already under doctor's treatment because my nerves had suffered so much owing to the rotten conditions there. They have not improved here, on the contrary, and this is the reason that my memory is playing me tricks. Even the most simpl [*sic*] things I cannot clearly remember and sometimes I suddenly find that I am confusing one thing with another. I feel however that they will regard me here as being ill and that I will not be released at all; I won't be able to stand this. Really Boys I cannot help it, don't be hard on me. I am greatly in need of sympathy; I am most anxious to find a solution for you two but I cannot think of one. In any case be convinced of my honest intentions; you need not doubt these at all although perhaps the people here think otherwise. As regards you two I am and remain your true friend and co-traveller.[18]

A cynic would likely say that this *cri de coeur* is simply a ploy; Dronkers is asking for sympathy because he claims he is not in his right mind and is confused about the facts. Being under stress will do that, but it is also easy to use his mental state to cover up for the fact that maybe he had been lying all along. Unfortunately, there is no mention in the files of any psychological examination being carried out by Dr Harold Dearden, the resident psychiatrist at Camp 020, which might have clarified whether Dronkers was as stressed as he claimed. De Langen also threw his hat into the ring with a letter dated 18 June in which he states:

> The undersigned, J.B. de Langen, herewith takes the liberty of writing you a letter which could be more aptly called a plea.
>
> The British Government, as well as its officials, are doing nothing but their duty by concentrating people who have escaped from occupied territory and then sifting the chaff from the corn.
>
> The undersigned and his two friends escaped with great courage and enthusiasm from their occupied fatherland in order to give England the benefit of their small but well meant efforts.
>
> Do you not think it a little too far fetched that because some points of our statement are not entirely uniform, we should be deprived of our freedom for such a long time and that even our good and honest intentions are being doubted? For the undersigned guarantees the honesty of his two friends, Mr Dronkers and Mr Mulder.
>
> It is quite true that he and his friends have had a great deal of luck but if they had not had this, they would now either be at the bottom of the North Sea or have received a bullet from the Germans.
>
> No sight must be lost of the fact that the boat by which they escaped was known to the Germans (I mean the rotten Huns), so that there was practically no fear of any control. They, therefore, had to risk it in this way as it was such a beautiful chance.
>
> That Mr Dronkers still returned to the village on the evening before departure is, in my opinion, completely justified, as he had lived in this village since Tuesday, and surely during the last night he had a right to have a good night's rest. For the leadership was entirely in his hands, such as for instance the matter of navigation.
>
> In the second place, the space in the cabin was very limited, hardly sufficient for two people.
>
> The undersigned has abandoned his mother who is ill, his family and friends, his position and everything, out of idealism for the rightful cause for which England is fighting and it is causing him great sorrow that he is doubted by those whom he loves.[19]

Jackson also discussed the forged passes and the fact that Dronkers' pass was conveniently missing. Dronkers claimed that when he saw the German guard-ship he became frightened and destroyed it along with other incriminating documents, instructing his companions to do likewise. They, however, denied he made such a request. Jackson refuted Dronkers' claim that the passes had been stolen six weeks prior to the escape, as the date on the one belonging to J. A. Mulder was made out on 27 April and the date had not been changed. After examining them under a magnifying glass he observed that the original names had been rubbed out and the new names typed on a different typewriter – a Remington, whereas the originals were typed with an Underwood – which was obvious from the different type characteristics. To Jackson, the original name on Mulder's pass was J. M. Noltes and that of de Langen, J. W. de Laeren, two names easy to alter without much trouble. When questioned about the passes, Dronkers maintained that the passes had been obtained from a man in the Maré Schaussee at Hoogvliet. This was the Koninklijke Marechaussee, known as the KMar, or Royal Military Constabulary in the Netherlands. It was this unknown man who had altered the passes. He claimed that it was only his pass which had been stolen six weeks before and not those of Mulder and de Langen.

A report from J. A. Riddell of the RVPS on 9 June posed a number of questions about Dronkers' motivation for escape and the voyage across the North Sea:

> It can be presumed that Dronkers Black Market activities must have called for a certain amount of intelligence or at leave [*sic*] low cunning. On the face of it it would appear that Dronkers is certainly not the type of man who could be used as an agent. But his demeanour during the first interrogation may have been due to his having a guilty conscience, and the period which elapsed between the the two interrogations may have enabled him to pull himself together.
>
> No satisfactory conclusion has been given for Dronkers reasons for escaping, his story of the arrangements for the actual escape is most unsatisfactory, and I suggest he be further interrogated on the following points:
>
> (a) His pre-war actvities.
> (b) His Black Market activities. Were they connected in any way with the Germans?
> (c) His domestic position. Was there any marital discord? Did he tell his wife his intentions to escape? Has he made any provision for her?
> (d) Investigation of Dronkers' Black Market activities.
> (e) Para.16 of the First Report shows that Dronkers left his two fellow escapees aboard the boat and returned to the shore and spent the night at the Café Mayer. This point should be explored.
> (f) De Langen should be closely interrogated on the point: Has Dronkers been away from the Post Office for any length of time during the last few months?[20]

None of these points appears to have been explored in any depth, judging from what is available in the files:

(a) His pre-war activities were what MI5 had already learned from the SIS trace: that he had allegedly been an active member of the NSB, or at least someone called Dronkers; also his work for his brother-in-law, Klever;
(b) His black market activities do not appear to have been connected with the Germans;

(c) There may have been some marital discord because Elise was always asking him for more money. Dronkers had told her that he was heading for Spain as a ruse to fool the Germans;

(d) Other than to mention the commodities in which Dronkers had been trading, there is no other information about his Black Market activities;

(e) Both Mulder and de Langen confirmed that Dronkers had left the *Joppe* and spent the night at the Café Mayer;

(f) If de Langen was questioned about any absences by Dronkers from the Post Office the information is not in any of the files.

In yet another account of his story on 16 June, Dronkers stated that the *Joppe*, which had been lying in Amsterdam, belonged to 'Dr Schneider' but he did not know who had taken it to Nieuwesluis. When he told 'Dr Schneider' that he could not sail the boat alone and needed at least two others to accompany him, 'Dr Schneider' first of all said he didn't have anyone and asked if Dronkers knew someone. Dronkers suggested de Langen since he knew that he was anxious to escape from Holland, so 'Dr Schneider' agreed. (The two used to meet for lunch and de Langen had expressed an interest in accompanying Dronkers to England.) Dronkers also claimed that de Langen did not know 'Dr Schneider' and was completely innocent. A few days later, 'Dr Schneider' said he thought Verkuyl could find someone else who also wanted to escape. This turned out to be Mulder who Dronkers met at Verkuyl's house on Sunday 10 May, a little under a week before their journey. Dronkers said he was pretty sure that Mulder knew nothing of his mission.

Here the story changes again. Dronkers said he went to Nieuwesluis on Tuesday 12 May and received the keys to the cabin and engine of the *Joppe* from a German guard, and not 'Jan' as he had originally claimed, on production of a letter from 'Dr Schneider'. He stayed at the Café Mayer until Friday 15 May when he took the *Joppe* to Hellevoetsluis where it was filled with petrol by the German Petrol Bureau, authorised by 'Dr Schneider'. Then he took the *Joppe* back to Nieuwesluis and moored her up.

Dronkers met Mulder and de Langen at 7.15 p.m. at the tram terminus in Heenvliet and took them to the *Joppe* where he hid them in the fore-peak. He then went back to the Café Mayer and at the suggestion of 'Dr Schneider', wrote a letter to his wife, Elise, saying that he was going to try to get to Spain. Elise knew that he was actually going to England, but this was so that she could explain his absence to friends. When he took some paper and envelopes to the boat de Langen wrote to his family, and Mulder to various friends.

Dronkers described 'Jan' to de Langen and Mulder as an 'ordinary fisherman' who would help take him through the lock; it was he who later posted their letters. However, neither of them ever saw 'Jan', only heard his voice as they were locked in the fore-peak the whole time. The following morning 'Jan' returned to take them through the lock and, once through, got off onto a coal barge lying just outside. Edward Cussen of SL(B), the Legal Section, prepared a Note to File on 18 June referring to Dronkers' confession in which he stated:

> The circumstances under which the confession at 20a at 10a was made were that Mr Pinto had obtained the assistance of a Dutch Intelligence Officer [Vrinten] who was aware of Dronkers' former connection with Dr. Hampkus of Cologne. This Dutch Intelligence Officer was brought to see Dronkers, Mr Pinto questioned Dronkers about this connection. Dronkers denied it and Mr Pinto pretended to become very angry and told Dronkers he was lying and that he was putting a rope round his own neck and said that he must now say exactly who had sent him to this country. Dronkers then broke down and said that he had been sent by the Germans. After an interval Mr Pinto saw him again and took the statement from him which contains the confession which is dated 16.6.42 at 20a 10a. He was cautioned before and after the statement was taken. He made it in Dutch and Mr Pinto translated it to a shorthand-typist who took it down. It was then typed in English and Mr Pinto then checked it with Dronkers in English. He then signed it. Only the word 'evidence' required further explanation.[21]

This is confirmed in the Registry list at the beginning of Dronkers' file (KV2/43), where there are two entries for 16.6.42 which are of special interest:

> Statement by DRONKERS at RPS: admitting that he is a German Agent and is identical with Karel van DONGEN (23a)
> B1d/RPS note on DRONKERS admission (23b)

7

The Radio Oranje Episode

In order to make it known that they had arrived in England safely, Dronkers and his compatriots expressed a desire to make a broadcast on Radio Oranje. This was a Dutch-language radio programme of the BBC European Service managed by the Dutch government-in-exile which broadcast to the occupied Netherlands each day for fifteen minutes at 9.00 p.m. from Stratton House, Piccadilly. On 30 May, Dronkers, Mulder and de Langen wrote to Jackson to protest the way in which they saw their case being handled:

> As loyal and Orange-minded Dutchmen, we wish to protest emphatically against the slow way our case is being dealt with. We should like to have <u>our</u> interests settled by the Dutch Authorities. Any suspicions on your side are ridiculous and absurd.
>
> Surely this cannot be the award for our patriotism which has manifested itself by an escape, nearly ending in a shipwreck, after two miserable days and nights on the sea.
>
> We have definitely informed those who remain behind in Holland, to listen for news from us to the 'Radio-Oranje' on the 2nd, 3rd or 4th of June. If they heard us it would mean that we were safe. If not, that we were taken prisoner by the Germans and executed.
>
> In the latter case, those remaining behind would be frightfully anxious and try to save their lives as the possibility could exist that that we might give their names to the Germans in consequence of torture.
>
> In order to prevent the complete suppression of our enthusiasm, especially of the first undersigned [Mulder], who secretly for 2½ years has served the interests of the House of Orange, risking his own life, we respectfully but emphatically request that our case be terminated, preferably to-day and not tomorrow.[1]

By the time Dronkers, Mulder and de Langen wrote to Jackson again on 3 June (the date in the file is actually 4 June as it had had to be translated) they were clearly getting anxious and dissatisfied with MI5's apparent intransigence in dealing with their request and the message they were supposed to send once they had arrived in the UK:

> With reference to our previous letter, we beg to point out that it is now the 3rd of June. This evening many will be listening in Holland to Radio Oranje for our voices; they will of course hear nothing. Tomorrow is their last chance. (you will probably receive this letter on the 4th June – therefore today). If the mother of de Langen does not hear anything of her boy on this day the shock may prove fatal to her as she is to undergo an operation.
>
> As regards Mulder's friends and the active members of his organisation, these will be extremely worried and unnecessarily try to hide themselves.
>
> Should we be unable to come before the Radio ourselves, could you arrange for the attached greetings to be broadcast this evening?[2]

The proposed announcement read as follows:

> From a harbour somewhere in Holland three Dutchmen, Carel, Theo and Bruno, have escaped. After having struggled for two days and two nights in a light sail and motor boat against engine trouble, stormy weather and leakages, they were picked up two miles from Harwich by a British trawler. Owing to circumstances, they cannot appear in person before the microphone; here are their greetings:-
>
> 1. Bruno greets Marie.
> 2. Carel greets Lies
> 3. Theo greets Knoertje; Theo greets Kondje: Remember my letter and rest assured that the time will come when all previous suffering will be forgotten. Theo further greets all his friends and compatriots and hopes soon to be able to return to their circle.

In fact Maria Margaretha ('Marie') de Langen (*née* Van Gorcom) died on 15 July 1942 in Leiden, although she was actually living at nearby Voorschoten. Her death in Leiden was reported by Carel Hendrik Wijkmans whose profession was doorman.

R. S. Sands of the RVPS, in the fourth report written on 5 June, elaborated on the names mentioned in the proposed broadcast on Radio Oranje:

> 'Bruno' = de Langen
> 'Carel' = Dronkers
> 'Theo' = Mulder

'Maria' is the mother of de Langen
'Lies' is Dronkers' wife [Elise]
'Kondje' is Stanny Van Meerwijk, 4, Lepelstraat Den Bosch, to whom
Mulder was originally engaged
'Knoertje' is Suzannah Henny the girl with whom Mulder has been going
lately and who is mentioned in the first report.[3]

On 23 July Captain McKinnell of Camp 020 interviewed Dronkers and
posed four questions related to the proposed broadcast:

a) Is it generally believed in Holland that if a refugee makes a successful
   escape to this country, he will be permitted to appear before the
   microphone in person and send a message of his own fabrication to
   his family in Holland? Can either Dronkers or Mulder confirm what is
   implied in this episode, that the Germans believe this also?
   Answer: According to Dronkers it is quite well known in Holland that
   BBC messages have been sent by refugees. He believes that the Germans
   know of this, but does not think that such messages would convey
   much information to them, owing to the fact that these refugees all use
   fictitious names.
b) If they had not been detained so long at the RVPS whom did they intend
   to approach with their request to send this message over the BBC? Was
   this channel suggested to them by Verkuyl?
   Answer: Dronkers stated that, had they been set free in time to send the
   message, they would have gone to the BBC offices and enquired if the
   message might be sent through Radio Oranje. They had not been told of
   any special person to approach.
c) At what hour and in what feature in the days in question was it intended
   that the message should be sent by Radio Oranje?
   Answer: Dronkers suggested that Mulder knew more about the times of
   sending than he did. All he knew was that Mulder had told his friends
   to listen in the evenings of the 2nd, 3rd, and 4th June.
d) Major Stimson has already pointed out the possibility that Mulder's
   BBC name Theo may stand in the same relation to an as yet unknown
   signature for secret writing letters as Dronkers' Carel van Dongen of
   the BBC message of his secret writing.
   Answer: On this point Dronkers merely confirmed that the name Theo
   was chosen by Mulder himself.

Various stories grew up around this mythical broadcast. A former supervisory
official at the Old Bailey claimed erroneously in 1957 that

Dronkers cultivated the friendship of the officials in charge of the
programme Radio Oranje, which was sponsored by the Netherlands

Government in London. He found to his surprise and excitement that his suggestion about broadcasting a message of greeting to his old comrades was accepted and a time arranged. He wrote his brief script and in the usual way submitted it for timing and censorship. Still everything appeared to be all right. The broadcast was scheduled and Dronkers duly arrived at the underground studio to give his talk. He spoke into the microphone – which unknown to him was dead. He was detained immediately afterwards, charged with espionage.[4]

In fact, Dronkers was incarcerated in Camp 020 and, unless the relevant page(s) from his file have been redacted, which is always possible, there is no mention of his ever being allowed to make his broadcast. This account also implied that until the time of the proposed broadcast Dronkers was a free man, which was never the case after he had been arrested on 18 May. Not only that, but it claimed he was an 'expert telegraphist' who had 'a scrap of paper signed by known leaders of the Dutch Resistance, which pronounced Dronkers a member of the Underground and in imminent danger of arrest by the Gestapo',[5] none of which has been substantiated by careful examination of his MI5 files.

E. H. Cookridge (Edward Spiro), in an article written after the war, also perpetuates this myth by saying that Dronkers had been allowed to go ahead with making his broadcast on Radio Oranje:

Only a few days later Dronkers stood before the microphone of 'Radio Orange', the transmitter sponsored by the Dutch Government at the BBC [*sic*].

In his hand he had messages of greeting he had written to his former comrades – or that was what they appeared to be. In the messages were cunningly inserted code words. They would be taken down by German monitors, recording every word of every broadcast throughout the 24 hours. In a matter of hours they would be in the hands of Nazi spy-chief Ritter, who would rush to his bosses the good news.

He made his broadcast without the slightest indication of the suppressed excitement that possessed him. He ended with 'Goud Mornjing' and turned away from the microphone. Then his face fell …

To his fear that the espionage charge might be proved was added the humiliation of learning that the microphone in which he had been speaking was connected, not to a transmitter, but simply to the room where intelligence officers had been standing watching him.[6]

The trouble is, there is no indication in the files that MI5 ever allowed him to make the broadcast, or that this spoof broadcast was engineered!

8

Who Was 'Doctor Schneider'?

There is much about me you do not know.

Spymaster (Ted Calloway), *Earth-616*

The mysterious 'Doctor Schneider' made his first appearance during a meeting with Agent SNOW (Arthur Owens) in Hamburg in August 1939:

> Ritter appeared the following morning accompanied by another Abwehr officer introduced as Herr Schneider ... Lily was handed a twenty Reichsmark note by Owens, who had received it from Schneider ...[1]

The same account describes 'Dr Schneider' as being Nikolaus Ritter's (alias 'Dr Rantzau' or Rheinhardt) replacement, based in Hamburg.[2] Ritter had been assigned to *Ast* Hamburg in 1937 and would remain there until June 1941 when he was in Libya.[3] 'Dr Schneider' is also referred to in an unofficial history of MI5:

> SNOW's principal contact in Germany was known only as 'The Doctor' ... he appeared to occupy the position of Leiter of I Luft, Hamburg ... He was introduced to various men by the names of Kurtz, "Schneider", Herr Doctor and Leitz ... At the meeting in Breslau the doctor described himself as Dr. Rantzau's secretary.[4]

So who was 'Dr Schneider'? Let us first take a look at the contenders and eliminate those who do not qualify. A chart of *Ast* Hamburg in the spring of 1939 shows that *Leiter* of Luft I was Major Ritter (alias 'Dr Rantzau'), who fell under the overall command of Herbert Wichmann. By the time Dronkers met 'Dr Schneider' Ritter had been posted out of the Abwehr and into Luftgau kdo Hamburg, where he worked in *Abt* 1c (1 April – 30 September). Therefore, the 'Dr Schneider' referred to by Dronkers cannot be Ritter.

There is a reference in the literature to a Major Hans Wagner (alias Hans Schneider or Hans Salzinger, also known as Dr Wagner) who was Abwehr Section III F (counter espionage) liaison officer in Stockholm dealing with the Scandinavian and Russian side of Abt III, and interrogated by the Allies in 1945, but he is not our man.[5, 6]

A Hauptmann (Captain) Dr Schneider is mentioned in the context of meetings held with representatives from the German cypher departments and the Abwehr to discuss Case Wicher, the name given to the German discovery in 1939 that the Poles had broken the Enigma codes and had been reading them up to the outbreak of war in 1939, and for some time afterwards. Wicher was the name of the Polish cryptanalytic organisation which had decyphered Enigma. Case Wicher was also the name assigned to the definite proof given in 1943 or 1944 that the Poles had found a solution to Enigma. Although *Der Fall Wicher* says that the Naval High Command (OKM) did not know about the Polish affair, the war diary of Inspectorate 7/VI (the German Army's code-breaking inspectorate)[7] for the month of April 1942 shows that a meeting took place between the naval officers Stummel and Singer, the Abwehr officials Hauptmann Dr Schneider and the Army cryptanalyst Dr Pietsch.[8, 9] This same Schneider also visited captured Polish intelligence officers on the General Staff in July 1942. In September 1943 he accompanied the OKM's Hauptmann Singer and Inspectorate's 7/VI Dr Pietsch to the Neuengamme concentration camp (near Hamburg) to interrogate the Polish intelligence officer Leja. However, this particular Schneider was an Army officer, but as we shall see, the 'Dr Schneider' referred to by Dronkers was most likely a naval officer.

Oreste Pinto believed Dronkers' contact to be Herr Strauch, who was in reality Kapitänleutnant Friederich ('Fritz') Carl Heinrich Strauch (1895–1959), alias Strachwitz, Strauchwitz, Stranz, Herr Doktor or Dr Rudi. During the First World War Strauch had served in the Das Kaiserlich Deutscher Marineoffizierkorps (Imperial German Navy Officer Corps) where he was listed as a Fähnrich zur See (Cadet/Midshipman (Junior Grade)). On 31 August 1939 he joined the navy and worked for the Abwehr. He was the officer who had recruited Pieter Jan Schipper, as we shall see in Chapter 26.

In the MI5 file on Hermann Giskes (1896–1977), it states he was stationed in the Netherlands and head of Abwehr Section IIIF; he was also responsible for the *Englandspiel* in 1942. A breakdown of the Abwehr's *Ast Niederlande* lists Strauch as being a Kapitänleutnant in Gruppe I, Marine, in the subsidiary *Stelle* in Amsterdam. Strauch was a reserve officer who had lived in Amsterdam prior to 1939. Giskes described him as being about 50, of medium height and slim build, about 1.75 metres tall, weighing about 75 kilograms, with grey hair, blue eyes and a weatherbeaten complexion, clean-shaven and always very neat in a naval uniform.

Englandspiel was the German operation (Operation Nordpol) conducted in 1942 in which Dutch agents sent by SOE to the Netherlands were captured by the SD. Controversy has arisen as to whether or not SOE was aware that these Dutch agents had been captured. Almost all were executed in Mauthausen concentration camp. Their tragic story, which would involve another book, does not appear to have had any impact on the Dronkers case.

The 'Dr Schneider' referred to in our story should not be confused with 'Dr Schneider', the pseudonym which General Rheinhard Gehlen assigned himself when he was recruited by the Americans after the Second World War. Gehlen helped to establish the post-war German intelligence service, the Abteilung Fremde Heere Ost (FHO), also known as the 'Gehlen Organisation', which was to become the Bundesnachrichtendienst (BND), the modern-day German foreign intelligence service, in 1956. Nor should 'Schneider' be confused with SS-Obersturmbahnführer Joseph Schreieder who was head of Amt IV (Gestapo) in The Netherlands, the reason being that apart from the names being spelled differently, the physical descriptions of 'Dr Schneider' and Schreieder are quite different. Schreieder, as described by Giskes, was a small, almost bald man, with a heavy round head, flabby well-manicured hands, slightly protruding rat-like eyes, a pasty face and red nose, aged 39.[10] Parts of this description seem to concur with a description in a CIA report made in 1955 of an interview with Joseph Schreieder which describes him as,

> Approximately 50 years old; 5'7" tall; 175 lbs; a little corpulent; ruddy complexion; dark eyes; wears glasses; balding, greyish-brown wisps of hair; speaks with a Bavarian accent; dresses a little shabbily and sloppily in comfortable fashion of some Bavarian officials; shrewd police-type; appeared to be ambitious and vain, profoundly convinced of his own professional skills.[11]

The plumpness (heavy, round head and flabby hands) and thinning hair agree, although height is different, but some people are not very good at judging height, so some leeway must be given here.

Silvio Ruiz Robles, Cornelius Evertsen and Peter Marcussen Krag,[12] who had arrived aboard the M/V *Josephine* which put into Fishguard on 12 November 1940 claiming that they were all refugees, described a 'Dr Schneiderwind'[13] as being between 45 and 50 (although Evertsen thought 35), between (1.74 metres and 1.80 metres tall, with grey brushed back hair, blue eyes, a sharp nose, clean-shaven, pale to fair complexion, sometimes dressed in the naval uniform of a Korvettenkapitän, probably promoted to Fregattenkapitän after a visit to Berlin) who spoke German, French and English (Dronkers said 'Dr Schneider' spoke broken Dutch). This trio was interned in Camp 020 until after the war.

Korvettenkapitän Schniederwind is shown in the organisational chart of *Ast* Hamburg 1939 as being Gruppe II *Leiter* but is not shown in another chart for May 1944. On 14 August 1940 there is an entry in the MI5 file for another contender for 'Dr Schneider' (see below) in an account of Korvettenkapitän Schniederwind and another agent in Brest, so Schniederwind cannot be 'Dr Schneider'. Schniederwind should also not be confused with Karl-Hermann Schneidewind, the U-boat captain (1907–1965), nor with Hermann or Kurt Schniedewind of the Luftwaffe.

Captain Eric Goodacre of Camp 020 drew up a comparison of descriptions as given to him by Dronkers, van Wijk, Pedro Hechevarria, Robles, Evertsen and Krag. 'Dr Schneider' as described by Dronkers and van Wijk was about 46, 1.70–1.71 m, with 'pepper and salt' hair brushed back, a sharp nose, thin and slim, who only wore civilian clothes, walked with a slight limp and always carried an attaché case under his left arm. This seems to concur with Robles, Evertsen and Krag. He was thought to be a naval intelligence officer, also known as Schneiderlin. Goodacre concluded that apart from any agreement over the limp, there was a 'considerable degree of resemblance between the descriptions'.

	DR SCHNEIDER The Hague Description obtained by VAN WIJK from DRONKERS	Captain SCHNEIDERWIND Brest Description by:		
		ROBLES 28.12.40	EVERTSEN 17.11.40	KRAG 11.12.40
Nationality	German	-	-	German
Age	46	45/50	About 35(?)	50
Height	1.70/1.71 m (5ft. 7ins)	1.74 m (5'9")	Tall	1.80 m (5'11")
Weight	-	-	-	75/80 kilos
Hair	Possibly 'pepper& salt' but is not sure; brushed back	Grey, brushed straight back	-	Greying; had been blond
Eyes	Does not know	-	Dark blue	Blue
Face	Sharp nose	Pointed	Sharp; clean-shaven	Clean-shaven
Complexion	-	Pale	Fair	Pale
Glasses	None	-	None	None
Build	Thin; slim	Very slim and straight	-	Rather slim
Uniform	Seen only in civilian clothes	-	Sometimes in uniform	Naval uniform; sometimes civilian clothes
Rank	Dr. Does not know if he is an officer; thinks he is a civilian	-	Navy Captain	Korvettenkapitän. Since visit too Berlin, probably promoted to Freegattenkapitän
Languages	Broken Dutch	Halting Spanish; French	English; a little Dutch	German, French, English
Peculiarities	Peculiar, limping walk. Aways an attache-case under left arm	-	-	Nervous, highly-strung manner; spoke in rushes
Aliases	-	-	SCHNEIDERLIN	SCHNEIDERLIN; Dr. SCHNEIDER
In civil life	-	-	-	Probably Naval Intelligence

Camp 020/24.7.42
KBG/MA

There are a few other probable non-runners who can be eliminated: a list of secretaries employed by *Kommando Meldegebiet* (Command and Report District) Hamburg formed from the Group I *Ast* shows a Herr Schneider attached to Leiter II/1; a 'Summary of Traces' dated 25 July 1945 shows that there was no trace of any Schneider in SHAEF's records; a list of minor characters in *Ast* Hamburg includes a Schneider who was aged 50 in 1944, height 1.68 metres, slim with light brown hair who worked as a draughtsman, is also unlikely. FBI files at the National Archives & Records Administration (NARA) list a number of other possible Schneider contenders, particularly those involved in espionage. There are also sixteen men named Schneider in *The Factual List of Nazis Protected by Spain*, but none of whom appear to fit the bill, so must be discounted.

A clue to the identity of 'Dr Schneider' may lie in the MI5 file of Herbert Wichmann, who seems to be the most likely candidate.[14] Wichmann, who was a Korvettenkapitän in charge of *Ast* Hamburg during the time that Dronkers was recruited, was formally arrested on 10 May1945 and later interrogated at Camp 020. His description also bears a striking resemblance to the one given by Dronkers *et al.*, apart from the fact that his photograph in the MI5 file shows him wearing glasses. However, since Dronkers was arrested in 1942 and the interrogations of Wichmann took place in 1945 this feature may have been new. This is borne out by a list of his personal property dated 9 July 1945 in which an optician's prescription is mentioned. A further list of property drawn up the following day when he was turned over to Camp 020 from the London District Cage on 22 June 1945 added '2 prs. spectacles, 1 leather spectacle case'. A CSDIC report by the 21st Army Group on Kapitän zur See Freiherr von Bechtolsheim describes him as nearly always wearing glasses.[15]

Herbert Christian Oscar Otto Wichmann, also known as Werner, was born in Hamburg on 18 April 1894 (although other sources say as early as 1882 or 1891) to Oscar Wichmann and Emma Wichmann, *née* Harbeck. The age given by Dronkers in 1942 for 'Dr Schneider' was 46; Robles and Krag said between 45 and 50 for Schneiderwind. Taking 1894 as his birth date makes Wichmann 48 in 1942, which makes it about right. Other characteristics were his height at 1.72–1.76 metres, which also concurs; his hair was dark grey, which also seems to agree (although Dronkers described it as 'pepper and salt'); sharp, pointed features and blue eyes, which concurs with Robles and Krag's description of Schneiderwind. In one of MI5's files on Ritter a CX report from MI6 dated 10 August 1942 and addressed to Major John Gwyer of MI5's B1a, in which the unknown MI6 author laments the scarce amount of knowledge they have on *Ast* Hamburg, gives Wichmann as being aged about '60 years of age, tall, slim, with dark grey hair, blue eyes, typical officer. He speaks fluent English and appears to be unmarried. He lives with his mother, Mrs O. Wichmann, at 39a Bellevue.' In fact, according to Wichmann's file, his mother's name was Emma. That being said, his MI5 file (KV2/103) records his address in 1942 as being 'c/o Mrs O. Wichmann (mother)'. Gwyer had in fact written to someone in MI6 on 26 March 1942 in response to a CX report on Ritter saying that:

> It seems very clear from your letter and the attached reports that the FBI has quite a quantity of information on the Hamburg Stelle which is new to us or complementary to what we have. Do you suppose that there is any possibility of the FBI emitting a report on this subject? If they do we should find it extremely interesting as we still have several cases on our hands which originated from Hamburg.[16]

According to a 'Secret MI5 Interim Interrogation Report' dated August 1945, Wichmann's aliases were Wegener, Wiesinger, Weber and Wolf. The report states that he could speak English and Spanish in addition to his native German. He began his career in the Imperial German Navy as a Midshipman on 1 April 1914, serving first on the ironclad warship *Hansa*, then on the König-class battleship SMS *Grosser Kurfürst* (1914–15). In December 1914 he was promoted to Färnricht zur See and in 1916 to Leutnant zur See while serving on the Pillau-class light cruiser *Elbing*. Between 1916 and 1917 he served on the Graudenz-class light cruiser *Graudenz*. At the end of the First World War he was discharged as an Oberleutnant sur Zee having become Flag Lieutenant to a torpedo boat flotilla leader.

In civilian life from 1919 to 1934 he worked for a number of different companies in Hamburg, Dusseldorf, Buenos Aires and Montevideo, marrying Lulu Bieber in 1922.[17] In spite of having a wife, he was later to have a girlfriend, Frau Marissal, who he referred to as *Schnutchen* while she referred to him as *Pumpelchen*. In 1934 he re-enlisted in the German Navy and became Naval Signals Officer at the Wireless Station Holtenau at Kiel. After attending the Naval Signals School at Flensburg, service at the wireless station in Tannenburg as Naval Signals Officer, and the destroyer torpedo boat *Kondor*, he was summoned in November 1935 to Berlin and informed by the *Amt/Ausland* Abwehr that he was being posted to the Hamburg Abwehrstelle to learn the ropes. He really began his career in the Abwehr in December when he was promoted to Korvettenkapitän and posted to *Ast* Lindau in Bavaria under *Leiter* Oberst Gombart and served in I Marine.

Between 1935 and 1936 he spent much of his time learning about the southern coast of France, taking over several agents from his predecessor, Korvettenkapitän Wendt. In February 1936 he was in Frankfurt am Main reporting to Kapitän zur See von Bonin. In April he travelled to Italy and Switzerland, as well as Budapest in July. In mid-November he was transferred to *Ast* Stuttgart, but only stayed a month.

When Korvettenkapitän Herbert Wichmann came to *Ast* Hamburg at the end of 1936, section I M(arine) only consisted of Korvettenkapitän Burghardt, Kapitänleutnant Ernst Müller (who organised a service to interrogate systematically all officers of the German Merchant Navy after their return to Hamburg, the so-called Schiffsbefragungsdienst), Hilmar Dierks and some secretaries. Later on the staff was enlarged.[18]

Hilmar Dierks, born in 1889 and a First World War spymaster, was killed in a car accident in early September 1940 on the eve of an operation involving three agents being sent to England via Scotland – Vera von Schalburg (alias Vera Eriksen, who had been married to Dierks), Theodore Drücke, and Werner Walti (alias Robert Petter). Drücke and Walti were hanged on 12 June 1941, while Vera disappeared.[19] Given her Russian background, it has been alleged that she may have been recruited by MI5 or MI6 to carry out Cold War spying for them. Could the following entry in Guy Liddell's post-war diaries for 30 October 1946 be a clue, and was it Vera?

> I went to see 'C' about the employment of [*redacted*], who is of Russian origin. We want to take her on for Russian work. We had made every enquiry that we could and were satisfied, as far as it was possible to be so, that she was all right. I did not, however, wish it to get round that we were employing a Russian woman and were consequently insecure. If, therefore, 'C' did not like the the position, on account of any opportunities which might give this woman access to his information, I would much prefer not to take her on. He said that he, in fact, had White Russians and Poles himself and that it was a risk he thought we both had to take.[20]

According to Wichmann, who became *Leiter* (Head) of Gruppe I in 1939 and Head of *Ast* Hamburg in May 1940, Dierks was specifically in charge of recruiting agents.

Until the beginning of 1937, Dierks had worked for both I Marine and I Luft, but in 1937, I Luft was established as an independent section headed by Hauptmann Nikolaus Ritter (also known as 'Dr Rantzau'). Both men took an active part in the extended recruiting activity of *Ast* Hamburg, travelling extensively between Germany, Belgium and Holland and using a variety of cover names and cover addresses. Interestingly, Dierks would sometimes use the name J. Van Dongen as a cover name, a name which Dronkers had been instructed to use. One of the MI5 files on Eriksen confirms this, saying that Dierks had used the alias in Holland in 1938/39.[21] Dronkers said he had no idea why that name had been chosen by 'Dr Schneider', but a memo from Ronnie Haylor to 'Buster' Milmo on 25 October gives us a clue as to where this might have originated:

> As spoken, Pinto, who is now with the Dutch Intelligence, informs me that in the course of the interrogation of a Dutch national named Tas, Louis (RVPS 6140)[22] who was released from the RVPS on 23.3.42, it was stated by Tas that he had distributed pro-Allied propaganda in Holland and had been assisted by his brother and a man named Dr. Karel van Dongen …

You will probably wish to arrange for Dronkers (RVPS 7411) to be asked to give the fullest particulars of the manner in which he came to receive the cover name of Karel van Dongen.[23]

It may also have been in tribute to Dierks that Wichmann chose to use the name as Dronkers' cover name.

In 1937 Wichmann was made *Leiter* I Marine under Korvettenkapitän Burghardt. At that time there was only a small staff, consisting of himself, Burghardt, Dierks (alias zum Stuhröck), Kapitänleutnant der Reserve Mueller, and a few secretaries. Wichmann mentioned that a Dutch art dealer named Reich had been sent to England in 1938 to try to recruit agents, but was not successful. This was the same year that Dronkers was supposedly first recruited by the Abwehr, although as was noted earlier he was not actually in England at that time. Unfortunately, there is no mention of Dronkers, Verkuyl or Dr Hampkus anywhere in the Wichmann file, or operations in the Netherlands.

During his interrogations at Camp 020 Wichmann does recall Ritter recruiting an agent (SNOW), and another known as DICK (CELERY – Walter Dicketts). As Lt Col Douglas Bernard 'Stimmy' Stimpson of Camp 020 noted in his file:

> Wichmann has appeared willing to give all information which he possesses, but the measure of its reliability is tempered by his faulty memory. Whether he has traded on this is difficult to decide, and such information as cannot be checked should be treated with reserve.[24]

In May 1940 Wichmann was promoted to *Leiter Ast* Hamburg and in July travelled to the Netherlands to look at Rotterdam. In September he was summoned to Abwehr HQ in Berlin and told that he was to be attached to Heeresgruppe 'A' and to make plans for Abwehr requirements for the invasion of Britain, *Unternehmen Seelöwe* (Operation Sea Lion). In early September he summoned Erich Pfeiffer to a meeting at the Hotel Lutetia on the Boulevard Raspail on the Left Bank in Paris to discuss the proposed invasion and the establishment of *Einsatz commandos* and Abwehr *Kommandos* which would accompany the army. Pfeiffer would be in operational command of *Sichtstellen* composed of officers of Abteilung I and all the sub-units, including III group, while Wichmann would be in charge, with the title of *Astleiter* z.b.V (Special Duties) at the HQ of the Heersgruppe.[25] The plan they drew up was delivered personally to Berlin by Wichmann. It seems from Pfeiffer's MI5 file that following the abandonment of Operation Sea Lion Wichmann wanted to instigate a smaller version of the invasion of Britain in 1941 during the invasion of Greece, and drew up plans[26] in collaboration with Pfeiffer and Major Praetorius, his *Leiter I*.

Towards the end of September 1940 Pfeiffer and Wichmann had been posted to the Heersgruppe, where they carried out radio tests, and waited until 10 or 11 October, when the plan to invade Britain was finally abandoned. Pfeiffer then returned to Brest and Wichmann to Hamburg. Pfeiffer noted that

> I arranged, as far as possible in 1941, to be in Paris when Wichmann, for one reason or another, might be there: on the whole Wichmann and I had the same point of view on our work, and were very much against the level of the officer corps of the Abwehr being reduced by the induction of unsuitable elements.[27]

Wichmann was to claim in his interrogations at Camp 020 in 1945 that 'all attempts to spy on England were disappointing, and that in spite of all their efforts the Germans achieved nothing'. Admiral Wilhelm Canaris, the head of the Abwehr, recorded that he was 'most displeased' with their work and that of the whole Section I of the Abwehr. This statement by Wichmann about intelligence failures is in sharp contrast to the findings in a recently published book by Monika Siedentopf,[28] so far only available in German. According to a review in *The Guardian* newspaper, her book focuses on Wichmann's role in sending spies to Britain (Operation Lena) who were of low intelligence but good National Socialists. If this is true, Wichmann's logic shows a certain prescience in doing so because he was afraid that Operation Sea Lion would fail, and at great cost to Germany, and would ultimately escalate into a full-blown world war. Sending agents with little or no knowledge of Britain would help in defusing the invasion plan. This lack of knowledge was borne out by the so-called 'Invasion Spies', as we shall see in Chapter 24 *et seq*. But was Wichmann acting on his own initiative, or on Canaris's instructions? By the time Dronkers was sent over, German plans for the invasion of Britain had long been abandoned and Germany was in the throes of a war with the Soviet Union on the Eastern Front.

Siedentopf's book also reveals that Wichmann was linked to Admiral Canaris and the Stauffenberg group who conspired to assassinate Hitler in July 1944. No mention of this can be found in Wichmann's MI5 file, although this could have been weeded out, nor in recent published accounts of Operation Valkyrie, the assassination plot to kill Hitler. However, a report dated 24 September 1945 which had been extracted from a BAOR report on GLASS on 2 February 1946 about Werner Wichmann (one of his aliases) suggests that the Gestapo had begun to compile a case against him with a possible link to the July 20 assassination attempt on Hitler:

> From July/44 to May 45 GLASS through WINDEL[29] kept abreast of the evidence which the Gestapo were compiling against WICHMANN and kept him informed of its extent.

GLASS knew of the existence of "documents" implicating WICHMANN from STAWITZKI, and finally persuaded WINDEL to show them to her. They were shown in her flat, but the accumulated evidence was not convincing. The Gestapo had proof that WICHMANN had passes made out in six different names, and that he had a cover address in MUNKCH [sic] under the firm CONTROLLCO. They had little knowledge of his visit to BERLIN on 20 July. There was also in the documents a Gestapo report on the activities of Hoib BERGEMEYER[based in Berlin], a friend of WICHMANN, wherein the foreign activities of B. [BERGEMEYER] had arouses [sic] suspicion and information from the RSHA had been asked for. On this report WICHMANN had taken the liberty of writing "So ein QUATSCH" in big red pencil [trs: What a load of crap!]. The details of this meeting were handed to WICHMANN by GLASS, and he was especially amused by the BERGEMEYER[30] report.

> Even our Kpt. Wichmann, for whom I had the greatest respect, was suspected of being pro-British by the Gestapo.[31]

This anti-Nazi, pro-British sympathy is borne out in a reference to an offer by the Allies to discuss peace if Hitler were to be overthrown (as reported by Boeckel's agent Oberstleutnant Raydt[32] via Christiansen in Norway). Christiansen was also known as Eisbär (polar bear), an *Ast* Hamburg agent for Norway and Sweden.

The offer was not passed on by *Ast* Hamburg, according to Major Julius Boeckel, because 'it was not felt it would be well received if it came from Abw, and especially from Wichmann who was known to be anti-Nazi'.[33] The rest of *Ast* Hamburg's activities during 1940–41 were spent sending agents to the Iberian Peninsula (Spain and Portugal). This may have been when the contact address in Bilbao was established.

Wichmann was promoted to Freegattenkapitän on 1 January 1941 with effect from 1 December 1940. On 1 November 1941 he was promoted to Kapitän zur See, and at the end of January 1942 he attended a high level Abwehr conference in Berlin. For part of March he was reportedly on leave skiing in Salzburg and Garmisch-Partenkirchen; in May/June he was again on five or six weeks leave in Bad Pistyan, Slovakia; Garmisch; and Lake Constance recovering from sciatica and lumbago.[34] Visas were issued on 12 March 1942 at Hamburg for a return journey to Mostyn-Lundenburg or Marchegg bahnhof (train station), from Mielland, Slovakia; on 16 April 1940 at Berlin to Slovakia, which was stamped at the German frontier on 7 May, with another stamp on 30 May, which concurs with Slovakian visas stamped on the same dates. This ailment may account for why Dronkers described him as walking with a limp whereas others did not. All that being said, one wonders why he would not have stayed around to monitor the progress of the Dronkers operation in May, unless his ailments were so severe he deputed someone else.

In his MI5 file Wichmann is described in 1942 by Josef Starziczny[35] as being *Ast Leiter* in SS Hamburg (although Wichmann claimed he knew nothing of the SS or Gestapo and worked for the Abwehr his entire intelligence career). Starziczny said that in 1939 Wichmann had been Chief of the Espionage Defence Section in Hamburg. Others, such as James Cromwell O'Neill, described him as a 'three-Ringer in the German navy' (i.e. Fregattenkapitän*)* and a 'big shot' in the Abwehr in Hamburg. O'Neill, from County Wexford, was one of a number of Irishmen, many in the British Army, who volunteered to work for the Abwehr II and were sent to Friesack Camp, designated Stalag XX-A (301), in the Brandenburg region to train in the use of explosives between 1940 and 1943.[36] After 1943 when the camp was dissolved they were either sent to fight on the Eastern Front or interned in a concentration camp.[37]

Captured Abwehr agent Janowski[38] reported Wichmann as being connected with Group I of the Abwehr in Hamburg and Kiel (a sub office) and was in Berlin in the summer of 1942. An Ultra intercept for 28 August may well confirm that Wichmann was in Berlin at that time:

28.8.42.
16964 WICHMANN (Berlin) to CUNO (Sofia): For AMBINK: MAX's date of departure unchanged.[39]

Jörgen Börressen, another Abwehr agent, described him as being the chief man in Hamburg in 1943.

If Wichmann is 'Dr Schneider' his entire career appears to have been spent in Hamburg. In 1944 he was reported to have been head of the Secret Service of MOK Nord (Abwehr III) (Naval Chief Command Baltic), head of the Abwehr in Hamburg (August), and in December the head of a new branch of submarine intelligence formed in Hamburg. Ironically, in a list of Wichmann's contacts there is a Clarens Schneider, a female friend of a friend of Wichmann's. Did he borrow her name, 'Schneider', as another alias?

Being a navy man, it would make sense that he might own the yacht *Joppe*, although it was more likely owned by the Abwehr. Another fact gleaned from the Wichmann file is that he had friends in the yachting community, namely Frau H. Waller in Göteburg whom he met in 1935 during a yacht race in Sweden, and Ebbe Wijkandler, also from Göteburg.[40] 'Consolidated Interrogation Report 039' from the Main HQ 30 Corps dated 21 June 1945 stated that in 1934, 'He had met naval friends in Berlin and had also kept up his interest in Yachting and even had visited Regattas in England, Sweden and Denmark.'

On 7 May 1945 Wichmann was captured by the 21st Army Group. The 2nd British Army sent a telegram to the War Room on 11 May to say that he had been traced to Hamburg and that 'The subject is prepared to talk'. He was transferred to Camp 031 at Barnstedt, near Westertimke, on 12 May,[41] the same camp that Heinrich Himmler would be taken to on 20 May. The War Room sent a telegram on 17 June 1945 to Major Noakes at the 21st Army Group with the following request:

> Would like Wichmann at 020. Although pressure of work precludes possibility of immediate interrogation, consider most desirable he should be segregated from colleagues and therefore suggest early transfer to UK.[42]

Wichmann was brought to England on Wednesday 20 June 1945 under escort of a Captain Hughes of the Intelligence Corps, arriving at RAF Hendon along with Dr Paul Dittel, an Obersturmbannführer in the SS, affiliated to the SD. In 1943 Dittel had succeeded Franz Six as head of the SS-Reichssicherheitshauptampt (RHSA), Amt VII. Ironically, Wichmann was described as a Category 'A' prisoner, whereas Dittel was an 'ordinary prisoner'. Owing to an administrative error there was no one to meet them from CSDIC, the Combined Services Detailed Interrogation Centre (also known as the London Cage), or Camp 020. Not only that, but two other prisoners had also arrived on the same aircraft – Korvettenkapitän Moehle [*sic*][43] and Kapitänleutnant Reber,[44] escorted by Lieutenant Jeffery, RNVR – who were supposed to have arrived at Croydon. When an escort did finally arrive from No. 2 Distribution Centre at Wilton Park, Beaconsfield, the instructions were to take everyone there, contrary to what had been expected. A note from Milmo on 22 June 1945 records:

> Major Le Bosquet rang me up this morning to state that Wichmann was in CSDIC. In view of serial 12A I expressed surprise and said I would look into the matter. I then ascertained from Major Ryde that he had not in fact carried out the instructions and had apparently acquiesced in the SCO allowing the DPW escort which arrived to take over Dittel and some other persons who were on the same plane, and bring them to CSDIC.
>
> I later confirmed with MI19, Major [Peter] Smithers, who eventually undertook to transfer Wichmann to Camp 020 and to see that he was not registered with DPW. I notified Camp 020, Colonel Stephens.[45]

On 26 June Milmo had scribbled a note on a minute sheet to Major Ryde of B1a,

> Ref 12a: Camp 020 informed regarding W. Can you say what instructions were given to 020? You will observe that at 14a that 020 say they received no further instructions about the collection of W.

12A (12a) was a minute to the NDO (Night Duty Officer) from Major M. Johnstone on 20 June 1945 regarding the possible arrival of Wichmann and Dittel during the night; 14a was the letter from Stimson to Milmo.

On 22 June, Stimson had written from Camp 020 to Milmo to clarify the situation:

> As requested, herewith the report from Capt. Moran who received the message on Wednesday evening at approximately 18.00 hrs concerning an escort for an incoming Category 'A' body.
>
> In view of these instructions the escort stood by until dark and was then stood down. No further messages were received that this body would arrive at Hendon Airport at 20.00 hrs, thus the escort was prepared to leave at any time.[46]

Milmo appended a note saying:

> Spoke Col. Stephens who confirmed that Camp 020 received no message from the NDO at Head Office; nor did they receive any message from anyone subsequent to Mr Horsfall's message.

St John Ratcliffe Stewart 'Jock' Horsfall (1910–49), the MI5 A3 Division, Transport officer had been a pre-war racing driver. Horsfall's message as stated by a captain [*signature illegible*] who had received the message at 18.00 on 20 June had said,

> Mr Horsfall informed me that it was not certain whether the body would arrive by that 'plane. The Security Officer at the Airport would see the 'plane in and inform the Night Duty Officer at St. James whether the prisoner was on it or not. The Night Duty Officer at St. James would in turn inform us of the arrival of the body and would we please stand by until we heard from the Night Duty Officer.

On 22 June Wichmann was received by Camp 020 from the London Cage.

In late June 1945 Wichmann's case was taken over by the War Room Registry (WRC1/C), which had been previously handled by WRC5. A 'Monthly Summary of Cases at Camp 020 and 020R (Hunterscombe)' for 1 July 1945, states that Wichmann was

> ... discovered in Hamburg in early May by the Second British Army and at once showed willingness to talk...Wichmann should prove a source of great interest, particularly in respect of activities directed against the United Kingdom from Hamburg before the war and in the first two years after the outbreak of war. There are a number of incompletely solved cases on which Wichmann can no doubt enlighten us. He should also provide useful particulars of Hamburg's activities against South America.

In 'Consolidated Interrogation Report 039' dated 21 June 1945, Lieutenant Findlay, his interrogator, concludes by saying that

> Wichmann has doubtless told his story honestly as far as it has gone. He knows that most of the facts he has given are either known or can be checked up. However, he is a wily customer who appears to be giving way on some points so as to cover his tracks on others.

Wichmann was able to provide both MI5 and MI6 with some information about the Abwehr's activities in South America; however, an extract from a monthly summary prepared by Camp 020 dated 1 August 1945 declared:

> This man, whose interrogation has been proceeding for over a month, has proved a disappointment as a source of information, particularly in regard to Ast Hamburg's activities against the United Kingdom in the early war years and those immediately preceding the war. Wichmann has, or finds it convenient to pretend to have, a very poor memory ... Wichmann has told us next to nothing about Hamburg's agent network in Brazil, Chile, Mexico and Argentina, and nothing at all of agents despatched on missions to the United Kingdom, such as UNLAND, SCHLUZ and SIMEN [sic], beyond stating that he believes the first two were controlled by Praetorius and that the third was controlled by the notorious I Luft official Ritter @ Rantzau. Of a list of 42 agents of Ast Hamburg operating in various parts of the world which Wichmann has provided during his stay at Camp 020, all were previously well known to us with the exception of 7, these being unidentifiable on the scanty information given.[47]

Werner Unland was believed by Wichmann to have been run by Praetorius. Schluz was Gunther Schutz and Simen was Walter Simon, trained by Nikolas Ritter ('Dr Rantzau').

A few days later on 3 August he was questioned about an assertion made by Walter Schellenberg that a Portuguese agent of *Ast* Hamburg had been sent to the USA from Bremen just four months before the end of the war. He was quoted as having no recollection of such an operation and suggested that it would have been more likely that Bischoff would have sent the agent from *Nest* Bremen. This is quite possible since *Ast* Hamburg and *Nest* Bremen operated independently of one another even though Bremen reported to Hamburg.

On 9 October 1945 Wichmann was returned to Germany via Buckeburg Airport. After the war the British gave him a job helping to rebuild the German shipping industry in Hamburg. It was later alleged that he had received top-grade information regarding Operation TORCH, the Allied invasion of French North Africa in 1942, from none other than Kim Philby.[48] Nigel West quotes Philby as saying, 'Vivian said that the Russians had known about Operation TORCH in advance, repeating what he had already told me – namely, that the Russians had accurate intelligence on the codes, beaches, medical supplies, etc., for the operation long before it was launched.'[49] This means the Germans must have had an agent also working for the Russians who passed on the information to them. The 'Vivian' referred to by Philby was Colonel Valentine Patrick Terrell Vivian (1886–1969), Vice Chief of MI6 and first head of Section V, Counter-espionage.

Author James Hayward cites German writer Gunther Peis, who claimed that former Abwehr officers, including Wichmann, had stated that they had received 'advanced warning from "a very reliable proven agent in the south of England"'. However, if Admiral Canaris or Field Marshal Keitel saw the report, no action on it was ever taken, and no evidence has come to light to support this theory. It was further suggested that Leonard Mosley had been inspired to build on this theory when he wrote his novel *The Druid*, in which there existed one spy during the Second World War who MI5 had failed to catch.[50] This myth is also debunked by John Campbell in *Dieppe Revisited: A Documentary Investigation*.[51]

Another suggestion as to the identity of 'Schneider' was offered by Edward Blanchard Stamp of B1b in the following note to a Miss Bingham of B1b on 10 October 1944 which can be found in the Schuchmann file from a Captain Marseille working at Camp 020:

MALBRANT
Captain Marseille rang up and told me that according to MALBRANT[52], SCHROEDER is the son of a shipowner at Hamburg.[53] The line in which he is interested is the SCHOENEMANN line. Captain Marseille added that the description of SCHROEDER appears to him similar to that of SCHNEIDER in the DRONKERS case.[54]

However, the description of Schroeder (or Schuchmann) in his MI5 file does not concur with that of Wichmann because their ranks were different (Wichmann outranked him), as well as Schuchmann not being in the Netherlands at the time (he was in Le Havre and Paris), so must be discounted as a possible contender:

Nationality: German; Age: 45 years; Build: Short, broad-shouldered, strong; Height: 1.68m; Hair: Fair, greying, not long; Eyes: Grey-blue; Face: Oval, broad; wide forehead, healthy complexion, straight nose, strong, square chin, good set of teeth, clean shaven; Hands: Short, broad, strong, rough, hard hands; Appearance: Soldierly figure; Clothes: Field-grey uniform, wears two stars and anchor (?) on shoulder; Voice: Powerful, heavy voice; Languages: German with Hamburg dialect.[55]

In summary, we can never be 100 percent sure who 'Dr Schneider' really was unless more information comes to light. However, none of the other contenders fit the bill as closely as Wichmann does, since they are either physically different, their age is wrong, or the position they occupied in the Abwehr is incompatible with his. Herbert Wichmann (1) bears a strong resemblance to 'Dr Schneider' both in physical appearance and age; (2) was also a naval officer as stated by others; (3) has a limp that can be explained by sciatica and lumbago; (4) is also possibly the owner of the yacht *Joppe*, given that he was a yachting enthusiast; (5) has a timeline that also fits, allowing for the fact that Wichmann's skiing trip must have been prior to his first meeting with Dronkers on or about 16 March 1942.

It is unfortunate that in Wichmann's file MI5 never made any connection between him and Dronkers during their interrogations, nor anything specific about operations conducted against Great Britain, apart from the references to his meeting in Berlin in September 1940 and the proposed establishing of an Abwehr *Stelle* in London following the successful completion of *Unternehmen Seelöwe* (Operation Sea Lion). As we all know, thanks to the contribution made by the RAF during the Battle of Britain, this never took place. Perhaps buried somewhere in the National Archives at Kew or in an archives in Germany are files yet to be discovered or declassified which may give us the answer once and for all.

9

'Playing With the Souls of Innocent Men'

On 19 July at 10.00 a.m. Mulder and Dronkers met in Room 41. As Stephens recounts in his story of Camp 020, 'A covered association between the two men was arranged. After a few banal exchanges, Dronkers finally confided to Mulder that he was a German agent and that he had already made a confession.' It would seem from the way Mulder keeps asking Dronkers to repeat the names of certain people or clarify certain facts that he may have been deliberately sent in to extract a confession from Dronkers. Unbeknown to Dronkers, however, others were listening. The account of the recorded conversation can be found in Mulder's file.[1] The key parts where Dronkers admits he is a spy are recounted here, with Dronkers beginning by stating that the reason he is in the camp is because of 'an old affair of mine':

> D. At one time I wrote a couple of letters for a certain VAN BAALEN, and that man has been a spy for the Germans.
> M. Yes?
> D. And it is because of that – well, you remember the chap who left —
> M. What chap?
> D. The chap at the Patriotic School —
> M. What chap? Oh, you mean the one who left?
> D. Yes. Well, I met a Dutchman there, who knew van BAALEN, and he knew all about the affair.

What exactly Dronkers' 'old affair' is he does not make clear, but it is most likely his involvement in spying for van Baalen in 1938. Annoyingly, he doesn't mention the name of the Dutchman he met at the Royal Victoria Patriotic School, unless it was van Wijk whom he mentions later on in their conversation and whom Mulder claims to have spoken to, except Dronkers says 'there is another Dutchman here', which could either mean he and van Wijk, or van Wijk and someone else as well as Dronkers. However, when

Mulder asks who van Baalen is, Dronkers dismisses him as someone he does not know:

> D: Well, anyway, he knew about the affair, he saw my photograph, and he said there was something wrong. That's why I'm kept here. Then I had to go to New Scotland Yard, and there I was interrogated all about Van Baalen, and I admitted it.
> M: And what was the address you had in the dictionary, and the letters?
> D: Oh, that was an address in Portugal.
> M: Yes, what is that? What does it mean?
> D: What do you mean?
> M: Yes, what does that address mean?
> D: Well, it is a proof that I am guilty.
> M: That is to say that you are a German agent?
> D: Yes, I am a spy.
> M: Do you mean to say that it is true?
> D: Yes.
> M: Then you <u>are</u> a spy?
> D: Yes. I was sent by them.
> M: My God! You dirty swine! What a filthy swine you are! Oh God! Oh God! And I – (breaks down and cries) – My whole future gone to the devil!
> D: Listen, if it had not been for that betrayal, nothing would have happened.
> M: Nothing would have happened? Damn it – and I am mixed up with you! (Swears)
> D: Do listen – I have always said that Mulder and de Langen are innocent.[2]

The conversation continued with Dronkers insisting that Mulder was innocent and that there were others in the camp, such as Gerth van Wijk, Commercial Attaché in Madrid for the Dutch government, who he proclaimed had done nothing.[3] Guy Liddell's diary entry for 12 July 1941 notes that van Wijk had recently arrived from Spain via Lisbon and had confessed to having been sent by the Germans. Van Wijk had been approached by a German agent called PABLO[4] in Spain and sent back to the Netherlands on a financial mission. Since that mission failed, the Germans suggested that he go to England and trained him in the use of secret ink. The van Wijk case will be discussed later.

Mulder was told by Dronkers that he had only been brought in to the arrangement through knowing Kuchlin[5] and Verkuyl. It incensed him that Dronkers had dragged him into it and that, like Dronkers, he had been accused of being a German agent by MI5. He accused Dronkers of allegedly being responsible for the death of twenty-one of his friends. When Dronkers protested his innocence, Mulder was having none of it, and reiterated his accusation, saying that he was now a broken man, both inside and out. He reproached Dronkers for not warning him, saying that had he known how things were going to end up, he would not have accompanied Dronkers on his voyage. Dronkers countered, saying that had he known the way things would turn out he would not have brought Mulder along either. Mulder also said he begrudged helping Dronkers and his wife financially. Dronkers admitted again that van Baalen was a German agent.

Dronkers' tone then became patronising, calling him 'young man', insisting that 'everything will come out all right'. Mulder claimed that he would never forget how Dronkers had ruined his life and expressed apprehension about how Verkuyl might find out about what had happened. Dronkers dismissed this, claiming that he hadn't even known that Mulder was in Camp 020. Mulder said he had been there since 29 June.

The remainder of their exchange was full of further recriminations. Dronkers admitted that his mission had been to send back military information and that Verkuyl was also a German agent. He tried to explain to Mulder why it was that he was to pay his wife Elise 2,000 guilders:

> M: And why was I to give the 2,000 guilders to your wife, if Verkuyl himself is a German agent, and so forth? Why can't the Germans themselves arrange all those things?
> D: Of course they will attend to them, but they had to make it look as if it was otherwise, isn't that so? Because you were not in it.
> M: Oh.
> D: If I told you that my wife was going to be cared for by the Germans, you would have known and informed the Consul when you arrived. It is because of that I kept silent. Do you understand?
> M: Oh well, <u>please</u> tell the authorities that!
> D: But, my boy, I have already done so a long time ago. They have all that information, and I have taken all the blame on myself ...[6]

Mulder accused Dronkers of 'playing with the souls of innocent men'. Dronkers rebutted him by saying that he wasn't going to do anything for the Germans because there would have been no results, no doubt meaning that he would have been unable to obtain the information they desired. Mulder sobbed as Dronkers continued to pronounce how he had been unwilling to follow through on the Germans' request. Mulder's performance became rather melodramatic at times, saying that he wanted to bash Dronkers' head in; that he was now a martyr; that he would die in a concentration camp, 'a poor boy of 21 years ... taken away from his mother in such a way'. His last words to Dronkers were that one day he would pay before God for his crimes.

'Tin-Eye' Stephens, however, seems unconvinced by this. In his report to Milmo dated 14 September and quoting Captain McKinnell, he notes that

Mulder is not capable of staging the scene with Dronkers to which the Association Report refers. This opinion is reached after (i) reading the transcript, (ii) hearing the record, and (iii) interviewing Mulder.[7]

Stephens recommended that, given the difficulties posed by releasing Mulder, he remain interned for the rest of the war. The cases of Mulder and de Langen will be dealt with in more detail in subsequent chapters.

10

Mulder's Story

There are currently no files available which deal specifically with de Langen. A file number in one of Dronkers' MI5 files refers to PF64893, which can only be about de Langen because the other numbers (PF64891 and PF64892) refer to files on Dronkers and Mulder respectively.[1] Apart from a few details mentioned in the files on Dronkers and Mulder, very little is known about his later life; what there is will be dealt with later. On the other hand, Mulder's background and how he became involved with Dronkers and others requires several chapters. Unfortunately, many documents that were in his MI5 file were destroyed in 1960, but there is still sufficient information available to be able to reconstruct how events came about and who was involved. However, some identities remain obscure as they were not fully revealed at the time of Mulder's interrogations. Nor has it always been possible to elaborate on existing information. The account of his life prior to his arrival in England also provides a useful insight into his character.

John Alphonsus Mulder was born on 29 September 1915 in Solo Seerakarta in the Dutch East Indies to Johan Alphonsus Mulder, a schoolmaster who died in 1936, and Lucia Geertruida Martherus, whose parents were Armenian refugees. Mulder had three brothers – Alex Avith, Rudi and Paul – and one sister, Mary, who were all living in the Dutch East Indies with their mother in Bandoeng, Java. Alex was reputedly in the Air Force and Rudi in the Royal Dutch Navy.[2] An extract from a Trace from the SIS Registry on 20 May 1942 states:

Our only trace is of a man of the surname Mulder (no initial) who, in April 1940, was reported as being the leader of Group of Dutch Nazis in Soekaboemi, Dutch East Indies.

John Alphonsus may be connected with Jan Mulder, (who is probably the father of Albert John (Jan) Mulder). Jan Mulder (father) was born Groningin [sic] 1865, address Oak Lodge, Blanford Road, Reigate, was reported to be pro-German in 1915. On 29.6.38 Albert John (Jan) Mulder (who is probably his son) – b.22.11.03. Dutch father; same address, instructor at Redhill Aero Club – was suspected of carrying out aerial photography. Whilst there is nothing from the file to suppose identity, there is reason to beleive [*sic*] they may be connected ...[3]

In fact, there appears to be no connection. As was stated earlier the Mulder in our story was born on 24 September 1915 to Johan Alphonsus Mulder. Once again, it seems that SIS sources were incorrect.

Mulder was educated first at the Lower School in Macassar, then the Hoog Burgher School in Bandoeng, Java. From the age of 18 he spent two years in the Royal Dutch Navy as a Vaandrig (Ensign), followed by a few weeks with the Air Force at Bandoeng training to be a short-distance pilot. During this time he was offered a job as a journalist, first by the Batavia *Nieuwsblad*, then at the end of 1937 as a correspondent for the *Javobode* in Bandoeng. Later, he decided that he wanted to study law in Leiden so on 31 July 1939, when he was supposed to be a correspondent for the *Nieuws Van der Dag*, he took a ship, the SS *Kasima Maroe*,[4] to Holland via Marseilles (he arrived there on 2 September 1939), arriving in the Netherlands around 6 September 1939.

Until the Netherlands were invaded by the Germans on 10 May 1940, Mulder was receiving 40 guilders a month from his mother. Following the invasion any transfer of funds was made impossible, and it also prevented him from any course of study. Nor was he receiving any payment for articles he had sent to Dutch East Indies Press. Not wishing to become destitute he began writing articles for Dutch newspapers in The Hague, together with doing some translation work that earned him 40–50 guilders a month. With a total of 80–90 guilders a month he was able to enjoy a decent lifestyle. However, the Germans' arrival put paid to that, and without his mother's support he was forced to seek help from the Department for Colonies. Being a Dutch East Indian he was entitled to receive 40 guilders a month from them. Eventually his journalistic efforts dried up, leading to his involvement in the black market. Tea, spirits and cigarettes were supplied to him by the bartender of the Café Brastagi that he frequented, and he sold these items to the café's customers.[5]

Things were about to change. In February or March 1941 Mulder received an unsigned letter which he claimed was from a secret organisation known as *Vrij Nederland*, requesting that he make copies of an enclosed pamphlet and distribute it amongst his friends.[6] He said he wrote out six or eight copies and distributed them, but later claimed at the RVPS that he made twenty-four or twenty-five copies. After he had copied out about ten articles he received no more pamphlets but only a copy of *Vrij Nederland*. He suspected his friend Henk Klatt[7] of delivering them but considered it 'too dangerous' to ask him about it. Exactly when the two men met varies, depending on when

Mulder tells the story. Initially, in a written statement made on 1 July 1942 at the RVPS, he stuck to his guns, saying that he had not met Klatt until after his trip to Paris in April 1941, yet later on 15 July he repeatedly contradicted himself, claiming to have known Klatt 'for a long time'.

From the time that the Germans invaded Holland Mulder had wanted to escape, and he discussed it with friends. One of these friends, Boy Bruining, introduced him to a man named Bisschop[8] who knew of an escape route: Breda–West Wesel–Antwerp–Brussels–Mons–Mauberg–Saint-Quentin–Paris–Biarritz–San Sebastián–Madrid–London. This seems to resemble the 'Comet' Line used primarily by Allied airmen and run by Andrée de Jong ('Dédée') (1910–2007). Bisschop told him that he and three others had been able to get as far as Saint-Quentin by hitch-hiking, a journey of ten days, after which he had run out of money to continue any further. Mulder said that he had saved enough money and was assured that the 80 or 90 guilders in his possession would be enough. Bisschop gave him the name of a woman in Saint-Quentin in the Rue des Faucons, 7 or 9, who he said would put him in touch with British Intelligence. This was to be another example of how Mulder kept contradicting himself.

While at the RVPS, Mulder had never mentioned Bisschop, but when questioned about how Bisschop had known Bruining, he maintained that they had met by chance on a train from Rotterdam to The Hague. During the course of the twenty-minute journey Bisschop had apparently introduced himself, given Bruining his address, told him about his trip to Saint-Quentin, and offered to help if he or his friends wanted to escape, which seems highly unlikely. Mulder also maintained that it was a man with whom he was supposed to meet in the Rue des Faucons, using the alias Mademoiselle-something (he couldn't remember the name). Then when he was at Camp 020 he claimed that his contact *was* in fact a woman; however, during the 15 July interrogation he stated that what he had said about Mademoiselle-something being the alias of a man was incorrect.

More contradictions were to follow. Mulder had asked Bisschop why the so-called members of British Intelligence were unable to help him by advancing him some cash to continue his journey. Bisschop told him that these people were unable to help unless they were paid for their trouble since it was highly dangerous being in Occupied France. He also told Mulder that a man named Vreede would be waiting for him at the Gare du Nord in Paris. Vreede frequently came to the station to meet the trains arriving and was instructed to meet anyone who looked like a Dutch East Indian. When interrogated about this at the RVPS, Mulder first made no mention of Vreede. He later said that he had been told about Vreede by a young man whose name he couldn't remember, but thought it might have been Henk Klatt who had told Vreede to expect him at the Gare du Nord. To compound this, he told another story of how he had first heard about Vreede at the house of a Mrs Stumpff. Also present at this meeting were his two friends, the Kaya brothers, and others whose names he couldn't remember. He maintained at Camp 020 that Bisschop had never visited Mrs Stumpff's house.

Bisschop told Mulder to call at a café in Wernhout where he would be able to change his money into Belgian francs. The café was a famous haunt for smugglers who, for a small payment, would take him over the border into Belgium.[9] He received no further instructions from Bisschop about how he should cross into France, apart from looking out for another smuggler in any of a number of cafés who could help him cross from Mons to Maubeuge. Bisschop demanded a payment of 30 guilders, stating that he had sold his information and the money was to go towards those who could not afford to pay for their escape. Mulder obliged, even though it left him with only about 50 guilders – scarcely enough for his trip.

At the RVPS Mulder first claimed that he had had no intention of returning to Holland. Yet later he changed his tune, saying that he had always intended to return so that his experience would help others, which did not seem credible to the people at MI5. This is borne out by his confession that he had lied about intending to return.

One morning in April 1941 (Mulder was uncertain of the actual date, but he said it was after Easter, which would make it after 13 April, Easter Sunday) Mulder set out by train from The Hague to Breda, taking with him no luggage or food, only his passport and *Stammkarte* (ration card). At Breda he took the bus to Zundert, then walked to the café, arriving at around 7.00 p.m. Bisschop had not given him the name of the café, only a description, but he found it anyway. There he changed his money and ordered a drink, watching to see who might be able to help him. In a corner he spotted a group of four men huddled in conversation. When three of them got up to leave he asked the remaining man if he could help him escape. The man agreed and Mulder paid him ten francs. Again, this story was later changed, with Mulder claiming that he had not changed any money at the café, and the man had not asked for any, the payment being only to buy him a beer.

At around 10.00 p.m. the two men left the café and rode on the smuggler's bicycle towards West Wezel. The smuggler was very drunk and got lost, then decided to turn back, but Mulder insisted that they continue. However, the smuggler insisted on going back, and they were taken into custody by the Dutch frontier guards. The Dutch police came to take the smuggler away, but allowed Mulder to stay overnight at the Customs post, where he was interrogated. He claimed to be a student on a hiking trip, but without any maps he had no idea he was so close to the border. The Customs officials, who were friendly towards him, suggested that he was not really a student and was actually trying to escape to England. When he admitted the truth, they offered to help him.

Early in the morning, around 5.00 or 6.00 a.m., he was shown how to cross the border by an official named Koppers. Unfortunately for Mulder, he was caught by a German patrol an hour or so later and arrested. The soldiers did not believe his story about being a student on holiday and took him over the border to the German post in Belgium and locked him up. That afternoon he was questioned by a sergeant. He stuck to the same story, which the sergeant believed, ignoring the fact that Mulder was carrying a large sum of money (900 Belgian francs). Mulder attributed this to the sergeant being 'of the stupid peasant type'. In a written statement made on 3 July 1942, Mulder said he had been arrested by a sergeant and not private soldiers, and questioned by the commandant. When MI5 questioned him during interrogations on 6 and 15 July about why the Germans had accepted his story, he switched his story to say that a German officer rather than the commandant had questioned him.

Eventually, at around 6.00 p.m. the Germans handed him over to the Dutch Customs. He went to Koppers' house where he was given two slices of bread – his first meal since leaving The Hague. Mulder said later that he had spent the day at Koppers' house. He waited until Jansen, another Customs officer, would take him back over the Dutch border. Jansen brought with him a bicycle for Mulder, so the two of them cycled through the night until they reached Polygom at around 7.00 a.m. On 31 May 1942 during another interrogation Mulder changed his story, saying that he had left with Jansen at around 8.00 or 8.30 p.m. and cycled for two and a half hours, arriving at Polygom at around 11.00 p.m. the same night.

After Jansen left him Mulder took the train to Antwerp, arriving at 8.00 or 9.00 a.m. the following morning, then another train to Brussels at noon, arriving at about 3.00 p.m. At the station in Antwerp he enquired about trains to Mons and was told there were no frequent trains to France so he waited and had a snack. At the RVPS on 12 June 1942 he said that there were special workers' trains running twice a day in both directions. He first denied having had anything to eat until he reached Saint-Quentin, then changed his story saying that he ate at every station where he had to wait.

At around 9.00 p.m. he caught a train carrying workers returning from Germany, to Saint-Quentin where he needed to go to pick up French francs, ration cards, and information he had been told would be forthcoming from the address in the Rue des Faucons. (During his interrogations at the RVPS he was vague about what he meant by 'information'.) He arrived in Saint-Quentin early the following morning, and it took him about half an hour to find the address in the Rue des Faucons. There he was greeted by a young Frenchwoman who informed him that Mademoiselle-something (her sister) had left, but she didn't know where she had gone. Had there actually been another woman, or was this person really Mademoiselle-something?

In conversation with the young Frenchwoman and her husband, Mulder learned that Bisschop's story of the British agents living there was a hoax. The couple changed some money for him and he went on his way, not sure what he should do next. They told him that there were prohibited areas between Saint-Quentin and Paris and it would be dangerous to proceed any further. After another meal of coffee and potato cakes (which seemed to be his staple diet) he bought a ticket to Paris at around mid-day, arriving there at about 6.00 or 7.00 p.m. Strangely enough, each time he says he had a meal, in the next breath he denies it; this time he said he had had nothing to eat since the two slices of bread given to him by the couple in the Rue des Faucons. The time of his departure also changed. He later said during an interrogation on 31 May 1942 that he had stayed overnight at the Gare du Nord and left the following morning. He had waited for Vreede to arrive, but after he failed to turn up decided to return to Holland.

On 19 May, 21/22 June and 3 July 1942, Mulder gave his interrogators at the RVPS several reasons why he decided to return to Holland: First, having found this easy way to Paris he decided this was the best way to escape; second, the rest of the way to Portugal would be just as easy; third, 'to tell my friends how to travel when they wanted to escape'; 'to make an organisation of loyal Dutch, including the Douane [Customs] and Marechaussee in Wernhout'; 'to punish Mr Bisschop'; and, 'I could not travel to Biarritz and so on to England, because I was afraid, if the people in Holland do not know anything about my journey, they would be in danger when they escape.' When pressed about this, he maintained that it was too dangerous.

Just before noon he took a workers' train to Brussels, travelling through the night and arriving around noon the next day. There he bought another ticket to Antwerp, from where he took a tram to Polygom and walked during the night until he arrived at Koppers' house in Wernhout the next morning. In all, his journey from The Hague to Paris and back had taken him seven days and six nights. He claimed that at no time had anyone challenged him about his journey as there were no control points at any of the stations.

He was unable to explain how he had been able to buy a train ticket in France when he apparently only had Belgian francs, saying that he thought he must have changed some money somewhere, perhaps at the house on the Rue de Faucons, which he had claimed earlier. There were other issues about the money in his possession which did not ring true, such as why he still retained some Belgian francs when his intention had been to head to Portugal. He explained away these inconsistencies by saying that Koppers had bought a train ticket or paid the bus fare for him. Nevertheless, he was still unable to account for where all his money had gone, or the cost of individual fares, which, as his interrogators pointed out to him, would have been useful information to tell his friends.

11

Mulder's Later Activities

At Koppers' house in Wernhout, Mulder told him that he was returning to The Hague and intended to set up a secret organisation. This contradicts his written statement of 3 July 1942, in which he claimed it was actually Koppers who had suggested setting up the organisation. Koppers told him that he would be happy to help any of his friends and would guide them across the border. A certain Dr A. de Weert would be appointed as head of the organisation for North Brabant. Koppers even went to Zundert where Dr de Weert lived and brought him to meet Mulder. Always contrary, Mulder later stated on 5 July 1942 that Koppers had actually phoned de Weert, and it was de Weert who had cycled to meet them. De Weert agreed to head the organisation and said he would put Mulder in touch with anyone who had access to weapons. Mulder said he would use a code with the words 'book' or 'examination' to mean the organisation. If de Weert received a letter from him saying 'that he had spoken to his friends and the examination would be OK', it would mean that his friends had agreed to supply weapons. Only two letters were ever written, but nothing is known about their content or to whom they were addressed.

Dr de Weert had a son, Jacques, who was born in Zundert on 10 April 1921 and had studied law at the Catholic University of Nijmegen from 1940 until 1943. Also listed as James or Jacobus, and known as 'Black Jacques' or 'Vick', he used the pseudonym 'Gemert' and was a source of forged coupons for illegal immigrants. It is likely he was co-opted by his father to assist. Jacques was arrested in Amsterdam in March 1944 and executed in Camp Vugt, the SS *Konzentrationslager*, at Herzogenbusch on 5 September 1944.[1]

They decided to include two Customs officers – H. Jansen, Koppers' colleague, and another – as part of their group; however, when Mulder wrote inviting Jansen to join them he received no reply. Mulder returned to The Hague and met with his friend Van Loo, who offered to help him and found him a room in Fahrenhertstraat where Mulder stayed until his second escape attempt in September 1941. While in The Hague he visited Bisschop whom he hit and called a liar. Yet in spite of this, he mentally included him in his organisation as he 'considered him to be a loyal Dutchman who could be trusted'! He then told Henk Klatt about the Wernhout members and also wrote to de Weert. This may have been a touch of hubris on Mulder's part, for if Bisschop had in fact been a trained intelligence officer working for SOE he would hardly have let Mulder get away with hitting him.

Klatt told Mulder about a man he knew, Burgwal, who had made an unsuccessful attempt to escape to England by boat and still wanted to get out. He thought Burgwal would be interested in the overland route. Mulder was introduced to Burgwal at his house in Populierstraat, 19, who expressed extreme interest in Mulder's plan. He also told him of others who might be interested, including Frederick Stumpff, who Mulder had already met through a man named Raden Sadell who was lodging at the Stumpffs' (see Appendix 8). A report from the RVPS dated 27 May 1942 stated that Burgwal had only met Mulder once at Mrs Stumpff's house.

In spite of Mulder's attempts to persuade him to take the overland route, Burgwal and Stumpff later successfully escaped by boat in September 1941.[2] There seems to have been some friction between Mulder and Burgwal, who Mulder called 'not a nice boy', 'jealous' and 'he has not a good character'. All this derived from Burgwal having accused Mulder of being a pathological liar.

From his return to Paris in April 1941 until September of that year, Mulder spent his time hanging around the Café Brastagi with Suurmondt, the bartender he had befriended who was keeping him supplied with cigarettes, etc. to sell on the black market, and providing him with free meals. When MI5 later questioned him about the identity of the café's patrons Mulder always became vague, claiming he couldn't remember, eventually saying that Boy Bruining, Commander North and Kuchlin were among them. He later added Mrs Dolly Beekema and her nineteen year-old daughter Willy to the list. Mrs Stumpff had warned him about both women being notoriously pro-Nazi, although Mulder claimed he only spoke to Mrs Beekema once when she had recognised him as being Dutch East Indian and spoke to him in Malay. A source at Camp 020 (identity unknown) revealed that the Beekema women were employed by the Germans to spy on Dutch patrons of cafés and bars and that Mulder had spoken to them on frequent occasions.

In fact, Dolly Beekema was really Dora Peekema, alias Durchlaucht, who worked for Major Rudolf Kratzer of *Ast* Brussels as well as for SS-Sturmbahnnführer Joseph Schreieder of Referat IV E of the Gestapo in The Hague. It comes as no surprise that she should have been interested in Mulder and spoken to him in Malay. She had been born in Tandjong Poera in the Dutch East Indies on 16 January 1898 and later married Wibo Godfried Peekema, the government delegate for the Algemene Zaken in Nederlands-Indië (General Affairs in the Dutch East Indies) in 1934. On 18 January 1939 they left Batavia and headed for The Hague, where Wibo was head of the legal department of the Colonial Office. When the Germans invaded the Netherlands Wibo fled to London, following in the wake of Queen Wilhelmina and her government.[3] However, Dolly stayed on and became the mistress of Seyss-Inquart, the Reich Commissioner in the Netherlands. She made a number of trips to Belgium and Spain on the Gestapo's behalf.

The section of the interrogation report on Protze[4] prepared by Chief Inspector of Police H. P. Drenthe and W. C. H. D. Hoogendijk, Chief, Case Work Department of the Netherlands Security Service (*c*. 9 May 1946) at Camp 031, a copy of which is now in his MI5 file, sheds more light on Dolly's identity and that of her daughter:

> 121. Hamer[5] introduced Protze to Mrs Peekema with whom Hamer entertained intimate relations, which was stopped by Schreieder. Mrs Peekema infmd suspect that she worked for Ast Brussels in Spain. According to her statements she was acquainted with the American Military Attaché and was able to supply her boss in Brussels with the plans for an American invasion with exact statement of the date. Prisoner never again met Mrs Peekema.
>
> 121a. Afterwards, having reported this case to Berlin, subject received orders by phone to change this case immediately into a 'Geheime Kommandosache' [secret commando operation] and NOT to drop the matter from then on. Subject concluded from this that Mrs Peekema was indeed an important agent. Some time afterwards he was infmd that Mrs Peekema was empld by Kratzer, Leiter I Brussels.[6] She addressed her infm to her daughter in The Hague [most likely Willy] who prob passed it on to Sonderfuehrer Crone[7] or anyway to Ast Niederlands, who in turn passed it on to Brussels.[8]

Guy Liddell reported in an entry in his war diaries for 18 August 1943:

> Dolly Peekema, the separated wife of an official of the Dutch government in London, is also coming here as an agent. She was scheduled to come some time ago but her mission was postponed, and she has worked as a German agent in Holland and Spain.[9]

Kratzer's MI5 file[10] notes that Dolly was 'Lost on her way to the UK via Spain'.[11] It further notes:

> In 1943, Hagerman undertook three journeys to Spain. He claims that all three visits were in no way connected with his work for the Abwehr and were made partly for pleasure and partly for business reasons ... Hagermann came into contact with the following persons: ... Major Kratzer, who was staying at the Hotel Ritz, Madrid with his mistress Peeckema. (See Appendix II)[12]

This would indicate that MI5 had read an ISOS intercept. However, so far no files in the National Archives at Kew have come to light to corroborate this.

Kratzer's file regarding communications in secret writing notes that 'DOLLY was provided with a dry point "like match with a yellow red head" but never wrote back with it.'[13] A report dated 17 December 1947 produced by the Headquarters, United States Forces European Theater, Military Intelligence Service Center, mentions the following:

6. @ DOLLY (female) Left PARIS end 1942 or beg 1943 as agent Belgian born 1920 vic BRUSSELS (?) 1.75 m blond hair blue eyes.
Career: Studied secret writing in Abw for assignment in England. Never heard from after she left PARIS.
Misc: Speaks German English and Flemish.[14]

And a message dated 18 June 1943 from Madrid to Berlin addressed to ERIZO, *Stelle* Brussels, states:

18.6.43 Madrid-Berlin. To ERIZO for Stelle BRUSSELS. A Belgian artist [obviously Remis Hennebert, see below] called here today and stated that he was travelling to ENGLAND with one DOLLY on behalf of Dr. KRUEGER of Stelle Brussels. The BRITISH Embassy, he says, rejected application for entry permit and is threatening to send him to the Belgian Congo. He says he has lost contact with DOLLY who has left the country, and requests instructions. As the matter is no known here, the man in question was sent away. KOSP.[15]

A further message from ERIZO for SOMOZA dated 12 August 1943 states that:

12.8. 43. Berlin-Madrid, For SOMOZA. Ref. your message 16/34 Secret of 23/6 and message no. 11 from 26/6. BRUSSELS reports that DOLLY had previously met with a mishap and is now living MADRID. Is to continue journey to ENGLAND in the near future.[16]

However, there were actually two women named 'Dolly': one was Dolly Peekema, the other, from a cross-check of the records at the National Archives of the annotation (PF66115) in Kratzer's file, comes up with an MI5 file on Elyane Duprez,[17] a Belgian woman with a number of other aliases, including 'Dolly' (her Abwehr cover name), who bears no resemblance to Dolly Peekema at all. Her other aliases were Mme Hennebert (she fell in love with conjuror Remis Hennebert in April 1941), 'Angelica' (used in Belgium), 'Ruth Lion' (used for correspondence with cover address), and 'Erika Erlach' (on German passport). This 'Dolly' appears to have been confused by the Americans who prepared the report mentioned above since their 'Dolly' is described as having blue eyes and blonde hair, whereas Elyane Duprez had blue eyes and *'chataine'* (chestnut) hair according to her Belgian passport. Clearly, if she was blonde she was Dolly Peekema, although her date of birth refers to Elyane Duprez.

Elyane Duprez was born Marie Angele Dauwe in Ghent on 19 May 1920 (one Home Office Suspects Index document dated 11 March 1947 gives the date as 25 May). Her Belgian passport gives her profession as 'artiste' and her place of residence as Lisbon. The passport was issued for a single trip to Great Britain and the Belgian Congo valid from 12 December 1943 to 11 February 1944. The British visa stamp shows she entered Lisbon on 13 December 1943; the other is a Portuguese exit stamp dated 14 December 1943. She was recruited by German Intelligence in September 1941 and worked for Dr Kruger (in fact a Lieutenant General), in charge of the Abwehrstelle Brussels, and became his mistress. On 16 December 1943 she flew to the UK on a Douglas DC-3 (G-AGBE) operated by KLM, accompanied by Remis Hennebert, arriving at Whitchurch (Bristol) Airport with a mission to work as a double agent and obtain intelligence on a variety of subjects for the Abwehr. However, MI5 suspected that she may be a triple agent and interned her in the UK under a Home Office Warrant and kept her in Holloway Prison until she was deported along with her illegitimate daughter Sonia on 11 May 1945. Her full story is not relevant to this book; it only serves to clear up the identity of the 'Dolly' with whom Mulder had become acquainted.

Dolly Peekema is also listed in the Kratzer file as 'Peeckema', alias 'Durchlaucht', and described as 'one of Major Kratzer's personal agents'.[18] After the war, when Wibo found out his wife had been a spy, he filed for divorce. The Dutch Secretary-General of Justice, van Angeren, wrote on 29 June 1945: 'Mr Peekema has a claim filed for divorce from his wife who is under suspicion of aiding the enemy and is wanted by the police.' She was arrested in a hotel in Milan on 14 July 1945 and on 7 August received a fifteen-year prison sentence, later reduced to eight years (minus the three years before her arrest) and the loss of voting rights for life.[19] She died in Rijnsburg on 19 March 1953, aged 55. Dolly Peekema also appears as a character in the second book of a factional trilogy (*For Queen and Country*) about the Second World War called The Carnation Code by Tomas Ross.[20]

Mulder was never very forthcoming about the activities of the secret organisation in which he now immersed himself, saying first that they held no meetings, then changed it to regular meetings being held at the Café Brastagi. He described it as a

> primitively formed little club of loyal men, willing to take their part in making free their country … When the time comes and the Allies land in Holland I will warn them to go to the places where the weapons can be found.[21]

He was also vague about the whereabouts of the cache of weapons and the addresses of the sixteen members of his so-called organisation. In the interrogation on 21/22 May 1942, he omitted mentioning Koppers and a fourth Customs officer as being members. More information regarding members of his organisation is included in Appendix 9.

12

The Further Adventures of Mulder

Mulder was restless. He wanted to escape again, but this time he chose a Jewish friend, Hans Nol, to accompany him. Nol was willing and said that should Mulder want to try again he would go with him. Mulder claimed that he had only known Nol a month, although on 4 July 1942 he claimed he had known him for about a year, saying that Bruining had passed on his name to him. They left sometime in September and headed to Breda. Koppers showed them a shortcut across the border after which they crawled through the undergrowth and onto a road leading to Polygom. It was there that they were stopped by some Germans in a car (or on motorcycles, depending on when Mulder tells the story), who told them they had too many Belgian francs. Their story was that they were students on a hiking holiday and had accidentally crossed the border. When questioned further they said they were actually looking for work in Belgium or France.

The Germans took them to a small town and put them on a train for Antwerp, where they were taken to a building and questioned by the Gestapo. The Gestapo accused them of sabotage, illegally crossing the border, and smuggling foreign currency. The whole interrogation, conducted separately, and involving seven men, took over three hours. After that they were taken to the Prison d'Anvers, on Beginjnenstraats, 19, dating from 1855, and put into separate cells. There Mulder spent two months, during which time he said he was only questioned once and never about his contacts in The Hague, which seems extraordinary. After two months' incarceration, the prison governor informed him that the charges had been reduced to illegally crossing the border and smuggling foreign currency; the charge of sabotage had been dropped. (Mulder always maintained that he had never been accused of sabotage.) The Gestapo confiscated his money and passport, but when he told them he was penniless they refunded 30 guilders of the 90 he had taken with him, warning him that they would be watching out for him in the future. They handed him over to the Belgian

Military Police at Wernhout who then took him to the main police station in The Hague.

After his release in November 1941, Mulder went to see Mrs Stumpff, who told him that her son had successfully escaped to England with Burgwal and eight other men. He stayed with her for two months before moving elsewhere, continuing with his black market activities at the Café Brastagi. At the RVPS he denied ever getting into trouble with the police apart from being taken to the police station in The Hague after he was released from prison. He would only admit to getting into trouble before his second escape attempt on account of some offensive remarks he had made about the morals of his fiancée, Stannie van Meerwijk, to some mutual friends. Stannie had threatened to sue him for slander, but they settled out of court, with Mulder withdrawing the remarks. At the time of his arrival in England he was still on friendly terms with Stannie but had become engaged to Susanna Hennie, a girl he had met at the café. She did not become part of his organisation, but he had recruited Jan le Heux, a lieutenant lodging with her mother.

Mulder said that he occasionally ran into Nol in the street but avoided having any contact with him since he, and likely Nol, was under surveillance by the Gestapo. It is interesting that, being Jewish, the Gestapo had let Nol go and not sent him to a camp. Another member of the organisation, Commander North, worked in a bank, but was always rather secretive about his affairs and where he lived. One evening in the bar of the café Mulder overheard North talking to the bartender, Suurmondt, about how he had ten shares for sale in the American Railway, worth 11,000–13,000 guilders, and would pay a 20 per cent commission to anyone who could find a buyer. (Mulder later changed this account on 31 May 1942 at the RVPS to 5,000 guilders and 10 per cent.) This was to dwell on his mind until he finally left for England. Writing at Camp 020 about his later activities in The Hague he said,

> I lived on, everywhere trying to get a chance … My plan now was to get a boat and escape over the Channel … Suddenly there came an 'officeele Duitsche Verordening' that people who had no work … or getting work without money (which I did) must go to to the 'Arbeidsbeurs' to present themselves, and within a short time they must work in Germany … I did not go to the 'Arbeidsbeurs' I thought one day … about the 'Dutch Legion in Russia'. It was called in Holland not the 'Dutch Legion' but the 'Legion van deserteurs' because many of the soldiers walked over to the Russians to try to escape this way … I went to the office and got my card, and I should be examined by the Doctor on Saturday, 16th of May 1942. So I saved my life for 10 days. [*sic*][1]

The *officeele Duitsche Verordening* literally means 'official German regulation' and the *Arbeidsbeurs* was the employment office.

On Thursday 7 May 1942 Mulder met Kuchlin for the first time at the Café Brastagi and got into a conversation about politics. Kuchlin invited Mulder to meet with him the following morning. He had been so drunk the night before that when he was sober he barely recognised Mulder. When Mulder reminded him about their conversation Kuchlin became more interested, saying that he had two machine guns and some hand grenades. He could also put Mulder in touch with someone who could help him to escape. It was at this point that Mulder considered Kuchlin to be another member of his organisation and confided in him that Henk Klatt was also a member. Kuchlin invited Mulder back again the following day. It was left to Kuchlin to arrange the transfer of weapons with Klatt. A further meeting took place on Saturday 9 May, when Kuchlin took him to Waalsdorperweg, 370, to meet Verkuyl for the first time. However, in his statement at the RVPS on 30 May, Mulder said that he had known Verkuyl three weeks before the escape and not just one week.

Verkuyl explained that a friend of his (Dronkers) wanted to escape, but it was complicated because he was married and also needed some financial provision for his wife before they departed. His friend also needed someone capable enough to handle a boat as he could not manage on his own. Mulder told him that he could navigate a boat and was also familiar with marine engines. As to the money needed, he was thinking about the sale of Commander North's shares which would make 2,000 guilders. Verkuyl liked the idea and said he would seek out a buyer. That same evening Mulder met North in the Café Brastagi and told him that he might have a buyer for the shares, but nothing was arranged until the following Wednesday. When questioned at the RVPS Mulder was characteristically vague about this. Dronkers, on the other hand, when asked the same question about the 2,000 guilders, told his interrogators that the Germans had told him to ask for that amount from whoever was to accompany him as his share of the payment for the trip.

At noon on Sunday 10 May, Mulder returned to Verkuyl's house where he met Dronkers for the first time. Again, when questioned later about their meeting, Mulder said it had been on 7 May. At this meeting Verkuyl promised to obtain a false pass for him and instructed him to call again on Wednesday 13 May. For whatever reason, Mulder did not sleep at the same place for very long: once at his own place, then with friends on Prinsesstraat, and at Verkuyl's house on the Monday or Tuesday (this would have to have been 11 and 12 May). While there on Wednesday Verkuyl gave him his false pass. It was arranged that he and Verkuyl would have dinner at the Café Brastagi with North where they would conduct their illegal transaction into selling the shares. It would not be until after Mulder's departure that the transaction was completed, and the money would be paid to Elise Dronkers by Verkuyl. Mulder said later that he did not know whether in fact the shares were ever sold.

At the meeting that evening Verkuyl told Mulder that he should leave the following day on the 4.42 p.m. train for Rotterdam. Verkuyl and de Langen would travel separately on the same train. On the station in The Hague Verkuyl arranged to chat with de Langen for a few minutes so that Mulder could identify him. At Mulder's suggestion, once they arrived in England the trio would make a broadcast on Radio Oranje. He told Susanna, his fiancée, and friends Henk Klatt, Droeke, and Stannie van Meerwijk, his ex-fiancée, to listen out for the message.

Captain R. J. McKinnell, the author of the provisional report from Camp 020 on Mulder, dated 5 August 1942, concludes,

> As will be seen by the foregoing report, the many interrogations have produced a maze of blatant contradictions and mis-statements...
>
> That Mulder is a congenital liar I am prepared to accept, but I do not agree with the suggestion put forward by his interrogator at the RVPS, that Mulder is a pathological liar. His stories about his all-white parentage, his journalistic achievements, and his secret-organisation activities are, perhaps, the lies of a braggart, but a close study of his file shows that the majority of the lies he has told have been deliberately thought out to cover up or distort statements he has made, and which he has later realised to be detrimental to his case ...[2]

Certainly there were too many contradictions to make some of his story plausible. In addition to the comments already noted in Mulder's accounts of his travels and dealings with others, McKinnell outlines the following which have not been satisfactorily explained:

> MULDER and DRONKERS both maintain that they thought the other to be loyal Dutchmen, anxious to escape. The reaction at their first meeting at Camp 020 (a covered association), tends to confirm this but does not rule out the possibility of the Germans' sending over two spies in the same expedition, leaving each in ignorance of the other's true role. [There is nothing in the files which outlines what, if any, role Mulder might have played, other than to assist Dronkers with crossing the North Sea.]
>
> 1. Mulder's part in distributing news and propaganda surreptitiously supplied from "Vrij Nederland" by some unknown person
> MULDER at first said that he suspected that this was his friend KLATT, whom he did not tax on the matter, as 'he thought this would be too dangerous'. It is very doubtful if he knew KLATT at this period, (February 1941); moreover his version of the whole affair is so vague and contradictory that it is possibly nothing more than a creation of his vivid imagination to give the impression of loyalty and anti-Nazi sympathies.

2. Mulder's trip to Paris and back

There are many points not cleared up regarding this trip:-

a) The circumstances of his arrest and subsequent release by the Germans

It is almost impossible to accept MULDER's story that he told the Germans that he had no intention of crossing the Dutch-Belgian frontier, and that they, inspite of having found that his money consisted almost entirely of Belgian currency, accepted his story without question. MULDER has tried to explain this by retracting an earlier statement that he was interrogated by a German officer, and substituting for it one to the effect that he was questioned by a sergeant, whose mentality MULDER has progressibly reduced to 'the stupid peasant type'.

b) The whole question of his finances during the trip

MULDER has been quite unable to give any reasonable story regarding his finances which could be accepted as being approximately correct.

The improbability of his first arrest by the Germans has already been mentioned under (a).

He is unable to give even the approximate cost of any of the railway tickets which he bought en route.

His accounts of how and when he changed his money vary with each telling, until they have become a maze of contradictions and lies. Even during the writing of this report, MULDER sent in a statement giving an entirely new version. He now claims that it was his intention to change all his guilders into the so-called 'Reichskreditkassenscheine' which, he says, were valid throughout Holland, Belgium and France. [Also known as RKK, was a military currency for use in German-occupied countries during the Second World War.] He was able to get only a few, which he retained until the return trip. He used them in part payment of his ticket Brussels-Antwerp, together with the Belgian francs 'which he naturally kept' when he changed his money at St.Quentin. He has been interrogated, but is quite unable to say how many guilders he exchanged for marks, stating that he did not count the money he received in the café near Wernhout.

He stated that he had received approximately 1,600 French francs for his Belgian money at St.Quentin, and that he had about 800 francs left when he returned to The Hague. He is quite unable to give details of how he spent the balance of 800 francs, vaguely stating that most of it was spent on 'tips' for coffee.

c) Time-table of the journey

MULDER's story of the trip to Paris and back is so vague and his time-table so full of contradictions that it leaves the impression that he did not, in fact, make the journey by train. Moreover, it is almost impossible to believe that on his return to KOPPER's house, after six days' journey without sleep and with very little food, and ending with 17 hours continuous walking, he was in a fit state either physically or mentally to discuss the formation of a secret organisation, before continuing his journey to The Hague.

d) 7 or 9 Rue des Faucons, St-Quentin

One of the few convincing points in MULDER's story is his description of the Rue des Faucons and of the house itself. He was able to describe the position of the street in relation to the railway station and main street. This has been checked with a town plan of St-Quentin, and found to be approximately correct. The impression he gives is that he has in fact at sometime or other visited this house. [The railway is on the opposite side of the Port Gayant.][3]

McKinnell continued in the same vein to deconstruct the rest of Mulder's account, first with Mulder's secret organisation. He considered the list of members of Mulder's organisation 'scanty', with most of the so-called members only existing in his mind. Mulder had stated that the purpose of the organisation was to form a 'second front', but McKinnell expressed doubt whether Mulder actually had any connection with any secret organisation, other than in his own mind. Certainly none of the known members of the Dutch Resistance appear in Mulder's list.

In discussing Burgwal and Stumpff, McKinnell found Mulder's attempts to persuade them to escape using the overland route implausible: Mulder had had no success through Holland, Belgium, France and Spain, but instead of attempting to escape overland again, he had finally decided to take a boat and opted for a sea crossing. Mulder's report of his relationship with the two pro-Nazi women, Dolly and Willy Beekema, did not concur with that of an unnamed agent at Camp 020. Not only that, but when Mulder first said he had known Hans Nol for over a year he had contradicted himself, as he later said he had met him through Boy Bruining only a month before his escape attempt. McKinnell also found Mulder's meeting and association with Kuchlin and Verkuyl incredible. Mulder had panicked when he thought the Gestapo was on to him and that he would soon be arrested, and decided to flee the country. His panic was also precipitated by having to register at the local Labour Exchange. That he should have told Kuchlin, who he had met for the first time at the Café Brastagi, about his secret organisation while Kuchlin was drunk also does not make sense. There was also the business of the sale of shares belonging to North, which Verkuyl had agreed to undertake for him after he had escaped, as well as the illegal possession of arms. Mulder had promised to give Dronkers some money (40 guilders) once they were in England which he would obtain from the Department for Colonies. However, this contradicted the promise of £50 which Dronkers said Mulder had made. As McKinnell summed up,

> While there is no concrete evidence of Mulder's being a German agent, he has contradicted himself to such an extent that he has given the impression of having something to hide.
>
> This may or may not be due to a congenital feeling, but under the present circumstances, it is impossible for me to recommend his release.[4]

13

The Case of Mulder and de Langen

On 19 June, Helenus 'Buster' Milmo wrote to Mrs K. G. Lee of the Home Office Aliens Department to apply for 12(5)(a) Detention Orders for Dronkers and Mulder. Dronkers had confessed on 16 June that he was a German agent and had been in contact with the German intelligence service since 1938. Milmo suggested that Dronkers must remain at Camp 020 for the duration of the war 'unless it is decided that the evidence against him warrants prosecution under the Treachery Act'.

The case against Mulder, who was transferred from the RVPS to Brixton prison on 17 June, was regarded as one of suspicion only. Jackson stated in a report dated 30 May that Mulder was not liked by Dronkers and that

Sipkes, a Dutch Flying Instructor,[1] whom he met here, had warned him [Dronkers] against Mulder and told him that Mulder has never been a flyer, although he pretended to have been a Pilot and Verkuyl had told Dronkers that Mulder was a Flying Officer. According to Sipkes, Mulder could not reply to the most elementary questions in connection with aviation.[2]

Milmo stated that it was likely that Mulder would be transferred to Camp 020 within a few days.

Mulder has shown himself to be a liar of no mean order, and it is worth recording that until Dronkers confessed Mulder was regarded as the most suspicious of the party.

With regard to de Langen we are at present disposed to believe that he was a genuine Dutch refugee, and was enlisted by Dronkers to afford cover to the party. At the moment, however, we think it would be premature to release him but it is expected that we will be able to put forward a definite recommendation with regard to him in the next week or so.[3]

The same day Milmo wrote to Stephens at Camp 020, sending him copies of MI5's files and stating:

> Although I am disposed to think that Mulder is probably all right I think there are circumstances attached to his case which renders it desirable that he should be transferred to Camp 020 for more thorough investigation. This is the very strong view of the RVPS examiners who handled his case. So far as de Langen is concerned I think there is no evidence which would justify his removal to your establishment, and everything points to his being innocent cover for the expedition.
>
> If you agree with my view as to the desirability of Mulder going to Camp 020 would you be good enough to let us know as soon as possible.[4]

On 21 August 1942 Mrs K. G. Lee wrote to Milmo enquiring about the case of Dronkers, Mulder and de Langen. The Home Office took the view that both Dronkers and Mulder should be charged unless the Director of Public Prosecutions found there was not sufficient evidence under the Treachery Act. Milmo replied to the Home Office on 31 August that the case against Dronkers was going before the DPP within the next week or so and that in due course the Attorney-General would issue his fiat for a prosecution under the Treachery Act. Some offences, in this case treachery, require the Attorney-General's permission to proceed; this is called a 'fiat'. Therefore, a group (i.e. MI5) applies for the Attorney-General to institute legal proceedings on their behalf. Milmo went on to say that their investigations into Mulder had not yet been completed but he doubted they would obtain any evidence linking him to espionage that would lead to his being interned for the duration of the war.

Stephens sent a secret report from Camp 020 to Milmo on 14 September in which he wrote:

> The case against MULDER is black. He was twice arrested by the German authorities. His benefactor VERKUYL is a known German agent... MULDER was examined at the RVPS and was held to be a pathological liar...He was patiently examined by Captain McKinnell at Camp 020, and the opinion given is that he is rather a liar whose intention is to cover up or distort statements which are detrimental to his case ... Now if justice is to be done, weight must be attached to this report. In my opinion it rings true and means much, for it is the abuse by a Javanese of a white man. Furthermore MULDER is not possessed of the histrionic ability to stage such a scene for the benefit of the authorities ...
>
> Captain McKinnell's report raises doubt, and in the ordinary course I would have recommended that doubt in favour of the State with the consequent detention of MULDER for the rest of the war ... His disposal, however, gives rise to a real problem, for MULDER in a European world

is a liability wherever he goes…What chance is there for him in England? I doubt whether the Dutch would enlist him and I certainly do not think it wise that he should be at liberty in England without means, for he is gullible, indiscreet and has no qualifiactions [*sic*] … In peace he would be marked down as a depressed subject and returned to Java. In war, it may well prove the kindest course, in his own interest, is to keep him interned.[5]

On 29 September 1942, an internal memo was sent by 2nd Lieutenant John P. de C. Day of B1b on behalf of Milmo to Herbert Hooper of E1a regarding the three:

At first sight the case against Mulder looked serious. Under preliminary interrogation at the RVPS he was found to be a pathological liar. The story he told there of somewhat vague activities in a patriotic resistance organisation did not ring true, and above all it became plain after Dronkers' confession that the man responsible for introducing Mulder into the party was the same German Secret Service representative as had originally recruited the spy Dronkers himself. In the circumstances, therefore, it was felt that Mulder could not be released until his case had been thoroughly examined.

This examination has now been completed and it is the considered opinion of the Security Service that Mulder is innocent of any connection with the German Secret Service, still less of having undertaken any commission on their behalf. The principal reasons which have induced us to arrive at this conclusion are first, the fact that Dronkers, though completely broken and no longer making any reservations in what he told the competent authorities, has [at] no time in the slightest degree implicated Mulder. Second, it is evident that regard must be had to Mulder's own position and character. He is a Javanese who has suffered rather than benefited from a superficial European education. The general result has been to produce a mind and character so confused that to attribute his inconsistencies under interrogation to insincerity would be beside the point. Moreover, from Dronkers' account of the matter it seems plain that although it is true that the German Secret Service representative was responsible for introducing Mulder in to the expedition, his motive was precisely the fact that such a character would offer ideal cover in virtue of the childish innocence of the subject.

The facts of the case so far as Mulder is concerned are that he is completely cleared; and this being so, we would appreciate the observations of the competent Dutch authority as to whether Mulder can be embodied in the Royal Dutch Navy.[6]

Turning now to de Langen, Day had this to say:

It was apparent from the first that de Langen was a quite innocent character; that if the expedition contained an agent, that agent was not he, and that his presence aboard the *Joppe* must be counted no more than cover. De Langen was accordingly released on 3.7.42.[7]

A statement written on 22 December, marked SECRET and annotated 'Top copy handed to Mr Newsam 22/xii/42 for infor[m] [*sic*] of the Home Secretary', set out further details exonerating de Langen and Mulder and explaining their connection with Dronkers:

This man [Mulder], though a Dutch subject, is half native having been born in Java on the 24th September 1915. Since the 6th September, 1939, Mulder was living at the Hague having come from Java to the Hague with the intention of studying law, and at the same time acting as newspaper correspondent for the Dutch East Indian Press. Owing to the war this plan fell to the ground as he was unable to receive remittances of money from his mother, and he accordingly made a living by writing stories in addition to which he received a small monthly sum from the Department of the Dutch Colonies.

After the invasion of Holland by the Germans in May 1940, Mulder decided to try and escape to England. On the first occasion, which was in 1941, he got as far as Paris by train by mixing with Belgian and French workers going on holiday from Germany. As he found this so easy to do he returned from Paris to Holland so as to tell his friends of the possibilities of escape. On his return his fiancée persuaded him not to try it again as it was too dangerous, and he made a living by indulging in black market deals in cigarettes and spirits. In September, 1941, in company with a friend, he again tried to escape, but was caught by the German Field Police and imprisoned in Antwerp for two months after which he was sent back to the Hague where he continued his black market business.

About 6th May, 1942, whilst sitting in the Dutch East Indies Restaurant in The Hague, from which he operated all his black market activities, a stranger, who afterwards told him his name was Kuchlin, asked him if he wished to escape as he knew of somebody who wanted to escape to England in a boat. The following morning Mulder went and saw Kuchlin who took him to see a Mr Verkuyl. Before then he had never met Mr Verkuyl in his life. Verkuyl introduced him to Dronkers. Verkuyl was, of course, a German agent, who had recruited Dronkers for his espionage mission. This fact threw considerable suspicion on Mulder, which was somewhat intensified at a later stage when it emerged as a result of interrogations of Mulder that he had volunteered for service with the German army on the Eastern Front in May, 1942.

Despite the various suspicious circumstances attaching to Mulder, a clear conclusion has been reached that Mulder is compeletely innocent; Dronkers in his various statements indicated that he required a third party to assist with the navigation of the vessel, and Mulder, who has some knowledge of engineering and navigation, having for a short period been in the Dutch East Indian Navy, was for this reason and because the Germans were aware of his previous attempt to escape, selected.

The position today with Mulder is that he is shortly to be released, and arrangements have been made with the Dutch Authorities for him to be sent to the Dutch West Indies.[8]

The statement went on to elaborate on de Langen's circumstances:

De Langen is a pure Dutchman born at the Hague on 21st April, 1921. In about 1938, when he was 17 years of age, he obtained a situation with the General Post Office at the Hague, and he continued in this employment until his departure with Dronkers and Mulder in May, 1942. For the last three years of this employment he was a close colleague of Dronkers' in the General Post Office in that they both worked in the same department. In about January, 1942 Dronkers expressed the wish to de Langen that he would like to escape from Holland, and de Langen intimated that he would like to go with him. One of the reasons that he gave de Langen was that his black market activities were such that the sooner he went the better, but de Langen at all times denied any knowledge of these, and it is fair to say that he knew nothing about them even if, which is extremely doubtful, they ever existed.

In early May, 1942, Dronkers informed de Langen that all arrangements for the escape were ready and that de Langen should come with him. De Langen agreed to go with him provided that his mother, who was ill, did not object. At first his mother did object, but finally she agreed. Dronkers handed to de Langen a pass, and he left the Hague for Rotterdam and from there went to Heenvliet. Dronkers informed de Langen that this pass which had had the name erased and de Langen's name inserted was a genuine pass which had been obtained by illegal means. No reason has been found for doubting de Langen on this point in his story. At no time was he ever aware that the pass deliberately altered in this manner was supplied by the German Secret Service.

De Langen met Mulder, about whom further reference will be made later on in this memorandum, for the first time at Heenvliet shortly before they left in the yacht 'Joppe'. Both de Langen and Mulder were hidden in the fore-peak of the vessel during the daylight hours. Dronkers supplied de Langen with note paper, and he wrote to his parents. After the yacht actually left de Langen and Mulder were still in the fore-peak and could not see very much of what happened. At no time did Dronkers tell de Langen that he was anything but a genuine refugee. Before de Langen left his mother he arranged to send her a message from England to Holland by Radio Oranje and to use his second Christian name, Bruno, as a code word. This accounts for his signing the joint protest by the party about their detention at the London Reception Centre.

Throughout his various interrogations de Langen was very frank, giving no cause for suspicion whatsoever, and, in fact, impressed his interrogators as being a genuine refugee and he was accordingly released. To-day de Langen is a corporal in the Dutch Army and was recently decorated with the Bronze Cross to mark his escape from Holland.

The Bronze Cross, instituted by Queen Wilhelmina on 11 June 1940, was the third-highest medal for bravery.

Following his release, de Langen had joined the Prinses Irene Brigade which would later land at Graye-sur-Mer in Normandy on 6 August 1944 as part of the 1st Canadian Army. It is likely he took part in the liberation of Pont Audemar on 26 August in which the unit was involved, and later crossed into the Netherlands on 20 September at Borkel en Schaft where the unit was met by the Dutch Waffen-SS *Landstorm Nederland*.

On 23 December Milmo forwarded to Stephens copies of the statement taken from Dronkers by Colonel Hinchley-Cooke, and that of Major de Vries. Dronkers' statement had been made under caution at New Scotland Yard to Sergeant Bertram Harris of the Metropolitan Police Special Branch on 19 and 20 June in the presence of Hinchley-Cooke and Inspector Bridges. All the details included in the statement have already been outlined in the various accounts of his escape. What did emerge, and not specifically mentioned earlier, is that the Germans were interested in the despatch of troops abroad, for instance to Egypt. As mentioned earlier, the North African Campaign was still underway at this time: various battles took place in May and June, including the Battle of Gazala (26 May – 21 June), and while his statement was being taken, the Second Battle of Tobruk (20 June) was under way. The Battles of El Alamein would take place on 1–27 July, and 23 October – 11 November. So it would seem that the Germans' priority for intelligence from Dronkers focused more on the North African Campaign than the raid on Dieppe.

14

Mulder's Future

Mulder's future hung in the balance. It was looking as if he was innocent but MI5 were still not sure what to do about him. Milmo reported on 21 November 1942 that Colonel Stephens at Camp 020 had rung up to say that he had discussed Milmo's letter of 17 November with ADB1 (Dick White) and was

leaving it up to us at this end to use our judgement as to what action was taken and that we should not expect to receive a written reply. ADB1 directed me to proceed accordingly and take such actions as might be necessary with the Dutch.

Having discussed the problem with Captain Brooke-Booth, it was arranged that the file should be sent to him and that he should see Derksema, the Head of the Dutch Security, personally and explain the position to him.[1]

Stephens' Camp 020 report on Mulder referred to earlier, dated 14 September 1942, had him calling Mulder a 'childish savage'. Milmo made reference to this report in his note to Captain Brooke-Booth of E1a on 21 November 1942 where he described it as a

vital document ... and I know you will not allow it out of your personal possession and treat it with all the appopriate secrecy ... a short summary will be found at 43a and the prima facie sound reasons put forward by the Dutch for keeping Mulder under lock and key for the duration which will be found at 47a.

It is our view, from which I do not think any fair-minded person can dissent, that the evidence at 41a establishes, beyond all question, Mulder's bona fides and loyalty, and completely outweighs his pathological tendency to lie and, indeed to convince himself of the truth of his lies.

We take the view that Mulder must be released, but if he is to be released, we must have the co-operation of the Dutch in finding him some employment, preferrably in the Dutch Navy. In these circumstances we would be very grateful if you would, personally, take an early opportunity of speaking to Derksema, who, I understand, is the Head of the Dutch Security Service, about the case, and you have our authority to reveal to him the evidence contained in 41a should it be necessary to do so, as I am afraid will be the case. Doubtless, you will impress upon Derksema that we regard this material as being highly secret and that we have hitherto invariably refrained from revealing it outside our own organisation, and that we are only doing so in the present case because we conceive that the interests of justice require us to do so and because we are placing full confidence in Derksema undertaking not to reveal its contents or nature to any other person.[2]

43a was a summary of the case dated 29 September 1942 sent by B1b to E1a to be passed to the Dutch; 47a was a report from the Dutch Security Service on Mulder dated 12 November 1942. Unfortunately, neither are now in Mulder's file (KV2/47), having been destroyed in 1960, but are listed at the beginning of it. 41a was a provisional report on Mulder from Camp 020, dated 14 September 1942. Brooke-Booth reported back on 26 November 1942 with the following:

I saw Captain Derksema today and referred him to his letter at 47a. I explained to him that we quite understood that the case as it then stood justified his unwillingness to see Mulder released and his refusal to permit him to be employed in the Dutch Forces. I also made it plain to him that we appreciated that Pinto's report was perfectly reasonable under the circumstances. I asked Derksema now to believe us when we tell him that we have what we consider to be proof of Mulder's complete innocence. Derksema's reaction was quite favourable and he expressed his appreciation at our letting him know, as he himself never believed that Mulder was a German agent, but favoured his internment as his association with Dronkers and Verkuuyl was not satisfactorily explained.

Although it was not necessary to produce the evidence at 41a, I imagine that Derksema has a shrewd idea as to how we procured proof of Mulder's innocence. His remark was: 'Of course you have ways and means of discovering things' and that 'he could not believe that further interrogation of Mulder would have convinced us of his innocence.'

Having accepted our decision, he made no trouble about the question of his employment by the Dutch, but in Mulder's own interest, did not think that it would be wise to send him to any of the Dutch Forces if anything else could be found. His solution, one which I think is quite satisfactory, is that Mulder should be sent to the Dutch West Indies.

He has asked us not to release Mulder until next week, to enable him to go into the question of his employment. He also asks to be advised if possible, the day before the release. Perhaps you will let me know and I will phone Derksema.[3]

The problem of what to do with Mulder would continue into the New Year. Edward Blanshard Stamp of B1b noted on 3 April 1943 that he had informed Mrs K. G. Lee of the Home Office Aliens Department that she should warn the Ministry of Labour for Belgian and Dutch Nationals that Mulder would be appearing there on the morning of Monday 5 April 1943. On 8 April 1943 Stamp arranged with Guy Liddell for a B5 officer to collect Mulder from Camp 020 and take him to an interview with Mono-containers Ltd at Willesden.[4] Stamp subsequently noted that Milmo had reported that the company had agreed to employ Mulder as soon as possible. MI5 then arranged with Mrs Lee to release Mulder the following Monday, 12 April 1943, and for him to report to the Dutch Employment Exchange at Rutland Lodge, Rutland Gate. The Employment Exchange would arrange accomodation for him and a pay advance. Stamp also arranged with Colonel Stephens that Mulder should be taken to the Oratory Schools before the release time of 10.00 where Captain Hindmarsh would ensure that Mulder report to the Dutch Employment Exchange. Mulder was granted a temporary AWS (Aliens War Service) Permit by Lieutenant Colonel C. F. Ryder of E4, and subsequently, a permanent permit by Mr Osborne, also of E4. He was duly released on 12 April,[5] having signed a promissory document requiring him

1. To maintain the strictest secrecy on any matter which may have come to my knowledge during my internment in this country.
2. Not to mention the name of this Camp to anyone.
3. Not pass any messages from/Not to do any act of any kind on behalf of/Not to mention the names of any internees in this Camp to any person whatsoever.

I understand that a breach of this promise will inevitably result in my return to this prison for such action as the British authorities may deem necessary.

I confirm that all my property has been returned to me and that I have no claim against the British Authorities.[6]

Major Stimson at Camp 020 confirmed that Mulder had been transferred to Camp 001 (the Oratory Schools) for release. Some documents (Dutch coupons and tram ticket) formerly in his possession were withheld and returned to B1b, adding that they 'may be of use in another quarter'. They returned to Mulder two letters addressed to him from an engineering officer (apparently a friend) named William H. Fokkink[7] of the Netherlands

Shipping and Trading Company who had sent them from the Regent Hotel, Piccadilly Circus on 22 June 1942 while Mulder was still in Brixton Prison:

> My Dear friend,
> I don't suppose you will be surprised when receiving this letter and parcel. Probable [*sic*] you are a bit surprised that I am writing in English but I do so because otherwise you will have to wait so long. I can not tell you what exactly will happen to me but as you can imagine I am glad to be out of there. I have not a fixed address yet as I told you the first thing I would do is to send you cigarettes and matches and here they are. It is not much of course but more will come as I am very short of money at the present. Well I hope you will be out one of these days and will enjoy your freedom as much as I do. I will end now with all the best of luck and quick freedom.
> Yours sincerely,
> William H. Fokkink
>
> My Dear friend,
> Again a few lines shortly after the parcel I send you After I had posted your parcel I went to the Office and I got a ship straight away and I am leaving tomorrow morning so I will not be able to visit you. I hope any how that you very soon be out of there. I don't know where I am going of course but I shall [*illegible*] my address so [*illegible*] in here. There is not much more to write about now so I will end with the best wishes and all [*illegible*] of luck.
> Yours sincerely,
> W.H. Fokkink
> Engineer Officer aboard s/s. 'Swasiland',
> c/o Netherlands Shipping & Trading Comm,
> (Crew Dept)
> 36 Bishopsgate, London E.C.3[8]

Mulder obviously could not settle, however, as Stamp spoke to Mrs Lee on 20 May 1943 to report that Mulder had quit his job. She informed him of the conditions of Mulder being 'landed' and they agreed to take the necessary steps to find out whether he had breached those conditions. They would not prosecute him unless he had misbehaved, but simply deliver a warning if he had broken any of the conditions. On 22 May 1943 Stamp wrote a note to Superintendent Leonard Burt of B5, Investigations:

> Smith sent us a note of an interview which he had with Mr Mailer at the Belgian and Dutch Section of the Ministry of Labour, on 15.5.43 regarding Mulder. The point was that Mulder left Mono Containers Ltd., and we are somewhat concerned about this.
>   I have found out from the Home Office that Mulder whose full name is John Alphonsus Mulder, was given leave to land on 12.4.43 upon

condition that he registered with the police, took up employment with Mono Containers Ltd. and did not change that employment without the permission of the Ministry of Labour.

We think that at some point Mulder should be given a serious warning if it appears that he has broken the conditions on which he was landed; and in view of the fact that Smith knows the man, we should, but at a slightly later stage, be grateful if Smith could administer the warning. In the meantime, however, it would probably be desirable to find out whether Mulder has registered with the police, where he is living and how, if he has left Mono Containers Ltd., he is obtaining money to keep himself. I wonder if you would be good enough to arrange to have these enquiries made by one of your officers.

I have spoken to the Home Office and I have arranged to have the matter dealt with in this way if you are able to do so.[9]

Milmo noted on 14 July 1943 that immigration officials had contacted Osborne asking for MI5's consent to cancel an Exit Restriction Stamp that had been placed on Mulder's Police Registration Certificate when he was granted his AWS permit. This was to allow Mulder to join a ship on 16 July 1943 belonging to the Netherlands Shipping Committee. Milmo had tried to speak to Edward Corin of E1b (which dealt with seamen) about whether the Dutch had kept MI5 informed of Mulder's plans but had been unable to contact anyone in that section. Given that it was an urgent request, Milmo told Osborne they had no objection to Mulder's permit being cancelled. In response to her letter of 24 August Milmo wrote to Mrs Lee on 10 September 1943:

I have now made enquiries as to what the Dutch have been doing in this case and I find that what has been going on is not quite so extraordinary as I had at one time supposed.

It would seem that prior to Mulder's release, at a time when we had asked the Dutch Security Service whether the man could be taken into the Netherlands Armed Forces, the Dutch Security Service approached their War Minister who, on reading the report concerning the man, refused to have anything to do with him. The Dutch Navy were then approached in a similar manner and with a like result. In view of the attitude adopted by the Dutch and our natural reluctance to put any pressure upon them to cause them to adopt a laxer view of security than they were themselves disposed to take, we then proceeded to make other arrangements with regard to Mulder's release and you are fully familiar with what subsequently occurred.

It would appear that after Mulder had been in the job which had been found for him for some little time he managed to interest a prominent Dutchman in his case and at the request of this individual was accepted by the Netherlands Shipping Committee for the Dutch Pool. Having accepted him the Shipping Committee then decided to have him vetted and approached the Dutch Security Service for a report, on receipt of which they decided they would have nothing further to do with him.

The Dutch Security people inform us, as I have no doubt is the fact, that they have no power to instruct any Netherlands Department concerning the acceptance or refusal of a Dutch national. If and when consulted in any case they make a report and it is for the department concerned [to] decide whether or not they will take the man on. In these circumstances, I am afraid that we are back where we started and that there is no propsect of our being able to get Mulder into the Dutch Mercantile Marine.[10]

But there was another twist to the story. Edward Corin wrote to Milmo on 8 December 1943 saying that he had been informed by a contact in Special Branch that Mulder had disappeared, likely two to three weeks earlier. He had been living in a Dutch hostel at 16 Harnton Street, apparently employed by Mono Containers of Cumberland Avenue, Willesden. However, this does not concur with information discussed previously, as he had supposedly left Mono Containers on 20 May 1943. Corin also reported that Mulder had been ordered to report to the firm of Opperman Limited of Boreham Wood, Hertfordshire, but had failed to appear.[11]

A note from B1b at the beginning of Mulder's file, dated 15 July 1943, indicates his employment on a Dutch ship. Another, dated 24 August 1943, is from the Home Office regarding his employment at sea. A couple of days later on 26 August there was an enquiry from B1b to E1aS asking for enquiries to be made of the Dutch regarding Mulder's employment. On 5 September E1aS wrote back to B1b stating that the Dutch had rejected him for employment. Finally, E1aA wrote to B1b on 10 December 1943 with information from Special Branch regarding Mulder's disappearance. However, none of these actual notes now exist so we are unable to know more about what happened.

On 4 February 1944 a note appeared on Mulder's file from a Captain R. N. Worton of C2b which states that it was proposed that Mulder be called up for service in the British Army under the Allied Powers (War Service) Act. Neither Milmo nor Edward Corin expressed any objection. The Personal Particulars page at the beginning of Mulder's file gives his address in 1945 as 23, Hyde Park Place, Paddington, W2.[12] This address now bears a plaque which reads:

ORANJEHAVEN
this building served as a club
endowed by QUEEN WILHELMINA OF THE NETHERLANDS
for dutchmen having escaped from their occupied country
to join the Allied Forces[13]

So where had he been in the meantime?

15

'As Sordid a Tale as Any We Have Had'

While all of this was going on, the case against Dronkers was building. MI5 was convinced of his guilt and was determined to bring him to trial. They had started out believing that he might be innocent, but as his story unfolded it was looking more like he was the only one of the three who was really culpable. The fact that he kept changing or embellishing the story of how he was recruited and how he had escaped had not done him any favours. However, in the higher echelons of MI5 not all agreed. In a statement taken by Jackson on 16 June, Dronkers was still professing his innocence:

> I declare that I had no intention of doing anything for the Germans, or carrying out any of my instructions once I had arrived in England. I accepted the proposition which was made to me because I did not earn enough money to keep myself and my wife decently in Holland and I could not bear to see my wife suffer. I thought by accepting to come over here, she would at least for a few months have no further financial worries. I am very sorry indeed that I did not tell the whole true story when first interrogated and realise that I should have done so but I did not think of it, and only hope and pray that my case may be judged mercifully.[1]

On 19 and 20 June (following the procedure outlined by Lord Swinton on 10 September 1940) Dronkers was taken to New Scotland Yard where he made another statement under caution, and witnessed by Colonel Hinchley-Cooke, Inspector Frank Bridges and Detective Sergeant Bertram Harris of the Special Branch. He was reminded that this statement would then be used as evidence for the prosecution. In it, Dronkers again told of his recruitment by the Abwehr, the financial arrangements 'Dr Schneider' had promised to make, what he was expected to find out while he was in England, the preparation of his secret communications in invisible ink, the contact addresses in Lisbon and Stockholm to which he was to send them, and how he was to try to seek employment with the Dutch government-in-exile. He explained the business of the passes and how they were obtained, the escape aboard the *Joppe* and the voyage across the North Sea, and their arrest and subsequent interrogations at the RVPS. He also explained how he was to use the Dutch–English dictionary to encode messages. He concluded:

> I wish to say that I agreed to come to England for the German Secret Service so that my wife should be supplied with money as she was always worrying me about money but I had no intention once I had got to England of carrying out Dr. Schneider's instructions or to act in any way for the Germans.[2]

Interestingly, John Day of B1b observed in a note to Herbert Hooper of E1a on 29 June, regarding Dronkers and his impecunity,

> He had led a conspicuously unsuccessful career and this fact, combined with the rapacity of his evil genius, his wife, had kept him more or less in continuously financial straits.[3]

This was further reinforced by Stephens of Camp 020 on 30 June when he denounced Dronkers' wife, describing her as

> ... a woman, as rapacious as she is evil ... In sum, the Dronkers case is as sordid a tale as any we have had to unfold at Ham [Camp 020]. Twice Dronkers has received money from the German Secret Service for espionage against this country, and twice, if he is to be believed, has he swindled them. In his duty in War, to give his Government, if not the Ally of his Government, the benefit of valuable information, he signally failed until the very last moment, when he sensed exposure was imminent. A redeeming feature, if such a term can be used in this case, is that he gave five-sixths of his filthy lucre to his wife, which she greedily accepted, notwithstanding the danger to the life of her husband. Quite obviously, however, this country should not be exposed to the danger of money-grubbers of this kind. Dronkers has been fairly and squarely caught as a spy and, as the element of patriotism is completely absent, there seems no doubt he deserves to pay the death penalty of a spy. My only regret in this case, if Dronkers must hang, is that his wife cannot hang too.[4]

Clearly, Stephens had the same chauvinistic opinion, verging on misogyny, of women that he had for foreigners in general, even though he was married. Ironically, his account of Camp 020 shows a photograph of him side-by-side with his wife and beaming, looking less terrifying than usual.[5]

When asked why he hadn't fulfilled his duty and volunteered information immediately on his arrival in England, Dronkers told N. Shepherd at Camp 020 that by saying nothing he thought he would keep out of trouble. Doing nothing would lead the Germans to think that he was under suspicion, thus ensuring that the monthly allowance they had promised to pay to his wife would continue. On 1 July Ronnie Haylor wrote to Captain Robert Derksema[6] of Dutch Intelligence, based at 82 Eaton Square, London, who had succeeded François van 't Sant in August 1941:

> I intended last week to write and thank you for the invaluable assistance given by Mr Vrinten in respect of our investigation of the case of Dronkers, Johannes Marinus. Indeed, I should like to to take this opportunity of letting you know how grateful we are for the continuous help which is being given to us by your office in the examination of cases of Dutch nationals who come to the RVPS. I am sure you will agree that this co-operation between us has been for our mutual benefit.
>
> So far as Dronkers is concerned, I think you are already aware this man has confessed that he was sent to this country as a German agent, and I should like in this letter to give you official notification that such a confession has been made.
>
> I am proposing within the course of the next few days to release one of Dronkers' companions, de Langen, Jan Bruno, who will of course be given permission to land in this country on condition that he reports to the Dutch Free Forces. Although we are satisfied that de Langen was not aware of Dronkers' mission and is an innocent person, no doubt you will wish to keep him under supervision. At the same time I should be very grateful if you would arrange for him to be kept in this country for the time being, so that if legal proceedings have to be taken in respect of either or both of the other members of the party, de Langen would be available if wanted to give evidence.[7]

Adriaanus Vrinten had been working for the Passport Control Office (PCO) in The Hague as assistant to William John 'Bill' Hooper.[8] According to an MI5 report dated 5 June 1946 entitled 'Protze Home Work', prior to working for the PCO Vrinten had been a counter-intelligence officer during the First World War, then a Dutch Customs official who had been dismissed from the service for an undisclosed reason. The report describes him as 'the most unfortunate man whom PCO ever employed'.[9] Up to the Second World War the PCO had served as a cover for MI6. Vrinten became the case officer for Folkert Arie van Koutrik, another PCO employee who had also been working as a double agent for the Abwehr with the code name WALBACH.[10] In 1938 Vrinten had recruited Van Koutrik as a sub-agent working for the then head of the PCO, Major 'Monty' Chidson.[11] This particular office was to become embroiled in the Venlo Incident in 1939, involving Captain Sigismund Payne Best of MI6 and Major Richard Stevens of the PCO who had been set up and kidnapped in a 'sting operation' by SS-Sturmbannführer Walter Schellenburg. As a result, SIS networks in the Netherlands, and possibly elsewhere, were 'blown'.

To tell the whole story of van Koutrik would require a separate book. Briefly, in May 1940 he and Vrinten fled to England, where van Koutrik was employed for a while by MI5 in E1c and B24.[12] In a letter to Herbert Hooper dated 17 March 1942, Nicholas Elliott of SIS informed him that van Koutrik had joined the RVPS as an interrogator working for SIS.[13] It would appear from correspondence between John Senter and Kenneth Younger, Assistant Director 'E' Division (ADE) of MI5, that van Koutrik had also been considered for employment by SOE. According to Christopher Andrew, MI5's official historian, van Koutrik made 'special enquiries' about foreign refugees flooding to Britain. However, Andrew notes that there was no compelling reason for his escape from Holland, except perhaps that the Abwehr wished to retain him as a penetration agent of MI5, thus preceding by one month the accolade normally accorded to Anthony Blunt.

Van Koutrik's involvement with MI5 was brief because of his antagonism towards his fellow officers. In 1946 Mrs D. M. Quin of MI5's B2b wrote to Kim Philby informing him that van Koutrik 'is under arrest in Holland strongly suspected of having worked for the German Espionage Service before the war, and having thus caused the loss of several Dutch lives'.[14] Philby wrote back on 11 September referring her to a letter written by Colonel Valentine Vivian, Vice Chief of SIS to Dick White. That letter is not included in MI5's file, although it is referred to in a letter to Vivian from Graham Mitchell of B1d, but mistakenly referenced as the Philby letter. At that time, according to Edward Corin, van Koutrik was working for the Royal Netherlands Navy as a civilian clerk. In 1948 SIS conducted an enquiry which concluded that he had been 'disloyal to the Dutch Government in exile' and in the words of Vivian, 'The man has blood on his hands.'[15]

On 2 July Herbert Morrison, the Home Secretary, issued a Detention Order for Dronkers under paragraph (5)(a) of the Aliens Order, 1920, as amended. Then on 8 August, Helenus Milmo (B1b) wrote to Dick White (ADB1):

Colonel Stephens in the course of a conversation the other day told me that he had now finished with the intelligence investigations of Dronkers and that the body could now be handed over to SLB in order that the law should take its course.

I respectfully agree with this conclusion and recommend that the case should now be handed to Colonel Hinchley Cooke.

To which Dick White had appended a handwritten note on 10 August saying:

SLB (through to B)
You will no doubt now wish to examine the possibilities of a prosecution in this case. As far as intelligence interests are concerned we have extracted as much as we consider we are likely to get at the moment.

Jasper Harker (DDG) added in a note written on 13 August to Guy Liddell (DB):

DDG

Unless there are very strong grounds for staging a prosecution under the Treachery Act in this case, I should be opposed to such a course. My main reason is, as you know, that people of this type are more use from an intelligence point of view on the shelf than under the sod. Dronkers was trained by the Abwehr at Antwerp a station about which we do not know a very great deal, and has given us the names and particulars of a large number of people in the German intelligence service with whom he came into contact. It may, in the future, be extremely valuable for us if we can refer to his knowledge of that locality and possibly confront him with other suspects who may come into our hands at a later date. It is quite possible that he may still have a good deal under his hat which he will only produce if his memory is refreshed.

DB

13.8.42

Harker seemed optimistic that there was more information of intelligence value that could be extracted from Dronkers if pressed; yet from the existing transcripts of his interrogations this does not seem to have been pursued, perhaps because, in fact, there was no more to be obtained. Harker mistakenly referred to Dronkers being trained in Antwerp. If that had been the case, it is not apparent from the interrogations, as all of his instruction appears to have been carried out in The Hague. Harker's statement 'a large number of people in the German intelligence service' implies there were others above and beyond those already mentioned in the files with whom Dronkers came into contact. Exactly who these persons were is not known because unfortunately that information does not appear in the files. On 17 August Harker wrote to the Director-General, Sir David Petrie:

DG

In his minute at 54, Captain Liddell raises a point which requires very careful consideration.

I have consulted Colonel Hinchley-Cooke, who tells me that, on form, there is sufficient evidence to put this case up before the Director of Public Prosecutions with a view to prosecution under the Treachery Act. From the ordinary point of view I cannot see any extenuating circumstances, and Dronkers, as an individual, does not appear to merit any particular consideration. On present form therefore, he would normally be tried and probably executed. Captain Liddell considers that, from time to time, we may extract further information from him and, for that reason, he suggests that no prosecution should take place and that Dronkers should remain in Camp 020 for the duration, to be referred to for further information as and when occasion arises.

   This proposal is a departure from the recognized procedure and, if you approve, on the grounds given by Captain Liddell, to refrain from putting this man up for trial, I feel that Mr Duff Cooper should be consulted and that probably it would be wise to carry the Attorney-General and DPP with us.
DDG
17.8.42[16]

Duff Cooper, married to Lady Diana Cooper (*née* Manners) and father of John Julius Norwich (2nd Viscount Norwich), was Chancellor of the Duchy of Lancaster (1941–43); he also took over from Lord Swinton as Chairman of the Home Defence (Security) Executive in 1942. Petrie responded the following day to Harker:

DDG
Director B's proposal really amounts to applying in a particular case a principle that has been rejected in the general. Beyond the fact that Dronkers was trained at Antwerp, I can see little to distinguish his case from any that have gone before.

   Director B's view is that no spy should be executed, the theory being that each one represents a reservoir of useful information which can never really be pumped dry. This is not my own view, and I should imagine that during the last 15 or 20 years of my time in India, we dealt with at least 20 such people for every one that happened in this country. There are prisoners who decline to talk at all and such are, of course, executed with valuable information in their possession, though they would have probably stuck to it just the same had they been left alone. In the case of people who have talked at all freely, I do not remember any single case in which, late in the day, a valuable piece of information was got. Nearly all of these people, however much they seem to 'come clean', do keep back some little details, often seemingly unimportant, and why they should choose to do so is an interesting point in phsychology [*sic*]. But major things are different.

   I do not believe then that Dronkers would prove to be a widow's cruise of information that would never run dry.* ['Widow's cruse': inexhaustible supply (*Merriam-Webster*)] It is to be remembered that the Germans are more careful than we are not to let their agents know too much; but even if Dronkers knows more than he has told us, such knowledge tends to become very speedily out of date.

   In the present case Colonel Stephens has finished with Dronkers and Mr White thinks we have extracted as much as we are likely to get. I see no reason to dissent from this view except on the general ground that no spy should ever be executed. I do not subscribe to this, and apart from the reasons I have given, such immunity would help to make spying a much "safer" profession, and so make it easier to get suitable results. On all these grounds, I see no grounds for interfering and the case should go to the DPP as usual.

DG

18.8.42[17]

Harker appended a hand-written note to the DG's minute commenting, 'To see previous minutes. SLB should now take up the case with DPP in the usual way,' to which Hinchley-Cooke added on 21 August, 'In accordance with DG's decision, this case will now be submitted to DPP.'

In a telephone message dated 16 September, Edward Cussen of MI5's legal section SLB recorded the conversation he had had with 'Tin-Eye' Stephens of Camp 020 in which he informed Stephens that papers were going to be submitted very shortly to the Director of Public Prosecutions. On 22 October the Attorney-General, Sir Donald Somervell, issued a fiat consenting to the prosecution of Dronkers:

In the Matter of Johannes Marinus Dronkers
And
In the Matter of the Treachery Act, 1940
Pursuant to the provisions of Section 2 (2) of the Treachery Act, 1940, I hereby consent to the prosecution of Johannes Marinus Dronkers for offences contrary to Section 1 of the Treachery Act, 1940.

Mulder and de Langen were required to make statements, which they did on 24, 25 and 30 June. De Langen had been approached to give a statement to Mr Maxwell, Dronkers' defence counsel, and Mr C. B. V. Head, his instructing solicitor, but in the end it was decided that he would not give evidence as a witness for the defence, although it is not clear why.

It was not until 2 November that Reginald Ernest Hedger, a chemist attached to MI5's Scientific section, was required to report on the examination of the invisible ink which Dronkers had been expected to use. He professed to having 'considerable knowledge of materials which may be used for "invisible" writing' and added that if the instructions had been followed correctly they would give 'satisfactory results'. Further discussion on the secret ink formulation is included in Appendix 3.

The following day, 3 November, at 8.30 a.m., Inspector Bridges received Dronkers into his custody from the military authorities where at 9.30 a.m. he was formally charged at Bow Street Police Court under Section 1 of the Treachery Act, 1940. In his answer to the charge Dronkers replied:

I say this. When I say 'Yes I agree with that' I would be guilty. I say when the Germans sent me from Holland to England to spy here I was not going to do so because I knew that when I should give the Germans informations [*sic*] they ask me I should bring a lot of trouble and perhaps death to a lot of people for this country and I don't like to do so.

At 10.00 a.m. he was brought before the Chief Magistrate at Bow Street Police Court, Sir Bertram Watson, together with Major de Vries, Lieutenant Cruickshank (substituting for Lieutenant Cannon who was in America), Sergeant Herrewyn of the Intelligence Corps, Reginald Smith of HM Customs, and Police Constable Knock of the Essex County Constabulary based at Parkeston Quay as witnesses. The charge sheet read:

Johannes Marinus Dronkers was charged for that he within the jurisdiction of the Central Criminal Court on the 18th May 1942, with intent to help the enemy did an act likely to give assistance to the Naval, Military or Air operations of the enemy and to impede such operations of His Majesty's Forces that is to say that he landed in the United Kingdom at the Port of Harwich.
Contrary to the Treachery Act, 1940, Section 1.

When asked if he wished to make a statement, Dronkers replied, 'I do not wish to say anything today, but I would ask if it is possible to have a lawyer. I do not wish to call any witnesses here.' Ironically, on that same day at 9.00 a.m., just an hour before Dronkers was brought before the Bow Street court, Duncan Alexander Croall Scott-Ford, a twenty-one-year-old British merchant seaman convicted of espionage under the Treachery Act on 16 October by Mr Justice Birkett, was hanged at Wandsworth Prison. It was to be a portent of things to come.

We come now to Dronkers' trial. All trial quotes, unless otherwise stated, are from TNA KV2/45.

16

The Trial, Day One

Friday 13 November 1942

The stage had been set. Inauspiciously for Dronkers, his trial had been scheduled to begin at 11.00 a.m. on Friday 13 November at the Central Criminal Court, better known as the Old Bailey. Statements had already been taken from all the key witnesses to be called. Lieutenant Cannon had given a statement at Ipswich on 25 June to Major de Vries prior to his being posted to America and was therefore unable to appear at the trial.[1] However, his chief officer, Lieutenant Ian Cruikshank, RNVR, who had since taken over command of the *Corena*, also gave a statement and was subpoenaed to give evidence on Cannon's behalf. Hinchley-Cooke would appear for MI5. However, there was no one who would appear in Dronkers' defence, not even his two compatriots, Mulder and de Langen, only his defence counsel, Mr Maxwell, instructed by Mr C. B. V. Head, a partner in Ludlow & Co. Solicitors of Broad Chambers, Bow Street, Covent Garden, who was provided under the Poor Prisoners Defence Act 1930.[2] Head would later appear as defence counsel for William Joyce ('Lord Haw-Haw') at his trial on 17 September 1945 and would author the book *Essentials of Magisterial Law* in 1949.

Among those who were permitted to attend the trial, MI5 was represented by Sir David Petrie, the Director-General, his deputy 'Jasper' Harker, Hinchley-Cooke, Derek Sinclair (from SLB who was Sir Hugh Sinclair's nephew), R. Butler (presumably the R. Butler who was Private Secretary to the DG), and Lieutenant Day. Sir Hugh Sinclair had been Chief of SIS (1923–39) after the death of Mansfield Cumming and was dismissed by Churchill in favour of Stewart Menzies. The City of London Police was represented by Captain H. P. Griffiths, Assistant Commissioner; the Metropolitan Police by Detective Inspector Frank Bridges and Detective Sergeant Bert Harris; the Royal Netherlands Security Service by Adriaanus Vrinten; and the Customs Service by Superintendent Charles Purser.

As noted earlier, Maxwell and Head had applied to Hinchley-Cooke for either Mulder or de Langen to be brought to the Old Bailey to give evidence on Dronkers' behalf, and de Langen had given a statement to Head after the court was adjourned on 13 November. But in consultation with each other, Maxwell and Head decided not to call de Langen to give evidence. As Dronkers lamented in his petition of 17 December,

> I stood alone without witnesses or any one [*sic*] to assist me except my lawyer ... I failed to ask for witnesses who could have been called ... These witnesses are officers of the Navy, RAF and Army to whom I gave the following important information against the Germans and in favour of England, the day after arrival at the Patriotic School, Wandsworth.[3]

It may have been pushing the point too far to expect that these officers could or would have remained impartial, given that they had interrogated him, although one or two were not totally convinced of his guilt.

Prosecuting counsel were Mr L. A. Byrne and Mr Travers Christmas Humphreys. Lawrence Byrne would go on to be the prosecuting counsel in the William Joyce ('Lord Haw-Haw') case in 1945, and judge in the *R. v. Penguin Books* case in 1960 when Penguin Books was prosecuted under the Obscene Publication Act 1959 for the publication of *Lady Chatterley's Lover*. Humphreys was Recorder of Deal in 1942, which was a part-time post. He later became Senior Treasury Counsel and secured convictions in such causes célèbres as Craig and Bentley, Ruth Ellis and Timothy Evans (accused of the 10 Rillington Place murders), although in the latter case it was later proved to have been John Christie who committed the crimes. He was also the prosecuting counsel at the trial of Klaus Fuchs, the atom spy, in 1950. In 1962 he became a High Court judge. A well-known leading Buddhist, he published extensively on Buddhism.

The judge was Mr Justice Frederic Wrottesley who later became a Lord Justice of the Court of Appeal. It is worth noting that he was the same judge who had heard the case of *R. v. Carl Heinrich Meier, Jose Waldberg, Charles Albert van den Kieboom and Sjoerd Pons* on 19 November 1940, with Lawrence Byrne as prosecuting counsel. Before the war Wrottesley was the judge who had presided over a number of murder trials and sentenced the convicted murderers to hanging; he would go on to sentence other felons to death later. This was not a good sign. Interestingly, Christmas Humphreys had appeared for both Kieboom and Pons as defence counsel. More about them later.

The first thing Byrne did at the start of the trial was to apply to the judge for the entire trial to be held in camera under Section 6 of the Emergency Powers (Defence Act), 1939, whereby only those who were authorised to be present in the court would be allowed to remain and anyone else, such as the press and public, would be ordered to leave. He also asked the judge for a non-disclosure order of all information pertaining to the trial except on the authority of the king. The judge ordered the court be cleared. The charge was then read out to Dronkers by the Clerk of the Court:

> Johannes Marinus Dronkers, you are charged that on 18th of May last, with intent to help the enemy, you did an act likely to give assistance to the enemy, that is to say, you entered the United Kingdom at the port of Harwich. Are you guilty or not guilty?

To this he replied, 'Not guilty.'

When the jury was recalled, the judge instructed them that Dronkers had been charged with treachery, explained the meaning of the non-disclosure order and gave them a stern warning of the penalty for anyone who disobeyed that order, which would be a fine and/or prison sentence. Byrne opened the proceedings by clarifying the charge of which Dronkers was accused:

> The charge which is in that indictment is framed under a Section of an Act of Parliament called the Treachery Act, which was passed in 1940, and Section 1 of that Statute provides as follows, that if with intent to help the enemy any person does any act which is designed or likely to give assistance to the naval, military or air operations of the enemy and to impede such operations of His Majesty's Forces or to endanger life, he shall be guilty of felony.
>
> Under that Section of the Statute this charge is made, and (to put it in the plainest possible terms) the allegation that the Crown make against the prisoner is that he came to this country with the intent to spy on behalf of the enemy.

He then went on to describe to the jury the circumstances in which Dronkers had come to England, and how the Royal Navy had taken his boat into tow approximately nine miles ESE of Harwich. He stated that on being taken aboard HMT *Corena* Dronkers had then exclaimed, 'Hurrah! We have escaped from the bloody Germans.' He had then shaken Lieutenant Cannon's hand and said, 'I very much appreciate what you have done.'

In noting the property that the Intelligence Corps had removed from Dronkers, Byrne mentioned the Dutch–English dictionary and explained how this exhibit, which the jury would see later, was significant to the case. He added that after being searched Dronkers had spoken in Dutch to Sergeant Harrewyn of the Intelligence Corps about the state of affairs in Holland and how it had been over-run by the Germans, but 'never at any time did he suggest that he was anything other than a refugee, in the sense that he had escaped from there without the knowledge of the Germans, to seek sanctuary in this country'.

When Dronkers had been interviewed by Major de Vries, he had told him about how 'Jan' had obtained the passes and the *Joppe* for him from Mr Nygh. Byrne suggested to the jury that if you accept that evidence from this Major in the Security Service, it is quite plain that the story the prisoner was making up at the time was that he had managed to get hold of this yacht in that way and, without attracting attention to himself, managed to get away without the Germans knowing that he had left the country.

Already, this would seem to be a leading statement, with the prosecuting counsel attempting to influence the jury's opinion by putting into their minds at a very early stage in the trial that the story was made up, without first giving them the benefit of hearing the accounts of witnesses and the defendant himself.

The jury learned that Dronkers had explained to de Vries that his reason for coming to England was to escape from the Germans and how he would like to obtain a clerical position working for the Allies. Byrne told them that, in his later conversation with the accompanying police officers on the train to London, Dronkers had explained about the letter he had sent to his wife Elise, saying that he had gone to Spain in order to put the Gestapo off the scent when his absence was noticed and they came looking for him. Dronkers had been dealing on the black market and it was only a matter of time before they caught up with him. Byrne summed it up:

> So there, you see, members of the jury, the picture that he was painting of his movements and of his reasons for coming to this country, putting himself forward as one of those persons who by good fortune, and perhaps skill, had eluded the Germans and so made his way to this country. I emphasise that matter in view of what I shall tell you presently.

In quoting the letter which Dronkers and his compatriots had written to Jackson in May regarding their desire to broadcast on Radio Oranje, and the fact that they were innocent of all charges, Byrne interpreted that as

> … Dronkers is putting his name to this document in which he is protesting that there is no reason at all for any suspicion with regard to him, and that in fact, he is what he had always said he was up to that time, a person who had escaped from Holland without the knowledge of the Germans and who wanted to assist the allies.

Then quoting from the report of 31 May regarding the escape from Holland as told by Dronkers and Mulder, Byrne said:

> Members of the jury, I have read that to you, not that there is so much interest attaching to the details of the journey that they made by means of this boat, but I read it to you so that you should realise that in this document, as in other documents, not one word is said as to the reason why they had left Holland. That you will hear presently.

Byrne made references to the coded message which Dronkers, Mulder and de Langen had hoped to broadcast once they had arrived in England. As he continued with his statement he suggested that, given the fact that Dronkers had been in custody since 18 May, and it was 3 June when the letter to Jackson was written, Dronkers had changed his story to include more of the truth, but in a way that would work to his advantage, given that his story was being treated with suspicion by his MI5 interrogators.

Byrne moved on to when Dronkers was cautioned by Hinchley-Cooke on 19 June and how he had told of his recruitment by his brother-in-law Klever, and his introduction to Verkuyl who had introduced him to the mysterious 'Dr Schneider'. The purpose of Dronkers' mission was outlined, as well as his instructions for using secret ink and sending messages to the contacts in Stockholm and Lisbon. The more detailed version of their escape was given to the jury, all of which has been mentioned earlier in this book. This included the fact that 'Dr Schneider' had apparently arranged Dronkers' journey to England, with the cover story that he was a refugee; the recruitment of the other two; the obtaining of the fake passes, and that Dronkers was acting on the instructions of 'Dr Schneider' when he destroyed his own pass while at sea. It was on 16 June that Dronkers was sent for again to see Jackson, where he was confronted with another man (most likely Vrinten), who asked him some questions about his family and people he had known in Holland. Dronkers admitted, 'I then decided to tell the truth about my coming to England.' At this point Byrne stopped reading the statement and, seizing this point, turned to the jury and said:

> Members of the jury, just let me pause there before I complete the reading of this statement to you: There, if you accept the fact that he made this statement, is, of course, a complete confession of guilt, as you have heard yourselves – a complete confession of guilt – and, of course, showing quite plainly that the story he told when he arrived here was a story that he had been told to tell by the German agent, Dr. Schneider.

He latched on to the fact that Dronkers had openly admitted in this statement that he had agreed to work for the Germans in order to provide his wife with money, while ignoring that in the next breath Dronkers had clearly stated, 'I had no intention once I had got to England of carrying out "Dr. Schneider's" instructions or to act in any way for the Germans.' He then continued to read to the jury the entire statement which Dronkers had made on the 19 and 20 June. While somewhat verbose and long-winded, Byrne's conclusion is worth quoting in full:

> Now, Members of the jury, therefore what you have got to determine in this case – and, in the submission of the prosecution, it must, upon this evidence, be a pretty easy thing to determine – is whether this man can possibly be heard by you, with any amount of credence being attached

to it, to say that he agreed to spy on behalf of the Germans, that he was sent here by the Germans for the purpose of spying, but that he had no intention of spying when he got here. It is, of course, the intention which is so important, and which you have to determine. What the prosecution say to you is this: You can only arrive at a person's intention, something that goes on in his mind, by his actions; you cannot see what is taking place in a man's mind; you have to judge what is in his mind by how he acts. What the prosecution say to you is this, that this man, if there had been a shadow of truth in the statement that he had merely agreed to spy for the Germans as a method of getting out of Holland and getting to this country, would have told his story when he arrived in this country. He might not have told it in the first five minutes to the captain of the trawler – no doubt he would have been very excited, and you possibly would not expect him to – but arriving here on the 18th May, and talking to a number of persons, as you know yourself from what I have told you, not only to the captain of the trawler, but to Major de Vries, to the Sergeant of the Intelligence Corps, to the Immigration Officer, to the police officers who took him to the Reception Centre, having arrived on the 18th May, he is here for a whole month at that Reception Centre before he tells this story of, as I say, first of all the truth, namely that he was engaged by the German Secret Service to spy here, but then secondly he attempts to get out of it by saying: 'Well, I only made use of that in order to get away from the Germans'. What the prosecution say to you is: If there was any truth in that part of the statement he would have made known how he came to reach this country long before he did, and that in fact he has told this story at the last minute, because he realised that he was not going to be released from this Reception Centre, in an attempt to get free and serve his masters in Holland, his German masters; he made this statement hoping it would be believed and that he would be accepted as a refugee, and that he had merely posed as a German spy, which is, in the submission of the prosecution, the reverse of the truth in this case, namely that he is a spy and had posed as a refugee.

There, members of the jury, is an outline of the facts of this case and the evidence, and now I will call that evidence before you.

In the absence of Lieutenant Cannon, the first lieutenant, James Ian Cruikshank, RNVR, now captain of HMT *Corena*, was the first witness called to give evidence. He was questioned by Byrne about the circumstances surrounding the discovery of the *Joppe* and its being taken into tow to Harwich. It appeared to come as something of a surprise to the judge that a small yacht should be sailing in the North Sea; remarkable, given that there was a war on, and there were mines in the North Sea! Cruickshank described how Mulder and de Langen were quiet and seemed nervous, while Dronkers was excited and singing. He was not cross-examined by Mr Maxwell, so the next witness, Major de Vries, was called.

De Vries told how he had informed the three seamen who he was, whereupon they were handed over to Sergeant Harrewyn, who had searched them and found a Dutch–English dictionary in Dronkers' possession, along with a Post Office identity card and some money. The judge seemed concerned as to whether the money (32.5 guilders) was in notes or coins, although why it mattered seems irrelevant. De Vries was then questioned about what Dronkers had told him about his escape, how he'd been able to enter a prohibited area of Holland, and the passes secured by 'Jan'. Maxwell cross-examined him about the dictionary, which de Vries said had been set aside, sealed, then given to the police officers who escorted Dronkers to London. There being no further questions, de Vries withdrew and the next witness, Robert Henry Charles Harrewyn, a sergeant in the Intelligence Corps, was called to the witness box.

Harrewyn told the court that he was present as part of the Intelligence Corps' detachment (123 FSS) stationed at Harwich and, since he spoke Dutch, was there to act as an interpreter should the need arise. During the twenty minutes or so that he was left alone with Dronkers, they spoke of the general situation in the Low Countries, but Dronkers, he said, had never once said anything about the Germans sending him to spy on Britain.

Maxwell cross-examined him about the property taken from the three Dutchmen, which was in the custody of two or three other sergeants from 123 FSS; these would have included sergeants Brown and Speirs. Maxwell and the judge expressed some concern about custody of evidence – how all this property had been documented and accounted for, particularly items such as handkerchiefs and cigarettes (perhaps because both items could be used as a means of carrying secret messages). Both tried to determine from Harrewyn whether any of the property had been handed back to any of the Dutchmen. Harrewyn's testimony was treated as slightly unreliable since, while he knew that the property had been sealed up, he could not state for sure whether any of the items had been returned since he was not the one having custody of them, nor actually saw them being sealed up. With that, he stood down.

Reginald Charles Smith, Preventive Officer for HM Customs, who was also acting as Immigration Officer at Harwich, had refused Dronkers permission to land. He told the court that during questioning Dronkers had told him that he was seeking work, possibly as a clerk, in England. There being no further questions, Police Constable John Albert Knock of the Essex Constabulary was then called.

Knock was questioned about how he and another police constable (Cecil Luke Scott of the Police War Reserve) had escorted Dronkers on the train to Liverpool Street Station in east London. During the journey Dronkers had talked about how he had been dealing on the black market and how the Gestapo were cracking down on black marketeers. He also mentioned the letter to his wife about his purported escape to Spain. There was even some slight levity when he made a joke about seeing cattle and the fact that Hitler had said that Britain had none. Again, he did not say anything to the witness about coming over to spy for the Germans.

Maxwell's cross-examination established that Dronkers was the most talkative of the three, but it was just general conversation; at no time had Knock carried out 'any sort of interrogation'. Maxwell returned to the question of custody of evidence. Knock explained that everything had been contained in two or three parcels which were in his care (it was later confirmed that there were three parcels, one for each man). When they arrived at the London Reception Centre these parcels were handed over to an Army officer. Maxwell questioned whether the parcels had been sealed with wax (which was customary at that time); however, Knock could not recall whether the parcels were actually sealed, even though having to escort three prisoners was a rare occurrence for him. Maxwell kept needling him about it, until the judge intervened. It would appear from the judge's questioning that the parcels were indeed sealed, although it was never really confirmed.

Samuel Lopez Salzedo, the translator of various documents, was called next to verify that all were true translations. These included Dronkers' Post Office identity card, a report of his escape and the message he was supposed to broadcast on Radio Oranje.

Reginald Ernest Hedger was attached to MI5 as a scientific officer. He had replaced H. L. Smith of MI5's A6 scientific section as an expert witness. Smith had written to Hinchley-Cooke on 27 October saying that he had had some throat trouble and as a result did not feel comfortable in giving evidence. 'Hedger has done a good deal of work on this [*redacted*] and has seen and approved of my report.' When questioned by Byrne about the description of how Dronkers was to prepare the invisible ink, he confirmed that the method described would produce the desired effect of 'invisible writing'.

The judge then reminded the jury about their obligation not to discuss the case with anyone outside the court, and adjourned the hearing until the following Monday.

Above: Johannes Marinus Dronkers as a younger man; portrait and fingerprints taken from his identification card. (The National Archives ref. KV2/45)

Below: Dronkers' Post Office identification card. (The National Archives ref. KV2/45)

STAATSBEDRIJF DER POSTERIJEN, TELEGRAFIE EN TELEFONIE

1523

IDENTITEITSBEWIJS voor

(NAAM EN VOORLETTERS)

Geboren:

(RANG)

(STANDPLAATS)

(AMBULANT)

(AANWIJZING OMTRENT UNIFORM)

Woonplaats:

AFGEGEVEN DEN

J.M. Dronkers (Johannes Marinus)
3.4.1896 te Nigtevegt
Arbeidscontractant

's-Gravenhage (Hoofdbestuur)
Aert v.d. Goesstr. 23 ggk

Valeriusstraat 55, den Haag.

16 Februari 1940

HET HOOFD VAN DIENST
INSPECTEUR, DISTRICTSHOOFD, DIRECTEUR.

HANDTEEKENING VAN DEN HOUDER:

HANDTEEKENING:

Algemeen Secretaris der PTT

Above: Jan Bruno de Langen's portrait and fingerprints taken from his identification card. (The National Archives, ref. KV2/46)

Below: John Alphonsus Mulder. (The National Archives, ref. KV2/47)

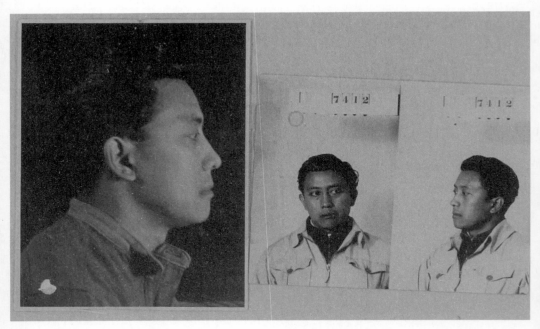

Above: Lt. Clifford Cannon, RNR, stood far-left. (Courtesy of the Bryans Knights' collection)

Below: Herbert Wichmann's portrait taken from his MI5 interrogation file. (The National Archives, ref. KV2/103)

Above: Jan Bruno de Langen in 1991 just prior to his death. (Courtesy of Peter Miebies)

17

The Trial, Day Two

Monday 16 November 1942

The first witness to be sworn in at 11.00 that morning was Colonel William Edward Hinchley-Cooke of MI5. Byrne questioned him about Dronkers' interview at New Scotland Yard on 19 and 20 June, whether he had been cautioned and who else had been present. Hinchley-Cooke confirmed that Dronkers had been cautioned and that Inspector Frank Bridges and Detective Sergeant Bertram Harris of Special Branch had also been present. Hinchley-Cooke said that during the interview on 19 June, after about an hour and forty minutes Dronkers had 'broke down completely', so the interview was adjourned until the morning of 20 June.

With the judge's consent, Byrne had the Clerk of the Court read Dronkers' statement to the jury. Dronkers interposed, correcting the clerk, who had not read out the date of the initial statement. After continuing, the judge then stopped the clerk to question the exchange rate between the guilder and the pound. This was in regard to the paltry salary that Dronkers said he was earning at the Post Office. Byrne then intervened to ask whether the address in The Hague – 11 Vondelstraat – was known to MI5. Hinchley-Cooke confirmed that it was the headquarters of the German Secret Service and 'the organisation in Holland operating against this country', to differentiate between the actual headquarters in Berlin and their regional *Abstellen*.

After a few more minutes the clerk read out the Swedish address to which Dronkers was supposed to send some of his messages. The judge asked whether Byrne thought that this might be an appropriate time to formally introduce the dictionary into the proceedings. There followed an exchange of questions and answers regarding the dictionary and the marked pages, an explanation of the marked letters, and also the address in Lisbon, with the jury being allowed to examine the dictionary. When asked by Byrne about both addresses, Hinchley-Cooke replied, 'They are both known as cover addresses used by the German Secret Service for receiving information from this country.'

When the clerk continued, the judge intervened to ask Hinchley-Cooke when exactly Dronkers' breakdown had occurred, which was after he had said 'and as a refugee I would be well looked after'. Throughout the clerk's reading of the statement Hinchley-Cooke continued to be somewhat nit-picky, correcting the wording of a particular phrase here and there, which, while it may have been grammatically incorrect, made little real difference to the overall meaning. For example:

Clerk: 'I was also …'
Hinchley-Cooke: 'I was told also …'
Clerk: 'He also gave me a pass for de Langen in which the name had been changed.'
Hinchley-Cooke: 'On which.'

Byrne turned to the subject of the passes and their wording which the clerk read out. Dronkers had said that on the instructions of 'Dr Schneider' he had torn his up and thrown it overboard. The journey from Hellevoetsluis to Harwich was outlined, as described in Dronkers' statement. Several aspects of this statement tended to incriminate him:

Before I left Holland Dr. Schneider instructed me what story to tell the English authorities on arrival in England. The story was that in Holland I had been mixed up in black market business; that two of the people with whom I had been associated in this business had been arrested by the German Gestapo; that I feared that I would also be arrested and that I had stolen the 'Joppe' and had escaped. Dr. Schneider also instructed me what to say about how I had stolen the boat. I was to say it belonged to a Mr Nygh, the President of the Dutch Fishery Board, that the boat was being looked after by a man called Jan, to whom I had given five hundred guilders to let me have the boat. That man does not exist; he is a fiction. But I was to call him Jan after the fisherman who had helped me with the 'Joppe' and who does not know anything about the story. Dr. Schneider also told me to say, if the English authorities asked about our passes, that they had been stolen by a friend of the fictitious Jan out of a small police office near Hoogvliet, who had also changed the names. Dr. Schneider also instructed me to tell the same story about the obtaining of the passes to de Langen and Mulder. I told de Langen and Mulder this story.

When we were taken aboard the British ship the captain asked us where we came from. I told him that we had come from Hellevoetsluis, and that we had stolen the boat. I was very tired at the time, and I don't remember all I told the captain, but it was all on the lines of what Dr. Schneider had told me to say. Of course, I did not tell the captain that I had really been sent by the Germans. I told the captain that I was pleased I had been picked up by him and that I was pleased that I had escaped from Holland and from the Germans.

Here we have an admission of how the passes were obtained, the acquisition of the *Joppe*, the spurious activities on the black market, and the fact that 'Jan' did not actually exist; all of it a cover story given to him by 'Dr Schneider'.

Byrne then questioned Hinchley-Cooke about Dronkers' identity cards and their wording: his PTT card and the other card about being a member of the 'Block Squad' in The Hague in 1941. He continued reading Dronkers' statement and the account of how he was first taken to the Royal Victoria Patriotic School and his interrogation by Jackson. He then addressed Mulder's report of 31 May on their escape and the illegal transaction of American railway stocks involving a friend of Mulder and a friend of Verkuyl. Although the names of the friends were not mentioned, one was obviously Commander North. In referring to the proposed broadcast on Radio Oranje, Dronkers had said, 'I had arranged with Verkuyl to listen in and to tell my wife and "Dr Schneider", of course.' Byrne withdrew, and it was the turn of Mr Maxwell to cross-examine Hinchley-Cooke.

Maxwell focussed first on the fact that the Netherlands was infested with German agents 'who either are, or pose as, Dutch subjects', and the activities of the Gestapo. However, Hinchley-Cooke refuted Maxwell's suggestion that if a Dutch citizen who happened to be a German agent approached another Dutch citizen to work for him, and that person refused, he might run the risk of suffering reprisals from the Germans. When Maxwell persisted with this line of questioning, Hinchley-Cooke pointed out that the inflicting of reprisals by the Germans on individuals and their families very much depended upon the circumstances. He did concede that it was possible, however, that the fear of reprisals was even more widespread 'than is even justified by what happens' and that anyone openly defying the Germans would be punished in some way. It seems that Maxwell was attempting to establish whether Dronkers had been coerced unwillingly into working for the Germans but had been too afraid to say 'no'.

Hinchley-Cooke would not be drawn into how the Germans controlled the coastal areas, other than to say there was a 'defence area'. Whether he did not know, or was not in a position to reveal what MI5 and other intelligence-related organisations knew, is hard to say; possibly a bit of both. Maxwell established that in order for Dronkers to have obtained fuel for the *Joppe* he would have had to either steal it, obtain it on the black market, or get it from the Germans directly, implying his collusion with the Germans. In the ensuing cross-examination Maxwell attempted to establish how Dronkers unwillingly became enmeshed in the Germans' web and his motivation for collaboration and escape, which is worth quoting in full:

Q. ... I think it more or less follows from what you have agreed so far – that once a person had agreed to work for the Germans, or had got into the sort of net of the German system, he would have to go on with it or else run a very great risk of reprisals or victimisation?

A. I do not agree altogether with that, because circumstances might arise which might lead to the breaking off of negotiations. After all, one must bear in mind that an unwilling tool is a very poor tool.

Q. Would you agree, then, that if a person wanted to escape from Holland, the facilities which the German espionage could afford him, if he appeared to be willing to work for them, would be the best possible means of escape?

A. Certainly; it would be better than stealing a boat, and stealing petrol, and getting away that way, although it is done quite frequently.

Q. Could I put it as high as this: Supposing you could imagine yourself in the position of a Dutch subject anxious to get away from Holland, would you consider it disgraceful to hold yourself up as ready to be a tool for the Germans in order to effect your escape?

A. No; if I wanted to do it in that way, I would probably do it, but immediately on my arrival in this country I would tell the first policeman that I had done so.

Q. Perhaps it is difficult to put yourself in the position of someone who has less experience of that sort of work.

A. Well, if I were a Dutchman I would go to the nearest Dutch Consul.

Mr Justice Wrottesley: What is the effect of your answer? You say there is nothing wrong, as far as you know, about a Dutchman pretending to be a spy to the Germans, but on his arrival in this country he would communicate the fact when he was safe from the Gestapo – temporarily, at any rate?

A. Quite, my lord; he would merely declare that he had made that arrangement with the Gestapo and that he had no intention of carrying out his bargain; he had merely done so to facilitate his escape.

Q. If he had done that, he would almost inevitably be detained for a very lengthy period whilst enquiries were being made?

A. Not in the very least. He would be detained for a short time so that his statements could be verified, but I think I can go as far as saying he would be welcomed with open arms.

Q. It would take a good deal of time to verify, would it not?

A. Oh, no; the Dutch authorities are established in this country; their Government is here; their Ministry of Justice is here; their police organisation is functioning here to some degree. There would be no difficulty whatsoever.

Q. Would you agree that a man who was not used to that sort of work, perhaps not very intelligent in considering those questions, might very well, even supposing he had good faith, be very timid about disclosing the fact tht he had been in touch with the Germans?

A. No I do not agree. Because he has been an employee of the Dutch Post Office for a period of years he knows he has colleagues in official circles, and he knows how to deal with officials. I should have thought it would have been the easiest thing out for him to go to an official, knowing how to deal with officials.

Maxwell's hypothesizing was attempting to establish the integrity and honesty of the defendant. However, when Hinchley-Cooke correctly stated that Dronkers would have been used to dealing with government officials, as would any public servant, he neglected to consider that Dronkers might have been afraid to report his recruitment to his superiors for fear of being betrayed to the Germans. As noted earlier, all public servants at that time had been expected to join the NSB so Maxwell was probably correct in assuming that Dronkers would have been very timid about his contacts with German intelligence, and being not particularly intelligent, would not have thought through all the consequences of his actions. As was confirmed later in the testimony, he tended to be an emotionally unstable individual, and likely panicked. If the boot had been on the other foot, with Hinchley-Cooke in that position, would *he* have gone to his superiors at MI5?

It is a moot point as far as the trial is concerned, but it is interesting to note that during these proceedings the German intelligence service is often referred to almost exclusively as the Gestapo, as a generic catch-all, yet the German intelligence service was comprised of many different services – the Abwehr (Dronkers' employer), the Sicherheitsdienst (SD) of the SS and the Gestapo, to name just three; other organisations involved signals intelligence.

Maxwell questioned Hinchley-Cooke about the dictionary and the fact that although it had intially been taken away from Dronkers during his journey from Harwich to the Royal Victoria Patriotic School, it had been returned to him there. It was not until 16 June that MI5 realised that, in Hinchley-Cooke's words, 'he was a man we wanted', even though roughly a week before Dronkers arrived, MI5 had seen an ISK intercept from GC&CS warning them of the arrival of someone who turned out to be Dronkers. Maxwell suggested that at any time between Dronkers' arrest on 19 May and 16 June he could have either destroyed it or tampered with it, removing incriminating pages that he had marked. Whether his captors had felt that he might need the dictionary in order to better understand what was being said to him is a possibility, but not very plausible since his comprehension of English was very good, according to all who dealt with him. Whatever the reason, this was, of course, a serious breach of custody of evidence.

The questioning then focused on de Langen and Mulder and how Dronkers had received the same treatment as them and many other refugees and escapees. Hinchley-Cooke said that he was now satisfied with de Langen and Mulder's bona fides and that de Langen was now serving in the Dutch army as a lance-corporal, having received the Bronze Cross to mark his escape from Holland, although Mulder was still detained. Maxwell concluded his cross-examination by asking first, whether the witness had any reason to suppose that there was any information that the accused or the others had withheld, to which Hinchley-Cooke replied that he was not in a position to say. Secondly, he asked about the accused's character, suggesting that he was 'an extremely emotional type – an emotional, hysterical sort of person, and very easily gives way to to his emotions,' to which Hinchley-Cooke replied that he 'became hysterical once or twice whilst I interviewed him.'

After Hinchley-Cooke had stepped down, Inspector Frank Bridges of Special Branch was called to the witness box and was required to produce the Attorney-General's fiat. He was then asked to explain the process by which Dronkers had been received into his custody on 3 November, and his being charged under the Treachery Act (1940). When asked if Dronkers had had anything to say, Bridges repeated what had been said at Bow Street court. There being no further questions from Byrne or Maxwell, Byrne concluded the case for the prosecution.

When Dronkers was called to the witness box some of his testimony was made through the interpreter, Mr Salzedo, to ensure that he understood everything being said to him. I will quote Dronkers' exact testimony where appropriate. He first confirmed that he had been in touch with his brother-in-law, Klever, since Klever's wife and Elise were sisters and quite close. When asked about his financial situation he replied that he had found it hard to make ends meet working at the Post Office, his wife having lost her money during the Depression, in spite of originally being quite well-off. This contradicts the earlier claim that he had lost her 'fortune' in his dubious business dealings with Klever. On the subject of Verkuyl, he said that Klever had spoken to him about his financial woes, and Verkuyl had asked whether he wanted to work as a spy for the Germans and go to England, to which he had said 'yes'. Maxwell asked him about his intentions. Again, this exchange is worth repeating verbatim:

Q. What did you have in mind when you said 'Yes'?
A. Well, at first I thought to myself: I can take the money and go, but they have to wait long if they will have any result of me; for I was not going to spy really for them.
Q. Had you any intention ever of actually furnishing information to the Germans?
A. Never. But my second thought was this; I thought: Here I am, knowing a German agent, and that is dangerous in Holland.

Q. In what way would that be dangerous?

A. Well, there are people shot for less knowledge than that.

Q. What, simply through –

A. Simply the knowledge that Verkuyl is a German agent is enough to bring you to a camp.

Q. If you had incurred the ill-will of a German agent. Is that right?

A. (Through the interpreter) If I would be able, knowing Mr Verkuyl as a German agent, to warn other people – the agents of England, for example.

Q. Verkuyl was a Dutch subject; is that right?

A. He was.

Q. And very much concerned in keeping his contact with the Germans secret; is that right?

A. Yes, of course.

Mr Justice Wrottesley: Do you say that people did not know that Verkuyl was a supporter of the Germans?

A. Yes; he thought so himself, for he told me that nobody knew him as an agent of the Germans.

Q. That is what he thought, anyhow?

A. That is what he said to me.

Maxwell turned to Dronkers' meetings with 'Dr Schneider' and the instructions he had been given. Dronkers replied that they had met about twice a week for about one and a half hours each time. When asked about why when he first arrived in England he had not declared that he was under instructions from the Germans he replied '... I knew when I gave the story that I was a refugee I would be free very soon, and telling the other way I was sure I would have been kept fast'. He said that he had hoped to obtain a job in business of some sort, preferrably working against the Germans. When asked what he had intended to do about 'Dr Schneider', Dronkers replied that he would have done nothing. When Maxwell pointed it out to him Dronkers admitted that he had been foolish not to have confessed to the authorities the moment he was arrested. 'Dr Schneider' had told him that it would be easy to get into England and to tell the authorities that he was a refugee and how pleased he was to be there. He had told him to speak of his dealings with the black market. When asked whether, if he was a free man, he would want to serve his country, he responded, 'I should like to do.'

Mr Byrne cross-examined him about his salary at the Post Office, the financial arrangements agreed by 'Dr Schneider' for his services, the payments to his wife while he was away, and that he was to try to return to Holland after September. He also quizzed him about how knowing a German agent would be dangerous and wanted Dronkers to explain it to him. The tone of his questioning appears particularly anal-retentive and one wonders whether he is being deliberately obtuse or cannot grasp Dronkers' answers, which seem simple enough to this author. Part of the cross-examination almost reads like Peter Sellers' Inspector Clouseau:

> Q. I did not understand something that you said a short time ago. Did you say that it is dangerous to be a German agent in Holland? Did you say that?
>
> A. I said that it is dangerous to know a German agent in Holland.
>
> Q. To know a German agent? Dangerous from what point of view?
>
> A. Well, the German Green Police,*['Green Police' may be a mistranslation for *Grenzpolizei*, or Border Police] the German Gestapo, because when I know a German agent I am able to - (Through the interpreter) I should be able in that case to betray to others who work for this country who that person is.
>
> Q. I do not follow that at all. I understood you to say, and you have just repeated it, that it is dangerous for anybody in Holland to know a German agent. Is that what you mean?
>
> A. That is what it is.
>
> Q. Where is the danger coming from while you are in Holland?
>
> A. Because Holland is occupied by the Germans, and there are a lot of people in Holland, and the Germans know that very well, who are working for the Allies, and knowing the names of those people, and telling the names of the German agents, that is where the danger is. The Gestapo would arrest such people and put them in a camp.
>
> Q. Would arrest whom? – not the Dutchmen who know the German agents? You do not mean that, do you?
>
> A. Yes, they would.
>
> Q. But why?
>
> A. That is what I tried to explain to you.
>
> Q. I am afraid I do not follow. Surely the Germans in Holland are in control of the country, are they not?
>
> A. They are, but when there are in England employed here German spies –
>
> Q. Do you say there are German spies in England?
>
> Interpreter: No, it is his Dutch way of saying 'if'.
>
> Mr Justice Wrottesley: Yes, 'if there were German spies' –
>
> A. They would not like to be known, would they, here in England? It would be very dangerous for them. So the same when in Holland; they are still in Holland, but it is not liked for them that the English Secret Service knows that.
>
> Q. I am afraid I do not follow that.
>
> Interpreter: It may be dangerous for them if they become known to the Dutch agents.
>
> Q. Well, that is common sense. Now I am beginning to understand. You mean that the danger to a Dutchman who has anything to do with a German agent in Holland is the fact that some patriot may put a bullet through him?

Mr Justice Wrottesley: No, I do not think he means that. What I gather he suggests is this; perhaps you would translate this suggestion of mine to him and see if I am right: He suggests that Verkuyl, knowing that this man knew Verkuyl was a German agent, would cause this man to be arrested by the Gestapo. I think that is the suggestion.

A. (Through the Interpreter): Yes.

[Thank goodness the judge saw fit to intervene and clarify matters!]

Q. Am I to take it from your answer that when you agreed to receive instructions from Dr. Schneider and come here to spy, you were running grave risks in Holland? Is that what you are saying?

A. Yes.

Q. Why did you undertake that risk? Was it because you were going to get 100 guilders a month while you were learning?

A. Not only for that 100 guilders but also for the rest, that my wife would have a living during the time that I was away.

Q. But, you see, if your story is true that when you got over here you were not going to spy, that would mean, would it not, that you would never send the Germans any information. Is that right?

A. (Through the Interpreter): They would never receive any information from me.

Q. If that were so, can you imagine for one moment that the Germans would have gone on paying your wife 150 guilders a month while you were away?

A. (Through the Interpreter): Yes, because Dr. Schneider told me that if I was being followed in any way, or was not free in my movements, or that I thought it dangerous to send any information, then I was not to do so.

Q. What I asked you was: Did you believe that if you did not send some information, the Germans would go on paying your wife 150 guilders monthly?

A. Dr. Schneider promised me that if I were not in a position to send information, as I have just stated, payments would go on just the same.

Q. Did you believe that?

A. I did. I had no reason not to believe it.

Q. You believed, did you, the word of a German that your wife would be paid whether you sent information or not? Do you tell the jury that?

A. Well, I hoped he would do.

Byrne had succeeded in showing just how naïve Dronkers had been in believing that 'Dr Schneider' would follow through with his promise of instant cash whether services were rendered or not, and humiliating him in front of the jury at the same time. He portrayed Dronkers as money-grabbing, trying to get something for nothing, but also deceitful, someone who could not be trusted with telling the truth.

Byrne turned to the subject of how Mulder and de Langen came to accompany Dronkers on his odyssey. Dronkers said he could not explain why he had not told de Langen the real reason for the escape from Holland; as for Mulder, he'd only known him for a week and didn't see the need to tell him. Byrne explained that he was trying to test the veracity of Dronkers' story and suggested that the story was a lie. Dronkers admitted that the story of his black market activities and being a refugee were what 'Dr Schneider' had told him to say. By sticking to his cover story Dronkers had believed that it would give him a better chance of being allowed into the country; to say otherwise would have led to his detention for a much longer period of time. He also admitted that 'Jan' was a complete fabrication.

Byrne suggested that the fact that Dronkers had arrived in England with the addresses of the headquarters of the Abwehr in The Hague, and the German intelligence service in Lisbon, should have been immediately conveyed to Major de Vries when he interviewed him at Harwich. In his defence, Dronkers replied that he had been unaware of the significance of those addresses, but Byrne suggested that Dronkers must have known of the latter's importance since it was where he was supposed to send secret messages to. This could be interpreted as 'need to know': Dronkers didn't need to know the significance of the addresses, only where to send the information. He asked Dronkers again why this information had not been conveyed to de Vries right away. Dronkers stuck to his guns and explained that it was for the same reason he had not told the truth about the other aspects of his story – that he believed it might jeopardise his chances of being a free man.

Q. If your story is true, you had been a very clever man, had not you?
A. Which story?
Q. The story that that you had made your escape from Holland by pretending to become a spy. It had been very clever, had it not?
A. I do not understand.
Q. Do not you? I have already indicated to you that, as I understand your case, it is that you escaped from Holland by the pretence of becoming a German spy, without any intention of spying.
A. Yes, that is true.
Q. What I am asking you – and it is quite simple – is this: Having been brought into Harwich by the trawler, and having seen the Security Officer [de Vries] why did not you tell him that you had tricked the Germans by pretending to spy for them? Why not?
A. Well, because I thought that when I would have told so I would not have been free after some time, I would be kept.

Dronkers reiterated what he had said earlier about seeking a job with the Dutch government-in-exile when he was set free. When asked whether he would have told them about his coming over to England pretending to be a spy, he replied that he would not, for the same reasons already stated. Byrne relentlessly pursued this and other points relating to it:

Q. So that nobody would have known at all that in fact you had arrived here, having got here upon the pretence of spying but that you had no intention of doing so; nobody would ever have known that. Is that what you are saying?

A. That is what I mean to say.

Q. Would you have assisted the Dutch Government or the British authorities by ever giving them the addresses of these places in Lisbon, Stockholm, and The Hague?

A. Not for that moment.

Q. I am not asking you about that moment – at any moment?

A. I cannot say that.

Q. Well, it would not be much good keeping that information to yourself if you wanted to help the Allies, would it, because addresses change quickly in the course of time? You would want to tell them pretty quickly would you not, if you were going to help them at all?

A. Yes. That is what I do not know, about the changing of addresses; I do not know anything about that.

Q. Were you proposing to tell anybody about Dr. Schneider?

A. Perhaps it is what I said for the last question: not at that moment. I do not know if I would have done afterwards.

Q. Or of Mr Verkuyl?

A. (Through the Interpreter) All those questions would have depended on circumstances.

Q. On what circumstances would they have depended?

A. (Through the Interpreter) That is difficult to say.

Q. Were you proposing to tell anybody at all that the Germans had given you a prescription for making invisible ink, as it is called?

A. The same answer as about the addresses and those things.

Dronkers was not helping himself with statements such as 'depending on circumstances', 'That is difficult to say', or when or if he would have told the truth, and was just digging himself in deeper. His obfuscation, whether intentional or because of something being lost in translation, was only leading to the belief of the prosecution, and no doubt the jury, that all along he had intended to remain a spy.

Byrne then went through the list of those with whom Dronkers had initially come into contact – Major de Vries, Sgt Harrewyn, Reginald Smith, the Immigration officer, and PC Knock, who had accompanied him to London – asking what he had said to them and whether he had told anyone about being a spy or the black market. Dronkers admitted he had mentioned to Constable Knock about dealing on the black market.

In reviewing Dronkers' first interview with Jackson at the RVPS, Byrne established that at that time Dronkers was still suppressing the truth, and also when Dronkers first realised Jackson was not buying it. He explored the circumstances of the Radio Oranje episode and the trio's need to make a broadcast, focusing on the words, 'If they do not hear in time through Radio Oranje, then I have friends who will have to conceal themselves.' According to Dronkers, there was never any suspicion on his part that Mulder was anything other than a refugee, and not a spy. It was Mulder who had initiated the statement which he and Dronkers had signed; the arrangements Mulder had made with friends were unknown to him. The court heard that the message to be broadcast would have been heard by Verkuyl, who would then have informed Dronkers' wife Elise, and 'Dr Schneider'. It is likely that the Germans would have been monitoring his broadcast anyway, as they had a sophisticated monitoring system in and around Hamburg.

Dronkers was questioned about Verkuyl being a German agent and the fact that he had first known this fact on 10 May. It had not occurred to him that his story and that of Mulder did not concur on several points, and was the cause of his continued detention. He reaffirmed that as far as he knew Mulder knew nothing about 'Dr Schneider', but could not speak for whether he knew Verkuyl. Even until 3 June he still believed that they would soon be released from the RVPS, but it did not occur to him to tell de Langen the real reason why they had escaped. Byrne wanted to know whether de Langen and Mulder were expecting him to help secure their release to which Dronkers replied, 'I do not know in what way I could have been of assistance in that respect.' The exchange continued:

Q. Well, you and de Langen and Mulder could not agree, could you, upon the statement that you were handing to the authorities?
A. (Through the Interpreter) As regards de Langen, I am not sure, because I do not know what he stated; but as regards Mulder, agreement had been reached, in my view, in the statement which was last referred to.
Q. It was quite obvious that in that statement Mulder was not concealing anything from the authorities, was he?
A. I am not sure of that.
Q. Why do you say that?
A. Because I do not know exactly what Mulder stated.
Q. But you saw the statement; you signed it. You have got it in front of you. Look at it, Exhibit 11.
A. You refer to this statement?
Q. Exhibit 11. You were looking at it a minute or two ago.
A. Yes, this was drawn up by us jointly.
Q. You knew whether that contained the truth so far as Mulder was concerned, did not you?
A. I had no reason to doubt it.
Q. What do you mean – that you had no reason to doubt that what he was saying in that statement was quite true?
A. That is right.

Q. On the other hand, you knew perfectly well that, so far as you were concerned, you were concealing the most important material?

A. No, because so far as I could judge, those were not directly important points.

Q. But you had concealed from the very beginning, and you were still concealing, the most important point, were not you, namely, that the Germans had sent you here?

A. Yes, but I had not stated this here, so that I could hardly be in disagreement on that point with Mulder.

Exhibit 13, the letter which Dronkers had written to de Langen and Mulder, was now read aloud to the jury, in which Dronkers admitted that the reason why they were all incarcerated at the RVPS was because of him:

It is my fault and you have become the victims. However, it cannot be helped, and it is difficult for me to personally to tell you the reason, but as you have a right to know I am writing to you at risk of being thought to be childish or cowardly.

During the last four months that I was in Holland I was already under doctor's treatment because my nerves had suffered so much owing to the rotten conditions there, which have not improved here. On the contrary, and this is the reason my memory is playing me tricks ... even the most simple things I cannot clearly remember, and sometimes I find that I am confusing one thing with another. I am afraid, however, that they will not regard me here as being ill, and that I will not be released at all. I will not be able to stand this. Really, boys, I cannot help it. Do not be hard on me. I am greatly in need of sympathy. I am most anxious to find a solution for you two, but I know of none. In any case, be convinced of my honest intentions. You need not doubt these at all, although the people here think otherwise.

When Byrne pursued this, Dronkers admitted that his contradictory statements were on account of the poor state of his nerves. The reason why he had kept the dictionary was solely for the purpose of translation and none other. When asked if he would have been able to remember the addresses to whom he was to send coded messages if it had been taken from him, he replied that he would not. Byrne suggested that he had held it back as a bargaining chip, 'hoping all the time to bluff your way out of this Royal Patriotic School and then be able to get on with your spying', which Dronkers denied.

Next under discussion was the origin of the name 'Carel': who had given it to him, and who had known about it. Dronkers admitted that 'Dr Schneider' had given it to him, but Verkuyl also knew about it and it had been his idea. According to the judge's notes, 'Carel' had in fact been the name of Verkuyl's wife.[1] The meeting with Verkuyl had been instigated by Klever, Dronkers' brother-in-law, mutually agreed by Dronkers and Verkuyl. That Dronkers should become a spy was, in his words, 'in name, at any rate, but not in fact'. The judge got him to admit that the object of the entire exercise was that he would spy for money. With that, the case for the defence rested.

Lawrence Byrne, on behalf of the Crown, rose to review the main facts of the case, followed by Michael Maxwell for the defence. Byrne began by reminding the jury that

> the prosecution have to satisfy you that in fact the prisoner did an act, that is to say, arrived in this country, with intent to help the enemy, namely, to spy on behalf of the enemy of this country, and what I ventured to say to you was this: You have got to say here whether the defendant's version is right, that is, that he was a refugee who got away from Holland by pretending to be a spy, or whether the prosecution have satisfied you that in fact he was a spy who arrived here pretending to be a refugee.

He went on to describe how, because of the state of affairs in the Netherlands at that time, many people were trying to escape to England, some with good intentions of serving the Allies, whilst others, he suggested, may have ulterior motives. In either case, these could be defined as refugees. It was put to the jury that the Germans were exploiting these refugees more than any other nation had ever done; that it was 'a marvellous opportunity for them [the Germans] to insinuate their spies into this country by getting persons willing to spy for them ... persons of the country they have over-run ... That is just what you have to determine here.' There was no necessity, he said,

> ... for this man to demonstrate his innocence, although he is charged with an offence which is as serious as, or, indeed, more serious than, most offences that one can imagine at the present time. There is no burden on him of proving his innocence; it is for the prosecution to prove his guilt; in other words, it is for the prosecution to prove that in fact he came here with the intention of spying on behalf of Germany.

The essence of the offence was the intention, and Byrne went to great pains to explore how the jury might arrive at whether there really was any intent or not:

> ... the only way that one can arrive in this world at the intention of any person is to look at his actions. You cannot look inside his mind; you do not know what is going on there; you look at his actions, and then you have to ask yourselves: Are those actions consistent with anything other than guilt? If they are equally consistent with innocence, then that means that the prosecution has not proved its case, and you will acquit; if those

actions are consistent, and only consistent with guilt, then that means that the prosecution have proved the case.

The remainder of his summary was to review the main facts as they had been presented in court. He placed emphasis on the financial rewards offered to Dronkers when he was recruited and how he had succumbed to the temptation, with the proviso that Dronkers had done so knowing in his own mind that he had never intended to follow through with it. Bryne also felt it necessary to ask the jury to imagine what they would have done had they been in Dronkers' situation:

> Using your knowledge of human nature, do you believe for one moment, putting yourself in his position, that, having made your escape and bluffed the Germans and arrived here, you could possibly have suppressed it that you had bluffed them and got away with it? If his story is true, is not that what you would anti[ci]pate he would have done?

Why would they not have spoken up the moment they had been taken into custody by the British, later while they were on the train, or at any other time? He suggested that it was odd not to have done so, given how pleased Dronkers must have felt about escaping. He said that the business of de Langen and Mulder not being kept informed of the true situation and the reason for wanting to make the radio broadcast were further grounds for suggesting that Dronkers had been lying about his situation. This was because it had been pre-arranged through Verkuyl and 'Dr Schneider':

> You may think that in asking for that announcement to be made on the wireless he was not only up to that time concealing the story of how he had come to leave Holland, but he was at that moment just obeying the orders of his German master, the spy organiser, by letting him know, if he could … that in fact his spy, Dronkers, had arrived in this country. If you come to the conclusion that that is the correct version of the matter, then, as I say, does not it throw a flood of light upon this case, and demonstrate quite plainly the falsity of his evidence when he says that he had nointention of spying on behalf of the Germans once he got here?

Turning to the letter that Dronkers had written to de Langen and Mulder accepting blame for the position in which they now found themselves, Byrne suggested that had Dronkers told them the truth he would have put himself in a difficult position. However, if his story, that he had bluffed the Germans, was true, why couldn't he have told them that? He posed the question, was this letter a final attempt to secure his release or a final attempt to bluff his way out of the London Reception Centre?

Dronkers' retention of the Dutch–English dictionary was another sticking point to be taken into consideration. His keeping it was a way of remembering difficult and foreign addresses that he would need when he managed to bluff his way out. To write down the information on a scrap of paper and then dispose of the dictionary would have further incriminated him. Byrne concluded his summing up by saying

> ... it must be perfectly plain that the story that this man has told, that he got away from the Germans by pretending to spy without any intention of doing so, cannot possibly be true. Judged by his actions as we know them from beginning to end of this story ... they are the actions of a person who is concealing the object of his arrival in this country, and only tells this story at the end because he sees that he is detained and is likely to be detained, and if he does not get out he will not be able to get on with his spying, and in trying to bluff himself out by telling this story he now finds himself in the dock charged with this offence.
>
> ... in the submission of the prosecution, it must be plain, on an impartial and just view of those facts, that the prosecution have established that which they set out to prove in this case, and that in fact this man in the dock is guilty of having arrived in this country with intent to help the enemy by spying.

Michael Maxwell rose to present his summary for the defence. He said that, in spite of the charge being very serious, the case must be dealt with just like any other, according to the rules of procedure. It was 'a devil's compact with the most unpleasant type of German spy', but it is also a story

> on which, of course, if you accept it without the reservation which the prisoner asks you to accept with it, there would be nothing more to address you, because the statement itself is the fullest possible confession of guilt. It would be the confession of a dishonest citizen of a brave country who has not only set out to undermine the forces of an allied country but who is an utter traitor to his own land and people, if you accepted his story of 'Dr Schneider' and the rest of it without the reservation; but, of course, if you think that in that reservation there is some ray of truth, well, then, the situation is entirely different, and the prosecution's case is, I will not say destroyed, but you are in a position where you are having to choose the two, and you are bound to find in his favour, and it is to a consideration of that reservation that I largely want to address myself.

Maxwell addressed the circumstances surrounding Dronkers' recruitment and the fact that he had not actively sought to become a spy, but the contrary: his brother-in-law, whom Maxwell described as a 'quisling', had acted as a 'catcher of victims' for Verkuyl, what today might be referred to as a 'talent-spotter'. The jury was reminded that the very fact that Dronkers had caught Verkuyl's attention had put him in danger and so, in order to alleviate that threat, had felt that he had to give the impression of co-operating. In other words, Maxwell was portraying Dronkers as an unwilling victim, at least initially. Like Byrne, he asked the jury to put themselves in Dronkers' shoes, to consider his mental state of mind, and what it must now be like to live under the repression of the Germans.

The Dutch were said to be 'stout-hearted' and of 'stout moral character', although Dronkers was perhaps not 'a person of high morals', so it was perhaps quite natural to behave in the way he had. What he might have told himself was:

> Well, I will appear to collaborate with the plans of these Germans but I will always keep, so far as I can, the reservation that once I get out of their power and clutches I will just let everything slide, and I will do nothing at all to betray my country.

After all, Maxwell posited:

> What possible reason can there be suggested why this man should want, not only, as I say, to betray, or do mischief, the greatest possible mischief, to this country, but also to prolong the time for which the Germans are going to occupy his own unhappy country? So, members of the jury, I do ask you to concede that at that time, at least – at the time he agreed, as I might call it, to this devil's compact – he could at least have had this reservation.

There was an attempt to inject an element of pity on Dronkers' behalf by outlining how hard up Dronkers had been and how he had seen this as an opportunity to crawl out of his penurious situation. At the same time, Maxwell was less than sympathetic about such a venture:

> Of course, I cannot help saying that it was an extraordinarily tainted and dishonourable source from which a Dutchman should really have been ashamed to draw any money, but he has told you quite openly that he did draw that money first of all in the period of his training, and secondly – and perhaps very naively – that he left the country under the impression that if things went on as they appeared, all he had to do was to sit fast and his wife would continue to draw some sort of stipend from the Germans.

He asked the jury to consider, as Byrne had done, why Dronkers had not opted to 'show his true colours' when he had come to England under a 'flag of good faith' and also to take into consideration that Dronkers had taken money from the Germans, allowed his wife to do the same, consorted with them, in the shape of his brother-in-law and 'Dr Schneider', and probably thought to himself that the British authorities would make extensive enquiries about him. Even though he was not a spy, he might not be believed and things would be made awkward for him: he would be held in custody and treated as if he *were* a spy, since he also had nothing on his person to prove he wasn't a refugee. Maxwell suggested what might have been going through Dronkers' mind:

> ... though genuinely I am not a German spy, the authorities may find it very difficult to believe that, and, whichever way they take it, whichever way they like to believe it, they may make things very awkward for me, and they may detain me for a very long time, and they may, in fact, treat the whole thing there and then as a confession that I am a spy; I have got nothing at all on me to show I am not a refugee, and if I am absolutely quiet, if I say nothing whatever about it, no one, perhaps, ever will be any the wiser.

It had been a foolish course of action to take, but having overcome the initial hurdle of de Vries's questions, it probably did not occur to Dronkers to tell the truth.

The jury was also asked to consider why Dronkers had said nothing to his compatriots about the real reason he had escaped. Perhaps it was because, had he done so, Mulder and de Langen could have made things difficult for him, and also he would have had no control over what story they might have told MI5. Dronkers had obviously convinced himself that there was no going back; therefore, he should stick to his story. However, the dictionary in his possession, with its addresses, was a 'very damning piece of evidence against him'. Given that he spoke reasonable English, why didn't the Intelligence Corps, or later MI5, take it from him and examine it at that initial stage? During his time at the Royal Victoria Patriotic School it was never subjected to any serious examination until Dronkers actually drew their attention to it. Did it not occur to them that this might have been used as a book code, or were they being charitable to him, thinking he might need it to translate something? As Maxwell put it to the jury,

> ... the more a spy carries about things that are marked, what I may again call his stock-in-trade, secret inks or instructions for using the like, the more he would be running into acute danger ...

In contrast to what Byrne had said about these being difficult addresses to remember, Maxwell suggested that they were in fact easy to remember over the course of about ten minutes. Therefore, Dronkers should have committed them to memory. However, he ignored Dronkers' mental state and the fact that quite possibly he would not have been able to remember them that easily. It seems to have been an oversight on the part of the intelligence authorities that they had not been more careful in what they allowed Dronkers to retain, and not to have realised the significance of the dictionary.

Dronkers was, according to Maxwell, 'an honest, but stupid, misguided man who thought he had been, perhaps a little clever and made some rather dirty money out of the Germans'. He was a 'very foolish and clumsy person, and a very obstinate one, and not a traitor'. The jury was asked to decide whether the fact that he had reversed his original statement and later 'confessed' after further enquiries had been made proved him guilty, or if the confession was simply that of a 'silly man at last casting aside his obstinacy'?

Maxwell concluded by saying that Dronkers had not been silly in drawing attention to his case when he signed letters of protest written by the other two, because he had no reason at that time to suspect that his situation was being treated any differently than theirs. It was only when he realised that this was not the case that he gave a clear account of himself. Had he not made that 'confession' he would likely have been sent to an internment camp on the Isle of Man until the end of the war and not appeared at the Old Bailey. He asked the jury to bear in mind that

> allowances sometimes have to be made for people in an overwrought and distressed state of mind: they are apt to do things and to come to conclusions which do sound, when looked at logically, rather absurd and quite understandable, and if you look in that way at this man's state of mind, you may … come to the conclusion that he, however foolish he was, at no time really enternatined the intention of spying against this country; and of course, if you have any doubt about that issue, you have only one possible thing you can do, and that is to acquit him.

The jury was dismissed for the evening on account of having to travel during the blackout and the court was adjourned until the following morning at 11.00.

18

The Trial, Day Three

Tuesday 17 November 1942

In his summing up on the final day of the trial, Mr Justice Wrottesley reminded the jury of the charge of which Dronkers was accused: that of entering the United Kingdom, an act intended to help the enemy. Technically, this charge was incorrect since the Immigration Officer at Harwich had formally refused permission for Dronkers and his compatriots to land under the Aliens Order, 1920. Therefore Dronkers had not actually *entered* the country, even though he was, of course, subsequently incarcerated on British soil, something which the defence should have argued during Maxwell's presentation of the case.

The judge suggested to the jury that they should not have any problems in determining the outcome of the case when he said, 'There is not going to be any difficulty in your way in this case in coming to a conclusion ...' This statement seems a bit ambiguous and the semantics leave it open to interpretation. It could be taken to mean that (a) the jury would reach the only conclusion they could, by finding Dronkers guilty as charged; or (b) the jury would arrive at the only just conclusion, either guilty or not guilty. Whatever the judge intended to mean, it looks as if he were directing the jury to find Dronkers guilty. The burden of proof, he said, rested with

the Crown, the prosecution, to satisfy you beyond all reasonable doubt that this man is guilty of the offence that is charged against him, and if, after weighing the evidence on either hand, the arguments addressed to you on either hand, and giving such weight as you think right to the observations which I make to you, if, after weighing all that, the conclusion to which you come is one of doubt, and you are not really sure beyond all reasonable doubt that this man was a spy, you have to give him the benefit of it.

He added that if the jury believed that Dronkers was in fact bluffing the Germans and had not really intended to spy, but was using it as a means of escaping from Holland and the Germans, then they would have to find him not guilty. However, if they were satisfied that the evidence caused them to believe that the bluff was a cover for the reason for his escape, then they must find him guilty.

The judge provided yet another review of the main points of evidence: Dronkers' motivation for working for the Germans being money; the meetings with Verkuyl and with his brother-in-law, Klever; the introduction to 'Dr Schneider'; the implication that at the point of recruitment, there was no suggestion of Dronkers *wanting* to escape from Holland [*my italics*]; the salary Dronkers had been earning; and the promises made by 'Dr Schneider' of financial remuneration. The judge reminded the jury of Dronkers' belief that, according to 'Dr Schneider', his wife would be paid even if he was unable to provide the information the Germans sought. The judge also reminded them of the prosecution's question of whether this could be seriously believed.

The prosecution had alleged that the whole thing was a 'cock-and-bull story'. The judge told the jury of a test they could apply to gauge whether this was correct: to ask themselves, 'Well, how did you behave? What did you do? A man's intentions can be judged from his actions, and are to be judged in that way.' The judge ridiculed Dronkers when he said that the man in the dock was 'a man of no intelligence … a fool; that is obvious from the way in which he gave his evidence before you'. He asked the jury to put themselves in Dronkers' shoes and to consider what they would have done, compared with what he actually did, beginning with how he had concealed the truth from de Langen and Mulder, and his arrival aboard the *Corena*. Was the song-and-dance routine he performed on the *Corena* an act?

When Dronkers had encountered Major de Vries and Sergeant Harrewyn, he stuck to the cover story given him by 'Dr Schneider', and did not reveal anything to Harrewyn, even though Harrewyn spoke Dutch. The judge asked the jury about the 'As loyal and Orange-minded Dutchmen' protest and whether this was the behaviour of someone who had just bluffed the Germans:

> You see, he is still concealing the truth, still concealing Dr. Schneider, still concealing the fact that he has addresses by which communications can be sent to Dr. Schneider, still hiding the fact that he had been promised money to come to this country and that by that means did he come here.

The judge said that the account of the escape written by Mulder and co-signed by Dronkers was a 'lying account' and yet another example of Dronkers' culpability, as was the request to send a coded message via Radio Oranje. Further damning evidence was the interview with Jackson, who basically told him to own up and in the fullness of time he would be set free; however, Dronkers apparently did not do so. Only when it became apparent to him that he would not be set free did Dronkers finally provide a true account to Hinchley-Cooke. The facts on which the Crown were relying were

> the clearest indications, to you that this man was really spying. They suggest to you that it is impossible that a man who behaved like that can have intended not to send information back to the Germans ... Would you, if you had been only bluffing the Germans, have kept all that information to yourselves for a whole month, long after the shadow of the Gestapo had disappeared, when you were safely inside this country and out of the reach of Holland's enemies?

The language of the judge here, in the opinion of the author, was tantamount to leading the jury. By repeating the things which Dronkers was allegedly concealing, the judge was putting into the heads of the jury the idea that this was part of the deception, without letting them decide for themselves whether this was indeed the case. By also suggesting that the account written by Mulder and co-signed by him was a 'lying account' it is more emotive language to direct the outcome of the decision the jury would have to make.

Dronkers had been afraid to tell the whole truth because he feared he would be detained much longer; this, of course, backfired on him. The judge instructed the jury:

> If you believe it, or if it even shakes you, you will say he is not guilty; but if the prosecution are right, then all this presistent course of concealment from the very first until he saw that there was no hope of his getting free because he was suspected, is consistent with what the Crown allege, that he was going to spy, and that by the skillful used of that dictionary...he would send such information as he could collect back to Dr. Schneider, that he was telling the very lies, you remember, that Dr. Schnieder [*sic*] had told him to tell and by that means trying to get his freedom...

Before sending the jury to the jury room to consider their verdict, the judge repeated that if there were any doubts they were to find Dronkers not guilty; but if they believed he came to England with the intent to spy and pass on information to the Germans, 'which would mean that more Englishmen and more Dutchmen would be killed', they would have to find him guilty. Again, more attempts to play on the emotions of the jury and, perhaps, misdirect their verdict.

The jury retired at 11.34 a.m. to consider their verdict, returning a mere thirteen minutes later at 11.47 a.m.! This, to the author, seems extraordinary. Were they in a hurry to get lunch? There can have been no proper discussion except for the foreman of the jury asking each person in turn whether

Dronkers was guilty or not guilty – they had all apparently made up their mind even before entering the jury room and were unanimous in finding Dronkers guilty. There followed the Proclamation that Dronkers was guilty:

> Prisoner at the bar, you stand convicted of treachery. Have you anything to say why the Court should not give you judgement of death according to law?
> Dronkers: I do not feel guilty, my Lord, because I say again that I had no intention to spy, and God hears me say so. He knows that I am speaking the real truth when I say that.

The judge then replied:

> Johannes Marinus Dronkers, I am bound to say that I think the jury have returned the only possible verdict in this case. The sentence is the sentence laid down for the offence you have committed.

The judge then placed the black cap, in fact a square of black cloth, on top of his wig and pronounced sentence:

> Johannes Marinus Dronkers you will be taken hence to the prison in which you were last confined and from there to a place of execution where you will be hanged by the neck until you be dead and thereafter your body buried within the precincts of the Prison in which you have been confined before your execution, and may the Lord have mercy upon your soul.

To this the chaplain said 'Amen'. Dronkers was then taken down to the cells below before being transferred to Wandsworth Prison to await execution.

19

The End of the Affair?

Dronkers now found himself condemned to death as a result of his folly in thinking he could persuade the British authorities that he was an innocent refugee. On 19 November Dronkers wrote to C. B. V. Head, his solicitor, saying:

> Referring to my sentening [*sic*] to death on 17th Nov. '42, I should like to have a talk to you one of these days, because I'm going to appeal against my conviction, what I must do within 10 days after my sentening [*sic*]. Some things came into my mind, which I remember now, that I cann ask [*sic*] 2 or 3 people as a witness in my favour, namely that I <u>shall be able to prove</u> that I gave, immediately after my arrival at Patriottic School very important informations <u>against the German</u> to officers employed at that School.
>
> Hoping to see you soon, and that you are willing to take up this case again, I remain with the best regards, Dear Sir, Yours faithfully (Signed), Joh. M. Dronkers

Written across the left-hand margin of a letter from C. B. V. Head dated 23 November regarding his appeal is the following, written by Dronkers:

> ... that I was exited when I was on deck of the Corenna [*sic*] is no wonder, when you know that we thought the boat small boat in which we came was not very much longer able to stand the waves. We had a terrible night in that lecky [*sic*] boat, and we feared shipwrecked. Had no sleep in 48 hours and were cold and hungry [*sic*].
>
> De Langen doesn't speak a word English and was not able to explain his excitement. Mulder is one [*Indian? Word is unclear*] and they never show any excitement, but are always calm and cool.[1]

The note continues on the verso:

When I came in Patriotic School, I am interviewed the day after by officers of the Navy, R.A.F. and Army. I gave them my important informations against the Germans in favour of the English [*sic*].

1. The place where the headquarters of the German Navy in Holland is, and know it is camouflaged.
2. In the dunes near Schevingen and Ymuiden several casements and bunkers are build, the places where they are build [*sic*].
3. When I was at Nieuwsluis I saw that the barges which the Germans wanted to use when they would invided [*sic*] this country and which were laid up in the canal there, were brought away. I very prudent [*sic*] questioned the skipper of the tug boat where he brought them to, and he said: All those barges must be brought to Waalhaven Rotterdam on command of the Germans.
4. I showed the officers on a map where on different places anti aircraft guns were placed, and how they are camouflaged.
5. Those and several other informations [*sic*] I gave to the above mentioned officers, who were very pleased with them it.

I proved in giving those informations [*sic*] that I was not such a German friend at all, for I was very pleased myself that I was able to give some important informations [*sic*] because I wanted to help.

I had no intention to spy in this country in favour of the Germans, because I'm not a friend of them, and only wanted their money.[2]

On 17 December, Dronkers wrote a petition from the condemned cell at Wandsworth Prison repeating what he had written on 19 November:

In submitting this petition, I beg you to give it your deep consideration, in the final hope that you will spare my life, as I swear before my Maker that I am fully innocent of the charge for which I know the penalty.

I beg to state that I am satisfied with the way my trial and appeal were carried out, but it was difficult for me to prove my innocence, because I stood alone without witnesses or any one to assist me except my lawyer.

At my trial, when I was fully confident that I would be set free, I failed to ask for witnesses who could have been called, and as I did not call them at my trial, I was not allowed to have them at my appeal. Those witnesses are officers of the Navy, RAF and Army, to whom I gave the following very important information, against the Germans and in favour of England, the day after arrival at the Patriotic School, Wandsworth.

1. The place where the headquarters of the German navy in Holland is, and how it is camouflaged.
2. In the dunes near Scheveningen and Ymuiden several 'casemats' and bunkers are built. I told the places where they are built.
3. When I was at Nieuweslins [*sic*], I saw that the barges which the Germans wanted to use when they would invade this country, and which were laid up in the canal there, were all brought away. I very carefully questioned the skipper of the tugboat where he was taking them and he aid: 'They all must be brought to Waalhaven Rotterdam on command of the Germans.'
4. I showed the officers on a map, where on different places anti aircraft guns were placed and how they are camouflaged. Those and other information I gave to the above mentioned officers, who told me they were very pleased with it.

This proves that I was helping England <u>whilst in Holland</u> before coming over, and therefor [*sic*] I had no sympathy with the Germans. I proved in giving information that I was not a friend of Germany at all, because if I wanted to help the Germans the first thing I would do on my arrival in England would be something in their favour, but this was not so.

It is important that you please verify the information I gave to the officers at the Patriotic School.

The reason I came to England is that I had to go when they forced me because the German agent [*Redacted*][3] knew very well that if I refused to go that I was able then to give his name as a German agent to English sympathisers in Holland and then very easy his name would be known in England. The only way to get rid of me was to hand me over to the gestapo [*sic*]. Knowing very well what that means, I had to agree with going to England, and of course I took the money they offered me, because I did not want them to know that I was going to deceive them.

I hereby declare again that I never had the intention to carry out the things the Germans asked me to do. I am therefor [*sic*] a victim of circumstances, which makes it very difficult for me to prove my innocence.

My intention on arrival in England was to report and vie the above information to the authorities and then get a job to remain in England till the end of the war [*sic*].

I therefor [*sic*] hope and pray that you will kindly show mercy in my case and thereby spare my life.

I swear before God that the above facts are true and that I am an innocent victim of the war.

In 'Minutes of Petition by Dronkers, 18/12/42':

> The prisoner alleges, in support of his story told at his trial that he had no intention to help the Enemy, that immediately on his arrival at the RVPS he did in fact give to the British authorities [*sic*] very valuable information about German military arrangements.
>
> Sqs [?] ought to know whether this is true and whether, if true, there is reason to think that Dronkers gave the information from any sinister motive.
>
> There is nothing in the petition to justify any interference.[4]

Was Dronkers a consumate liar? Perhaps, but it was clearly a case of too little, too late. Obviously the so-called 'important informations' he had allegedly given the officers at the RVPS was either already known to them or of no strategic importance. The wheels were in motion and the hangman had already been contracted to carry out his deadly deed. If any of the information Dronkers claims to have told his captors is true, the details are missing from the official files, with no indication that they had been redacted under the Public Records Act, 1958 or the Freedom of Information Act, 2000. It is also unclear exactly when these files were handed over by MI5 into the custody of the Public Record Office/National Archives, Kew. There is the distinct possibility therefore that this information had already been weeded prior to its being handed over, although one wonders why. What possibly could be gained by shielding information about German wartime defences on the coast of Holland? Unless some of these defences were still in use by the Dutch at the time the files were weeded, which is always possible, although, again, what possible secrets could they hold?

This was a man now clutching at straws, desperate to save his neck from the gallows, like someone dangling from a cliff-top about to fall, clutching a tuft of grass in the vain hope that it would save him. Who were these witnesses he intended to call on his behalf? The so-called 'very important information' to which Dronkers referred was included in his petition on 17 December. On the day Dronkers had been condemned to death, Hinchley-Cooke wrote to de Vries thanking him for his help and co-operation.

In the letter of 23 November previously mentioned regarding his intended appeal Head wrote to Dronkers in Wandsworth Prison:

> I am in receipt of your letter dated 19th instant and not that you intend to appeal.
>
> You will find that the Governor of the Prison will give you the necessary form.
>
> With regard to my calling to see you, the position is that if you appeal, the Registrar of the Court of Criminal Appeal becomes your Solicitor to conduct the hearing but if he thinks you ought to be interviewed, he will probably delegate me to come and see you.
>
> In any event, if I can assist you at all, please let me know when I will do so.[5]

On 24 November the Governor of Wandsworth Prison wrote to Hinchley-Cooke to inform him that Dronkers had launched an appeal against his conviction under the Criminal Appeal Act, 1907. The appeal was filed with the Criminal Appeal Office on 26 November in which it contained

1. Particulars of Trial
2. Criminal Indictment
3. Original Depositions
4. Original Exhibits[6]

The appeal was heard on 14 December by the Lord Chief Justice, Thomas Inskip (Viscount Caldecote of Bristol), Mr Justice Christmas Humphreys and Mr Justice Asquith. In the document submitted by SL(B), MI5's Legal branch, it was stated that the application itself was treated as the appeal. Lawrence Byrne appeared for the Crown, and Michael Maxwell for the defence. Maxwell argued that there had been misdirection by the judge at the trial during his summing up to the jury. Like the trial, the appeal was heard in camera under Section 6 of the Emergency Powers Act, 1940. The court dismissed the Appeal without calling on counsel for the Crown. The Judgement which was handed down by the Lord Chief Justice is worth recounting in full, and comprises the next chapter.

20

Judgement Day

IN THE COURT OF CRIMINAL APPEAL

Royal Courts of Justice.
Monday, 14th December, 1942.

Before:-
THE LORD CHIEF JUSTICE OF ENGLAND.
(Viscount Caldecote of Bristol)
MR JUSTICE HUMPHREYS, and
MR JUSTICE ASQUITH.
REX
-V-
JOHANNES MARINUS DRONKERS

THE LORD CHIEF JUSTICE: In this case the Appellant was charged under Section 1 of the Treachery Act of 1940, that he was a person who, with intent to help the enemy, did an act which was likely to give assistance to the naval, military or air operations of the enemy.

The circumstances in which he came into the custody of officers of His Majesty's Services are not in dispute. On the 18th of May of this year, the Commanding Officer of one of His Majesty's trawlers saw a small yacht some miles north east of Harwich. The yacht was flying a Dutch flag, and somebody on board her was sounding a horn with the SOS signal. Eventually three men were taken off the yacht on to the trawler, and the present Appellant was one of the three men. He was described by the Commanding Officer, who gave evidence at the trial, as behaving in an excited manner, and with great heartiness thanking him for what he had done. He made no statement, except to the effect that the three of them had escaped, to use his own words, 'the bloody Germans'.

On reaching Parkestone Quay [sic], Major de Vries took charge of the men, and handed them over to another officer, I think to a non-commissioned officer. Upon the Appellant was found a dictionary which contained certain markings and an identity card. The Appellant gave Major de Vries a story of escape from Germany, to the effect that the yacht which had brought them from Holland had belonged to a lawyer, who was one of the German agents, and that a caretaker named Jan had made plans to enable the yacht to become available for himself and his two comrades to escape. He further told a story of permits being forged which were intended to facilitate their escape. He told Major de Vries that he was a servant of the General Post Office in Holland. Nothing whatever was said to the effect that he had been sent with the object, so far as the German power in Holland was concerned, as a spy. The Appellant had further opportunities of making a disclosure of the true facts relating to himself, but although in one case, at any rate, the officers with whom he had contact were able to speak his own language, Dutch, he said nothing whatever to them to suggest that he had come ostensibly, so far as the Germans were concerned, as a spy, but that he had no intention whatever of acting as a spy.

Sergeant Harrewyn, who spoke Dutch, saw him. Another official was told that he had come to work possibly as a clerk in this country, and a police officer who took him in charge on the journey from Harwich to London, who had heard nothing about his training as a spy, or his intentions, was told a story which afterwards it was admitted was a false story, about the Appellant's connection with black market operations and the Gestapo in matters of that sort, but nothing to show he had been sent as a spy.

Some four weeks after he had reached this country in the circumstances which I have stated, he saw an officer of His Majesty's Army in military intelligence, with police officers who were present, and made a full statement which was taken down in writing. It was a long and full statement. It began one day and finished the following day, an interruption having taken place owing to some emotion, or something of that sort, felt by the prisoner, and in that he told a story that he had a brother-in-law who had been asked by a German agent if he could introduce somebody to spy for Germany by coming to this country. The prisoner in due course was taken to see a Dr Schneider who, the prisoner said, was the head of the Secret Service at The Hague. He was given certain inducements to act. He was to receive a course of instruction as a spy, and while he was receiving that instruction, in addition to his salary as a Post Office servant there was to be paid into a bank a monthly sum of money. If and when he undertook his duties, he was to receive good employment at a higher rate of pay than he was then receiving when he returned to Holland, and his wife also was to be paid a considerable sum of money. On these terms, which the Appellant said he accepted, he was given instruction. He was told the matters about which he was to pass information back to German agents, relating to motorised troops, tanks, petrol and ports, and the numbers of American and native troops, and a great many more matters of the same sort. He was furnished with two cover addresses, one in Portugal and one in Sweden, to which he should address his communications. The dictionary was marked in such a way as to contain a sort of code which recorded these cover addresses. He also stated that he was given instructions as to the use of invisible ink which, by the proper process, could be brought to light. All his previous stories, he said, had been untrue. He said he had told them because they had been suggested to him by the head German agent as to the stories which he should tell, and finally he made a statement which has formed the basis of his defence to the charge on which he was convicted as to what his intentions were. He said this, and this was the first time he said it, being more than four weeks after his arrival in this country: "I wish to say that I agreed to come to England for the German Secret Service so that my wife should be supplied with money, as she was always worrying me about money, but I had no intention once I got to England of carrying out Dr Schneider's instructions or to act in any way for the Germans".

Upon this statement having been made, he was charged with the offence which I have stated. He was convicted. The Jury found him guilty of the offence with which he was charged. He made two defences. He was defended by learned Counsel, the same learned Counsel who has appeared for him to-day, and who has said everything possible on his behalf, and two points were made. The first was an explanation of his long slience as to the truth of the circumstances in which he had come to this country. His reason was that he feared long detention by the military authorities here if he disclosed the facts. Going back to the circumstances in which he agreed with Dr Schneider that he should act, he said that that assent was dictated by the fear of consequences in Holland, for if he refused, and it was known, as it would necessarily be known, to the German authorities that he was acquainted with the personnel of the Secret Service, he would be a marked man, and would be likely to suffer some evil consequences. When the question was put to him by his learned Counsel in examination-in-chief as to his reasons for not declaring immediately that he had been given instructions by the Germans, he gave the answers which are the basis of what I have stated as his two main points. He said: 'Well, I knew that when I gave the story that I was a refugee I would be free very soon, and telling the other way I was sure I would have been kept fast. (Q) What were you going to do when you were free? (A) When I would have been free I would have asked for a job, for a business occupation, and I would prefer a job against the Germans. (Q) Were you going to do anything about Dr Schneider if you got free', and the answer was 'Never'.

The rewards which he was promised were substantial; I have stated them, and the fact remains that he came here, so far as the German authorities were concerned, with apparatus and with knowledge which would have enabled him to set up as a spy, and to communicate with Germany if he had not been discovered. He did not tell his story to either the military or the police officers with whom he had contact and in whose charge he was. He did not even tell, so far as the evidence goes, his story to his two companions, and perhaps it is not surprising that the Jury in these circumstances found that his actions spoke louder than his words, and that he was guilty of the offence, a necessary element in which he was intent to help the enemy.

Mr Maxwell has taken three or four points, with which I think I can deal briefly. He suggests that the learned Judge, in describing the offence charged against him as that of being a spy, led the Jury to think that the question they had to decide was whether he was a spy in fact. Put as a proposition, we think there is nothing objectionable in it. The word 'spy' is not used in the Act, but it was directing the mind of the Jury, perhaps not with verbal accuracy but substantial accuracy, to the provisions of the Act. The question was whether he came here as a spy, that is, as somebody who was going to help the enemy by passing information to Germany. The learned Judge put quite clearly to the Jury that they must find intent and, as he quite rightly said, you could best judge a man's intention by seeing what his actions were.

The next point that was made was that the learned Judge begged a question which was for the Jury by describing the long statement made on the 19th June as a confession. The learned Judge used that expression, 'a confession', in the same sentence in which he made it quite plain that it was a confession except for the last sentence of that statement. The last sentence of the statement was the sentence which I read earlier to-day, to the effect that he never intended to carry out the duties for which he had been assigned by the Germans. We see nothing at all which was inaccurate or misleading in the passge to which our attention was called in which the learned Judge referred to the statement as a signed confession, that is, except with regard to one sentence, which he read out in full to the Jury.

It was then said that the point which the Appellant made through his Counsel at the trial, that he had to agree to do it, or to be victimised in Germany, was never put to the Jury, but in our Judgement the point was not one which would have afforded an answer to the charge made against him. The fact he had to face was that he had not for one month, or rather more, disclosed the facts relating to his preparation for coming to this country, and the reasons which led him to agree to act as a German spy threw no light upon that point which he had to meet.

Finally, the learned Judge's observations about some evidence which Col. Hinchley-Cooke gave is said to have been an arrogation to himself of the decision on a question which was for the Jury and not for him. Col. Hinchley-Cooke in cross-examination had been asked a question as to whether or not it was true that he would have been kept longer in confinement if he had stated the facts. Col. Hinchley-Cooke said: 'No, so far from being kept longer in confinement, he would have been received with open arms', and the learned Judge reminded the Jury of that passage in the evidence in a sentence to this effect: "It is true, of course, as Col. Hinchley-Cooke told you quite fairly, that he would have been received with open arms". The learned Judge is there quite accurately stating the evidence which had been given, and if he introduced it with the words 'It is true', it is merely an indication to the Jury which they could form an opinion about as well as the learned Judge as to whether the evidence satisfied them on that point.

We think that in this case, which has been carefully put before us by learned Counsel, there is nothing whatever which would justify us in interfering with the verdict of the Jury and the consequences of that verdict. The whole question at this trial, having regard to the long statement which the Appellant made, was: 'I never intended to do any spying, although I came here equipped with the knowledge and means of spying'. That was a question which was quite fairly and fully put by the learned Judge before the Jury. The Jury held that the offence was proved. We think there was plenty of evidence to justify that conclusion, and we further think there was nothing inaccurate in any of the observations in the Summing Up to which our attention has been drawn. We must therefore dismiss this appeal.

21

The Death of a Spy

Hanging is quite all right for Englishmen; they actually seem to like it; it is only the foreigners who cause trouble.

Arthur Koestler, *Reflections on Hanging*

Examination of the judge's note book from the trial is quite revealing. Mr Justice Wrottesley wrote: 'I can find no grounds for clemency,' to which H.M. (Herbert Morrison, the Home Secretary) added the footnote, 'I agree. Where are the other two. Is there no case against them? 18/12.'

On page 8 of the notes F.A.N. (Frank A. Newsam) had written on 19 December:

I can find no grounds whatever which would justify any interference. The prisoner is a man aged 46 and I have no doubt from reading all the evidence that he deliberately came to this country to spy on behalf of the enemy for the purposes of gain.[1]

The judge added: 'No suggestion of wanting to escape to leave Holland or to get to England or to join Dutch line here. Simply money.' He applied what he referred to as the 'Fair Test':

(1) He concealed truth from fellow travellers even after he was beyond reach of Gestapo.
(2) He danced on deck to denote he was a bona fide refugee.
(3) He told Major de Vries the lying story Schneider had recommended though he was an officer of the country he had come to help.
(4) He failed to tell Harroweyn [sic] who spoke his language the truth.
(5) He signed passport protest to tell Mr Jackson.
(6) He signed the long account of escape written by Mulder on 31ˢᵗ May.

(7) He joined in request on 3rd June for sending a message which he knew would get through to Schneider using his code name, Carel.

Also equipped with lying story, picture pretence of refugee 'Black Market' 'Afraid of Gestapo'. Two confessions are found. One an admittedly loyal Dutchman. He <u>arrives</u>. He now tells us, I never intended to send information. Asked how in that event he was to get the money, and told S. it would be quite easy. All he had to do was to pretend he was to be a refugee – Dutch Gov. would befriend and employ him – and if so!

(8) He does not even tell Mr Jackson who explains – if tell truth you will be free.

(9) Not even in letter Ex.13 does he tell his fellow travellers the truth. Not till it is clear that he will not be set free does he start to tell the truth, <u>adding that he never</u> really intended to send information to Germans.

You have heard his explanation. Col. H. Cooke said 'If he had told us on landing, he would have been received with open arms.' For he would have given best possible proof of his loyalty. Information not much. But if prosecution are right concealing truth then you can understand his conduct.

Telling the very lies his instructor Dr. S had told him to tell. Holding on to this means of communicating with his --- Actually sending or trying to send that wireless message and using the code signature which the German espionage knew.

<u>GUILTY</u>

Summing up after the sentence was proclaimed he said,

(10) I am bound to say that I think the jury have returned the only possible verdict in this case.[2]

Arrangements were being made for Dronkers' execution. On 4 December Herbert Hooper of E1a wrote to Hinchley-Cooke requesting permission to release information about the outcome of Dronkers' trial to Captain Derksema of the Netherlands Security Service and Johannes Regnerus Maria Van Angeren, the Dutch Minister of Justice. After discussion with Dick White and 'Buster' Milmo it was decided that Kenneth Younger, Assistant Director, E branch (ADE), should receive a short statement which he could pass on to the Dutch. On 14 December Hinchley-Cooke wrote a memo regarding whether or not the Dutch authorities should be informed of the execution prior to the news being released in the Press.

On 17 December a letter from Major Grew, Governor of Wandsworth Prison, advised Hinchley-Cooke that the execution was scheduled for 9.00 a.m. on 31 December. It had originally been intended for 8 December but owing to the Appeal, had had to be postponed. Hinchley-Cooke wrote to Major Grew on 27 December to find out whether it would be the Under Sheriff or Deputy Sheriff for the County of London who would be attending the execution, as required by the Capital Punishment (Amendment) Act of 1868, and to offer him a lift in his car. The Governor confirmed that the Deputy Under Sheriff, Mr Gedge, would be present at the execution. While this was going on, a meeting was held to discuss how the execution should be announced and the wording of the statement to the Press. The Home Office announcement stated:

> For Press and Broadcast
> Execution of a Spy
> The Home Office announces that a German Secret Service agent was executed at Wandsworth Prison this morning. He was
> Johannes Marinus DRONKERS
> a Dutch subject, born at Nigtevecht, near Utrecht, on 3rd April, 1896. He was convicted under the Treachery Act, 1940, after a trial before Mr Justice Wrottesley and a jury at the Central Criminal Court, London, on 13th, 16th and 17th November, 1942. His appeal against the sentence of death was heard by the Court of Criminal Appeal on 14th December, 1942, by the Lord Chief Justice, Mr Justice Humphreys, and Mr Justice Asquith, and was dismissed. Dronkers was represented by Counsel at the trial and in the Court of Criminal Appeal. The proceedings at both Courts were held in camera.

The statement then went on to describe 'For the information of the Press' the circumstances under which Dronkers had arrived in England and his mission. In the original manuscript, various parts have been underlined in red pencil, probably by Hinchley-Cooke, viz:

> He was a member of the Dutch Nazi Party before the war; ... it [the *Joppe*] was flying the Dutch flag and giving out signals of distress. On being brought aboard the British trawler Dronkers expressed his joy, danced on the deck and began singing; ... to whom he posed as a refugee who managed to escape from Holland by obtaining a yacht from a fisherman whom he had bribed. He said that he hoped to get some useful work in this country with the British or Netherlands Governments, possibly as a clerk; under caution; the yacht in which he came to this country had been provided for him by the German Secret Service.
> ... Dronkers several times protested both verbally and in writing about the slowness of the investigation of his case; which were in reality intended for his German masters.

On 27 December Hinchley-Cooke wrote to George Griffiths at the Home Office Press Department:

My chief, Brigadier Sir David Petrie, however, strongly urges that the very last paragraph of part II should be amended to read as follows:-
While detained pending enquiries, Dronkers several times protested both verbally and in writing about the slowness of the investigation of his case, at the same time affirming that he was a loyal Dutch subject. Moreover, he made more than one request that he should be allowed to broadcast messages over Radio Oranje to his relatives and friends in Holland which were in reality intended for his German masters.

The reason for this amendment is that, as far as I understand, there have been some complaints regarding the delay at the London Reception Centre (Royal Victoria Patriotic Schools) and that, therefore, this case is an example which illustrates the necessity of careful investigation. It is, therefore thought that the above would assist last not least your own Department vis-à-vis the various Allied Governments who are apt to grouse about the combing-out process at the LRC.

Griffiths had also written to Hinchley-Cooke on 29 December saying that Frank Aubrey Newsam, the Deputy Under-Secretary at the Home Office, agreed with the amendment to the Draft Press Notice. In his absence, Griffiths' colleague, Mr Keefe, was to see that the Press Notice would be sent to the Ministry of Information once Hinchley-Cooke had agreed to release it.

There was not going to be any Royal Pardon as was evident from a letter written by Frank Newsam to Justice Wrottesley on 28 December 1942 which stated:

I have the honour by direction of the Secretary of State, to inform your Lordship that he has given his careful consideration to all the circumstances in the case of Johannes Marinus Dronkers, convicted at the Central Criminal Court and sentenced to death, and that he has failed to discover any sufficient ground to justify him in advising His Majesty to interfere with the due course of law.

Copies were also sent to the Governor of Wandsworth Prison, High Sheriff of the County of London, Secretary, Prison Commission, DPP (Devonshire House, Mayfair Pl., Piccadilly), and the Commissioner of Police for the Metropolis. The copy addressed to the Secretary of the Prison Commission based at Oriel College, Oxford, was worded slightly different:

Sir,
I am directed by the Secretary of State to inform you that, having had under his consideration the case of Johannes Marinus Dronkers, now lying under sentence of death in Wandsworth Prison, he has failed to discover any sufficient ground to justify him in advising His Majesty to interfere with the due course of the law.

The day before his execution, 30 December, Dronkers wrote a note listing all his belongings and instructing that they be sent to his wife in The Hague. He also wrote to his wife a touching letter:

My darling,
I don't know when you will receive this letter, neither do I know whether it will be before or after the end of this war, but in any case I shall not be alive when you do. It is, therefore, my last farewell in this life and it is very difficult for me to leave you behind alone.

I have been accused of having come here with the intention of committing espionage and for that I have been sentenced to death and to-morrow the sentence will be carried out exactly on the last day of the year.

I have constantly maintained my innocence but was not believed and therefore, I also will fall as a victim of this war.

I am, however, completely prepared to depart, because I know in "whom" I have believed and God will accept me in his eternal paternal house where my father went before me.

You may be certain that God will also look after you whatever may happen, always ask him for help and guidance and you will go short of nothing.

All my property here will be sent to you and anything at home now belongs to you and you can do with it as you please.

My darling, I know that whatever I may have done against you has been forgiven by you, because I know that you have always loved me and I also know that my love for you is still complete and that I have always done my best to give you to the best of my ability. Whatever you may think; I wish I had never done or said this or that, you must realise that I am convinced that you have always tried to act in my best interests and that I have forgiven you all. Give a hearty greeting from me to all and until we meet again up above, Mother, Annie and Henk, Harry and his little wife and the little one, they are all very dear to me, Bets and Piet and the boys, tell them also that I have forgiven them their silence.

And now, my darling, a farewell to all friends, Marie a last greeting. What more can I write, except that I have spent a time here which can be called good in all respects, sufficient food, my cigarettes at the right time and good treatment. I have made friends here especially the clergyman of this Prison. He has been like a father unto me [Chaplain Basil Hilliard].

And now my dear wife, I take leave of you for ever. Do not weep for me because I shall be happy and your sadness would hamper my happiness.

God be with you and help you in your after life, have faith in him, he will provide for you. Be sensible and live humbly, that is the only advice I can give you. We shall see each other again, that is certain and I shall always be near you, though you cannot see me. Goodbye, my darling, your always deeply loving husband,
Johannes Dronkers[3]

Whether Elise ever received a copy of the letter is unknown as the original is still in his file.

Recommendations for the services of Albert Pierrepoint as executioner, to be assisted by Stephen Wade, were made in a document signed by the prison governor and countersigned by the Secretary of the Prison Commission. Paragraph 3 of the document noted:

> If the execution is to take place at 9 a.m., the Commissioners request that you will arrange for the usual prison routine to be followed during the time of execution so that prisoners will be scattered over the prison at their respective tasks. Their minds will be occupied; and any noise caused by the trap-door should pass unnoticed. The following arrangements are suggested:-
>
> Early morning exercise as usual; associated labour at 8.35 a.m. Prisoners normally employed near the execution shed given a period of additional exercise in a yard remote from it and the prison clock chime disconnected for the hour of nine. The executioners lodged so that they neither have to enter the prison nor cross the yards.[4]

Pierrepoint had already despatched several others convicted of treachery or treason, and would go on to hang over thirty people (not all for treason or treachery) during the war, and 200 Nazis following the Nuremburg Trials. For his services he was paid between 10 guineas (£10.10 shillings) and £15 for each hanging. Molly Lefubure, in her book *Murder on the Home Front*, originally published in 1954, described Pierrepoint as, 'short in stature, but powerfully built, with a ruddy face, a round head, bright blue eyes and a quick, cheery manner. There was nothing mawkish about him'.[5]

On the chilly, damp morning of 31 December just before 9.00, with a light wind blowing from the west, Johannes Marinus Dronkers was led from the condemned cell adjacent to the execution shed. There he was met by Albert Pierrepoint and his assistant Stephen Wade, and made to stand over the trap door. Present were the prison Governor, Major Grew; Deputy Under Sheriff H. N. Gedge; the prison chaplain, Basil Hilliard, and the prison warders escorting him. A white linen hood was placed over his head and his hands pinioned behind him with a leather strap; his legs were also secured with a strap. The noose was then placed around his neck and the coils tightened. Given Dronkers' weight at 182 lbs, Pierrepoint had calculated that the drop should be exactly 6 feet 3 inches. At precisely 9.00, Pierrepoint pulled the lever and Dronkers dropped to his death.

As required, the body was allowed to hang for an hour before being taken down to allow total body death to occur.[6] The autopsy was performed by Dr John Joseph Landers, the Medical Officer at HM Wandsworth Prison. The Coroner's Inquisition was composed of the following:

L.Hallows
C.Hall
A.Horsman
C.R.Bowdler
F.H.Kimber
[*illegible*] Lyall
[*illegible*]
[*illegible*]
[*illegible*]

It reported 'that the cause of death was injury to brain and central nervous system consequent upon judicial hanging'. It was reported in the 'Records of an Execution carried out in Wandsworth Prison' that the actual length of the drop was 6 feet 4½ inches; the cause of death was 'Dislocation of vertebrae', specifically,

Transverse rupture of spinal cord at juncture of medulla and cervical portion. Spine dislocated at 1½ ins. Extensive injury to medulla and brain stem. Fracture of hyoid and thyoid.[7]

The body was buried in an unmarked grave within the prison's precincts.

22

Fall-out and the Media

Following the execution a notice was posted outside the prison announcing Dronkers' death. That day, and in the days thereafter, the execution was widely reported in the media; however the Press Association and the BBC managed to incur the wrath of MI5 for disclosing details of Dronkers' operation which MI5 had tried to suppress. George Griffiths of the Press Department at the Home Office in a letter dated 26 January 1943 wrote to Hinchley-Cooke regarding the memo he had promised to send him:

The BBC in the 6 pm News on 31st December broadcast an account of the Dronkers case which included the following:-

'Dronkers made repeated requests to be allowed to broadcast messages to his Dutch relatives over Radio Orange [sic]. Actually, these messages were intended for his German employers – but they didn't get through. He probably didn't know that all messages going through Radio Orange must pass through the finest mesh of double British and Dutch security control. He also didn't know that our Dutch Allies work in close collaboration with the British authorities in checking up on Dutch people who arrive in Britain.'

In reply to our enquiries the BBC stated that they had got this additional piece of information from the Press Association and that as it had been passed by the Censor they felt they were entitled to use it.

Several of the morning newspapers on 1st January published the following as an addition to the authorised version:-

'The unmasking of Dronkers was the result of very successful co-operation between the Dutch security authorities and the British. The Dutch security authorities from the beginning have taken, in close collaboration with the British authorities, all possible steps for a thorough investigation into the reliability of Dutch refugees arriving in Britain.' (*Manchester Guardian*, *Eastern Daily Press*, *Scotsman* and *Liverpool Post*; shorter versions in Birmingham Post and Yorkshire Post.)

The *Daily Telegraph* said:-

Last night it was stated in London that the Dutch security authorities had always taken, in close collaboration with the British authorities, all possible steps to investigate thoroughly the reliability of Dutch people arriving in Britain after escaping from Holland. Before being broadcast over Radio Orange all messages, even ordinary greetings to families first pass through the finest mesh of double British and Dutch security control.

We took up the matter with Admiral Thomson, Chief Press Censor, who at once agreed that the publication of these statements was inconsistent with his Private and Confidential Memo to Editors warning them against any additions to the officially-supplied story. He undertook to make enquiries.

Later, Admiral Thomson telephoned the result of his enquiries. He said that the Press association had submitted a follow-up story about Dutch co-operation, that it had been referred to a Duty Assistant Director who was new to his job, and that unfortunately he had passed it. The DAD was wrong, said Admiral Thomson, in giving this decision. Moreover, the Press Association were at fault in submitting the story. Admiral Thomson apologised for the DAD's error and said he would speak to the Editor of the Press Association and call his attention to the fact that the whole arrangement about these spy stories was based on the understanding that no details additional to those contained in the official version should be published.

It was left to us to deal with the BBC. I spoke to the News Editor who explained that they had used the Press Association's text as it was more clearly printed than the Ministry of Information's 'copy', and had, apparently, failed to detect the presence of an unauthorised paragraph in the former. He said that steps will be taken to ensure greater care in future.

It has been ascertained that the source of the Press Association's follow-up story was the Netherlands Press Agency.[1]

The information to which Griffiths may have been referring was an article in the *Vrij Nederland* on 9 January 1943 which mentioned the proposed Radio Oranje broadcast.[2] A letter written by Kenneth Younger (ADE) to Hinchley-Cooke on 30 December 1942 sheds more light on this:

I passed the press statement to the Dutch (Capt. Wolters) this morning. To-night he telephoned to say that his Minister of Justice thought that the second part gave away too much. He felt that it would indicate to the enemy what not to do next time.

Wolters could give me no details of the Minister's objections, [an]d my impression is that Wolters was merely passing on the oder [*sic*] without any expectation that we would pay any attention to the Minister's view. I explained that no other statement had been agreed by the Court, the Home

Office, and the officers in charge of the case, it would be very difficult to alter it now, especially as the press would be getting it tomorrow morning.

Wolters clearly appreciated this difficulty. Having passed the message on, I have no doubt that he considers that honour is satisfied.

I do not intend to take any action – even if it were practicable to do so.[3]

Montague Lacey, reporting in the *Daily Express*, suggested that Dronkers may have been influenced by stories of Elizabeth Büttner, the German woman expelled from England before the war and denounced at a sensational Paris spy trial.[4] Lacey also suggested that Dronkers may have read the cables he (Lacey) had sent from The Hague when he interviewed Büttner in 1939, although he does not explain how this may have occurred.

The *Daily Mirror* echoed the *Daily Express* when it said 'Spy danced for joy when picked up by Navy' and mentioned the proposed use of invisible ink and the Radio Oranje broadcast, as did the *Daily Sketch*, although *The Times* was more circumspect. The *News Chronicle* report was short to the point of a few lines only, as was the *Daily Mail*. The *Evening News* went into greater detail, also publishing part of the notice posted outside Wandsworth Prison and listing Dronkers as 'The twelfth to die', with a list of the other eleven who had been executed to date. Other reports appeared in *The Star*, *The Evening Standard*, and again another article in the *Evening News* saying that the news was announced at 9.15 a.m., when two civilians (presumably Pierrepoint and Wade) emerged and were driven off in an Army car.

The news was also widely reported in the international media, such as the *Evening Independent* of Massillon, Ohio ('British Execute Dutch Subject as Nazi Spy'), on 31 December; the *Herald and News* from Klamath Falls, Oregon; the *Panama City News-Herald*, Florida; and the *Western Australian* in Perth on 1 January. These reports would have undoubtedly attracted the attention of the Germans, who would have discovered the fate of their 'agent', as noted in ISK intercepts of 5 and 10 January 1943:

5.1.43

27284 Lisbon – Berlin. RADER KRAIS LUDOVICO to GRUBE for KERSTEN. For information THEODOR.Ref. THEODOR GRUBE 857 (ISK 26835). In re. MARCEL ask KERSTEN. LONDON reports on 1/1 the execution of a German agent, the Dutchman MARIUS DRONKERS. [*sic*] Does GRUBE require details? For control purposes the SIMA letter identification mark of BILLY of GRUBE is needed.

10.1.43 Berlin – Lisbon. From BRUNO No. 16. For LUDOVICO, RADER, KRAIS. In re. Lisbon No.15. RADER, KRAIS T 509 (above message) BILLY has not yet set out, therefore letter identification concerning Dronkers not required. GRUBE, Leiter 1.[5]

Interestingly, there is no mention of *Ast* Hamburg or any of its staff.

One person who heard the news on the radio was double agent Eddie Chapman (Agent ZIGZAG) at his safe house at 35 Crespigny Road, Hendon, London. According to Alan Tooth,[6] his MI5 handler, 'He was obviously very shaken. I had not seen him like this before.'[7] Chapman was probably breathing a sigh of relief and thinking, 'There but for the grace of God go I.'

Over the following weeks there was an exchange of correspondence between MI5, SIS and the US Embassy in London. MI5's nose was clearly out of joint by the way in which protocols had seemingly been breached in the exchange of information, with requests being channelled through SIS instead of MI5. On 14 January 1943, Peter Ramsbotham in B3 wrote to Reginald Gibbs of B1b drawing his attention to 'our American friends' and their having seen reports of Dronkers' execution in the press. The Americans were also requesting details about Dronkers' recruitment and training. Rambsotham describes this as annoying and that

1. It shows that S.I.S have not attempted to turn up their own records, although the Camp 020 reports on Dronkers were almost certainly passed to them.
2. It shows that a month after Thurston's arrival in this country, and in spite of his assurances that all exchange of espionage material between us and the FBI would be passed through his hands and would not be referred through Stephenson, nevertheless the old channels of FBI, DSC and S.I.S are being used. This is presuming that 'our American friends' is a reference to the FBI [*sic*].

In the belief, however, that the FBI would not have approached Stephenson but Thurston, for a report on Dronkers, I suggest that 'our American friends' is a reference to Donovan, and that Stephenson has perhaps been deliberately misleading in putting forward this request, since it may be that we would not care for Donovan's people to have a full report on the Dronkers case.

Perhaps we should suggest to S.I.S that they have already had the report on this case, but that as it is our material, we should be grateful if they would ascertain from the DSC that it is the FBI and no other US authority who is making this request [*sic*].[8]

The people Ramsbotham was referring to were Arthur Thurston, who was the FBI's first Legal Attaché (or 'Legat') at the US Embassy, London; Sir William Stephenson, head of British Security Coordination (BSC), based at the Rockefeller Center in New York (DSC appears to be a typo for BSC); and William 'Wild Bill' Donovan, head of the Office of Strategic Services (OSS), the USA's wartime equivalent to SOE and the forerunner of the CIA. In a redacted report of 4 February 1943, Gibbs wrote to SIS regarding a CX report:

Dear [*Redacted*],

Confirming our conversation this morning in the course of which you told me that the query regarding Dronkers emanated from the FBI in New York, it was suggested that you would check up in your office to find whether the ordinary routine had been followed in this case which would have provided for your office receiving copies of any interrogation reports relating to Dronkers whether interim or final.

As explained, we do give to Thurston specific reports relating to characters in whom he takes a special interest, but apart from this we have always relied on the system above described to ensure that Section V.A. may be in a position to pass on to the Americans any general product of interrogations at Camp 020 which strikes them as being relevant.[9]

Gibbs also sent a memo to Ramsbotham confirming that 'our American friends' were indeed the FBI, saying that perhaps they needed to talk about it once he had seen Gibbs' letter to SIS. Gibbs was also under the impression that Arthur Thurston was not particularly interested in the Dronkers case. Ramsbotham scribbled a note at the bottom saying, 'It is curious that the FBI did not put their enquiry through Thurston. Will be interested to see S.I.S. reply to you.' The following month, on 3 March, Thurston wrote to Gibbs reminding him that the report on Dronkers which they had discussed in January had still not been sent and that he was still expecting a copy. Gibbs replied tersely that

I must remind you that we discussed this matter at the time when you made your original request, and you then agreed that you could arrange with S.I.S. at Glenalmond to forward to your Bureau their copy of the case summary on Dronkers if it was finally considered necessary to do so on what you agreed was a hangover request from the FBI dating from before your appointment over here.

If this is not satisfactory and you let me know, we can probably arrange to have another copy made.[10]

Glenalmond House in St Albans was the home of SIS's Section V (1940–43) and also their Registry (1940–45). Gibbs then wrote back to his contact at SIS the following day expressing his irritation at being sent a reminder by Thurston, enclosing a copy of his communication to Thurston and referring to the CX report and his reply of 4 February. Clearly, this was a case of SIS dragging its heels and not being up front with MI5.

Later, on 10 July, Thurston wrote to Gibbs, referring to a recently made summary report on the Dronkers case, and requested information on the secret ink found in Dronkers' possession. This may have been the FBI's *Bureau Bulletin N°.15*, addressed to 'All Investigative Employees' and marked 'Strictly Confidential', dated 24 March 1943, or another document altogether. The *Bulletin* contained information obviously gleaned from MI5 or SIS, in which it incorrectly stated that Dronkers had been sighted on 16 May 1942 and apprehended by a 'vessel of the United Nations'. It also reiterated how he had posed as a refugee, how he had repeatedly requested to make a broadcast, and the messages he was supposed to send in secret ink.[11]

It can be inferred that MI5 had obviously not been in a hurry to send the FBI a copy of their report, and neither was SIS. MI5 was also not in a hurry to reply to this latest request as it was not until 26 July that 'Buster' Milmo replied to Thurston. Interestingly, Milmo said that Dronkers had not brought any materials with him to make the ink, being expected to purchase them in England; however, he added that Dronkers would have encountered problems since one key ingredient (see Appendix 3) was only available with a doctor's certificate.

While all this was going on, Herbert Hooper of E1a wrote a memo to Hinchley-Cooke on 20 January 1943 to arrange a meeting with the Dutch Minister of Justice, Johannes van Angeren, presumably to discuss how information from the Dutch had been leaked to the Press. The dates the Minister was available were Thursday 28 January, Friday 29 January, or Saturday 30 January, at 11.00 a.m. However, it is not known the outcome of the meeting nor on which day it took place. On 17 November 1945, Baron van Moyland wrote to Captain Edward Corin of E1b from his office at 82 Eaton Square, London:

I am sure you will remember the case of Dronkers–the man who was sent to England by the Germans, and eventually discovered here and hanged as a spy.

I should be most grateful if you will please obtain for me a copy of his whole case including his interrogation, as it would be very helpful to us in our efforts to sort out details concerning other people with whom he had been in contact.[12]

Corin replied to van Moyland on 29 December:

In connection with the Dronkers case, you asked me about one Nygh.

We have a trace of Hendricus Nygh, a journalist and a director of Nygh and Van Ditmar, Advertising Bureau. This man was born in 1873 at Rotterdam.

We also have a trace of a Mr Nygh, a lawyer, said to have been Director of Fisheries at Rotterdam or Ymuiden.

Dronkers was asked about Mr Nygh on 10.6.42. He said at first that he knew nothing, but that he had heard from Jan (who was caretaker of the yacht Joppe) that Mr Nygh was a lawyer by profession and that he was then director of Fisheries at Rotterdam. It was suggested to Dronkers that as the fishing industry was under the control of the German Naval authorities, there could be no doubt about Mr Nygh working for the Germans. Whereupon Dronkers said he fully agreed that Mr Nygh was very pro-German indeed, and added that he could not understand why Jan, whom he believed to be generally pro-British, was employed by a man in a responsible position working for the Germans. He admitted that this made no sense at all, but offered no explanation.

Dronkers did not know whether Mr Nygh was a partner in the well-known firm of Nygh and Ditmar.[13]

As late as 14 July 1947, Mrs D. M. Quin of B2b wrote to Joan Chenhalls, also of B2b, regarding a request she had received from Baron van Moyland of the Dutch Security Service for copies of all the RPS interrogation reports on Dronkers and all statements he had made. Van Moyland explained that they were needed in connection with some other cases the Dutch were investigating and requested which papers they could send to him. One of these cases may well have been about Schipper. A few weeks later on 31 July, Joan Chenhalls wrote to Bernard Hill in SLB, the Legal section, stating that she had had a copy made of the statement Dronkers had given in the presence of Hinchley-Cooke (presumably she meant the one made at New Scotland Yard in June, when he was formally cautioned), and requesting Hill's approval to send it to the Dutch, 'and adding no other remark concerning other original statements held by us, but made at Camp 020'. Hill added on 7 August that

> it was agreed that we would not send to the Dutch the RPS interrogation reports, but would confine our information to the statement made by Dronkers under caution. I have read this statement and there seems no objection to this being passed to the Dutch.[14]

The following day a copy of the statement was sent to Baron van Moyland by Mrs D. M. Quin saying that she hoped it would prove of assistance to him. There is no further correspondence in the file to indicate whether indeed this statement was satisfactory to the Dutch security authorities.

As a footnote to the case, a letter dated 27 April 1950 from a Mr A. Stanowsky of Weissenbruchstraat 23, Amsterdam, which was originally sent to the War Office, requesting information about Dronkers ' ... in order to arrange some family-matters as marriage a.s.o. [and so on]' was forwarded to the Under-Secretary of State for the Home Office, on 20 May 1950:

> I am directed by Mr Secretary Ede to send you a copy of a letter which he has received from a Mr A. Stanowsky of Amsterdam and to request that you will be good enough to inform Mr Stanowsky that Johannes Marinus Dronkers was executed at Wandsworth Prison on 31st December 1942.[15]

However, there is no indication in this file or any other that any information was sent to Mr Stanowsky or any clues as to his identity, although it must be assumed he was a lawyer. The address in Amsterdam is now a bicycle repair shop. It is interesting to note that the letter refers to marriage, because it would appear that according to information uncovered by the author, Elise Dronkers had died in 1944.

23

'The Kent Spies', 1940

Before drawing any conclusions on the Dronkers case, it would be useful to take a more detailed look at three other cases in the order that they occurred – Pons *et al.*, van Wijk and Schipper – and compare their stories of how they became spies, their activities and inevitable outcome, with the Dronkers case.

When Pons, Waldberg, Meier and Kieboom landed on the south coast of England in September 1940, the Battle of Britain was raging overhead, with RAF Fighter Command pitted against the might of the German Luftwaffe. For months there had been the threat of invasion hanging over Britain's head. The Wehrmacht (German Army) had overrun all the neighbouring European countries; it was thought to be only a matter of time before Britain succumbed. Fear of German spies was rampant; everywhere it seemed they were parachuting into British fields, some reportedly disguised as nuns. Rallied by Winston Churchill, the newly appointed Prime Minster, Britain put up a massive fight for its survival. Yet the arrival of this quartet of spies was far from dramatic, and patently amateurish.

Interrogations at Camp 020 established that two of these men had landed on 3 September 1940 between Dungeness lighthouse and Lydd coastguard station. Some documents in the files state it was 5 September, but this was likely when Waldberg, Pons and Kieboom were actually captured. The two in question were Jose Waldberg, aged twenty-seven, born in Mainz, and Carl Heinz Meier, aged twenty-five, a Dutch subject of German origin born in Coblenz. Their arrival coincided with the planned German invasion of Britain, *Unternehmen Seelöwe* (Operation Sea Lion) scheduled for 15 September. Also aboard the motor cutter *Mascot* were the crew, comprising a Russian captain, two other Russians and a Latvian, although none of these were ever named, nor is there any information about them in the files. Onboard another unnamed cutter were two other spies, Charles Albert Van den Kieboom, aged twenty-seven, a Dutch 'half-caste from the Far East' born in Takaramuka, Japan; and Sjoerd Pons, aged twenty-seven, born in Amsterdam. These last two landed near the Dymchurch Redoubt. Both vessels were flying the Norwegian flag, with the white flag of surrender above it. All had travelled from Boulogne. A *Sunday Express* article, 'The Kent Spies', published on 14 June 1941 stated that Waldberg, being German, was the only one

> with heart in his work and determination in his mind ... He was the brains and natural leader of the expedition, and he was working for his country, not just for money like the renegade Dutchman [Meier], who went rather in fear of his overbearing colleague.[1]

In a somewhat sensational article which appeared in the *Evening Standard* on 11 May 1954, Sir William Jowitt, the Solicitor-General who had been elevated to the peerage as Earl Jowitt in 1951, described them as 'brave men', and revealed for the first time the fourth man, Pons, as the one who was acquitted.[2]

Each of the four had a different role to play, with Meier, who spoke good English with a Canadian accent laced with some American slang, tasked with being the intelligence-gatherer. He was to frequent pubs, cafés and railway stations and collect information from, primarily, soldiers who liked to talk about 'things that are better left unsaid in public places'. All four were expected to focus on airfields and camps, troop concentrations, ammunition dumps and other military defences.

Walberg and Meier carried with them a Morse transmitter and a battery case. By his own admission, Waldberg had been a professional spy for two or three years and claimed to have worked behind French lines, until the capitulation of France in May 1940. It would appear from his notebooks that at least some messages were sent back to the Germans and

> Our own radio sleuths also claimed to have picked up the messages, the first of which read:
> ARRIVED SAFELY. DOCUMENTS DESTROYED. ENGLISH PATROL 200 METRES FROM COAST NO MINES. FEW SOLDIERS. UNFINISHED BLOCKHOUSE.[3]

These presumably were maps, charts and codes. The codes found in Waldberg's possession were a simple substitution code, while the other used a grid whereby a stencil was placed over a message to decode it. He also had fixed times for sending messages.

Meier's undoing, which has been recorded in other intelligence literature about the Second World War, has become almost legendary. His first mistake was to go into The Rising Sun pub at 9.00 in the morning and ask for a drink.[4] Finding that it was not open until 10.30, he committed his second error by asking for a bath, something unheard of at an English country inn.

Indeed it could be said it was unusual anywhere as the British tended to only take a bath once a week at that time. He again raised suspicion when he returned to the pub at opening time and asked for a champagne cider, settling instead for a half a pint of mild and bitter. The landlady, Mrs Mabel Cole, invited a customer, Mr Horace Mansfield, to strike up a conversation with him, causing Meier to move out of the pub. His final mistake was to leave half a crown (2s 6d) on the bar, asking if that was enough for the beer, which only cost 4½d!

Mansfield decided to follow him out of the pub and watched as Meier purchased a few items (biscuits, grapefruit, and cigarettes) from a grocer's and asked the way to Dungeness. It was then that Meier received a tap on the shoulder and Mansfield produced his Air Ministry identification card (he worked for the Short's aircraft factory at Rochester as an aircraft examiner). When Mansfield challenged him about being in a prohibited area, Meier, somewhat astonished, produced his passport (he had no registration card) and claimed to be a Dutch refugee who had escaped from France via Brest in an 8-foot dinghy; he also produced £50. Mansfield drove him to the local police station in his car, where Meier was given breakfast. When questioned, he broke down and changed his story to the escape from Boulogne, telling the police that he had been intimidated into coming across the English Channel by the Germans, and revealed the presence of his other three colleagues.

The police relieved Meier of a pistol he was carrying and took him over to Dymchurch in Mansfield's car. It emerged at the trial that this was actually Waldberg's pistol, Meier having thrown his overboard during the voyage. But although the striker had been removed from the pistol and Meier could not have killed anyone with it, it was still considered a lethal weapon. Waldberg, meanwhile, saw his colleague being driven past and sent off the following message:

MEIER ARRESTED. POLICE SEARCHING FOR ME. CAN HOLD OUT TILL SATURDAY. SEND PLANES. LONG LIVE GERMANY.[5]

It is unclear what was meant by 'send planes', but Saturday 7 September 1940 is known as 'Black Saturday', when the East End of London was subjected to daylight bombing raids and the official start of The Blitz. It may have been just coincidence that on that hazy but fair day, three Messerschmitt Bf 109 fighters flew over the Dungeness area and strafed with machine-gun fire the water tower close to Waldberg's hide-out.[6] This attack most likely occurred between 11.00 and 12.00 in the morning, according to RAF reports documenting the first attack of the day. These fighters would have been escorting the Heinkel bombers on their way to bomb London and may have seen the water tower as a 'target of opportunity'. It was also the day that Herman Goering said would be 'one of the greatest days of his life'.[7] At 4.16 p.m. the Observer Corps had reported 'many hundreds of aircraft' approaching the Kent coast from Deal to the North Foreland, and a minute later eleven squadrons from Fighter Command were scrambled. This was the same day that the classic photograph of a Heinkel bomber over the U-bend of Wapping and the Isle of Dogs was taken.

Waldberg was tracked down two days later by troops searching for him. Shortly thereafter, Pons and Kieboom were rounded up by Private Sidney Charles Tollervey and initially interrogated by Second Lieutenant Eric Arnold Batten of the Somerset Light Infantry.[8] Pons, it appears, was the designated radio operator, but neither he nor Kieboom had had much enthusiasm for putting their radio into action and had deliberately dumped it in the long grass, hoping the dew would ruin it. They had also managed to ditch their codes, believing that they would have compromised them if found. However, the prosecution at their trial suggested they would have been better off dumping the radio in the English Channel.

When first interrogated, all four tried to dissociate themselves from one another. The three Dutchmen pleaded that they had been severely coerced into travelling to England, but Waldberg said little and seemed resigned to his fate. Little by little, Meier revealed later to Detective Inspector Frank Bridges of Scotland Yard's Special Branch that he had begun to work for the Germans shortly after the invasion of Holland in May 1940. He was recruited while working as a clerk in the Dutch Food Ministry by a friend who had introduced him to a German cavalry officer who was a 'talent-spotter'. Meier was sent to Brussels to learn Morse code at a school for spies under a man named Schroeder.

Schroeder, based on a description in a CIA document declassified in 2000, was probably Behrend Schuchmann, born on 12 June 1898, although it was more likely Heinrich (Behrend was his brother)

... who served in Freegattenkapitän Pfeiffer's Einsatzkommando [Operation Force] in France in May and June 1940. Subject went to France with a mobile unit of the German Naval Intelligence at Bremen, Germany, which established posts all along the Channel coast and the Atlantic. In August, Subject was posted to Le Havre branch of the I. M. and in December of the same year, he became the leader or director of that branch. [I. M. – Marine Section of Department I which was the most important department of the Abwehr, the espionage organization of the German High Command; the I. M. had as its function espionage against foreign navies and a subsection that dealt strictly with technical matters.] Subject frequently visited Spain in 1941 and was interested in fitting out small craft, principally at Brest and Leticia, France, and even in Spain, with wireless transmitter sets and operators for observation in the Channel and possibly for landing agents in the United Kingdom. In this connection, an Allied source whose information was affirmed by a captured German who had been an Abwehr typist and a naval intelligence report translator, indicated that Subject had six ships or yachts under his control for the transportation of agents, surveillance of fishing boats, and the reporting of weather conditions.[9]

The key part of this description being 'interested in fitting out small craft, principally at Brest and Leticia, France, and even in Spain, with wireless transmitter sets and operators for observation in the Channel and possibly for landing agents in the United Kingdom'. Pfeiffer, it should be remembered, was a close friend of Herbert Wichmann. As an Interim report in Schuchmann's file on Eitel, a German agent working for Bueking, *Leiter* IM in Lisbon, originally dated 11 November 1944 confirms:

> Schuchmann and Pfeiffer soon began to train and place W/T operators of the Schuchmann company operating off the French, Belgian and Dutch coasts. Together they had elaborated a private code for the use of these operators, who kept them fully informed on all shipping movements and coastal installations in that area. Additionally Pfeiffer was employed in a number of cover addresse[s] in Belgium and Holland.[10]

A description in the file on MEISSTEUFFEN written by E. M. B. Hall of B1b on 7 May 1942 provides further information:

> Our information about this man, who has been known to us for some time as the head of the German S.S. in Le Havre, has recently been augmented by the statement of a certain Hans von MEISS … From his information it appears very probable that SCHUCHMANN is a member of the SCHUCHMANN Reederi of the STEWART case[11] … MEISS states that SCHUCHMANN was a native of Hamburg, where he was a partner in a big shipping firm, which specialized in salvaging wrecked ships. He describes him as immediately recognizable as a Navy man, not very tall, sturdy built, bright blue eys, speaks German with a Hamburg accent. Is inclined to boast; fond of good living; jovial and good natured. According to MEISS he is the right man on the right job, as he knows how to handle all kinds of seamen.[12]

MEISSTEUFFEN also confirms that Schroeder was Schuchmann in a statement given to MI5 on 11 April 1942:

> The man who came to see me when I came the second time (for the final departure) to Bayonne and Biarritz was one of the bosses from Cologne, who also handed me my final instructions, what I should find out for them in the Congo (microscopic film). In his company was the Chief of the Marine Secret Service from Le Havre…His name is in

the Secret Service Kapitanleutnant Schroeder [sic], but his real name is – I found out Schuchmann and he comes originally from Hamburg having a big shipping firm there, which specializes in salvaging shipwrecked ships.[13]

While Meier was studying in Freiburg as a medical student, the Gestapo became aware of his criminal record as a money and jewel smuggler and confronted him with a complete dossier on all his crossings to a border town. They offered him the choice of going to England as a spy or facing the death penalty. But Meier also had an ulterior motive: to give Waldberg the slip, get a job on a ship and work his passage across the Atlantic where he could be reunited with his girlfriend in America, Margaret S. Moseley of Greencastle, Indiana.[14]

At Wimille, a coastal resort three miles north of Boulogne, the four collaborators were wined and dined at the Hotel Metropole, courtesy of Schroeder and a naval officer thought to be called Kuehlint, Kühling or Kuehling – or was this Kuchlin? The name certainly sounds similar when spoken. When it came to signing an agreement to spy, Meier wrote, 'I am not a confirmed Nazi.' On 4 September when they departed for England they were given a farewell lunch complete with champagne at a restaurant in Le Touquet before sailing off that evening between 10.00 and 11.00. When asked why he had not gone straight to the police on landing, Meier replied that having seen how successful the Germans had been in invading France, Belgium and the Netherlands, he was convinced that the same would happen to Britain. Had he betrayed the Germans, when they invaded Britain he feared he would have suffered a worse fate than being captured by the British. Does this sound familiar?

24

'The Kent Spies' on Trial

The trial at the Old Bailey began on 19 November 1940 before Mr Justice Wrottesley. The Solicitor-General, Sir William Jowitt, KC, and Lawrence Byrne appeared for the Crown as prosecuting counsel; Stephen Gerald Howard, KC, for Meier; a Mr R. H. Blundell[1] for Waldberg; and Christmas Humphreys for Kieboom and Pons. As with the Dronkers trial, it was held in camera.

Only Waldberg pleaded guilty, although Meier and Kieboom fought hard not to be executed. Kieboom had also been coerced into spying because of smuggling. He said he would have given himself up but he was also afraid of what vengeance the Gestapo might have brought upon his wife and child. One can only imagine what likely happened to them once the Germans learned of his arrest and execution. Initially, he appealed his death sentence, but later withdrew it and was executed on 16 December at Pentonville Prison, six days after Waldberg and Meier. The coroner was Mr Bentley Purchase.[2] The *Sunday Express* report wryly noted of Kieboom:

> It must have been the hand of fate that he came from the same country as Mata Hari, the notorious woman spy executed in France during the last war.[3]

The first witnesses to appear were the various members of the Army who had arrested the spies: Privates Tollervey, Arthur Richard Chappell, James McDonnell, Lance Corporal Reginald Goody and Second Lieutenant Batten, all of the Somerset Light Infantry. They were questioned and cross-examined about the circumstances of Kieboom's and Pons' arrests, what the two were carrying (binoculars, sack of food for ten days), the gun with which Kieboom was armed, and the discovery of the radio. Lance Corporal Robert Henry North of the Royal Engineers was also called to testify. He too had been on patrol in the area and had arrested Pons. Byrne and the judge expressed some interest in where Pons was standing when challenged by L/Cpl North, as well as the state of his trousers and whether they were wet.

After the soldiers' testimonies it was the turn of Horace Rendal Mansfield,[4] the aircraft examiner who had become suspicious of Meier in The Rising Sun pub. He was questioned about how as a civilian he had challenged Meier and taken him to the police station. When it came to the turn of Sergeant Joseph Henry Tye of the Kent County Constabulary, he was asked about when Meier took him to find the upturned boat where he had hidden a sack of food, a boat which had been washed ashore after the Dunkirk evacuation. Waldberg had been apprehended the following day, 4 September, while walking along the beach in an area between the Coastguard station at Lade and the Littlestone pumping station situated half-way between Dungeness and Littlestone close to Lydd (now London Ashford Airport). On the road from Lydd to Dungeness, Waldberg had hidden two black cases in the hollow of a tree; these were the radio and its accompanying battery. Other witnesses were also questioned: Denis Henry Hayles, living at the Coastguard station, who had found one of the rowing boats used to bring the agents ashore, and George Frederick Bunstone, who had found a brown paper parcel containing maps, a stone and a sheet of white paper.

Sergeant Frank George Robertson, the police officer who had taken Kieboom into custody from the Army, was questioned mainly about access to the restricted area where the accused had been found. When it came to Police Constable Alfred Frank Pearman, Byrne focussed on the contents of Meier's pockets and whether or not he had examined his Dutch passport, to which Pearman replied he had not. Meier said the money in his possession, amounting to £44 16s 7½d, had been sent to him from friends in Scotland. Byrne suggested that he had meant Holland, but Pearman denied that he had misheard what Meier had said.

Leonard William Humphreys, an Inspector with the Radio Branch of the Post Office Engineering Department, was called to speak about the radios that had been discovered. He testified that they were both in good working order and confirmed that they were designed to send or receive Morse signals, with a range of up to about 100 miles, adding that the dry batteries could last up to two weeks.[5]

It was now MI5's turn, in the shape of Seymour Bingham, described as a civil assistant attached to the General Staff of the War Office, but who in fact worked in B1d, Special Examiners.[6] Waldberg had handed him a notebook when he was interviewed at Seabrook police station, which Bingham had later handed to Hinchley-Cooke. However, there were no questions about the contents of the notebook. These were revealed in a supplementary statement made by Hinchley-Cooke, who was called to testify on the second day of the trial. The translations of the notes from French, some of which have already appeared earlier in this chapter, are as follows:

Page marked 'A':

ARRIVED SAFELY DOCUMENT DESTROYED ENGLISH PATROL TWO HUNDRED METRES FROM COAST BEACH WITH BROWN NETS AND RAILWAY SLEEPERS AT A DISTANCE OF FIFTY METRES NO MINES FEW SOLDIERS UNFINISHED BLOCKHOUSE NEW ROAD WALDBERG

Page marked 'B': Same message, encoded for transmission.

Page marked 'C': Two messages, one on the left, one on the right. The one on the left:

MEYER PRISONER ENGLISH POLICE SEARCHING FOR ME SITUATION DIFFICULT I CAN RESIST THIRRST [*sic*] UNTIL SATURDAY ~~AM THREE KM KM~~ IF I AM TO RESIST SEND AEROPLANES WEDNESDAY EVENING AM ~~BETWEEN TWO LARGE~~ IN THE NEIGHBOURHOOD OF ARRIVAL THREE KM KM FROM COAST WALDBERG

The one on the right:

MEYER PRISONER ENGLISH POLICE SEARCHING FOR ME AM CORNERED SITUATION DIFFICULT I CAN RESIST THIRST UNTIL SATURDAY IF I AM TO RESIST SEND AEROPLANES WEDNESDAY EVENING ELEVEN O'CLOCK AM THREE KM KM NORTH (of point of) ARRIVAL LONG LIVE GERMANY

On the opposite page, marked 'D':

THIS IS EXACT POSITION YESTERDAY EVENING SIX O'CLOCK THREE MESSERSCHMIT [*sic*] FIRED MACHINE GUNS IN MY DIRECTION THREE HUNDRED METRES SOUTH WATER RESERVOIR PAINTED RED MEIER PRISONER

'E' is the same message marked 'C' but encoded for transmission; 'F' is a copy of 'E'.[7]

Hinchley-Cooke produced a copy of the code, which had also been translated. The judge then instructed him to explain it to the jury.

Byrne questioned him about his interviews with the four accused, the method of his questioning and which languages were used (French and German), since Waldberg said he did not speak English. When it came to

Christmas Humphreys' turn, he closely questioned Hinchley-Cooke about the information extracted from the accused. It appears from the transcripts that none of the spies seemed reluctant to withhold information and gave of it quite freely, with a bit of occasional prompting to maintain the flow.

Humphreys focussed on the fact that because of conditions now prevailing in the Netherlands and the fact that two of them were known to the Gestapo as having been smugglers, the threat of reprisals against them and their families would have been severe. Therefore, they were under pressure to cooperate with them and the penalty for not doing so was in some dispute. He also suggested that the penalty would have been death, which Hinchley-Cooke refuted, suggesting instead being sent to a concentration camp. It is perhaps a somewhat moot point as to which would have been worse. His exchange with Humphreys verged on the sarcastic when it was suggested that a camp would not have been 'very pleasant'; Hinchley-Cooke replied that he had never been in one, so couldn't comment.

There followed some discussion regarding the quartet's training as spies, their previous military training as ambulance drivers, and whether they were simply conscripts or more experienced soldiers. Hinchley-Cooke also admitted that the Germans preferred using Dutch nationals since they were able to produce genuine documents, such as passports, which the Germans could not unless they were forged. On arrival in Britain, Dutch nationals could then try to claim refugee status. Humphreys suggested that being in possession of a loaded firearm would not reflect very well on someone who claimed simply to be a refugee. Hinchley-Cooke offered to have the firearm tested during the lunch hour to ascertain its workability.

Another bone of contention seemed to be the suggestion that the food and other items found in their possession had been 'looted' from items left behind during the retreat from Dunkirk. This was refuted as being fair pickings for anyone who happened to find them. What may have contributed finally to Pons' acquittal was the line of questioning which followed regarding his willingness to (a) give himself up, and (b) his explanation of the code. Humphreys:

Q: Did it not strike you as odd that a spy upon his first voyage should be informing the British Intelligence Department about how to use a code?
A: He is not the first enemy agent we have caught who was very anxious to tell us immediately all that happened to try to save his skin.
Q: That is a different point of view. Was he not almost like a small boy with a new toy, something he had just been taught and wanted to tell you all about it?
A: I do not think so.[8]

Turning to describe Waldberg, Humphreys suggested that his attitude had been completely different and one of 'contemptuous indifference' towards his fellow spies because he was a self-described professional spy. (Waldberg had explained that he had worked for the 'German Espionage Bureau' for two years.) Humphreys based this so-called indifference on a statement made by Waldberg when he was questioned after his arrest, saying that he couldn't remember the names of all of them as he had only met them on the journey from Brussels. This remark provoked scepticism from the judge.

The various police officers from New Scotland Yard – Detective Sergeants Stanley Buswell and William Allchin, and Detective Inspector Frank Bridges – all gave testimonies of being present when the accused were questioned by Hinchley-Cooke. Bridges was asked about a visit Meier had made to New York in February 1939, as evidenced by a visa stamp on his passport. When at last his turn came, Meier was also asked about this trip to the USA and the girl he had fallen in love with while studying in Freiburg and Brysgall. He admitted that he had been recruited by a group leader in the NSB and was aware that the training he had been given in Morse and military matters was for the purpose of espionage. Meier claimed that 'I had never wanted to go in for this spying business at all', but saw it as a means of going back to America if he could get to England. He also claimed that he had been afraid of Waldberg who had been his senior officer.

The Solicitor-General covered much of the same ground during his cross-examination, going over the circumstances of Meier's recruitment and the apparent hold the Germans had over him. Like Dronkers, he had been promised a good job at the end of the mission. The remainder of the questioning was about his recruitment and the fact that he had knowingly signed up with the Germans to carry out a mission in England. He was firmly of the belief that with the imminent invasion, to have betrayed Waldberg and then been discovered would have resulted in the Germans punishing him when they arrived.

Kieboom said that he had first met Pons when the Dutch Army was mobilised in September 1939. Both he and Meier had said that after the Dutch had capitulated they had been unsuccessful in finding work (Meier had eventually found work as a clerk in the Dutch Food Ministry, and Kieboom as an ambulance driver, which is what he had been in the Army). He said that when the Germans started training them he thought they were just going to listen in to radio messages, but when they discovered what their ultimate task was they had refused. However, the Germans had an ace up their sleeve with their knowledge of his money smuggling between Holland and Germany. Faced with the prospect that under the German Military Code the penalty was death if they did not cooperate, they were given several days to think it over. Their decision was to appear to cooperate and use the trip to England as a means to escape, with the goal of reaching America. Unlike Meier, Kieboom claimed he had never signed any document accepting 'this mission voluntarily to go to England'. Both of them kept their secret from Waldberg and Meier, whom they had not met before. Kieboom also stated that he had thrown away his code so that it did not fall into British hands, which would have been a punishable offence had the Germans ever found out.

Before the court adjourned for the day, Robert Churchill, a well-known firearms expert,[9] was allowed to interpose before further questioning of Kieboom so that he could explain about the pistol, a special type of Belgian Browning, which had suffered considerable wear and tear. This, he explained, was why it was not working properly. It is interesting to note that a receipt from S. Reisen to Hinchley-Cooke dated 1 January 1946 mentions a Mauser pistol on loan to the Imperial War Museum for a Security Services exhibit. Whether this was meant to be the same pistol is unknown. The following day, 21 November, Kieboom revealed that both he and Pons had agreed not to concoct a cover story, but to come clean and tell the truth. Quoting what Pons had said in his statement to Hinchley-Cooke and the Special Branch, the Solicitor-General said,

> It was my meaning to go to England, for when I did not go to England I go to Germany for smuggling affairs, and they say, 'If you don't do it we will get you later when we come to England', but I did not believe that they would come here ... It was a way of escape from the Germans, so I said I would do it, so I had the meaning to go to the Police directly and report myself.

Kieboom contradicted that statement to some extent because when challenged by the Solicitor-General, although he admitted to having seen a copy of Pons' statement and that it applied to him too, he said that it was not directly his intention, but first to find a port such as Liverpool or Bristol, to embark for America.

The Solicitor-General questioned the plausibility of his story about getting to a port and then departing for America. Why wouldn't he simply have told the British authorities that since he had been to America before, could they possibly help him to get back there? And like Dronkers, Kieboom said that he didn't think the British would believe his story. Jowitt suggested to him that his intention of telling the whole truth the moment he was taken into custody was, in fact, not the case: he had told the soldiers that they had come from Brest, not Boulogne (for some reason not explained to them, the Germans had not wanted them to mention Boulogne); he had neglected to mention that he had a compatriot who was also a 'refugee'; and he had also lied about paying a fisherman to take them across the Channel. Kieboom replied somewhat appositely, 'If I told them directly we had come across for the Germans with a radio, they would probably have treated us as spies, Sir.'

Pons claimed that he too had been threatened by the Germans over his smuggling and would have been sent to Germany to face prison had he not agreed to carry out their mission to England. He said the Germans agreed to overlook his previous record if he cooperated. When he asked them what the nature of the work would be they had assured him that it was not against England, but to do translations. When the true nature of the work became apparent from a senior officer brought in to explain, he also said that he had refused and corroborated Kieboom's story of being given a few days to think it over.

On the subject of the radio set, he was asked why he hadn't simply thrown it into the sea instead of into a drainage ditch. He replied that he wanted to be able find it again to show to the authorities. By ditching it in the sea this would have been impossible. The judge appeared a bit irascible and disagreed with him. Parts of his statement were read to him in which he stated that he had never intended to help the Germans in any way once he had arrived, which he said was true.

The Solicitor-General in his cross-examination seemed preoccupied with Pons' jewel and gold smuggling, demanding to know details of what type of jewels, the address in Köln of his contact, how he was supposed to deliver them, etc. All of this seems irrelevant to the case in hand. It should have been sufficient to establish that this past crime was the reason why he had been coerced into working for the Germans.

In his summing up to the jury, Gerald Howard, speaking of his client Meier, stated that it had not been proved 'beyond reasonable doubt that he intended in the real sense of the word – not pretended – that he intended to help the enemy and do something injurious to this country, his mind going with the act ... ' Meier did not dispute the fact that he had landed with Waldberg in England, it was 'with what intention did he do that thing and agree to come'. He went on to say that 'the Prosecution have not proved beyond reasonable doubt that this man, Meier, when he came to this country, came with the real intention of helping Germany or of harming England'. To justify why he came over to England equipped with a radio and supplies etc., Howard said it was only because Meier had to be seen to go along with the sham: 'It has nothing to do really, has it, with what his real intention was if you are satisfied ... that he embarked upon this business without any real intention in spying in this country at all.' He used the justification heard earlier why Meier had not given himself up immediately, that he was expecting the Germans to invade at any time soon, and was afraid of the consequences. When it seemed as if he would never let up, the judge called for an adjournment to dismiss the witnesses and other officers. When they resumed, Howard added that Meier had never assembled the radio, thus making it workable to transmit any messages.

Christmas Humphreys then spoke of his two clients, Kieboom and Pons. He began by reading to the jury the first section of the Treachery Act, and also focused on the issue of intent, asking them to note

the very wide scope of the acts which a person may not do, but note that every one of those acts before it becomes an offence must be based upon this fact, that it is done with intent to help the enemy; in this case Germany ... You are not trying a man for acts, you are trying these two men for the state of their minds in the dark in the early hours of the 3rd September as they approached the English shore and when they landed. What is in a man's mind can only be known by what he does or says … You have to decide what was in their minds, the intent, to the extent that any was formed, with which they came to this country or conspired in the way alleged in the Indictment. I for one make no difference between the two counts, because as they approached our shores and came within the three mile limit they are automatically in this country, and if they set up a wireless set with that intent, or if they land here with that intent it is all the same, it make [sic] no difference on either charge if you find them guilty upon either.

He emphasised that just agreeing to something does not actually mean that the act will be carried out, saying that there is a 'big distinction between agreeing to come to England and the real intent with which you propose to come England so far as your own true mind is concerned'. Their lack of training as spies was another point in their favour. The fact that they (well, Kieboom, as Pons was unsure of the proposal) had planned to abscond to America the moment they arrived in England was more proof that they had no intention of carrying out the Germans' wishes. Their not signing the document which the Germans had thrust at them was also an indication of not following through with their assignment.

Jowitt's summing up began on a patriotic, almost Churchillian, note when he said that 'although the Germans may bomb this building brick by brick they will never succeed in destroying the heritage we have handed down to us and will hand on of British justice and British fairness'. (Shades of 'we shall fight them on the beaches … ') He attempted to clarify to the jury the facts of the Treachery Act. Jowitt made the distinction that if their boat had been captured by a Royal Navy vessel within British territorial waters (the three-mile limit) before they had landed, depending on whether they had committed anything referred to in the Act, the case would then have to rest on conspiracy to commit an act. He explained that 'conspiracy is an act of the mind, but it is an act of the mind which is proved by what we call overt acts, that which a man does, because in no other way can you try what a man's mind is'. He went on to say that in not all conspiracy cases do all the conspirators know each other, but at the same time are equally guilty, citing the case of R v. Meyrick and Ribuffi as an example.[10] In describing the sort of person who becomes a spy for the Germans, and one which is worth bearing in mind, is that

what the Germans want are quite unscrupulous people, but they want clever people, intelligent people who may see the thing through. After all, even these things cost money, you know, and they are not going to give this to an absolute dud.

Again, the whole business of intent was forefront in Jowitt's argument, stressing once more that what is in a man's mind cannot be tried; it can only be known by his actions. By the time the jury had heard this from all counsel it must have been firmly instilled in their minds.

The following day when the judge began his summing up he reiterated the two charges: first of conspiracy to commit espionage, and second of landing, with the intention of spying. As if to put ideas into the jury's mind prior to their making it up for themselves, he said:

> As a matter of fact I am satisfied that it could, subject to what I have to say to you about the intention of these three men which is an important thing in this case, because the conspiracy, if it were one, was undoubtedly still on foot [*sic*] while these men were in this country, and subject to what I have got to say about their intention there is ample evidence upon which you could say they were planning in conjunction with one another and in conjunction with those who sent them, after they arrived in this country.

The judge added that to claim they had been under duress by the Gestapo was no excuse. He went over the facts of the case again, one defendant at a time, finally reminding them that if there was any doubt as to the guilt of any of the accused they must not find him guilty.

The jury retired to reach their verdict and returned an hour and twenty-five minutes later with the foreman of the jury saying that they had come to the conclusion that one of the accused (Pons) was guilty of the 'conspiracy' but had not intended to do anything against England upon his arrival:

> What should they do, the foreman asked, if they thought that one of the defendants had originally conspired with the others to spy for Germany – but that 'when he arrived in England he decided that he would not do anything to help the enemy but he would make a clean breast of it here.' Sir William Jowett, [*sic*] solicitor general and prosecuting counsel in the case, stood and said that would be a 'Not Guilty' verdict.[11]

Mr Justice Wrottesley then turned to the Solicitor-General and stated, 'That means a verdict of "not guilty,"' to which Jowitt agreed. Pons was acquitted but afterwards rearrested and detained at Pentonville Prison, mostly in solitary confinement, under the Aliens Order, 1920. An application for his internment was made to the Home Office under Article 12(5) (a) of the Aliens Order, 1920, and he was detained until the end of the war in Europe, when he was deported to the Netherlands on 2 July 1945.[12] His fellow compatriots, Jose Waldberg, Charles van den Kieboom and Carl Meier, were found guilty as charged and sentenced to death, without making any comment. The phrase, 'when he arrived in England he decided that he would not do anything to help the enemy but he would make a clean breast of it here' is worth remembering as we shall return to it later. Humphreys' statement about intent should also be remembered for future reference.

There were some interesting comments post-trial which emerged regarding Pons's acquittal. An account dated 27 November sent to Sir Alexander Maxwell at the Home Office on behalf of Sir Norman Kendal of the Special Branch and signed by Inspector Frank Bridges states:

> Their respective Counsel [Meier, Kieboom and Pons] each said that there was no dispute as to fact but held contended that the prosecution had not proved beyond reasonable doubt that the 'intention' of the prisoners was to assist the enemy ...
>
> Pons, the only man acquitted, adhered in the witness box to what he had said in his statement to Lieutenant Colonel Hinchley Cooke, and Mr Christmas Humphreys on his behalf, said that his whole conduct was consistent of a man acting under duress. Pons had, said Counsel (under pressure from the Nazis), landed at the Dymchurch Redoubt which he must have expected to find bristling with soldiers. This was a prohibited area and Pons could not have expected to get far without being challenged. His first act on reaching shore, Co[unsel] was instructed, was to immerse the radio set in water and then approach the witness Lance Corporal North. This was in accordan[ce] with his original intention and was referred to in his statement to Lieutenant Colonel Hinchley Cooke.
>
> Counsel's pleas as briefly outlined in the foregoing paragraph must have carried some weight with the Jury, who although[h] they could safely have found a verdict of 'guilty' on Mr Justice Wrottesley's summing up, no doubt were over impressed by his reminding them that Pons was the only one of the four who when arrested had volunteered that he had a companion.
>
> Sir William Jowitt in his cross examination had thrown doubt on Pons' evidence that the Gestapo had a hold on him because he had been engaged in smuggling jewellery from Germany to Holland; and asked him why, if it had been his intention to give himself up on arrival in England he had not rowed his boat slower so as to arrive in daylight or struck a match and shouted when he arrived in the dark.

A post-trial document summarising the outcome, which appears to date from 28 October 1941, states:

> Although there is no doubt that Pons was as guilty as his three confederates, the Jury unfortunately believed his evidence, given under oath, that he had been blackmailed by the Gestapo and that he had come to England with the intention of giving himself up immediately on landing.

The author Joshua Levine noted that

> Pons may well have cut a more sympathetic figure than Kieboom, and it is perfectly possible that the jury simply didn't want to punish him with death. It is not unknown for juries to decide cases on emotion rather than brutal logic. It is certainly true that while the other two defendants had made attempts to hide their equipment, or conceal their identities, Pons had been unresisting and co-operative.
>
> Whatever the reason for his acquittal, though, it stands as an extraordinary testament to the independence of these jurors – and a testament to the jury system itself – that Pons was acquitted as the Germans stood poised to invade.[13]

Initially, however, the whole episode became the subject of an official cover-up. The public were kept in the dark about the fact that there had been an acquittal, and in light of invasion fever (which had actually dissipated by the time the trial took place), it was important for public morale that Pons's identity not be disclosed. For a time, immediately following the trial, it was also decided not to reveal that a trial had even taken place. In a revealing letter that Sir Alexander Maxwell wrote to Lord Swinton on 3 December he asked,

> I wonder if you could assist the Home Secretary by letting him have a letter giving a reasoned statement of the purposes for which, in the view of the Security Services, it is necessary to keep the public and the Press entirely unaware of the trial of the German spies who were recently caught on the coast of Kent…One of the prisoners has now appealed and I have written to the Registrar of the Court of Criminal Appeal asking that similar exceptional measures shall be taken to prevent any knowledge reaching the Press and the public that such a case is before the Court of Criminal Appeal…From the judge's notes and from the transcript of the interrogation by Colonel Hinchley Cooke it appears that before Waldberg was arrested he had sent out a message stating that Meier was a prisoner and that the English police were searching for him. It is therefore arguable that the enemy must know that some at any rate of this party were captured.
>
> In addition, numerous members of the public know, including many people in the Kent area. We may, therefore, have to answer the argument that we are taking great pains to conceal something which the enemy must be presumed to know.
>
> In addition there are important considerations in favour of publicity: (1) it would be advantageous to the morale of the people of this country to know that some spies had been caught and brought to justice; (2) the deterrent effect of the sentences will be lost if the trial and the sentences are kept secret – it will be said that publicity ought to be given to these sentences as a warning to any other persons who may be induced by enemy threats or promises to follow the example of the men who have been caught; (3) it is

of course as a general proposition wrong that a sentence of death should be passed and executed without the public knowing anything about it. Such sentences, it will be said, are of great importance, and the Government and the Courts ought to know what is the public opinion thereon. Public opinion and public criticism is the most important safeguard for the proper administration of justice, and to carry out sentences of this kind in secrecy is contrary to all our traditions.[14]

In his reply to Maxwell on 5 December Lord Swinton was equally revealing, and it would set the tone for future trials; it is worth reproducing in full:

In the particular case of the three men, we have come to the conclusion that it will be possible to publish the conviction; and we propose that should be done in a carefully prepared statement, to be issued to the Press on the day the execution is carried out.

The fact that a conviction and sentence can be published does not affect the importance of the trial being conducted in secret. It is very difficult in a genuine spy case to select any part of the proceedings which can be conducted in public. Something may slip out which is most desirable to keep hidden; and even in passing sentence a judge may inadvertently err, from a security point of view if he makes any observations.

I fully share your view that the fact of conviction and the execution of sentence should be published wherever possible; and also that this should be accompanied by such statement of the case as can be made public. What can be given in such a statement requires very careful consideration in each case.

As you know, the policy which is being followed is that when an agent is caught, he is thoroughly examined. The first and overriding consideration is what information can we get to build up our knowledge of enemy plans and organisation. On this the Secret and Security Services and the Directorate of Intelligence work in co-operation; and the examination often takes a considerable time.

In some cases it is both possible and necessar[y] to use the man and his equipment. In other cases the man can ultimately be brought to trial. Even where a man is tried and convicted, it may be absolutely essential to keep the fact secret; it may be necessary to the whole chain of counter-espionage that the enemy should believe him to be still at large. But even where this is not so and the conviction can be made public, many of the facts disclosed at the trial must be kept secret.

I want to make it plain that there is much more in this than keeping the enemy in doubt as to the fate of his agents, as in the case of the submarines. The combined work of all the Services as built up, and is continually adding to, a great structure of intelligence and counter-espionage; and a single disclosure, affecting one individual, might send the whole building toppling. I have no love for unnecessary secrecy; but in this matter we cannot afford to take any avoidable risk.[15]

Someone else who had a vested interest in learning more about what happened was Horace Mansfield, the aircraft examiner who had initially detained Meier. Writing from Gloucester on 6 September 1941 to the News Editor of the *Sunday Express*, he enquired as to when the Censor would release information about the case. Mansfield had originally written to the *Sunday Express* on 10 June and again on 18 July, regarding whether they would be interested in hearing his story. On 9 September the *Sunday Express* News Editor, J. L. Garbutt, replied that in his opinion nothing about the case would be released until the end of the war. It also appears that Mansfield had written an article about the arrest of Meier which he had given to William Kerr Bliss, a journalist working for the *Evening Standard* but attached to the *Sunday Express*.

On Thursday 10 June, Bliss travelled down to Gloucester to interview Mansfield, who was accompanied by his wife, both at his digs and also over a drink at the New Inn Hotel. There Mansfield handed over some pencilled notes and showed Bliss the subpoena he had received to give evidence at the trial. In due course, Bliss wrote two articles, one long, one short, from notes he had taken at the interview and submitted them to the *Sunday Express*. In consultation with Mansfield he had omitted certain facts, although it is unclear what these were. When he returned to the office on 24 June, having been engaged in other matters, Bliss was summoned to the War Office to meet with Hinchley-Cooke who informed him that there was a judge's order banning any publication, and ordered him to hand over all his notes.[16] There is no indication in the files what sort of warning Mansfield received from MI5 about his articles, particularly given that he would have signed the Official Secrets Act when he began work as an aircraft inspector.

The question now was, what to do with Pons? A report from Inspector Frank Bridges of Special Branch dated 22 November 1940, the day after the trial concluded, states:

> From my enquiries and from the evidence I am satisfied that Pons was as culpable as his three confederates, but that he owes his life to the scrupulous fairness of the jury ... He is a dangerous man and obviously should be kept in custody until the cessation of hostilities.[17]

On 24 November 1940, Major Langdon of B1b stated that Pons was in Pentonville Prison. Herbert Hooper of E1a noted that Pons should be moved since there was a 'stool pigeon' in the prison who had belonged to the same organisation as Pons and was afraid that Pons might start talking to others. This prompted a letter from the Governor of Brixton Prison, G. F. Clayton, on 27 November who told Hinchley-Cooke,

> I thought you would be glad to know that Pons has had no conversation with anyone concerning his case, and through methods I had better not disclose,

I feel certain he will not do so in the future. [Hand-written note added: I succeeded in putting the wind up him and am quite satisfied and am pretty certain he was telling the truth. I thought this might relieve you of anxiety.][18]

A little bit of friendly persuasion, perhaps? Clearly, Major Langdon had got his facts wrong about in which prison Pons currently resided.

On 10 December 1940 the Chief Officer at Brixton Prison, George Watson, wrote to Hinchley-Cooke asking whether Pons should be kept in solitary confinement.[19] That same day 'Jasper' Harker wrote asking what they should continue to do with Pons, 'as I feel the Home Office will begin to get a bit querulous about this and we must decide exactly what we want done'. A handwritten note was appended saying that the Home Office was trying to set up a 'House for Incurables' on the Isle of Man.[20] Harker had spoken with Lord Swinton, who told him that the Solicitor-General was of the opinion that the jury had acquitted Pons because they

> did not feel keen on his execution. Had there been the possibility of a lesser penalty the Solicitor thinks he would have been convicted.
>
> As a result of this case I am inclined to think that that we should probably be better off if these cases could be tried by a Tribunal of three judges and the jury eliminated, and I gather the DPP is of the same view. Whether this is a practical proposition at the moment I do not know, but I would like your views.[21]

A reply at the bottom of this document dated 27 November 1940 made the following points:

> From a practical point of view and as an immediate objective such an arrangement would suit us admirably. On the other hand I feel there may be political difficulties even if the technical ones can be got over. Would it [not - *added in ink*] be a dangerous precedent to establish? You would certainly meet with trouble if the accused had any political background.

Waldberg and Meier were both hanged at Pentonville Prison on 11 December, Kieboom on 17 December. He had decided to appeal his conviction, but on the advice of Christmas Humphreys withdrew it. All three were the first to be executed under the Treachery Act, 1940. In another part of the official cover-up, M. H. Whitelegge of the Home Office informed Hinchley-Cooke at MI5 that the Governor of Pentonville Prison had been requested to dispense with the usual notice of execution posted outside the prison and that the Coroner had been instructed 'to ensure the preservation of secrecy in connection with the inquest.'[22]

There is a note in the Home Office Prison Commission file regarding Waldberg and Meier stating, 'Mrs A. McGrowther protests against

execution' and 'Miss G. Freeman protests against execution', but the latter
note has been crossed out. It is not known who these ladies were, other than
Mrs McGrowther was from Glasgow. A copy of Mrs McGrowther's letter
dated 11 December 1940, the day Waldberg and Meier were hanged, is
included in the file:

> Sir,
>
> I wish to protest to you against the execution of the two men who were
> trying to wireless information to Germany. It was a quite cruel and needless
> punishment they could have been kept as prisoners till the war was over.
> The worst bit about it too was that we the British nation were art and pert
> in their crime providing pubs and drink to loosen mens tongues to give
> away news [sic]. Actions like that will not help Britain nor the Labour Party
> who will soon be kicked out of office by their sometime friends the Tories.[23]

It is interesting to note that a letter signed 'MHW' (M. H. Whitelegge, Home
Office) addressed to Hinchley-Cooke on 17 December 1940 stated,

> Waldberg, however, while testifying to the good treatment which he
> received in prison, complains that English Justice failed him at his trial. He
> alleges that inter alia he was deceived into pleading guilty and that his trial
> only took three minutes.[24]

This has been marked with an asterisk and a handwritten note appended
to the bottom of the page saying, 'I [illegible] from our papers that he had
previously tried his complaint on us.' Another note also added, 'I am not sure
from recollection in what form this complaint appeared [?]'

With the beginning of the New Year MI5 returned to the old question
of what to do with Pons. Clayton, the Governor of Brixton Prison, wrote
to Hinchley-Cooke on 3 January 1941 asking whether Pons should remain
in solitary confinement. He was referring to instructions he had received
from Hinchley-Cooke on 14 December stating that Pons should be isolated
until after Kieboom's execution, when the situation would be reviewed.
As of 24 January 1941 Pons was at Camp 006 on Lingfield racecourse in
Surrey. In February 1941 there was an exchange of correspondence between
MI5 (mostly Hinchley-Cooke), Sir Alexander Maxwell and Lord Swinton
about what to do with Pons and his possible transfer to 'a segregated house
we hope to establish in the Isle of Man', which had been referred to as the
'Black Sheep Pen' and a 'Home for Incurables'.[25] As of 24 November 1943
he was still at Camp 020. Author Joshua Levine has reported that contrary
to popular belief, Pons's wife was not executed in a concentration camp
in 1943. He was repatriated to Holland on 2 July 1945 on a flight from
Hendon Airport. He and his wife were divorced in 1951; later, he remarried
and moved to Spain in 1983, where he died.[26]

25

The Self-Confessed Agent

Willem Adolph Theodor van Wijk was born in Bangkinang, Sumatra, on 24 April 1903, and came to England in April 1941. His case is worth comparing to that of Dronkers as there are many parallels. What the Director of Public Prosecutions (DPP) had to say about the van Wijk case, and how MI5 reacted to the case and the DPP's comments, is quite revealing and worthy of examination.

Without elaborating too much on the van Wijk case, essentially the MI6 station in Madrid had established that he had been working for the German Intelligence Service and that he had received financial remuneration from them. In September 1939 he had been living in Spain but had returned to Holland in February 1940 and served in the Dutch Army. He returned to Spain on 28 September 1940. Three weeks later he was visited by PABLO, who blackmailed him into working for them on account of his being allowed to return to Spain with the permission of the German authorities. Van Wijk was threatened that his family (father, married sister and her children) still in Holland would suffer if he were to refuse. A letter from the British Embassy in Madrid dated 3 December 1940 explained the situation:

> Van W. is suspected of carrying on pro-German activities in Spain and is stated to be in German pay and to be ingratiating himself with members of the German Embassy … in arranging for the deblocking of some important Dutch funds in Spain, which would be a severe blow to the Dutch Government … Dutch Legation say that Van W. is a menace to our common interests … On the other hand, the British A.A. [Air Attaché][1] in Madrid gets information from Van W. about bombing raids on Germany and Holland and is inclined to think him genuine.[2]

In early 1941, on the instructions of PABLO, he travelled to Tangier to find out whether his cousin, Frederick Gerth van Wijk, the Dutch Consul-General and Minister in Tangier, was pro-German or anti-German; he reported to PABLO that his cousin was anti-German. This may have been on account of Frederick's sister Selina marrying Lord Rhidian Crichton-Stuart, younger son of the 4th Marquess of Bute, in 1939.[3] On a second trip he was sent to establish whether the British had designs on Spanish Morocco. There then followed a discussion amongst British authorities as to whether Willem van Wijk should be brought to England. The Dutch government was requesting that the Passport Office at the British Embassy in Lisbon issue him with a visa to do so. This is important because this means that van Wijk, as opposed to Dronkers, came legitimately to England with the permission of the British government.

Van Wijk flew to England from Lisbon on 5 April 1941, landing in Bristol, and was taken to the Royal Victoria Patriotic School before being transferred to the Oratory Schools. A Home Office Detention Order was issued against him on 20 June 1941. Other evidence soon began to emerge of van Wijk's activities. A report dated 28 June 1941 from Seymour Bingham of MI5's B24k stated that

> According to MI6 Gerth van Wijk has contacted a number of enemy agents in Madrid and endeavoured to penetrate the British Embassy, going as far as to offer his services for espionage activities ... The information on this file gives us to believe that Gerth van Wijk is, in fact, an agent provocateur...[4]

In one of his 'Yellow Perils' written about van Wijk on 7 August, Stephens, the Commandant of Camp 020, had this to say:

> The espionage story of GERTH VAN WIJK is somewhat remarkable. He is a self confessed German agent. He did not, however, confess on arrival in England that he was a German agent, nor was that information elicited from him in interrogation either at the Royal Patriotic Schools or at the Oratory Schools. Indeed, for some reason best known to himself, GERTH VAN WIJK elected to give this information at the Oratory Schools 98 days after arrival in this country. The true active for this somewhat sudden confession is difficult to ascertain, for his explanations are contradictory. His first explanation is that he was blackmailed by that capable German S.S. official PABLO to the extent that if his mission failed his family in Holland would suffer ... His second explanation is that he was a good Dutchman and wished to revenge himself upon the German authorities, wherefore he determined to confess on arrival in England. He attributes his failure to confess to two incidents. The first of these incidents is that on arrival at the Royal Patriotic Schools he was greeted by the news that the British authorities had already hanged two Dutchmen, and GERTH VAN WIJK admits he was shaken thereby.

Stephens goes on to add,

My own reading of his motive is simple and yet has not be[en] properly met by GERTH VAN WIJK. In effect, GERTH VAN WIJK f[aced] with the possibility of interminable incarceration, took the risk of divulging he was a German agent ...[5]

He recommended that van Wijk be kept in British custody with the possibility of being 'turned' as a double agent:

As however GERTH VAN WIJK (in his statements of July 23rd and August 1st) has made detailed proposals for his use as a double cross agent in Madrid which raise the question of his reliability I must add, that after hearing his explanations, I am disposed to accept his statement that he had intended confessing immediately on arrival in this country ... I also believe the present offer of his services to be honest, though I am not convinced that he possesses the necessary strength of character to carry out a mission successfully ... If the above-mentioned offer is not accepted, I suggest that GERTH VAN WIJK could be a most valuable addition to our own string of inside agents ...[6]

However, Milmo disagreed, commenting on 11 August that

I do not see that there is any possibility of using Gerth van Wijk as an agent, either here or abroad ... it would hardly be possible to send him back to Lisbon as an external agent. As an internal agent, I do not see what use would be made of him, since it would be practically impossible for him to regain the confidence of his previous employers having failed to obey his very express instructions that he return to Spain at all costs.

   The question of whether Gerth van Wijk is to be prosecuted will have to be decided by the DPP, to whom I suggest that it [*annotation illegible*] should be submitted without further delay now that it has been liquidated from an Intelligence standpoint. In view of the delay which has occurred in other cases I feel that it would make a favourable impression if this one were to be put forward with expedition. I may say that I think it improbable that the DPP will decide to prosecute, and in any event, the prospects of a conviction are, I think, very remote.[7]

Dick White was also of the same opinion and wrote to Stephens on 11 August:

Dear Robert [*sic*],
Will you please refer to your letter of 26th July concerning Gerth van WIJK.
   I have considered and discussed Van WIJK's proposals very carefully and can see no way of implementing them. I do not see how you can risk letting this man go free of control. It is true, as he argues, that the Gestapo would shoot him if they caught him and that he has no reason to love the

Germans, but I see no reason why he shouldn't manage to elude both the British and the German Intelligence Services and find a perfectly good hide-out in Spain until the war is over. I prefer to have him nearer at hand and to treat him as a reference library. He appears to be one of our principal sources of information on the German S.S. in Spain.[8]

Hinchley-Cooke wrote to the Director of Public Prosecutions, Sir Edward Tindal Atkinson, on 23 September 1941 the following:

You will observe that this is the case of a Dutch National who came to this country from Spain, and who, since his arrival, has admitted that at the time when he landed he was a German Agent. The only evidence available in regard to this matter is to be found in the various statements which he has made.

I shall be grateful if you will kindly read the papers and let me know your view as to whether it is practicable to institute proceedings against him under the Treachery Act. In its general features, this case is not dissimilar to the case of the "TAANEVIK"[9] which you are now considering.

It would be of great assistance to the Security Service if, when giving your decision in connection with these two cases, you would be good enough to lay down some general principles as to the possibility of taking proceedings under the Treachery Act, in cases where the evidence available consists only of admissions by prisoners and is unsupported by other evidence.[10]

To which the Director of Public Prosecutions replied the following day:

I have considered your letter of the 23rd. instant with the accompanying report about this Dutchman. I have come to the conclusion that, on a broad view of these facts, it would be undesirable to institute proceedings under the Treachery Act or under Defence (General) Regulation 2A mainly because I feel some doubt as to the certainty of a conviction upon the grave charges arising under the Statute and the Regulation.

The case is an unusual one but it may, I think, be used as affording some guidance in solving the general problem mentioned in the concluding paragraph of your letter.

To deal with the particular facts, I observe that what one may term the physical evidence, as apart from admissions, is not strong. We have the fact that van Wijk landed in this country but, in the circumstances, the fact of his landing throws no light upon any treasonable intentions which may have been present in his mind because it could not be suggested that the landing per se gave rise to suspicion; van Wijk arrived in a passenger 'plane from Lisbon, not having upon him any espionage apparatus, any unusual amount of money or any document which, upon search, might have been held to have been incriminating.

After landing, van Wijk committed no act which could be regarded as consistent with a real intent to assist the enemy. In this respect, the absence of any such act must be regarded as in his favour when viewed as part of the evidence in a possible prosecution, although we know quite well how his passge to this country was brought about.

I now turn to the question of his admissions, evidence of which would form practically the whole basis of a possible prosecution. Broadly speaking, the main of such admissions is his statement that he was acting on the instructions of the German secret service. I think we should want more than that admission to prove to a jury his intent after landing to assist the enemy. The only light which can be thrown on this intent, since his immediate intention deprived him of any further activity, is the fact that he made no immediate and affirmative effort to report his intention not to carry out the instructions mentioned above although, even on this issue, one cannot ignore his request for an interview or interviews with some superior officer in our own intelligence service.

I cannot help thinking that, if properly defended, he might induce the jury to accept as true a contention that from the time he last contacted with his German superiors he never intended to do anything which would come within the terms of the Treachery Act or the Regulation.

It is rather on these lines that I view the case as unfavourable from the aspect of prosecution.

With regard to the concluding paragraph of your letter, you will appreciate that it would be difficult to lay down very definite general principles of the kind indicated in that paragraph because, of necessity, cases of this character must inevitably vary in the particular circumstances of fact disclosed in each case. In proof of proceedings under the Treachery Act I have always felt it desirable to lay, as it were, a greater emphasis on the physical facts rather than upon statements by way of admission made by the proposed defendant. The physical facts mentioned above may, by way of illustration, be summarized in the following manner:-

(a) Circumstances of suspicion surrounding the manner in which the proposed defendant landed in this country.
(b) The dress and equipment of the proposed defendant and any materials found upon him clearly indicating the possibility of espionage activities e.g. false identity papers, materials for secret writing and, in particular, wireless equipment.
(c) Obviously false statements made when first questioned as to his identity and the objects of his visit.

You will appreciate my comment as to the variation of facts in these cases by my drawing a rather marked distinction as to (a) between an apparently innocent landing at a port from a ship, and a landing by a parachute from an aeroplane. Little comment need be devoted to the factors (b) and (c) mentioned above. The strongest case against the proposed defendant would obviously be one in which factors (a), (b) and (c) were all unfavourable to him and added thereto if an admission of definite instructions to operate as a spy had been given to him by the German secret service.

The weakest case would be represented by circumstances in which factors (a), (b) and (c) were all, so to speak, favourable to the proposed defendant, and the evidence would, in effect, solely rest upon some admission by him made under caution. I obviously ignore a case in which no admission is made by the proposed defendant.

Where, in my illustration of the weakest case, an admission is made, the proposed defendant would be in a position to hold up two possible lines of defence until the trial viz., either that his landing in this country was due solely upon a purpose to escape without any intent to carry out espionage activities, or possibly where the whole of his journey on instructions from the enemy on the basis that if he did not obey the orders of the enemy he would be killed.

It seems to me impossible to ignore these possible lines of defence whether or not they had emerged in the proposed defendant's admission.

In so far as I can lay down any general principle, I should be disinclined to institute proceedings the evidence in which consists, in effect, only of admissions made after an interview under caution. I should like to have the opportunity of discussing with you the general comments which form the second part of this letter.[11]

The Observations section (VI) of a report on van Wijk prepared by MI5 (most probably by Hinchley-Cooke) in September 1941 elaborates on what the DPP had outlined:

The following comment may be made on the position of this man so far as a possible prosecution is concerned:-

(a) There appears to be no doubt that he did commit the act of 'landing' in this country. He was, of course, unaware that the door had been deliberately opened for him, and evn though this was in fact the case, it would not emerge in the course of any trial, so far as can be seen.
(b) Is there evidence available to show that he landed with intent to help the enemy? Certain points arise here:-
   (i)   His statements on July 8th and July 14th show that when he landed he was in fact acting upon the instructions of the German Secret Service.
   (ii) On the other hand, as he was detained immediately he stepped from the aeroplane, there is no physical evidence available which would help a court to ascertain by his acts what his real intent was.
   (iii) By examining his conduct during detention from April 5th to July 8th it may be possible to ascertain what his intent was

when he landed. It could be said that had he not intended to carry out the orders of the German Secret Service he would at the very first moment have asked to see someone in authority so that he could tell them the truth about himself. Instead of doing this he makes a number of statements, in the course of which he appears to tell the story which he had be instructed to tell by his German superiors, that is that it was essential for him to see the Netherlands authorities in London about frozen funds in Spain. Even on July 7th one finds him saying: 'I want to give every help to the Allied cause and take every oath that I was never a German agent or was offered to work for them'. On the other hand it will no doubt be said in his defence that he was frightened by his immediate detention, confused by the number of interrogations to which he was subjected, and, as is the case, that he did make more than one request to see a senior official of the British Intelligence Service. Furthermore he does, on July 8th and subsequently, make full and frank admissions as to his true position. It is felt that reliance upon these statements alone, after an immediate detention upon landing, may prove to be somewhat unsatisfactory from the point of view of the prosecution.

(iv) It will not be possible to call evidence from Spain in regard to his conduct there with a view to associating with the German Secret Service.

(v) It would seem, therefore, that the evidence available as to intent, were a prosecution to take place, must come from the accused himself. The prosecution would say of him: 'You have kept too silent too long so far as the truth is concerned. You were hoping to be released, having deceived the authorities, so that you could carry out the orders you had been given by your German masters.'

(vi) It is suggested that before any consultation with the Netherlands authorities as to the possible prosecution of GERTH van WIJK, it would be desirable to place the facts of this case before the Director of Public Prosecutions.[12]

Let us deconstruct these statements and examine how they might be applied to the Dronkers case.

(1) Hinchley-Cooke's comment to the DPP: 'in cases where the evidence available consists only of admissions by prisoners and is unsupported by other evidence'.

In the Dronkers case there was other evidence, in the shape of the Dutch–English dictionary serving as a code book, and the recipe for secret ink. However, no one, it appears, had latched on to the former until Dronkers had pointed it out to them during one of the interrogations, evidence that was staring them in the face. The dictionary had even been taken from him temporarily by the Intelligence Corps during his arrest at Harwich, but returned later, and its chain of custody was brought into question at Dronkers' trial. In Dronkers' case the presence of the dictionary code book and the recipe for secret ink are strong physical evidence as they were something intended to be used to communicate with the Germans, but they were the only real physical evidence.

(2) The DPP's comment that 'the fact that van Wijk landed in this country but, in the circumstances, the fact of his landing throws no light upon any treasonable intentions which may have been present in his mind because it could not be suggested that the landing per se gave rise to suspicion'.

If we remove the name van Wijk and substitute Dronkers, the act of Dronkers arriving in England was in itself not entirely suspicious if he and his compatriots had been treated as refugees as they claimed, except that van Wijk had been granted a visa by the British authorities in Spain. Both Dronkers and van Wijk had been refused permission to 'land'.

(3) The DPP's comment, 'van Wijk arrived in a passenger 'plane from Lisbon, not having upon him any espionage apparatus, any unusual amount of money or any document which, upon search, might have been held to have been incriminating'.

The dictionary code book in Dronkers' possession was, belatedly, acknowledged as being 'espionage apparatus'.

(4) The DPP's comment, 'After landing, van Wijk committed no act which could be regarded as consistent with a real intent to assist the enemy. In this respect, the absence of any such act must be regarded as in his favour when viewed as part of the evidence in a possible prosecution, although we know quite well how his passage to this country was brought about.'

As with van Wijk, once he was in England Dronkers had no chance of committing any act 'which could be regarded as consistent with a real intent to assist the enemy'. However, unlike van Wijk, this was not regarded in his favour when viewed as part of the evidence in his prosecution. The fact remains that he did not use the physical evidence, so does possession, but not use, incriminate him to such a degree that he needed to hang? Put another way, is the possession of a firearm or edged weapon, legal or illegal, proof that someone intends to commit a homicide with it?

(5) The DPP's comment: 'Broadly speaking, the main of such admissions is his statement that he was acting on the instructions of the German secret service. I think we should want more than that admission to prove to a jury his intent after landing to assist the enemy. The only light which can be thrown on on this intent, since his immediate intention deprived him of any further activity, is the fact that he made no immediate and affirmative effort to report his intention not to carry out the instructions mentioned above although, even on this issue, one cannot ignore his request for an interview or interviews with some superior officer in our own intelligence service.'

Dronkers, too, was acting on instructions of the German Secret Service and had stuck to his guns about escaping because of his activities on the black market, asserting that he had had no intention of following through with the Germans' instructions. Did MI5 and the DPP get more out of him 'to prove to a jury his intent after landing to assist the enemy'? It seems unlikely, at least from the evidence available today. The jury accepted his admissions at face value that he had allegedly spied for the Germans in 1938, which had nothing to do with the case in hand, and had come to England with the intent to spy again.

(6) The DPP's comment, 'I cannot help thinking that, if properly defended, he might induce the jury to accept as true a contention that from the time he last contacted with his German superiors he never intended to do anything which would come within the terms of the Treachery Act or the Regulation. It is rather on these lines that I view the case as unfavourable from the aspect of prosecution.'

Clearly, this did not happen at the Dronkers trial. Dronkers' protests about his lack of intent were ignored or disbelieved. Either he was not properly defended by Maxwell, or the prosecution was just that much better at presenting their case.

(7) In the DPP's summary of the 'physical facts' it is worth noting those in (b) regarding 'false identity papers, materials for secret writing', and (c) the 'obviously false statements made when first questioned as to his identity and the objects of his visit'.

Dronkers had genuine identity papers, claiming he had thrown his false ones overboard shortly after they set off, and he never claimed to be anyone other than who he was. He did, however, have materials which were later identified as being compatible with those which could be used for secret writing, but so did van Wijk. He also made a series of false statements about his true intentions in coming to England.

(8) As the DPP said, 'The strongest case against the proposed defendant would obviously be one in which factors (a), (b) and (c) were all unfavourable to him and added thereto if an admission of definite instructions to operate as a spy had been given to him by the German secret service.'

It would seem that, in part, all three of these criteria, (a), (b) and (c), applied to Dronkers in making a strong case against him, although as the DPP admitted, 'of necessity, cases of this character must inevitably vary in the particular circumstances of fact disclosed in each case'. Therefore, it was impossible to provide guidelines or criteria which would apply across the board. Nor were any of these guidelines or criteria in the van Wijk case taken into consideration by MI5 when it approached the DPP with its case against Dronkers. On 13 August Guy Liddell had expressed his objection to bringing a case under the Treachery Act 'unless there are very strong grounds for staging a prosecution' but he was overruled by 'Jasper' Harker when he wrote on 17 August 1942 (and referred to earlier),

... there is *sufficient evidence* to put this case up before the Director of Public Prosecutions with a view to prosecution under the Treachery Act. From the ordinary point of view I cannot see any extenuating circumstances, and Dronkers, as an individual, does not appear to merit any particular consideration...

to which Petrie added,

Director B's proposal really amounts to applying in a particular case *a principle that has been rejected in the general*. Beyond the fact that Dronkers was trained at Antwerp [*sic*], I can see *little to distinguish his case from any that have gone before*.[13] [*My italics*]

What was the 'sufficient evidence' to which Harker referred, and how did it differ from the van Wijk case? The code book and secret ink recipe? Is the 'principle that has been rejected in the general' one of those mentioned by the DPP in discussing the van Wijk case? Harker also referred to it being 'a departure from the recognized procedure'; however, this principle does not seem to have been rejected in the case of van Wijk. If there was 'little to distinguish his case from any that have gone before' (i.e. the van Wijk case), it could be argued, as Guy Liddell had done, that the Dronkers case should have been treated in the same way, and a case made to intern him in Camp 020 for the duration of the war instead of to hang him.

When Harker said, 'I feel that Mr Duff Cooper should be consulted and that probably it would be wise to carry the Attorney-General and DPP with us',[14] if there was any correspondence in Dronkers' files to or from Duff Cooper, the Attorney-General or the DPP, it has been destroyed prior to being deposited with the National Archives in order to conceal a cover-up in MI5's desperation to secure a conviction. Had the documents been redacted by the National Archives, a blank or semi-blank sheet would have been inserted bearing the stamp, 'THIS IS A COPY/ORIGINAL RETAINED/IN DEPARTMENT UNDER SECTION/3(4) OF THE PUBLIC RECORDS/ ACT 1958' and a date appended when this was done. There is certainly evidence from the registry list at the beginning of van Wijk's file that many documents had been destroyed in February 2002 prior to their being handed over to or released by the National Archives. Some documents from the Dronkers files were partially redacted in November 1998, although the registry list does not indicate that whole documents are missing.

On 21 August 1942 Mrs K. G. Lee of the Home Office had written to Milmo enquiring as to the status of the cases against Dronkers and Mulder saying,

In our view these two men should be charged unless the Director of Public Prosecutions advises that there is not sufficient evidence to base a charge under the Treachery Act.[15]

To which Milmo replied on 31 August:

> The case of Dronkers is going to be placed before the Director of Public Prosecutions in the course of the next week or so and I have little doubt that, in due course, the Attorney General will issue his fiat for a prosecution under the Treachery Act.[16]

As noted above, there are no comments or advice available from the DPP regarding the Dronkers case, only the Attorney General's fiat issued on 22 October. Nor is the 'sufficient evidence' elaborated on. MI5's observations in their report are also revealing:

1. Their first point (b) (i), 'Is there evidence available to show that he landed with intent to help the enemy?' When van Wijk landed he was in fact acting upon the instructions of the German Secret Service. This is borne out by his statements on 8 July and 14 July. The same could be said for Dronkers in the various statements he made to MI5.
2. Their next point, (b) (ii), 'On the other hand, as he was detained immediately... there is no physical evidence available which would help a court to ascertain by his acts what his real intent was.' This could also be applied to Dronkers. If 'by his acts' MI5 or the DPP meant the act of actually using the dictionary code book and materials for secret writing (the so-called 'physical evidence'), which Dronkers did not, and which, therefore, they should have discounted, then Dronkers' real intent by these acts could not have been ascertained either.
3. Let's look at MI5's next observation, (b) (iii), 'By examining his conduct during detention from April 5th to July 8th it may be possible to ascertain what his intent was when he landed. It could be said that had he not intended to carry out the orders of the German Secret Service he would at the very first moment have asked to see someone in authority so that he could tell them the truth about himself. Instead of doing this he makes a number of statements, in the course of which he appears to tell the story which he had be instructed to tell by his German superiors, that is that it was essential for him to see the Netherlands authorities in London about frozen funds in Spain.' Dronkers did not ask to see someone in authority, but as with van Wijk, he made 'a number of statements, in the course of which he appears to tell the story which he had been instructed to tell by his German superiors ...'
4. Continuing on from that same paragraph with the observation, 'I want to give every help to the Allied cause and take every oath that I was never a German agent or was offered to work for them.' Dronkers also claimed he had given whatever help he could to the Allies by providing them with intelligence about the defences around the port from which he departed. This information seems to have been rejected as being not useful. He also claimed that he was never a German agent.

5. '... it will no doubt be said in his defence that he was frightened by his immediate detention, confused by the number of interrogations to which he was subjected'. Van Wijk said in his statement of 8 July that 'I was afraid that when telling this story to the British authorities they might take a wrong point of view and being a Dutch subject I felt that I had to inform my Government about the above first'. Dronkers also became frightened and confused, as acknowledged by his interrogators at Camp 020 and the RVPS, such as F. Jackson, who said he was 'a mental case ... a dithering fool, old before his time, a bundle of shaking nerves'. However, he had not asked to tell the Dutch authorities first, nor had he admitted as such to Vrinten or Pinto, the two Dutch officers who had also interviewed him.

6. 'Furthermore he does, on July 8th and subsequently, make full and frank admissions as to his true position.' Dronkers also made a full and frank confession as to his true position, both to MI5 and to Mulder.

7. 'It is felt that reliance upon these statements alone, after an immediate detention upon landing, may prove to be somewhat unsatisfactory from the point of view of the prosecution.' So what exactly did MI5 rely upon if not Dronkers' statements and confession? Depositions by Mulder and de Langen were taken but not presented during his trial at the Old Bailey, although no reason was ever given. It suggests that MI5 was relying solely on the only other incriminating evidence – the dictionary code book and materials for secret writing – to reinforce their case, evidence which, if there is even a modicum of truth in what Pinto said, should have been thrown out as inadmissible because they had potentially been tampered with. More about this later.

8. (b) (v), 'You have kept too silent too long so far as the truth is concerned. You were hoping to be released, having deceived the authorities, so that you could carry out the orders you had been given by your German masters.' The same accusation was levelled by the prosecution in Dronkers' trial. It was what they deemed his major faux pas – he had obfuscated too long. However, whether he had actually intended to carry out the orders given to him by Dr Schneider, is highly questionable.

Thus we have a number of areas where the van Wijk case and the Dronkers case are not dissimilar:

1. Both were blackmailed into working for the Germans; indeed, van Wijk had been working for them for much longer than Dronkers and been paid by them. Although as Stephens noted in his report of 4 August,

> ... it would appear that with the exception of his two missions to Tangier (which produced nothing of great value) GERTH VAN WIJK has not yet been used by the Germans as an *active* agent ... [*My italics*][17]

2. (a) Van Wijk, came to England with the permission of the British authorities; Dronkers did not; (b) Like Dronkers, van Wijk had been refused permission to 'land'; (c) Like van Wijk, Dronkers had not become an active agent.
3. Both took their time in confessing the true nature of their coming to England. In the case of van Wijk, it took ninety-eight days, which was considerably longer even than Dronkers. Yet this was held against Dronkers, but not against van Wijk.
4. Both admitted to being frightened by the number of interrogations to which they were subjected, with van Wijk being told that two of his compatriots had already been hanged (probably Meier and Kieboom), which was designed to intimidate him and elicit a confession. In none of the files is there any mention of Dronkers being told the same thing.
5. Both had also claimed that they had no intention of following through with the Germans' instructions.
6. Both had materials or a recipe for secret writing. As Stephens also noted later on in his report,

> ... he [van Wijk] has made one damaging admission, namely, at the Oratory Schools he obtained a piece of caustic soda through the canteen-man with the intention of writing a secret message to his contact in Madrid informing her that he could not return for some time. The purpose of this would have been to save his family from immediate reprisals ...[18]

The only real difference seems to be that Dronkers had in his possession physical evidence with which to commit espionage (the dictionary code book), although, as noted earlier, he did not have a chance to use it. Should this have been enough to convince the jury of Dronkers' guilt and secure a capital conviction? Based on the statement made by the Lord Chief Justice regarding Dronkers' appeal, had van Wijk's case gone to trial and he had appealed a guilty verdict, he too might have ended up on the gallows.

Van Wijk was deported back to the Netherlands from Hendon Airport on 2 July 1945 along with thirteen other Dutchmen including Pieter Jan Schipper, of whom we will hear more in the next chapter. The case of van Wijk was investigated by the Dutch Political Investigation Department and he was released on 12 July 1946 pending further investigations, according to an extract of a report sent to MI5 by the Royal Netherlands Embassy on 4 October 1947. The remainder of the report in the file appears to have been destroyed in 2002.

26

Three Men in a Boat

A few months before Dronkers arrived in England another spy case had reared its ugly head. This was the arrival of Pieter Jan Schipper, David Davids and Arthur Pay aboard the Dutch steel launch *Ariel 209* at Margate on 24 March 1942. Schipper was born in Amsterdam on 6 February 1906 and owned a Dutch fishing boat. Prior to his arrival in the UK, he had been in the employ of the German Secret Service, reporting to Kapitänleutnant Friederich ('Fritz') Carl Heinrich Strauch of the Abwehr. Pay, described as a 'negro', was born in Paramaribo, in Dutch Guiana (now the capital of Suriname), on 9 November 1910 and a musician (drummer) by profession, although his documentation showed him as being a seaman; Davids was a Jew.[1] The three men were arrested and Home Office Detention Orders issued under paragraph 12(5) (a) of the Aliens Order, 1920.

Schipper's career as a spy makes for interesting reading, although his MI5 file has been heavily redacted and one feels that there must be more that could have been revealed. An interim Camp 020 report dated 23 April 1942 stated that Schipper had been recruited by Strauch in December 1939. He and his family, consisting of his wife Marie Annie de Vries and four children, had settled in Howth, Ireland, in 1937 to fish. However, when he returned to Holland in September 1939 there was very little international trade and his prospects were not looking good. He was introduced to Strauch through Strauch's brother-in-law, Alff, who was the General Manager of the *Nordsee Fischerei Gesellschaft* in Wesermünde, Germany. When the two men met Strauch produced a file on Schipper which the Abwehr had already compiled. Strauch explained that he was about to start a fishing business in Ymuiden and invited Schipper to take part in this venture. Having submitted plans, Schipper did not hear from Strauch again apart from the offer of another job in the interim.

In late June 1940 Schipper was summoned to The Hague to 13, Parkweg, the headquarters of The Hague *Abwehrstelle*, where he met Strauch in a room marked M1 (for Ein Marine, the naval section). Strauch instructed him to return a few days later in July, where he found other Dutch sea captains present. Strauch told him that his first task was to act as an interpreter at the *Hafenüberwachungstelle* in Amsterdam (Port monitoring body), reporting to a Leutnant Ossenbrueken and advising on British goods in Dutch warehouses and to whom they were consigned. A secondary task was to denounce his fellow-countrymen who might be dealing with the British. This did not sit well with Schipper so shortly afterwards he terminated the contract.

Around the middle of August he again approached Strauch in The Hague for more work. In Ymuiden a month later he met up with Alff and another Dutchman, van den Oever, with whom he purchased a fishing smack named the *Sursum Corda*. Strauch instructed Schipper and van den Oever to act as observers for the SS and report on anything of interest, such as convoys, ships, seaplanes, the position of wrecks and buoys. He was given the code name 'Piet'. Unbeknown to Strauch, between the two Dutchmen they concocted a plethora of false information which they passed on to him.

Schipper was later introduced to a Hauptmann Stein, also known as Dr Hille, a wireless specialist who explained to him the principle of short-wave transmission. This in turn led to an introduction to Schule, also known as Jap, who was a radio instructor at the German radio school in Vondelstraat, an address which was already known to MI5.[2] Schule showed him a special, luxury type of radio transmitter and tested him on Morse code transmissions. He was also trained in the use of secret inks by someone he described as 'The Professor'. The plan was for Schipper to eventually replace 'The Professor', who was required urgently in Yugoslavia. Strauch, it appears, saw him as being an able recruit of the SS. It should be noted that it is unclear whether 'SS' here means Secret Service or *Schutzstaffel* (the SS), although it is most likely the former since Strauch worked for the Abwehr not the SS.

Just before Christmas 1940, Stein and Schule went to Ymuiden to install wireless transmitters on various Dutch fishing boats, including the *Sursum Corda I*. Each boat was assigned an SS wireless transmitting agent from Vondelstraat, known as *Vertrauensmänner* ('Confidential people', sometimes referred to as *V-Männer*; singular is *V-Mann*.) At the beginning of March 1941 Strauch suggested that Schipper try recruiting his friends to work as wireless operators and spies, but he was unsuccessful. A couple of weeks later Strauch suggested that he should become a German agent, which he accepted. At the end of March he was told he would be sent on an assignment abroad. While he was away his wife would be paid 300 florins in monthly instalments (although this was never fulfilled). The object of this mission, which would take him to Lisbon, would be to persuade ships' officers to desert their ships and return to Holland via Berlin, bringing with them their logbooks that could be used by the Germans to trace the movements of Allied convoys. It also served to immobilise the ships in Lisbon and clog the harbours. But the trip to Lisbon did not go as planned. In fact, Schipper never made it there owing to difficulties in obtaining a Portuguese visa.

Together, Schipper and Strauch had taken the overnight sleeper from Paris to Hendaye, France, where Schipper crossed the border into Spain and Irun in the Basque region. The following day he proceeded to San Sebastián where it became apparent that his documents were not up to the scrutiny of Spanish officials, so he abandoned the idea of trying to get to Lisbon and headed to Bilbao instead. By the time he reached Bilbao he had become so disenchanted with the whole venture that he returned to Paris. After a debriefing there on his failed mission, he returned to Holland with a case of cognac which the Paris *Abstelle* had asked him to deliver to Strauch.

According to MI5, he was now under the direct influence of Strauch. Schipper and Strauch purchased two more fishing boats, the *Sursum Corda II* and *Sursum Corda III*, each of which was equipped with the same radio equipment and *Vertrauensmänner* as the first. While he claimed he did not receive any further payments from Strauch, Schipper did benefit from the profits of the fishing fleet, with Strauch taking a 10 per cent share. While at Camp 020, Schipper claimed that the SS had had a plan to introduce a spy into Britain in either July or August 1941 using a speedboat belonging to Prince Bernhardt of the Netherlands. The three-man mission was a failure, with the boat capsizing and the crew being rescued by an E-boat from Ymuiden.

Things came to a head in November 1941 when the two men quarrelled over their nefarious dealings, with Strauch finally insisting that Schipper either buy a boat or go to sea again. In Amsterdam Schipper was also told in no uncertain terms to produce better results. A naval officer subordinate to Strauch by the name of Bucking (also known as Becker) contacted him and arranged for a meeting in The Hague. There Schipper also met a Dr Korrell who questioned him about secret inks and accused him of disclosing information (although it is not clear to whom or the nature of the information), indicating that there would be further complications as a result.

The matter did not end there. Two days later Schipper was arrested by a naval officer and an Oberfeldwebel (Chief Petty Officer) of the Kriegsmarine (German Navy) and imprisoned in Haarlem, where he was questioned by field police. He was unable to establish why he had been arrested, so appealed to Strauch to have him released, which Strauch did. That being said, Strauch refused to have anything further to do with him. Future control then fell to Bucking, who informed him that his imprisonment had had nothing to do with the idle threats made against him previously. Schipper was assured that if he agreed to cooperate there would be no further action taken by the Gestapo. He was next sent to The Hague where a certain Willem Grohn of Buitensluisstraat, Katwijk, was prepared to buy his boat, the *Ariel 209,* but for some reason Schipper delayed applying for a permit.

Schipper had made two attempts to escape prior to his imprisonment in March 1942, and was now even more determined. His crew would consist of his long-standing Jewish friend David Davids, who had approached him to help him escape because he had been in trouble with the Gestapo, and

Arthur Pay, whom he had met in the street in December 1941, and who also wished to escape. There was supposed to have been a fourth member, a Dutch Army officer named Captain Schumacher, but he failed to turn up on the day they were due to set sail. At 12.45 on Sunday 23 April 1942, the three set off, having managed to obtain the permit required to sail. Unlike the Dronkers case, there is no detailed account of the voyage, no stories of false papers; however, the voyage was not without difficulties. Navigational aids aboard the *Ariel 209* were inferior, and they lost their bearings. When they arrived in Margate, Schipper had thought they were off the coast of Norfolk. The report from Camp 020, dated 23 April 1942, concludes with the statement:

> Considerable doubt naturally was felt about the genuineness of Schipper's 'escape' from Holland, but the details of his voyage have been carefully checked and it was decided that Schipper's own description is probably accurate, although the motives which prompted the departure are still open to doubt.[3]

It is curious that, even without the missing documents, presumably destroyed, Schipper was not considered worth trying under the Treachery Act, nor, it would seem, was it worth turning him over to 'Tar' Robertson as a potential double agent. It was considered simply enough to intern him for the duration of the war. There is a handwritten note in Schipper's file dated 9 April 1942 written by Helenus Milmo which bears this out:

> I spoke to S.L.(B), Major Cussen, about this case and, having given an outline of the facts, asked him to read Schipper's signed statement (serial 10c). Major Cussen stated that no useful purpose could be served by S.L.(B) taking a statement under caution at this stage. I undertook to keep S.L.(B) informed of any developments which might alter the position.

A report dated 2 May 1942, sent to Mrs K. G. Lee at the Home Office Aliens Department and prepared for Helenus Milmo by J. P. de C. Day (John Day) of B1b, about Schipper concludes:

> It is improbable that Schipper on arriving in this country ever had any intention of carrying out a mission on behalf of the Germans, and although at one time we were disposed to take a contrary view, we now feel that it is on the whole unlikely that he was sent here on behalf of the enemy ... Schipper seems to have been in trouble with his German employers shortly before his departure, and there appear to have been some grounds for his desiring to make a get-away, despite the fact that he was leaving his wife and children behind him.
>
> Schipper admits to having worked for the German secret service for more than a year, and it is quite possible that this may be a considerable

understatement. The fact that he has been able to give us detailed descriptions of no less than 50 officers and agents of the Abwehr is an indication of the closeness of his connection with the organisation.[4]

Unfortunately, his MI5 file does not include a list of these personnel. A further report from B1b dated 17 September 1942 added:

> On his own admission therefore Schipper is a man who has voluntarily and fruitfully co-operated with the German Secret Service for a period of a year and a half. This fact in itself is more than adequate to justify his detention for the duration of the war. In addition to this there remains an element of doubt as to the genuineness of his alleged escape to this country. As has been pointed out above, his account of the circumstances and reasons for this escape are decidedly implausible so that it cannot be said with any certainty that it was not as a German agent that Schipper arrived over here. At the same ti[me] he has not yet been induced to give an account of the purpose of his mission, if mission it was.

This seems extraordinary when one compares these circumstances to the Dronkers case. Here was a man who had been associated with the German intelligence services for much longer than Dronkers and had been trained more extensively. The irony is not lost on the fact that he had almost certainly gathered information during his fishing trips and profited from them. He also claimed that he had had no intention of continuing to work for the Germans after he escaped. How else would he have legitimately obtained a permit to sail if he hadn't agreed to spy for the Germans? And why was it considered any more improbable that he should have had 'any intention of carrying out a mission on behalf of the Germans' than Dronkers?

Dronkers, in contrast, had had less involvement with the Abwehr, was inadequately trained and also expressed his intention not to work for the Germans, albeit belatedly. Surely, given that the two cases occurred almost at the same time, the same criteria should have been applied and a case against Schipper brought before the DPP, particularly as John Day says that, 'This fact in itself [his co-operation with the Germans for over a year and a half] is more than adequate to justify his detention for the duration of the war.' Day's report for Milmo contradicts what Stephens' report later had to say about Schipper. In this case, there might have been some merit in considering turning him into a double agent.

Schipper was transferred from the Oratory Schools, otherwise known as the London Reception Centre (LRC), on 13 April to Camp 020. Stephens' report on Schipper states that

> The Schipper case is rich in information from a contre-espionage Naval and Air Force point of view ... In so far as contre-espionage is concerned, the

present papers contain considerable background of German SS activities in Holland and France and the descriptions of no less than fifty contacts have been obtained.[5]

Having milked him dry of any intelligence he could provide, he was considered surplus to requirements and interned. Schipper did, however, get his comeuppance from the Dutch after he had been repatriated to the Netherlands on 2 July 1945 on a flight from Hendon Airport, along with Pons, van Wijk and a number of others. Responding to a request made by Mrs D. M. Quin of MI5, Baron van Moyland of the Royal Netherlands Embassy informed her on 10 June 1949 that Schipper had been imprisoned by the Dutch at a camp at Laren from 2 July 1945 until 21 February 1948. On 25 March 1948 a court in Amsterdam sentenced him to two years and five months' imprisonment and deprived him of citizenship rights for ten years. This was also confirmed by Thérèse Adams of the Home Office Aliens Department.

Further developments were to ensue. On 16 June 1949, writing to W. M. Perks, Chief Inspector of the Home Office Immigration Branch, on behalf of Hinchley-Cooke, an unnamed MI5 officer (the name has been redacted from the file) expressed no security objection to Schipper's case being removed from the Home Office Suspect Index. On 9 March 1950, Thérèse Adams wrote to Joan Chenhalls, now in C4a at MI5, regarding the possible revocation of his Deportation Order and enquiring about what he had been charged with by the Dutch authorities.

Between 1950 and 1953 there was also correspondence relating to his case between British immigration authorities at Newcastle-upon-Tyne, Middlesbrough and West Hartlepool regarding his status, and being refused entry to land, since he was still covered by the Aliens Order imposed on him in 1942 which had not been revoked. On one occasion his ship, the MS *Geziena*, had arrived at West Hartlepool from Rotterdam late in the evening of 11 May 1952. Early the next morning he was visited by Immigration Officer T. W. Yeldham, who refused him entry into the UK. The ship sailed later that day for Stockton-on-Tees, en route to Copenhagen.

Schipper, now captain and owner of the MS *Geziena*, wrote to the Home Office Aliens Department to protest, claiming that he did not deserve this sort of treatment; that he had always been 'true and faithful to Great Britain'; that he had 'never done or said any harm, untruthfulness or damages to British persons or property', even citing that three of his four children had British names as proof of his Anglophilia. On 20 March 1952, R. L. Jones of C4a wrote to the Home Office suggesting that Schipper's file be downgraded from Secret to Confidential, to which the Home Office showed no objection.

After interrogation at the RVPS, Arthur Pay was released on 13 April 1942 to the Dutch HQ in London where he joined the Dutch seamen's pool. It is unclear when Davids was released, but both are referred to in correspondence between MI5 and SIS in 1947.

27

'The Greatest Living Expert on Security'

Before concluding this book, perhaps this is a good time to set the record straight about several books which purport to tell something of Dronkers' story, but appear to have distorted the facts into fantasy. The episode with the Radio Oranje broadcast has already been dealt with. As mentioned at the beginning of this book, the first of these perpetrators was Oreste Pinto.

Much to the consternation of the Dutch authorities, and presumably MI5 as well, Lieutenant Colonel Oreste Pinto achieved a certain undeserved fame from his books *Spycatcher* and *Friend or Foe?*, both published in 1953, as well as the television series of the same name broadcast by the BBC between the years 1959 and 1961, with Bernard Archard in the title role. Interestingly, Archard had been a conscientious objector during the war and had been sent to work on Quaker land. I well remember the TV series, but cannot remember whether the Dronkers case was ever covered in any of the episodes. However, it was featured as part of the *Spycatcher* radio series broadcast at 9.30 p.m. on Friday 7 April 1961, entitled 'One Must Die', with veteran actor Carleton Hobbs playing the part of Dronkers and Bernard Archard as Pinto. The script was written by Robert Barr. In it, some details, such as the contact addresses found in the Dutch–English dictionary, and the Café Atlanta, are correct. The names of Mulder and de Langen were changed for the broadcast to Hans Delden and Jan Leuven respectively, perhaps because they were still alive at the time. Listening to the recording now, available as an MP3 file on YouTube, it sounds tame and amateurish.

Oreste Pinto, born in Amsterdam on 9 October 1889, was the youngest in a modestly wealthy Jewish family. His parents were Louis Pinto, a stockbroker, and Annette Abigael Roozeboom. After completing his secondary education in Amsterdam and his military service with the 7th Infantry Regiment, he obtained a bachelor's degree in literature from the Sorbonne, Paris. Shortly before the First World War he worked for the Deuxième Bureau, the French intelligence organisation. While in Paris he met Anne Brookes, a young

British teacher, whom he married on 5 May 1914, and who later bore him a son. From about 1915 he worked for the Sûreté du Territoire behind the lines on the Somme interrogating people who had come through the front line.

During the interwar years Pinto owned a large translation agency in London. As a director of several companies dealing mostly in tropical fruit, he was several times convicted of embezzlement. This is obviously what Guy Liddell and Leonard Burt alluded to when they talked of his dubious character. Before the Second World War he was attached to MI5, although neither the internal history by Curry nor the official history by Andrew mention him at all. From April 1941 he served at the Royal Victoria Patriotic School (RVPS), but when forced to give up his Dutch citizenship, he resigned in September 1942 and went to work for the Dutch Security Service, which reported to the Dutch Department of Justice, with Adriaanus Vrinten as his deputy. According to Nigel West, it was Vrinten who recognised Dronkers as having been a leading fascist before the war.[1] This allegation is repeated by author J. Robert Nash:

Dronkers had been active for many years in the National Socialistische Beweging, a group of Dutch Nazis headed by Adrian Mussert with widespread operations throughout Holland ... several of Mussert's most fanatical followers volunteered to act as spies in England. One of these was Dronkers.[2]

Nash repeats the account of Pinto's interview with Dronkers, with Pinto bringing in Adriaanus Vrinten, now a member of the Dutch Intelligence Service, who had been a detective before the war and had investigated Mussert's Nazis for the Dutch Justice Ministry:

'I know who you are, Dronkers,' Vrinten told the man. 'You were a leading Party member when we first met in Holland and you are now a German spy.'[3]

As was mentioned earlier, a register of known members of the NSB had listed a Johannes Dronkers, born 14 January 1914, which may have actually been the man to whom Vrinten was referring, but not the Dronkers central to our story, who was born earlier in 1896. It should be noted that Vrinten, when he escaped to Britain in 1940, had kept ledgers of all known agents in Holland.

From late December 1944 to March 1945 Pinto stayed in Britain to recover from severe bronchitis. In April 1945 he returned to the Politiebuitendienst (Police Field Service), which had been renamed Section IIIA of the military government. After the liberation of Holland, he joined the Bureau Nationale Veiligheid or Office of National Security (BNV), where he trained the staff, was engaged in some espionage cases, and was promoted to lieutenant colonel. When the war ended he left the intelligence world, and in 1946 became the head of the Commissariaat-Generaal voor de Nederlandse Economische Belangen in Duitsland (Crime Investigation Department of the Commissioner General for the Dutch Economic Interests in Germany). He was fired in 1948 when he was caught trying to smuggle paintings, and resettled in England.

His other dubious claim to fame is the unmasking of four Dutch spies in 1940 – Kieboom, Pons, Meier and Waldberg – claiming to have received a radio message from an Allied agent in France. As has been discussed earlier, the spies were caught by the British Army soon after landing and confessed. There is also nothing in the MI5 files connecting Pinto to the case. Interestingly, his account of the Dutch spies in 1940 was removed from later British editions of *Spycatcher*, but remains in the American edition. An article which appeared in 1976 entitled 'German Spies in Britain' states that:

> When the manuscript for 'Spycatcher' and 'Friend or Foe' was submitted to the War Office in 1950 for approval by Pinto's publishers [*sic*], it was returned with a note saying there was nothing which H.M. Government objected to ... One person closely concerned with the events at the time [the Pons, Waldberg, Meier, Kieboom case] has said that 'Publication of Pinto's accounts was only allowed because they were a pack of lies'.[4]

Pinto also expressed his suspicions about Christiaan Lindemans, exposing him as 'King Kong', the 'traitor of Arnhem'. As the official SOE historian M. R. D. Foot said of him,

> Oreste Pinto, early in the field of inaccurate story-writing after the war about intelligence affairs, has this to be said for him: instinct told him Lindemans was a traitor.[5]

As will be seen, Pinto's account of the Dronkers case is one of self-promotion and semi-fictional, while purporting to be true. Consequently, it must be considered unreliable. Indeed, it might even be considered a greater work of fiction than the initial stories told by Dronkers and his compatriots. What is interesting about his *Spycatcher* book is that, in spite of the many errors and embellishments, there are some facts about the case which are basically correct. Does this mean then that Pinto did actually play a bigger part in interrogating Dronkers? Pinto left the intelligence field in 1946 and died in 1961 so it is unlikely that Pinto had access to MI5's files after the war when he wrote his books as these were only declassified in 1999. The alternative explanation is that he kept notes on his cases, something which would have been forbidden then as now, but still possible. It was alleged in 1983 by Kenneth de Courcy, editor and proprietor of *Intelligence Digest*, that Pinto had been his most important source of intelligence.[6]

It is worth examining Pinto's involvement in this case if only to dispel a few myths and try to set the record straight once and for all. The quotes here are all taken from Pinto's book.[7]

1. Pinto recalls being contacted by an RAF intelligence officer who had just been interrogating Dronkers. The only mention of an RAF officer in any of the documents in the official files is that of Flight Lieutenant Charles Cholmondeley, and that is in reference to the Vultee Vengeance aircraft about which Dronkers was supposed to find out. While Cholmondeley may have assisted his MI5 colleagues with information about this aircraft, none of the interrogation reports that are available appear to have been compiled by an RAF officer.

2. The Dutchmen arrived off the south east coast of England. Harwich has always been geographically part of the east coast; the south-east coast would be regarded as Kent and Sussex.

3. 'Apart from the fact that he was Dutch and his name was Dronkers, the intelligence officer could get no sense out of him.' Dronkers had appeared at times to his interrogators as somewhat maudlin, and occasionally erratic, but he seemed to be making sense, even if what he said was sometimes contradictory or, to coin a much-used phrase by Sir Robert Armstrong, the British Cabinet Secretary during the other *Spycatcher* trial in Australia in 1986, he was being 'economical with the truth'.[8]

4. Pinto's description of Dronkers. Pinto's description of Dronkers being tall and thin is borne out by the photographs on file (he was a little over six feet) as well as having white (the file says grey) hair and he looked a great deal older than his forty-six years. However, the description of his bursting into the room 'like a whirling dervish, waving his arms and skipping to and fro, shrieking in his cracked voice an old Dutch song' seems like pure melodrama and not recorded in any of the interrogation reports.

5. 'It was nerve-wracking to see an elderly, dignified man so completely out of control...' He was forty-six (see previous point) for goodness sake, so not that old! Pinto was older than him. Whether Dronkers could be described as 'dignified' is open to debate. There was certainly nothing dignified about his alleged spying for the Germans.

6. 'They had always had a struggle to make ends meet by pinching and scraping ... Life which had always been a drudgery now became a nightmare and his wife was wasting away before his eyes.' It is true that Dronkers had been unsuccessful in employment, had never earned very much money, and the privations of war in the Netherlands were horrendous. There is some suggestion from Dronkers that his wife was always after him for money, but to say that his wife was 'wasting away' never appears anywhere in the official record and again, is somewhat melodramatic on the part of Dronkers, or perhaps Pinto as well.

7. 'The Gestapo was on to him and that the penalty for Black Marketeering was death.' Not according to MI5, who stated that unless they were Jewish, anyone caught dealing on the black market would be imprisoned for a couple of months. That is not to say, of course, that the Gestapo were always that lenient, given how mercurial they could be.

8. The man known as 'Jan' is referred to here as 'Hans'. Since Dronkers claimed he never knew 'Jan's' real name, why bother to change it for the book? Nash also refers to 'Jan' as 'Hans'. Of course, 'Jan' later on turned out to be pure fiction, invented by Dronkers, so the name is moot.

9. Hans worked for someone who supplied petrol to ships in the harbour. True, according to the earlier statements made by Dronkers. The supplier of petrol was Mr Nygh.

10. 'They evolved a simple plan.' Pinto implies that Dronkers and 'Hans/Jan' concocted the plan between them, yet it was more likely concocted by 'Dr Schneider'.

11. 'I was not much of a hand at navigating and nor were the others. The first thing we did was to run on to a sandbank.' Dronkers obviously didn't learn much as a mate's assistant in the Dutch Merchant Navy. By all accounts, this was a deliberate act by Dronkers and not accidental.

12. 'I even know who has sent you on this errand. Herr Strauch of the German Secret Service, wasn't it?' As has been discussed earlier, it could not have been Strauch for the reasons already stated.

13. Dronkers' letters. Pinto mentions that Dronkers wrote letters to King George VI, Queen Wilhelmina of the Netherlands, and Winston Churchill, although these were never delivered. Whether they ever existed, there is no mention of them in the files and they may have been weeded from the official record. If they existed at one time, what they contained is a matter of conjecture. Nash claims that the letters stated that Dronkers was complaining about his treatment by Pinto and that the august royal figures and the Prime Minister were 'harboring a Himmler' (presumably he was referring to Pinto).[9] The only letters on record were (a) one of protest by Dronkers, Mulder and de Langen complaining about how their case was taking too long; (b) another that they should be allowed to broadcast their coded message on Radio Oranje; (c) Dronkers' letter to his solicitor, and (d) his final letter to his wife. It is unknown how Nash saw these alleged letters, or if they ever existed.

14. 'Every day I made him repeat his story over and over again.' Contrary to what Pinto would have the reader of his books believe, there are few mentions of him interrogating Dronkers in the official files, while claiming he was the one to have broken Dronkers' cover story. While it is always possible that Dronkers *was* interrogated every day (but not by Pinto), the dates on the reports of his interrogations do not bear this out. Pinto has put himself into the role played by Jackson at Camp 020

and others at MI5 who actually interrogated Dronkers, and invented most of the dialogue, perhaps to add verisimilitude and credence to his supposed involvement, but also because the real MI5 officers could not be identified for security reasons.

15. Removing evidence. Pinto refers to taking home a parcel of Dronkers' belongings every night to examine in his Chelsea flat. This is contrary to the recognised practice of preserving 'continuity of evidence'.[10] All personal property regarded as evidence should have been kept under lock and key when not being examined by *qualified* professionals, which Pinto was not, and a log kept of everyone having access to it. Items examined by him should have been excluded as inadmissible evidence in Dronkers' trial because there existed the potential that they might have been tampered with.

16. The watch and other property. Pinto mentions one of Dronkers' possessions as being a silver watch and chain. According to the inventory, it was a gold watch inside a leather pouch. He even gives the cigarettes a different name. Pinto states they are cheap Dutch cigarettes called 'North State', while the inventory lists them as 'Winchester'. This is interesting since Winchesters are American cigarettes. How did Dronkers get hold of them? On the black market?

17. 'I had now got on to the newspapers and maps he had brought ... ' Dronkers claimed not to have had any maps on his voyage; nor is there any mention of any maps or newspapers in the inventory of the *Joppe* compiled by MI5.

18. 'On the twelfth evening I had come to the last of Dronkers's possessions. It was a bulky copy of Kramer's Dutch–English dictionary.' Pinto then describes how he had found tiny pinpricks on certain pages, indicating a code. In decoding the letters he purportedly uncovered, they spelled out two addresses, one in Lisbon, the other in Stockholm, which is true. However, during one of the interrogations it was actually Dronkers who pointed this out to Jackson.

It would seem that Pinto in his vainglorious account of events was guilty of the 'tissue of lies' of which he accused Dronkers. He has taken facts gleaned by the real interrogators, glossed over others, and generally presented the entire story as one in which he single-handedly achieved success when others had given up, perhaps to make amends for his own murky past and a need to be rehabilitated as a professional into the intelligence hall of fame.

'An ambitious and diligent pupil'?

Pinto was not the only author to misrepresent the facts. After the war an article by the journalist E. H. Cookridge, real name Edward Spiro (1908–79), author of several spy books, appeared entitled, 'How we beat the spies. The Spy in the BBC' and containing tall tales of the Dronkers case.[11] According to him, General Joseph von Tippleskirch,[12] a close friend of Admiral Canaris, the head of the Abwehr, ordered SS-Gruppenführer (Group leader or Major General) Josef Schreckenberg and Nikolaus Ritter to find a suitable man to be smuggled into an Allied government-in-exile to make daily broadcasts from Britain. Ritter, in turn, got in touch with SS-Obergruppenführer Walter Rauter, the SS and Police Leader in the Netherlands.[13] Rauter turned to Adriaan Mussert, one of the founders of the Dutch National Socialist Party, whom Dronkers apparently knew.

As the story goes, Dronkers was sent for training to a Nazi espionage school in Mülheim, Westphalia,[14] proving to be 'an ambitious and diligent pupil' – a far cry from the story we already know! The basic story of the escape is correct, apart from the distance from the English shore at which he was arrested (Cookridge claims it was 30 miles, but Cannon's statement says 9 miles ESE of Harwich). Cookridge then claims that Dronkers had torn apart the seams of his sou'wester and

> brought out some papers and displayed a letter from the Utrecht HQ of the Resistance movement, confirming that he had taken part in the underground fight against the Nazis, had been arrested by the Gestapo and managed to escape. The letter recommended him to the British and Dutch authorities because his life would be in danger if he were again caught by the Germans.

There is no mention in the files of any letters or any such incident, no such training in Germany, only in The Hague, no contact with the Dutch Resistance, nor the requirement to make daily broadcasts. Given Dronkers' level of intelligence, he can hardly have been described as 'ambitious and diligent'.

'Hollywood's version of a sinister Nazi officer'

Three books featuring Wichmann should be also mentioned, if only to dispel the misinformation they include. The first, *Burn After Reading: The Espionage History of World War II* by best-selling author Ladislas Farago, describes Wichmann as

> big and bluff, with a Prussian cropped head and duelling scars, heavy-set but agile, heavy-handed but alert, not exceptionally brilliant but industrious and efficient; the very prototype of the competent, hard-working German staff officer. He was chief of the British desk at the Abwehr.[15]

The late former soldier, journalist and military historian William Breuer's *Deceptions of World War II* describes Wichmann as 'industrious, loyal, but not too cerebral, looked like Hollywood's version of a sinister Nazi officer: closely cropped hair, dueling scar, even a monocle on occasion', which seems to borrow heavily from Farago;[16] whereas Breuer's other book, *Daring Missions of World War II*, describes Wichmann as 'a dedicated and brainy operative'.[17] So which is it?

None of the physical descriptions concur with the descriptions of those who had met him nor the photographs in his MI5 file, and are in sharp contrast to David Kahn's assessment of Wichmann as being 'versatile, erudite and reliable'. If he had duelling scars or a monocle they tend to stand out and would have been remarked upon by those who had met him and visible in the file photographs. Clearly, Breuer's creation was a complete fantasy, as was that of Cookridge.

An even more spurious story which is still persistently circulating on the internet is that Dronkers was connected to the 'Hagley Wood Mystery' and the 'Who Put Bella in the Wych Elm?' claim. It has been alleged that 'Bella' was a Dutch woman named Clarabella who was a Nazi spy, and may have been Dronkers' wife, who had been murdered in about 1941 and her body stuffed in a wych elm (really just an elm) in Hagley Wood, part of the Hagley Hall estate, near Kidderminster, in the West Midlands. The story, perpetrated by a number of websites, is so ridiculous that no further discussion is warranted. But whoever she was, she was not Dronkers' wife.

Postscript

By the time Dronkers was executed, eleven others had also been convicted and executed under the Treachery Act (1940), with Pons being the only one to be acquitted. When Dronkers was caught in May 1942, the war had not been going well for Britain and the prevailing mood was at a low ebb. Spies and saboteurs were being conjured up out of thin air almost everywhere. Churchill and the public were not too sympathetic to aliens of any particular stripe and were looking for revenge. During the Phoney War in 1939–40, everyone waited on tenterhooks to see what Hitler would do next and whether he would invade the British Isles. The country had seen the rise of Sir Oswald Mosley and his British Union of Fascists, whose membership was later interned en masse when the government's patience wore thin and they dispensed with the niceties of civil liberties. The threat of fifth columnists had led to the discovery by MI5 of the Wolkoff-Tyler Kent affair[1] and a conspiracy of traitors within the country. It was time for the British government to clamp down before things got out of hand. Defence Regulations in 1940 were strengthened, and the Treachery Act was passed. As Seaborne Davies remarked in his article reviewing the Treachery Act,

> The recollection of the harsh necessities of the times must silence arm-chair criticism of its [Treachery Act] enactment and content. It was the creation of the Parliament of a free nation superbly determined, in an extremity of circumstances, to defend its liberties and its life.[2]

In Norway, the Narvik campaign in 1940 had largely been a failure, and the humiliating débâcle at Dunkirk had resulted in the heroic armada (Operation Dynamo) which had rescued so many British troops from French beaches. Many, however, had not been so lucky and would spend the rest of the war in prisoner-of-war camps. Much of the British Army's matériel was depleted, abandoned on the beaches of northern France, and it would take some time to rebuild its stock of artillery and tanks. The Battle of Britain immediately followed and had been won by the daring and bravado of the young RAF pilots of Fighter Command. With that, the threat of a German invasion subsided. At least this had given everyone a temporary ray of hope, or so they thought. But as if this wasn't enough, London, cities in the industrial Midlands and parts of the North were being pounded by the Blitz, which lasted from 7 September 1940 until 21 May 1941. People's patience and nerves were wearing thin.

To compound these problems, petrol rationing had been introduced in 1939, with food following in 1940, and coal in 1942; clothing was also rationed. By 1943 many of the quantities of food and other commodities were reduced owing to more people being conscripted. Imports suffered because of heavy shipping losses to U-boats sinking the Atlantic convoys, although this was offset somewhat by the resumption of success in breaking the German naval Enigma codes. The war in the Western Desert of North Africa had not gone very well to begin with in 1940 and 1941, and with the fall of Tobruk in June 1942, things were not looking good. In the Far East, the Japanese were rapidly encroaching into British territories: Hong Kong fell in December 1941; between December 1941 and May 1942, Burma was overrun, sending the British Army retreating back to India. This also coincided with the fall of Singapore in February 1942. It was against these hardships, and perhaps a natural xenophobia towards foreigners, that Churchill and the British public demanded revenge against anyone caught as a spy or saboteur.

Overall, the Dronkers case is a sorry account of a pathetic individual; in the words of his defence counsel Michael Maxwell, he was a 'very foolish and clumsy person, and a very obstinate one, and not a traitor', who thought that he was smarter than both the Germans and the British whom he had tried to deceive, but whose plan would backfire badly and eventually cost him his life. He would not be the last to hang at the end of a rope for his alleged crime, and doubtless would have been punished in some way by the Dutch after the war, as they had with Schipper and van Wijk.

The questions that must now be asked are those which were posed at the beginning of this book: First, was Dronkers really a spy; was he really guilty of the charges laid against him? Did British authorities go too far in this particular case, or were they justified in their actions?

Was Dronkers really a spy?

Whether Dronkers was really a spy depends on how the term 'spy' is defined. No actual definition of a spy or what constitutes espionage appears anywhere in the Treachery Act – it seems to have been taken for granted that anyone investigating or trying such a case knew exactly what was meant by these terms

– but they are spelled out in the Official Secrets Acts of 1911 and 1920, as cited on MI5's official website and others (see Appendix 6). By these definitions it would appear that Dronkers was indeed a spy. He had been hired by the Abwehr, with whom he had entered into a financial agreement for the purpose of obtaining information about British defence capabilities, etc., an 'act preparatory' to spying, even though he hadn't actually sought to obtain any, collected any or been caught in the act of doing so. Was, then, that agreement with the Abwehr proof of intent? The 1911 and 1920 Official Secrets Acts as cited by MI5 on their website (see Appendix 6) state 'those who intend to help an enemy'. Whether he had the intent to communicate it to a 'hostile party' is the crux of the whole matter. It all comes back to proof of intent.

The definition in the Treachery Act of 'intent to help the enemy' is unclear, as Seaborne Davies observed earlier. Dronkers always maintained that he had never intended to go along with the Germans' request to provide information; that notwithstanding, by his own admission he did *conspire* with the Abwehr to supply information, and admitted to Mulder that he was a spy. Therefore, on that count it probably makes him guilty of conspiracy, but then by that same token so was Schipper. The only distinction between Dronkers and Schipper is that Dronkers did not make this clear to MI5 from the very beginning, but only about a month later; Schipper admitted it right away but it took van Wijk ninety-five days to come clean. By this logic it would seem that it is all right to be a spy provided you admit to it right away.

Nor were there were any 'grievous cases of sabotage', which Sir John Anderson had talked about, since no act of sabotage was ever conspired or committed. He said that 'an act of treachery can be made the subject of a charge under Clause 1 but the charge must be of a grievous description'.

When the jury failed to convict Pons in 1940 they said that the Crown had not proved that while he had originally conspired to spy for Germany, his intent had been to 'make a clean breast of it' when he arrived in England, when he was, in all likelihood, as guilty as his comrades. Christmas Humphreys' declaration that just agreeing to something does not actually mean that the act will be carried out is germane here. He also said that there is a 'big distinction between agreeing to come to England and the real intent with which you propose to come to England so far as your own true mind is concerned'. Dronkers had claimed the same defence but had been found guilty of intent and executed, largely one supposes, because he had not made a 'clean breast of it' when he was first arrested, but then neither had van Wijk, Schipper *et al.* had been interned when, if anything, they had been more fully trained as spies – by his own admission Schipper had been a professional spy. So why had MI5 considered Schipper devoid of any intent to commit espionage once on British soil when he had so obviously been working for the Germans for about a year and a half? The reasons for not 'turning' him have already been dealt with, and Milmo considered it unsafe to send van Wijk back to Lisbon. Dronkers, in comparison with Schipper, had been a neophyte in the intelligence game. Perhaps the reason why he was not 'turned' is because, 'Some however had to perish, both to satisfy the public that the security of the country was being maintained, and also to convince the Germans that the others were working properly and were not being controlled.'[3]

Given that these cases overlapped, the authorities must have realised that they had made a grievous mistake with Schipper and van Wijk in not sending them for trial and were determined not to make the same one with Dronkers. Never mind the fact that Pons had been acquitted in 1940, Dorothy O'Grady's sentence had been commuted to fourteen years' penal servitude, or Schipper, Davids and Pay had been detained in 1942 under Regulation 18B until the end of the war, it was necessary to stop all this nonsense and make an example of Dronkers as a deterrent to others. Following the Dronkers trial there would be no further acquittals on charges of treachery. From this it could be inferred that the government may have put pressure on the judiciary and the prosecuting counsel to secure a conviction no matter what the cost. In the files available on Dronkers and his trial there is no 'smoking gun' which actually proves this was the case, but it is evident that the Home Office, in the shape of the Home Secretary, Herbert Morrison, his Deputy Under-Secretary, Frank Newsam, and Mr Justice Wrottesley, all considered Dronkers guilty as charged, and the suggestion that the judge attempted to influence the jury to that effect was dismissed during Dronkers' appeal.

What led the WWII British authorities to want to secure a capital conviction against Dronkers, rather than simply to 'turn' him, as they had done – and would continue to do – with many others?

In spite of whatever information Dronkers may have given MI5 about German defences in Holland during his many interrogations – information which he claimed at his trial should have been of use to British authorities – they did not consider him to be a particularly stable individual and therefore of no use to them as a double agent. With his nerves in shreds even before he started out, what hope could he have had of following through? MI5 even said that he was, to borrow a phrase from Graham Greene, a 'burnt-out case'. He was not a well-trained spy, therefore the expected outcome would create more stress: How was he going to obtain information? If he was confident he could pull it off then the stress would go down; if not (and he doesn't come across as being very confident) then the stress would go way up. Perhaps this was why he opted to claim that he had never had any intention of going through with the deal. That being said, many of those whom MI5 had 'doubled' were prone to histrionics, egomania, lying, cheating, licentiousness and promiscuity, so was Dronkers really any different? Given his lack of experience and mental state should we then draw the conclusion that he had been deliberately set up by the Germans to fail?

Why didn't the Double Cross Committee choose to feed Dronkers with disinformation about the subjects the Germans had asked him to find out about, or do the same to Schipper for that matter? As noted earlier, 'Jasper' Harker seemed to think that Dronkers was still capable of providing more information of intelligence value. However, Dick White concluded that MI5 had extracted as much as they were likely to get out of him. In the words of Sir David Petrie, 'Mr White thinks we have extracted as much as we are likely to get.' MI5 was also of the opinion that there was enough evidence for a prima facie case against him and to be able to secure a prosecution.

In choosing not to 'turn' Dronkers, did MI5 fail in this instance to live up to the Twenty Committee's creed as outlined in Chapter Three? On the plus side, it did catch a fresh 'spy'. It also gained some knowledge of the personalities and methods of the German Secret Service, as noted in the conclusion of a copy of a report from B1b on the Dronkers case dated 4 January 1943 and given to Arthur Thurston on 11 March 1943:

> From the intelligence aspect, the case is chiefly of interest for the light it sheds on the activities of I.M. The Hague. Dronkers' case should be compared with those of Schipper, Grobben, Dijkstra,[4] and above all with that of the Brothers Erasmus. From these emerges a general picture of the 'Ueberseedienst' [Overseas service i.e. foreign intelligence], character of the undertakings of I.M. The Hague – that is, an organisation primarily, but by no means exclusively, naval in its own composition and in the objectives it sets itself. So far as concerns the refugee-agents as distinct from the trawler or seamen agents employed by I.M. The Hague, the evidence of the *Dronkers and Erasmus cases does not lead one to regard them as a particularly serious menace* [my italics]. The low quality of the material employed and the carelessness in the organisation of the mission point to a different conclusion.[5]

What is curious about the statement 'the evidence of the Dronkers and Erasmus cases does not lead one to regard them as a particularly serious menace', is why they would then take it as far as the Director of Public Prosecutions, the Old Bailey and judicial hanging. If the threat each of them posed was not 'particularly serious', why then did MI5 not simply intern Dronkers for the duration as they had with Pons or van Wijk? Since MI5 was comparing the case of Dronkers to those of Grobben and the Erasmus brothers and their involvement with the Abwehr, it may be useful to provide a brief explanation as a sidebar; however, they will not be discussed in detail.

***

Jacobus Johannes Grobben was a Dutch merchant seaman born 10 January 1904 who was recruited by the Abwehr in Rotterdam in 1942 by Becker, who had been involved with the Schipper case. Grobben was instructed to carry out espionage on the east coast of America and then the UK. In Genoa he had missed his ship, the *St Cergue*, and had joined the Swiss ship *Albula* bound for Gibraltar. The Royal Navy boarded the *Albula* while it was at sea in June 1942 where he informed them of his recruitment by the Abwehr and his espionage training. The Navy then transported him by HMS *Icarus* to Britain, where he was detained at Camp 020 for six weeks, during which time he provided MI5 with a good deal of intelligence. The ensuing investigation by MI5 concluded that the Navy had mishandled the case and that it should have been turned over immediately to them or MI6. As a result, Masterman reported that Grobben could not be 'turned' by the Double-Cross Committee because

> (a) He would be of little use to us and (b) because we considered that, having regard to the method of his arrest, it was almost impossible that the Germans would believe he was acting still in their interests. No doubt the case was handled clumsily in Gibraltar, and this was the main reason which ruled out Groben [*sic*] as a possible candidate for us.[6]

The fact that Grobben had 'come clean' with both the British authorities and the Dutch Secret Service had stood him in good stead. He was extensively debriefed by Stephens at Camp 020 before finally being released. On the recommendation of 'Buster' Milmo he was compensated to the tune of £100 from Sir David Petrie's funds because as Petrie said, Grobben had 'played a straight game with us'. Stephens had suggested that £50 would be sufficient but Milmo thought that 'somewhat parsimonious'. Following his release Grobben began working for the Dutch Security Service, but MI5 later reported in March 1943 that the Dutch no longer trusted him.

* * *

The Erasmus brothers – Abraham Janni and Jacobus Cornelis – were recruited by the Abwehr in The Hague in the spring of 1942. Abraham was born on 20 June 1914 and was approached by a member of the NSB called Jan Kielema (1892–1965) who asked him whether he was prepared to go to England. Abraham saw this as a means of escaping from Holland and accepted. On 6 June he was introduced to 'Beckers' (Becker), asked to sign a document agreeing to be paid for his services and sent for training in secret inks. Jacobus, who was born on 6 October 1919, had been working in Germany on the railway and while on leave with his family in the Netherlands was contacted by his brother. He also agreed to work for the Germans and met with Kuechling and Coenrad. MI5 reported that both

> Dronkers and Mulder have mentioned a man of this name [Kuechling] in the Hague whom they know to be in touch with the Germans. Dronkers,

however, cannot describe him, as they never met; and Mulder's description does not check with those given by the Erasmus brothers.[7]

In an Internal Memorandum from Captain Winn to Colonel Stephens on 7 November 1942 he states,

> On comparing the descriptions given by MULDER and the ERASMUS BROTHERS of KUECHLING, it is evident that these two men are not the same. The address – Waalsdorperweg 283 – given by MULDER as KUECHLING's, conveyed nothing to the two brothers.[8]

On another name mentioned in the brothers' file, Clevers, MI5 had this to say:

> This description checks well with that given by Dykstra[9] of Klever, Hiller's assistant and wireless instructor at Cornelis Jolstraat, which is known to be connected with 1, Johannvan Oldenbarneveld-laan [sic] [in Scheveningen]. Erasmus' Klever is more likely to be identical to this man than with the Klever mentioned by Mulder and Dronkers.[10]

The description, as included in Appendix III of a Camp 020 report, states that Clevers was aged between 30–35; thin and 1.70 m tall; 60–75 kg in weight; fair hair, somewhat sparse in front; pale eyes (mostly likely blue); with a pointed nose and chin, who was exceptionally polite and wore grey plus-fours – baggy trousers extending four inches below the knee (hence the name), longer than knickerbockers, which originally appeared in the 1920s and were much favoured by golfers.

The brothers were given contact addresses in Lisbon and Lugano, Switzerland, to send information relating to naval affairs, such as shipbuilding, submarine bases, convoy assembly points, American ships in port, and much more. When they arrived at Ramsgate on 2 October 1942 they turned themselves in to the authorities. On 7 October MI5 made an application to the Home Office for Detention Orders under Article 12(5) (a) of the Aliens Act. Interestingly, the 'Supplementary Report on the Case of the Erasmus Brothers' prepared by Captain T. L.Winn[11] at Camp 020 dated 19 December 1942 raised the questions of whether the brothers should be prosecuted under the Treachery Act or whether they should continue to be held at Camp 020 because they were suspected of being German agents on the grounds

(a) that they were recruited by the German Secret Service to act as agents against this country; that they were trained by the Germans in the writing of secret ink messages, and were sent to England in the guise of refugees from Holland;

(b) that it was their intention on arrival in this country to carry out the agreement made with their German employers to act as spies against this country.

The charges in (a) are admitted by Abraham Jannes and Jacobus Cornelis Erasmus. With regard to (b) they state that their intention was not to act against this country, but to use their employment by the German Secret Service as a means of escaping from Holland to England, where they would put themselves and their knowledge at the disposal of the British Government.

It thus follows that the sole issue to determine is their intention on arriving in this country.[12]

Evidence against both brothers was presented:

1. Abraham had in his possession very friendly letters from Germans who frequented his café;
2. His name had been given to the German agent Kielema as a suitable employee of the German Secret Service;
3. After he had broken the specially prepared match (with which to carry out secret writing) he made a trip to The Hague to obtain another;
4. Jacobus had volunteered to work for the Germans;
5. He possessed a note of the fishing vessel KW 116, known to be in the Germans' service;
6. Both of them on arriving in Ramsgate stated they had escaped from Holland but not that they were in the service of the Germans;
7. Not until '*some days later* at the RVPS' did either of them make any mention of their employment by the German Secret Service. [*My italics*]

However, various excuses were made in the report to justify why this evidence 'seems a reasonable explanation' or 'understandable' in both brothers' cases. Winn concluded that

> It is not possible to know the motives which made them undertake this trip. If patriotism is not accepted as an explanation, there is the possibility that their circumstances in Holland had become so intolerable that they had to escape at any cost. However, it appears improbable that they had any intention of working for the Germans, and results of investigations here suggest their innocence.[13]

He recommended that 'I feel justified in recommending the release of these two men.'[14] These conclusions could equally apply to Dronkers. Indeed, the 'Provisional Report on the Case of the Erasmus Brothers' (no date) states that

> Abraham is most emphatic that it was his intention from the first to gain as much information about the German S.S. [Secret Service] as he could and to give this information on his arrival in this country.[15]

Their recommended release from Camp 020 where they were being held came in early February 1943. As John Day reported on 15 January 1943:

> The same general intelligence observations hold for this case as for Dronkers (q.v.). Further, as in the case of Dronkers, there is evidence of carelessness in organisation, due to lack of attention to detail; namely failure to vet either spy before engaging him, entailing the employment of a pair of anti-Nazis, and failure to provide a complete cover-story or a plausible subject for the en clair text they were told to use for their secret writing letters.[16]

In both the Grobben and Erasmus cases, B1a decided against using any of them as double agents, nor were there any prosecution proceedings filed, as MI5 felt that there was 'no possible chance of success'.[17] With the imminent execution of Dronkers in mind, Milmo pointed out to Mrs Lee of the Home Office, Aliens Department on 30 December 1942 that

> ... it is not proposed to prosecute either of these men there being no evidence upon which any prima facie case could be established in a criminal court.[18]

Milmo's comments are interesting since they are in direct conflict with the Dronkers case if we compare the evidence. Like the Erasmus brothers,

1. Dronkers' name had been given to a German agent;
2. Dronkers had in his possession materials for secret writing;
3. Dronkers had agreed to work for the Germans as the Erasmus brothers had done, although he had been blackmailed into working for them, not volunteered;
4. Dronkers had also said that he had escaped from the Germans, but not about working for the German Secret Service; but
5. Unlike the Erasmus brothers, it was not until about a month later that he admitted to working for the Germans.

How then could his case be any different from that of the Erasmus brothers? The only real difference here seems to be that Dronkers had lied and obfuscated until he realised much later that MI5 did not believe him, whereas Grobben and the Erasmus brothers had been up front with MI5. They had each professed to want to impart the intelligence they had obtained to British authorities as soon as possible. Their full co-operation during interrogations meant that MI5 were inclined to be more lenient towards them, even though initially there had been some suspicion, particularly in the case of the Erasmus brothers and their recruitment by the Abwehr. In each case, as with

Dronkers, the question of intent always existed. But as Mr Justice Wrottesley said at the end of the Dronkers trial, 'A man's intentions can be judged from his actions, and are to be judged in that way'; MP Thomas Harvey had posed the question in 1940 during the Treachery Act debate:

How is any court to make a perfect judgment as to intention? In most cases it can be only by inferring it by a process of reasoning deduced from acts.

So what were these 'actions' upon which Dronkers was to be judged?

First, Dronkers had entered into a financial arrangement with the Abwehr, where it could be argued that intent was there. But what really was the intent? To spy for Germany? To cheat the Germans out of some money? He certainly attempted to do that, but he was never allowed to carry out any spying. Second, as a result of that arrangement, he had sailed to England with the alleged intent of spying for Germany. Sailing to England in and of itself was no illegal act, although there must have been some collusion with the Germans through 'Jan' so that he could sail past their coastal defences with a fully fuelled boat unchallenged. Third, he had consistently lied to MI5 about his so-called reason for escaping from the Netherlands, which would suggest that he had had something to hide. But if he was to be judged on these actions then surely all it proved was that he was a bad liar, not that he was a spy. Of course, what we can never know is, at what point did he not intend to spy for the Germans? Immediately, when he first entered into the arrangement? Just after it, before he set sail? Whilst on the journey? Once he was first arrested? During his first interrogation, or later when he realised that lying was futile and his stories cut no ice with MI5? That he took to his grave.

Finally, did the climate of that time predetermine Dronkers' fate and amount to a miscarriage of justice being committed?

The outcomes of the van Wijk, Pons and Schipper cases were clearly not what MI5 and the British establishment had hoped for. Whether the judge had misdirected the jury in his summing up of the Dronkers case is perhaps a matter of conjecture. That was certainly the claim during his Appeal, but it was rejected. It does seem as if the judge were biased and looking for a conviction when he said to the jury, 'There is not going to be any difficulty in your way in this case in coming to a conclusion … ' as if urging them to find him guilty.

Did the prosecution fulfil 'to the last scintilla' (as the Attorney-General, Sir Donald Somervell, had put it in 1940) the burden of proof that Dronkers was guilty? Guilty of what? In *Cases and Materials on Criminal Law and*

Procedure, M. L. Friedland cites Kennedy, who gives a model example of the burden of proof:

> The onus or burden of proving the guilt of an accused person, beyond a reasonable doubt, rests upon the Crown and never shifts. There is no burden on an accused person to prove his innocence. The Crown must prove beyond a reasonable doubt that an accused person is guilty of the offence with which he is charged, before he can be convicted. If you have a reasonable doubt as to whether the accused in this case committed the offence with which he is charged, it is your duty to give the accused the benefit of the doubt and to find him not guilty.
>
> In other words, if after considering all the evidence, the arguments of counsel and my charge, you come to the conclusion that the Crown has failed to prove to your satisfaction, beyond a reasonable doubt, that the accused committed the offence with which he is charged, it is your duty to give the accused the benefit of the doubt and to find him not guilty.
>
> A question that may come to your minds is, what is meant by the words 'reasonable doubt'. A reasonable doubt is an honest doubt, not an imaginary doubt conjured up by a juror to escape his responsibility. It must be a doubt which prevents a juror from saying, 'I am morally certain that the accused committed the offence with which he is charged'.[19]

However, Lord Goddard (Rayner Goddard, 1871–1971, Lord Chief Justice, 1946–58) following an Appeal at Surrey Quarter Sessions in 1952, offered this opinion:

> I have never yet heard a court give a satisfactory definition of what is a reasonable doubt, and it would be very much better if summings-up did not use that expression, for it seems to me that, whenever a court attempts to explain what is meant by reasonable doubt, it gives a definition or tries to explain the term in a way which is likely to cause more confusion than clarity. It is far better, instead of using the words 'reasonable doubt' and then trying to explain what is meant by reasonable doubt, to direct a jury: 'You must not convict unless you are satisfied by the evidence that the offence has been committed.' The jury should be told that it is not for the prisoner to prove his innocence, but for the prosecution to prove his guilt. If a jury is told that it is their duty to regard the evidence and see that it satisfies them so that they can feel sure when they return a verdict of Guilty, that is much better than using the expression 'reasonable doubt' and I hope in future that that will be done. I never use the expression when summing-up. I always tell a jury that, before they convict, they must feel sure and must be satisfied that the prosecution have established the guilt of the prisoner.[20]

If we take Kennedy's definition of 'reasonable doubt' and apply it to Dronkers' trial, it would appear that the accused person (Dronkers) *did* have to prove his innocence. The Crown did not, and could not, in this author's opinion, prove 'beyond a reasonable doubt' that he was guilty of the offence with which he was charged, because the charge of treachery as laid down under the Act was so ambiguous; it was really only Dronkers' word against the Crown's whether he had intended to commit that act, and no one could possibly know that, only Dronkers. Therefore, he should have been given the benefit of the doubt and acquitted.

A number of other mitigating factors had also contributed to Dronkers' downfall. Like his compatriots, he had had to suffer the privations of living through the Nazi occupation of Holland. Throughout his life he had been unable to hold down a steady job for very long, although it seems that this was not always his fault. Because of this ill luck he was always financially strapped, not helped by the fact that his wife was (apparently) always demanding more money, or that he had lost her so-called 'fortune' in a failed business venture with van Baalen, which probably caused much friction between them. Whether Elise Dronkers was really as rapacious and the 'evil genius' she was portrayed as being by Day and Stephens, or by prosecuting counsel during the trial is unknown: this was perhaps emotive language designed to stir the jury.

When Dronkers fell under the clutches of the Germans, he naively saw this as a means to extricate himself from his impecunious situation and an opportunity to earn some extra money by escaping from the misery of living in occupied Holland as he later claimed, and live out the rest of the war in England. He was, as Michael Maxwell said, 'an honest, but stupid, misguided man who thought he had been, perhaps a little clever and made some rather dirty money out of the Germans'. And in the words of P. Van Dyck at the RVPS, 'he revealed himself as a very shifty and subtle man … also a very unscrupulous man'.

This naivety was a reflection of Dronkers' own weak character and level of intelligence. He felt, perhaps justifiably, threatened by what punishment the Germans may inflict upon him from his dealings on the black market, given how menacing the Gestapo could be. But MI5 had thought he was making too much of this. His punishment was likely to be a few months in prison, so why give up such a lucrative existence? Yet his so-called dealings on the black market may just have been part of his 'cover story'. However, he had maintained this 'cover story' too long, until about a month after his arrest. In British custody he was conscious of not being believed, as there were too many inconsistencies and contradictions in the accounts of his escape.

The question of Dronkers' honesty is perhaps moot. He had certainly not been honest with the British authorities, nor with Mulder and de Langen about his true reason for escaping, until Mulder had prised it out of him. That he was cheating the Germans, the Allies' sworn enemy, in this climate of war should have been considered 'fair game'. After all, the Double-Cross

Committee was also cheating or deceiving the Germans, albeit in a different way. The statement 'all's fair in love and war' seems appropriate here.

What of Dronkers' wife, Elise? In escaping from Holland without her there is also an element of selfishness. His innate naivety allowed himself to believe that while he was conducting his mission the Germans would honour their promise to support her, then reward him with a good job when he returned. In becoming a victim of their blackmail, he failed to realise that the Germans were only using him as a pawn. Did he seriously believe that they would take care of Elise and provide her with a stipend all the time he was in England? He claimed they were happily married, but did he not realise that she would be held hostage while he was away? He was putting not only his own life but that of his wife in danger. It had not occurred to him that once he reneged on the deal or failed to provide useful intelligence to the Abwehr they would have punished her. It all seems a bit too naïve to be credible.

Yet there must have been some feeling of guilt for what might be happening to his wife in Holland as he said to Major de Vries several times during his arrest that 'my poor darling wife is left behind'. He had abandoned her to her fate, whatever that was likely to be – possible starvation, prison or concentration camp. Did that expression of guilt also extend to his fellow countrymen? The stories he told did not hold water. Why did he, the 'simple-minded Dutchman' that he was, think that he could hoodwink both MI5 and the Germans, both of whom were much smarter than him?

The 'traces' of his alleged activities before the war in 1938 and his alleged membership of the NSB should have remained inadmissible at the trial at the Old Bailey as they were far from conclusive or fully proven. With hindsight, it is easy to say that he was not the Dronkers referred to as a member of the NSB. But these 'traces' stuck and would serve as a reflection of his own lack of trustworthiness and reliability: he had allegedly committed espionage before, therefore he was perfectly capable of being a recidivist and committing it again in wartime. Yet the so-called act of espionage in 1938 in which Dronkers played a part by translating documents was a scheme concocted by van Baalen and Klever to cheat the Germans, and only provided false information invented by them. Did that make Dronkers guilty of espionage and being a spy if the information was false? No national security was compromised, so where was the crime? If anything he was surely aiding and abetting an act of fraud on the part of van Baalen and Klever. And how much did these alleged activities really contribute to the episode in 1942 anyway? Were they proof that he was already a closet Nazi supporter? That he was guilty of being a spy by association? It was, from the Germans' point of view, proof that he could be easily manipulated. Others, such as Schipper and van Wijk, had been far more active than he, so why was it much worse for Dronkers? There was also the foreknowledge by British intelligence through ISK decrypts of his arrival. When he arrived in Britain he was automatically treated with suspicion as a possible spy rather than as a bona fide refugee.

Then there is the clumsy chain of custody of evidence exercised by MI5 and the Intelligence Corps when they failed to exhibit sufficient care or attention to items confiscated from him, which in a modern court of law would surely have been thrown out as inadmissible. The 'discovery' of the dictionary is a case in point. That it had been removed from him when he was first arrested by the Intelligence Corps then returned is inexcusable, and, as was suggested by the prosecution in court, he could have tampered with it or destroyed it.

Dronkers had not asked for any witnesses at his arraignment at Bow Street Magistrates' Court. Would the fact that there were also none who would speak up for him at his trial have made any difference? Who was there anyway? Mulder certainly would not have done, based on his reaction to their 'association' on 19 July, and de Langen was already serving in the Dutch Army. Statements had been taken from both of them but not used at the trial, although it is unclear why. Perhaps his defence counsel thought they might have further incriminated him, although there is nothing in either statement which appears to do so. Dronkers had said later that he had hoped that the various officers who interrogated him might have spoken up for him. It is hardly likely, even if some of them did express reservations about his guilt. When it came to the crunch, would they have actually risen to his defence with a clear conscience? After all, he wasn't playing on the same side. Again, another example of his innate naivety.

Was there a miscarriage of justice? Yes, in the sense that the trial was far from perfect or wholly impartial. As noted earlier, there was likely no consideration of the general guidelines the DPP had offered regarding van Wijk when MI5 considered submitting Dronkers' case to the DPP. The dice were, in a sense, loaded, with shades of a 'kangaroo court' about it. It is also unfortunate that in the climate of the Second World War, the British government deemed it necessary to inflict such a harsh punishment when the question of intent was so ambiguous, with the lives of the accused at the mercy of slick-tongued lawyers and judges who may have been ordered to toe the party line. Although he was certainly culpable, Dronkers served to make an example to others, but I remain unconvinced that he was totally guilty of the crime with which he was charged. If anything, he should probably have been convicted of conspiracy only, and given a lesser sentence, or acquitted and interned for the duration of the war, then repatriated to face the consequences in Holland.

What happened to them?

Jan Bruno de Langen
After the war he lived in The Hague and was a member of the Society of Engelandvaarders, an organisation formed from men and women who escaped occupied Europe to fight against the Axis countries. He became

a recluse, who collected old newspapers and rags and was surrounded by hundreds of mice. He died as a result of injuries sustained in a fire to his house on 19 May 1993 which he had set deliberately.

John Alphonsus Mulder

After the war he returned to The Hague on 7 December 1946, having been registered as 'having departed with unknown destination'. His Civil Registry card shows that he continued to live in The Hague at eight different addresses until he died. However, during the period 16 September 1950 – 28 August 1951 he left again for an unknown destination. On 11 July 1962 in The Hague he married Erika Hedwig Sauer, born Bad Kreuznach (Germany) on 14 August 1940. The couple had two daughters both born in The Hague: Hedwig Elisabeth Lucia Maria Mulder, on 11 January 1963, and Lucia Maria Christina Petra Mulder on 18 May 1964. The marriage was apparently not a stable one and around 8 July 1964 the preliminaries for a divorce were set in motion. During her second pregnancy Erika left her house and moved into an institution for unmarried mothers in the Scheveningen part of The Hague called 'Maria Stella'. Mulder visited her there twice a week and tried to convince her to return. Frustrated, on 9 August 1964 he returned, went to his wife's room and killed her with an axe, before killing his eldest daughter. He then went to the department where his youngest daughter stayed and killed her as well. Returning to his wife's room he was cornered by a policeman and a bystander. He jumped out of the 8-metre-high window and died of his injuries.

Dora 'Dolly' Peekema Dibbets

Died in Leiden on 19 March 1953, aged fifty-five.

Elise Antoinette Eleonora Seignette

Died in Amsterdam, although her death was registered in The Hague, on 18 December 1944. The cause is unknown.

Directory of Key Personnel Mentioned in Official Documents

Intelligence Services

ADAM, LIEUTENANT COLONEL JOHN H.: MI5 officer in charge of D4, Port Control, at sea ports and airports.

BINGHAM, MAJOR SEYMOUR (1898–?): B1d, Special Examiners; later head of N (Dutch) Section, SOE.

BINGHAM, MISS L.: Officer in B1b.

BROOKE-BOOTH, CAPTAIN SEPTIMUS PAUL, MC: E1a, Nationals of Western Europe. Northumberland Fusiliers, 7th Battalion, in First World War; also listed as Intelligence Corps (*London Gazette*, 19 January 1945). Succeeded Maj. Kenneth Younger as Assistant Director, E Division (ADE), in 1943. Later Lt Col.

BUTLER, COLONEL R: DDG's office, MI5.

CHENEY, CHRISTOPHER ROBERT (1906–87): E1b. Later Chair in Medieval History, University of Manchester and Professor of Medieval History, University of Cambridge.

CHENHALLS, JOAN, MBE: MI5 officer in B2b, later C4a. Daughter of a Methodist minister, spinster. Friend of Jona 'Klop' Ustinov; worked with Dick White after the Second World War tracking Nazis; later chairperson of the executive committee of the International Girl's Brigade.

CHOLMONDELEY, FLIGHT LIEUTENANT CHARLES (c. 1918–82): RAF section of MI5's B1a; member of the Twenty Committee; later worked with Lieutenant Commander Ewen Montagu on Operation Mincemeat.

CLEGG, M. H.: Officer at Camp 020.

CORIN, CAPTAIN EDWARD JOHN RONALD: MI5 Officer in E1b (Seamen). 2nd Lieutenant in cavalry, 1916; Lt 1917.

COWGILL, COLONEL FELIX: Former Indian Army officer. Head of SIS Section V, Counter-espionage, in 1940.

CUSSEN, MAJOR (LATER LIEUTENANT COLONEL) EDWARD JAMES PATRICK, KC (1904–73): MI5 Legal Advisor in SLB, MI5's Legal section. Interrogated P. G. Wodehouse in September 1944; later became a Circuit Judge (Additional Judge, Central Criminal Court).

DAVIDSON, M.: Officer at Camp 020.

DAY, 2ND LIEUTENANT J. P. DE C. (JOHN DAY): MI5 officer with B1b, later with K7, dealing with Soviet penetration.

DEARDEN, DR HAROLD GOLDSMITH (1882–1962): Resident psychiatrist at Camp 020; former Captain, RAMC, attached to 3rd Battalion Grenadier Guards during First World War.

DE VRIES, MAJOR REGINALD 'REX' FALLOWS: Commissioned to the General List in September 1939 from the Royal Field Artillery; July 1940, Intelligence Corps and OC 123 FSS and Security Control Officer (SCO), Harwich.

GIBBS, REGINALD D.: MI5 officer in B1b, Espionage, Special Sources.

GLASS, ANN CATHERINE (LATER ELWELL) (1922–96): MI5 officer in B2b (1940–58); Foreign Office, Information Research Department (IRD), 1959 – late 1970s.

GOODACRE, CAPTAIN ERIC BRERETON (1901–79): Intelligence Corps officer, Camp 020.

GROGAN, ALAN: MI5 officer in B3d, Censorship Liaison.

GWYER, MAJOR JOHN M. A.: MI5 officer in B1a, Research Section who carried out research on the organisation of the German secret services. Post-war he was in F2c.

HARKER, BRIGADIER OSWALD ALLEN 'JASPER' (1886–1968): Deputy Director-General, MI5, 1940–47.

HART, HERBERT LIONEL ADOLPHUS (1907–92): MI5 officer in B1b, Espionage, Special Sources; later, Professor of Jurisprudence at Oxford University and Principal of Brasenose College.

HAYLOR, MAJOR E. R. OR H. V. 'RONNIE': MI5 officer in B1d and Commandant of the Royal Victoria Patriotic School (RVPS).

HERREWYN, SERGEANT ROBERT HENRY CHARLES: 123 FSS, Intelligence Corps, Harwich.

HILL, BERNARD A. (1904–78): MI5 officer in SLB, MI5's Legal section (1940–64). Belonged to Gray's Inn. Described in 1950 as the MI5 officer in charge of planning.

HINCHLEY-COOKE, LIEUTENANT COLONEL WILLIAM EDWARD (1894–1955): MI5 interrogator and Legal advisor in SLB, MI5's Legal section (SLB1).

HOOPER, HERBERT: MI5 officer in E1a, Nationals of Western Europe.

JACKSON, F.: MI5 officer at the Royal Victoria Patriotic School (RVPS).

JEFFREYS, M. E.: MI5 officer in B1b.

KNOX, ALFRED DILLWYN 'DILLY', CMG (1884–1943): Classical scholar and papyrologist, King's College, Cambridge; codebreaker at GC&CS and breaker of Abwehr Enigma; member of First World War Room 40 codebreaking unit; helped to decrypt Zimmermann Telegram.

LIDDELL, CAPTAIN GUY, MC (1892–1958): Director, MI5 B Branch; later Deputy Director-General, 1945–53.

MACALISTER, LIEUTENANT: Officer, Camp 020.

MACDONALD, MISS: IRB, Inter-services Research Bureau (cover name for SOE).

McKINNELL, CAPTAIN: MI5 officer, Camp 020.

MASTERMAN, (SIR) JOHN CECIL (1891–1977): Chairman of the Twenty Committee/Double Cross Committee; later Provost of Worcester College, Oxford and Vice-Chancellor of Oxford University; knighted 1959.

MAYOR, TESS (1915–96): MI5 officer in B1c and assistant to Victor, Lord Rothschild, later Lady Rothschild.

MILMO, HELENUS PADRAIC SEOSAMH 'BUSTER' (1908–88): Assistant Director, MI5, B1; later a High Court judge and part of the prosecution team of the Nuremberg Trials. While with MI5 unsuccessfully investigated Kim Philby.

OSBORNE, MR: MI5 officer, E4, Aliens War Service permits.

PETRIE, BRIGADIER SIR DAVID, KCMG, CIE, CVO, CBE, KPM (1879–1961): Director-General, MI5, 1940–45; Indian police, 1900–36.

QUIN, MRS D. M.: MI5 officer in B2b. Investigated case of Marina Lee, a Russian-born dancer, who penetrated the British command in Norway in 1940.

RAMSBOTHAM, PETER EDWARD, 3RD VISCOUNT SOULBURY, GCMG, GCVO, DL (1919–2010): MI5 officer in B3, Foreign journalists (1941) then E1a, Alien Control. Commissioned in the Intelligence Corps, 1944, later becoming a lieutenant colonel. Member of 106 Special Counter Intelligence Unit (SCIU) running double agents, liaison officer to French counter-espionage; mentioned in dispatches (MiD), 1945, Croix de Guerre, 1949. Later, High Commissioner to Cyprus (1969–71), Ambassador to Iran (1971–74), the United States (1974–77), Governor of Bermuda (1977–80).

RIDDELL, J. A.: MI5 officer in B1d, the Royal Victoria Patriotic School (RVPS).

ROTHSCHILD, VICTOR, LORD (1910–90): MI5 officer in B1c; later married Tess Mayor; implicated in 'Cambridge Spies' case.

RYDER, LIEUTENANT COLONEL C. F.: MI5 officer in E4, Aliens War Service permits.

SAMPSON, MAJOR GEORGE F. (1883–1948): Assistant Commandant, Camp 020.

SANDS, 2ND LIEUTENANT R. S.: Officer at the Royal Victoria Patriotic School (RVPS).

SENTER, COMMANDER (SIR) JOHN WATT, RNVR (1905–66): Member, Army Officer's Emergency Reserve, 1938; civilian assistant attached to General Staff, War Office, 1940–41; Naval Intelligence Division, Admiralty (HMS *President*), 1942–45; Director of Security, Special Operations, SOE, August 1942. Called to the Bar, 1928; resumed practice 1945, Queen's Council, 1953; knighted, 1958.

SHEPHERD, N.: Officer, Camp 020.

SINCLAIR, D. H.: MI5 officer in SLB, MI5's Legal Branch.

SMITH, H. L.: GPO; also MI5 Scientific section, A6.

SPEIRS, SERGEANT ROBERT BROWN: 123 FSS, Intelligence Corps, Harwich.

STAMP, EDWARD BLANCHARD (1905–84): Officer, B1b. Later, Sir Edward Blanchard Stamp, Rt Hon Lord Justice Stamp, a Lord Justice of Appeal and Privy Counsellor.

STEPHENS, COLONEL ROBIN WILLIAM GEORGE 'TIN-EYE' (1900–?): Commandant, Camp 020; formerly, Captain, 18th Royal Garhwal Rifles (formerly 2/2 Gurkha Rifles).

STIMSON, MAJOR DOUGLAS BERNARD 'STIMMY' (1897–1979): Officer at Camp 020.

STRACHEY, OLIVER, CBE (1874–1960): Brother of Lytton Strachey; codebreaker in First and Second World Wars at GC&CS, where he was head of ISOS unit decrypting Abwehr cyphers; Ottawa, December 1941 – September 1942 as chief cryptographer at the Examination Unit.

VAN DYCK, P.: Officer at the Royal Victoria Patriotic School (RVPS).

WHITE, (SIR) DICK GOLDSMITH, KCMG, KBE (1906–93): Head of MI5's B1b and assistant to Guy Liddell; Director-General, MI5, 1953–56 and Chief of MI6, 1956–68, the only person to do so.

WINN, CAPTAIN THOMAS LEITH (1894–1964): Camp 020, who also worked as a dentist at the camp.

WORLLEDGE, COLONEL JOHN PENRY GARNONS, OBE (d. 1957): Formerly Royal Engineers; head of MI8c (1939–41 when control was taken over by MI6); commanded No. 2 Wireless Company, Royal Signals, in Sarafand, Palestine, in

1923; 2nd Lieutenant, 23 July 1907; Captain, 1919; Acting Major 21 January 1918; Fellow of the Royal Geographical Society, 1920.

WORTON, CAPTAIN: MI5 officer in C2b.

YOUNGER, MAJOR THE HON. KENNETH J. (1908–76): Second son of James Younger, Viscount Younger of Leckie; Major, Intelligence Corps; Assistant Director, E branch (ADE). Labour MP for Grimsby in 1945; 1950, Minister of State at Foreign Office; Director, Royal Institute for International Affairs (Chatham House), 1960.

The Dutch

DERKSEMA, CAPTAIN ROBERT PIETER JAN: Officer with Dutch Intelligence-in-exile (CID); took over from François van t'Sant on 14 August 1941. TNA file closed until 1 January 2031.

PINTO, LIEUTENANT COLONEL ORESTE (1889–1961): Officer of Dutch counterintelligence who worked with MI5 interrogating spies. Author of *Spycatcher* and *Friend or Foe?*, both published in 1952.

VAN ANGEREN, JOHANNES REGNERUS MARIA (1894–1959): Dutch Minister of Justice, 1942–1944.

VAN MOYLAND, BARON HENRY ADOLF ADRIAAN GUSTAVE STEENGRACHT (1905–77): Dutch Intelligence.

VRINTEN, ADRIAANUS JOHANNES JOSEPHUS (1893–1981): Dutch Intelligence; former private detective, apparently the main recruiter for the Passport Control Office (PCO) in The Hague, which was a cover for SIS.

WOLTERS, CAPTAIN ARNOLDUS 'NOL' (1912–94): Royal Dutch Navy; Dutch Intelligence; liaison officer with No. 2 Dutch Group, 1st Airborne Division at Arnhem; also attached to the RVPS.

Royal Navy

CANNON, T/LIEUTENANT CLIFFORD KENNARD, RNR (1903–?): Born, Woolwich/Plumstead. Captain of HMT *Corena* (4 February 1941 – July 1942). Mentioned in Navy List for 18 Sept. 1940 as Probationary Temporary Lieutenant (2 Sept.). Received 2nd Mate's Certificate of Competency, 1 November 1922; 1st Mate's Certificate of Competency, 17 November 1924.

CRUICKSHANK, LIEUTENANT. JAMES IAN, DSC, RNVR: 1st Lieutenant, later Captain, HMT *Corena* (mid-July 1942 – mid-1945; Mentioned in Despatches (MID), 1 July 1941; DSC, 1 January 1944.

GLOVER, ROBERT LAWRENCE: Steward, HMT *Corena*.

GODFREY, VICE-ADMIRAL JOHN, CB (1888 – 1970): Director of Naval Intelligence (DNI), 1939–42.

JOHNS, COMMANDER PHILLIP: Assistant Director of Naval Intelligence (ADNI).

ROGERS, REAR ADMIRAL HUGH HEXT, RN, MVO, OBE (1883 – 1955): Flag Officer-in-Charge, Harwich; promoted Rear Admiral, 2 October 1935.

SMITH-GORDON, LIEUTENANT SIR LIONEL ELDRED POTTINGER, Bt, RNVR (1889–1976): Staff Officer Intelligence, Harwich Naval Base.

The Police

BRIDGES, INSPECTOR FRANK: Metropolitan Police Special Branch, Scotland Yard. Chief Inspector in 1945.

FIRMIN, SERGEANT: Essex County Constabulary, Parkeston Station, Clacton Division.

HARRIS, DETECTIVE SERGEANT BERTRAM: Metropolitan Police Special Branch, Scotland Yard.

KNOCK, POLICE CONSTABLE JOHN ALBERT: Essex Constabulary.

SCOTT, POLICE CONSTABLE CECIL LUKE: Police War Reserve (PWR).

Legal officials

ATKINSON, MAJOR SIR EDWARD HALE TINDAL, KCB, CBE (1878–1957): Director of Public Prosecutions (1930–44).

BYRNE, (SIR) LAWRENCE A. (1896–1965): Barrister, prosecuting counsel. Also prosecuting counsel in the William Joyce ('Lord Haw-Haw') case and judge in the *R* v. *Penguin Books* case (1960) under the Obscene Publication Act 1959 when Penguin Books was prosecuted for the publication of *Lady Chatterley's Lover*. Recorder of Rochester, 1939; High Court judge, 1945.

CALDECOTE, VISCOUNT, THOMAS INSKIP (1876–1947): Lord Chief Justice (1940–46).

HEAD, C. B. V.: Solicitor, partner in Ludlow & Co.; Dronkers' solicitor. Also defence counsel for William Joyce ('Lord Haw-Haw'). Author of *Essentials of Magisterial Law. A Reference Book for Counsel, Solicitors, Lay Magistrates, Police Officers and Other Engaged in the Administration of Magisterial Law*, 1949.

HUMPHREYS, TRAVERS CHRISTMAS, KC (1901–83): Prosecuting counsel.

JOWITT, 1ST EARL (WILLIAM ALLEN) PC, KC (1885–1957): Solicitor-General, 1940–42; later Paymaster-General (1942–45) and Lord Chancellor (1945–51).

MAXWELL, MICHAEL: Dronkers' defence counsel.

SOMERVELL, SIR DONALD BRADLEY, OBE, PC, KC (1889–1960): Attorney-General, 1936–45. Later Baron Somervell of Harrow.

WATSON, SIR BERTRAM: Chief Magistrate, Bow Street Magistrates' Court.

WROTTESLEY, THE HON. MR JUSTICE FREDERIC JOHN (1880–1948): Judge hearing the Dronkers case. Later a Lord Justice of the Court of Appeal and Chairman of the Quarter Sessions for the County of Stafford, 1939–48.

Other officials

BRISCOE, HENRY VINCENT AIRD (1888–1973): Professor of Inorganic Chemistry, Imperial College of Science & Technology, London (1938–54). Undergraduate in the Department of Chemistry (1906–09). Carried out research into arsine; purification of boron; the chemistry of thorium; phosgene gas, etc. Analysed secret inks for MI5 during First and Second World Wars.

COOPER, ALFRED DUFF (1890–1954): GCMG, DSO, PC; 1st Viscount Norwich. Minister of Information (1940–41); Chancellor of the Duchy of Lancaster (1941–43); Chairman of the Home Defence (Security) Committee (1941–45).

GEDGE, H. N.: Deputy Under-Sheriff for the County of London, who attended Dronkers' execution.

GREW, MAJOR B. D.: Governor, HM Wandsworth Prison.

GRIFFITHS, GEORGE: Press Dept., Home Office.

HEDGER, REGINALD ERNEST, BSc: Fellow of the Institute of Chemistry; attached to MI5.

LANDERS, JOHN JOSEPH, OBE, MB, BCh, DPH: Medical officer at HM Wandsworth Prison. Also later served as Medical Officer at Dartmoor and Parkhurst prisons. Awarded OBE in 1952 Birthday Honours.

LEE, MRS K. G.: Home Office, Aliens Department. Possibly formerly of MI5 G Branch (June 1917).

MORRISON, HERBERT, CH, PC (1888–1965): Home Secretary, 1940–45.

NEWSAM, (SIR) FRANK AUBREY, GCB, KBE, CVO, MC (1893–1964): Deputy Under-Secretary of State, Home Office.

PEAKE, OSBERT (1897–1966): Under-Secretary of State for the Home Office (1939–44); later Viscount Ingleby.

PIERREPOINT, ALBERT (1905–92): Public hangman.

PURSER, CHARLES RICHARD, OBE (d. 1959): Superintendent, HM Customs Service.

SALZEDO, SAMUEL LOPEZ: Translator and interpreter.

SMITH, REGINALD CHARLES: Preventive Officer, HM Customs & Excise Waterguard, also acting as Immigration officer, port of Harwich.

SWINTON, LORD, GBE, CH, MC, PC (1884–1972): Philip Cunliffe-Lister; Chairman of the Home Defence (Security) Executive.

THOMSON, REAR ADMIRAL GORDON PIRIE (1887–1965): Chief Press Censor, 1940–45, Ministry of Information.

THURSTON, ARTHUR M.: First FBI Legal Attaché, US Embassy, London (Nov. 1942 – 45).

WADE, STEVEN (1887–1956): Assistant to Albert Pierrepoint.

The Role of the Intelligence Services

MI5, being responsible for domestic security, would play the lead role in investigating Dronkers' claims. The official files which they compiled on him contain a plethora of names, sections, and an alphabet soup of acronyms which may require some explanation, as do the roles and responsibilities which they performed. Therefore, for the benefit of the reader, some brief explanation is offered of who did what, based on John Curry's official history of MI5 and other sources.

The Security Service, better known as MI5, had been created in October 1909 as MO5, part of the Special Intelligence Bureau or Secret Intelligence Bureau. During the First World War it fell under the Directorate of Military Intelligence (DMI). Its mandate was to curb what was thought to be an impending threat from the Germans, a scare often attributed to authors such as William Le Queux, in *Spies of the Kaiser*, and Erskine Childers' *The Riddle of the Sands*, both published in 1909. It started out as a small operation working in conjunction with its counterpart, known then as MI1c, later to become known as MI6, or the Secret Intelligence Service (SIS) under Captain Mansfield Smith Cumming of the Royal Navy.

From its inception MI5's Director had been Major General Sir Vernon Kell, late of the South Staffordshire Regiment. Kell was sacked on 10 June 1940 by Prime Minister Winston Churchill, replacing him temporarily with Brigadier Oswald Allen 'Jasper' Harker, followed in 1941 by Sir David Petrie, formerly head of the Delhi Intelligence Bureau, with Harker agreeing to stay on as Deputy Director-General. On the same day that Kell was sacked Eric B. Holt-Wilson, the former Deputy Director-General, resigned.

During the First World War MI5 had been extremely active against foreign, mainly German, spies but also those within the United Kingdom, and achieved many successful convictions, executions and deportations as a result of Defence Regulations then in place. After the First World War its staff was cut back from 544 at the Armistice in 1918 to 151 in 1920.[1] It also underwent several major reorganisations as well as attempts by the government for it to be subsumed by MI6. It was to 'B' Division (sometimes referred to as 'B' Branch) that the investigations of Dronkers largely fell, primarily B1b and B1e (Latchmere House, also known as Camp 020, where he was later interned); sections of 'D' (D4) and 'E' (E1a; E1b) also occasionally feature in the official documents. Counter-espionage had been the responsibility of 'F' Branch (Preventive intelligence) and 'G' Branch (Investigations) in 1916. In 1931 'B' Branch became responsible for Defence security intelligence, Communism in Great Britain, Russian espionage, and Comintern secret agents. It was not until 1941 that the new 'B' Branch was formally charged with counter-espionage. This reorganisation came about as a result of proposals made by Lord Swinton, Lord President of the Council. On 22 April 1941, the title of Director was upgraded to Director-General, with Directors being appointed to 'A', 'B', 'C' and 'D' Divisions, with some sections of 'B' being placed under the control of a Deputy Director 'E' Division or 'F' Division.

'B' Division

In charge of 'B' Division, as its Director (DB), was Captain Guy Liddell, who had won the Military Cross (MC) during the First World War while serving in the Royal Field Artillery (RFA). His diaries would later become an important unofficial record of MI5's wartime activities. His deputy, as Assistant Director, (ADB1) was Dick Goldsmith White, later to become Deputy Director (DDB), who also ran B1 (Espionage). Other principal sections of 'B' were B2 (Agents), run by Major Maxwell Knight (ADB2); B3 (Communications), run by Major Frost (ADB3); and B4 (Espionage, Country Section), run by Major Dick Brooman-White. B5 (Investigations) was under Superintendent Leonard Burt, seconded from Scotland Yard; B6 (Watchers) and the Press Section, under Captain Derek Tangye, all came under the direct control of the Director (DB).

Further broken down into its subsections, Major Thomas Argyll 'Tar' Robertson was in charge of B1a (Special Agents), responsible for running double agents 'turned' as part of the Double Cross system; B1b, run by Herbert Hart, was responsible for Espionage, Special Sources; B1c Sabotage and Espionage, Inventions and Technical, was run by Victor, Lord Rothschild, and assisted by Tess Mayor, later to become his wife; B1d was Special Examiners under Major Seymour Bingham; B1e was Latchmere House, otherwise known as Camp 020, under the formidable Lieutenant Colonel Robin 'Tin-Eye' Stephens, because of the monocle he always wore in his right eye. The work of B1f, B1g and B1h are not important to this case; B3d was Censorship Liaison.

As part of its remit, B1b handled 'Most Secret Sources' or ISOS transcripts. John 'Jack' Curry's official history of MI5 commissioned after the war outlines the work of the principal sections of B1:

1. The study of ISOS or the intercepted wireless system of the Abwehr and the Sipo und SD (B1B);
2. The examination of persons (including refugees from enemy-occupied Europe, whether arriving by regular means, by sea or by air, or by an 'escape' boat or 'escape' plane) by the SCOs at the ports working under the direction of ADD4;
3. The interrogation at the LRC of British and alien subjects and all persons arriving from enemy-occupied territory or neutral countries otherwise than on fully authenticated business (B1D);
4. The interrogation of suspected known spies at Camp 020 (in close association with B1B);
5. The investigation of cases of enemy sabotage (B1C);
6. The employment of captured enemy agents who had been "turned round" with a view to using them to supply the enemy with false information or to carry through deception plans (B1A).[2]

B Division, Espionage, as of July 1941

Under control of Director B (DB):

B5 (Investigation Staff): Superintendent Len Burt
B6 (Watchers): Harry Hunter
PS (Press Section): Capt. Derek Tangye

B1 (Espionage): Asst Dir. (ADB1): Dick Goldsmith White
B1a (Special Agents): Maj. T. A. Robertson
B1b (Espionage, Special Sources): H. L. A. Hart
B1c (Sabotage & Espionage, Inventions & Technical): Lord Rothschild
B1d (Special Examiners): Ronald Haylor
B1e (Latchmere House) (Camp 020): Lt-Col. R. W. Stephens
B1f (Japanese Espionage)
B1g (Spanish, Portuguese, S. American Espionage): Dick Brooman White
B1h (Ireland): Cecil Liddell

B2 (Agents): Asst Dir. (ADB2): Maj. Maxwell Knight
B3 (Communications); Asst Dir. (ADB3): Maj. Malcolm Frost
B3a (Censorship): Roland Bird
B3b (Illicit Wireless Investigations); RSS Liaison: R. L. Hughes
B3c (Lights and Pigeons): Fl. Lt. Walker
B3d (Liaison with Censorship): Alan Grogan
B3e (Signal Security): Col. Sclater
B4 (Espionage, Country Section): Maj. White, officer-in-charge (OIC)
B4a (Suspected cases of espionage by individuals domiciled in UK; espionage in British possessions abroad): Maj. Jock White

'D' Division

The Director of 'D' Division was Brigadier Allen, with Lieutenant Colonel Norman as his deputy. D4, Security Control at Sea and Airports, was run by Lieutenant Colonel John Adam (ADD4) whose Security Control Officers (SCO) stationed at ports and airports reported to him.

The need to control travel had first been established during the First World War as a preventive measure for counter-espionage, and it was Adam who had worked out the plans before the Second World War as a result of work carried out by the War Emergency Legislation Committee. Their aim was to control the entry to and exit from the United Kingdom under the Aliens' Order 1920, as amended from the Aliens Restriction Act of 1919, by preventing travel except through an 'approved port' (in all, twenty-three including airports, some accounts say twenty-seven). All docks and airports were declared protected places by Leslie Hore-Belisha, the Secretary of State for War, shortly after war was declared in 1939.

D4 and its Security Control Officers worked to prevent the illicit entry or departure of enemy agents or known suspects, who may have passed unnoticed to 'B' Division. D4 referred them through Immigration Officers to the London Reception Centre (LRC) at the Royal Victoria Patriotic School (RVPS), as well as supplying intelligence to other divisions of MI5 when required.[3] The work of D4 and the SCOs they were responsible for was:

a. Documentary control of travel into the United Kingdom;
b. Documentary control of travel out of the United Kingdom;

c. Control of travel through the military Permit Office;

d. Physical control of travel at ports;

e. Censorship;

f. Security of military embarkations and operations;

g. Security of shipping;

h. Collection of intelligence;

i. Liaison with Government Departments and Allied Services;

j. Maintenance and distribution of a Black List of suspects for use at ports in this country and aboard.[4]

'E' Division

'E' Division, created in 1941 and run by Major the Hon. Kenneth Younger (later run by Captain Septimus Paul Brooke-Booth as ADE from April 1943), was responsible for 'alien control' and internment. E1a, Nationals of Western Europe, was responsible for French, Belgians, Czechs, Dutch, and Scandinavians and run by Peter Ramsbotham (later ran the USA section as E1a). E1b was responsible for seamen, run in 1943 by Christopher Robert Cheney.

Legal Section

The Legal Section, under Henry 'Toby' Pilcher (SLA), as part of the Secretariat and reporting to the Director-General, handled decisions to bring formal charges of espionage, treason or treachery against captured spies. The half-German Colonel Edward Hinchley-Cooke (as SLB), an old hand who had joined MI5 in 1914, would give evidence at several spy trials as MI5's public spokesperson.

On 27 August 1939 MI5 moved out of its Millbank address at Thames House, London (where its present refurbished headquarters are located), and operated from Wormwood Scrubs prison in west London. First to move in was 'A' Division's Registry; some personnel (such as Colonel Adam's D4) moved to Blenheim Palace, Churchill's birthplace in Oxfordshire, in October 1940, while others were located at Keble College, Oxford. However, later in the war MI5 relocated back to London to 57–58, St James's Street, which is found in many of the documents in the files, including 'Box 500' as part of the address. Today, within the British intelligence community MI5 is still sometimes referred to as 'Box' as a result of this.

Intelligence Corps

The Intelligence Corps had been re-established in 1940, having been disbanded after the First World War. Within it, the Field Security Wing had numerous Field Security Sections stationed around the country and abroad, such as 123 FSS based at Harwich:[5]

It is thought that all section personnel were recruited locally by Captain Rex De Vries, who was the first SCO Harwich. The section's first HQ was in the 'Elco' Restaurant on the Marine Parade in Harwich. In 1940, the HQ suffered bomb damage and moved, firstly to 'Fairhaven', also on the Marine Parade, and later to 'Horley', a large house on Crane Hill in Ipswich. The section initially covered the coastal area from Southend up to Norfolk, but in early June 1940, elements of 123 FSS moved to Yarmouth and formed 138 FSS (HPSS) which then took over the northern part of what had been 123 FSS's area, covering Lowestoft and Kings Lynn.

In 1940 [*sic*], two NCOS were on duty at Harwich when three men were brought ashore, two Dutchman and one Javanese, who had been picked up by the Royal Navy. The NCOs decided that one of the Dutchmen, Jan Dronkers, seemed very suspicious and all three were taken to London for a detailed interrogation. Here, Dronkers, admitted that he was a German agent and he was tried at the Old Bailey for espionage, found guilty and hanged.

The Royal Navy maintained a large presence in Harwich. This included the MTB base at Felixstowe, and the SCO worked closely with the Senior Naval Officer, Harwich. During the course of the war, detachments were set up in a number of locations, Harwich, Ipswich, Woolverston (for the D-Day LCT trials), Rivenhall, Maldon, Brightlingsea, Aldeburgh, Burnham on Crouch and Rowhedge. In January 1945, 123 FSS probably became part of the Port and Travel Group. However, the Section is believed to have disbanded by the middle of 1946, and some members were posted to 138 FSS. In 1946 the section was known as the Eastern Command Field and Port Security Section, with the role to check the paperwork of all service personnel passing through the port. [6]

Other organisations

To a lesser extent, the Special Operations Executive (SOE) and the Secret Intelligence Service (MI6) are mentioned in the files, but their involvement seems to have been minimal. There was also an exchange of information with Dutch Intelligence (CID).

For the most part, co-operation between the intelligence services was fairly amicable; however, there were times when it would appear that MI6 was being somewhat obtuse when it came to exchanging information. There was also some mistrust by British Intelligence of the Dutch intelligence service, most likely due to the *Englandspiel* perpetrated by the Germans, with the capture of British and Dutch agents sent into Holland. However, *Englandspiel* does not appear to have had a direct bearing on the case of Dronkers. MI5 also liaised with the FBI's Legal Attaché at the US embassy, although, as we shall see, this was not always an agreeable arrangement.

Dronkers' Instructions on How to Use Secret Ink[1]

For writing, I was to take an ordinary quarto sheet of non-glazed paper. On one side of this sheet I was to write an ordinary innocent letter and I was to finish off this innocent letter with a few lines at the top of the back of the sheet.

The real message I was to write on the remainder of the back of the sheet with invisible ink. To get this ink, I was to take some alcoholic beverage such as Gin, but not containing sugar, say half an eggcupful. Into this I was to put one tablet of [redacted] after having scratched off the sugar coating. I was to buy the [redacted] in England. I had to pulverise the [redacted] and then dissolve the powder in the alcoholic solution.

I then had to take a little sliver of wood such as a toothpick, with a very sharp point. Put some cotton wool round the tip for protection against scratching. Dip this in the solution and write. I had to write my message in block letters. I had to let it dry for at least half an hour.

Once it had dried in, I had to pull the whole sheet through a bath of the same kind of alcoholic solution, such as Gin, in which a little Soda had been dissolved.

Then I had to put the sheet between two sheets of blotting paper and put a glass plate on top. I had to do this twice to demonstrate that I had everything right and I did it to his satisfaction.

As John Day was to add in a note on 27 June to H. L. Stephens, the scientific officer from the GPO, attached to A6 at MI5,

He adds that he was to buy the [redacted] in England ... Despite his statement that he was to have purchased his ink here in England it is none the less felt that there may be among his property some second substance useful for secret writing.

Day's report to Stimson at Camp 020 on 14 July explains the results of the Scientific Section's analysis of other substances found in Dronkers' possession:

1) The material in the powders is sodium calcium lactate, known to be used in medicine. It does not make a satisfactory secret ink.

2) Block of alum. This seems to come up every time. It can be used for a crude-secret ink to be developed by heat. Though I call it crude, unless a heat test was applied it might not be found. Apparently both we and the Germans hesitate to mark papers by charring when testing for secret ink. It is rather a drastic test.

The remainder of the material is genuine, innocuous and of no interest in secret writing.

Author's note: I was curious to know what the substance might have been which the censor had redacted from the text. Dronkers had been told to remove the sugar coating first. That meant it was probably some sort of pharmaceutical product, since most pills are sugar-coated to make them more palatable. In the inventory of Dronkers' possessions I found what I thought I was looking for: Carter's Little Liver Pills, an over-the-counter laxative which contained bisacodyl, now sold as Dukolax or Durolax. An old recipe from 1890[2] revealed that the pills contained:

Podophyllin 1½ grs (grains)
Aloes, Socotrine 3½ grs
Mucilage of acacia q.s. (*quantum satis* or *quantum sufficit* – the amount which is needed)

The instructions called for these to be mixed together, divided into twelve pills and coated with sugar. Further investigation when I consulted a pharmacist friend confirmed my suspicions:

The 1940s formulation contained Phenolphthalein (long since removed from the product – it was nasty stuff) which has the property of being an indicator. So dissolved it should produce a colourless solution which could have been used as an ink. Exposure subsequently to a weak acid – such as lemon juice – would then produce a red colour which could be seen.[3]

Phenolphthalein:
Chemical formula: $C_{20}H_{14}O_4$.
Uses:
As an indicator in acid-based titrations and as a universal indicator, along with methyl red, bromothymol blue and thymol blue;
As a laxative, but is no longer added because it is considered carcinogenic;
In toys as a component of 'disappearing inks', and a disappearing dye in Barbie dolls' hair.
Properties: It is only slightly soluble in water and best dissolved in alcohol (hence the gin). In secret ink it is dissolved in sodium hydroxide (hence the use of soda water) or ammonium hydroxide[4], which reacts with carbon dioxide in the air to produce a range of orange to fuschia (pink) depending on the pH (acidity or alkalinity):
OH^- (aq) + CO_2 (g) CO_3^{2-} (aq) + H^+ (g)   (aq = aqueous solution; g = gas)
pH <8.2 (acidic) = colourless; pH 10.0 - 13.0 (highly alkaline or basic) = fuschia; neutral is pH 7.0.
Soda water has the chemical formula of H_2O + CO_2 <-> H_2CO_3 (carbonic acid, pH 5.5 – 5.6, a weak acid)
A seemingly innocuous inventory, but when connected with a recipe, it was possible to join the dots. Therefore, Dronkers would have taken one of the

Carter's Little Liver Pills and scraped off the sugar coating first. The alcohol in the gin would have rendered the ink colourless; the soda water as the developer, which is essentially carbonic acid, would have produced the pink colour. *QED*

NOTE: A recipe for invisible ink, using Ex-Lax, another laxative, is included in 'Appendix III, Secret Inks', in MI5 file KV3/413 *German Saboteurs Landed in the USA from U-Boats in boats in 1942 – Report of operation.* The page concerned has been redacted to remove some of the ingredients.[5] The recipe given to Dronkers varies from the one given to Grobben in which ½ pint of pure alcohol (whisky or gin can be substituted) is used to dissolve a quinine pill once the sugar has been removed (the instructions recommend sucking it off). Quinine glows under ultraviolet light. It seems a lot to expect anyone to legally obtain pure alcohol; even using ½ pint of whisky or gin would mean obtaining a whole bottle. Matchsticks removed from the Erasmus brothers also reveal the presence of quinine.

APPENDIX 4

Abwehr Structure:
Ast Hamburg Spring 1939

GENERALKOMMANDO X. ARMEEKORPS (10th Army Corps)
I c/A.O. Hauptmann i. Hans G. Crome (Abwehrstelle im Wehrkreis X)

Gruppe I: Espionage
Leiter I: Korvettenkapitän Wichmann
I H (Heer/Army): Hauptmann Lips
Angest. Moll Angest. = Angestellter (Civil Servant)
I M (Marine): Korvettenkapitän von Wettstein
Kapitänleutnant A.R. Mueller
Angest. Hilmar Dierks Angest. = Angestellter (Civil Servant)
I L (Luftwaffe): Major Nicholas Ritter
Obertleutnant Schaarschmidt
I Wi (Wirtshaft/Economy): Hauptmann Dr. Friederich Karl Praetorius
Ii (Communications): Hauptmann Werner Max Trautmann

Gruppe II: Sabotage
Leiter II: Korvettenkapitän Schneiderwind (only from about 1939–40)

Gruppe III: Counterespionage
Leiter III: Major Dr. Dischler
III H: Hauptmann Dr. Hainrich
III L: Major von Sommerfeld
III M: unknown
III C: Hauptmann Dr. Eucker
III F: Oberleutnant Adolf von Feldmann
Kapitänleutnant Freund?
III C2: Hauptmann Giskes
III Wi: Korvettenkapitän Liebenscheutz
Korvettenkapitän Haun? With AO III

Hamburg: Korvettenkapitän Bracht
Bremen: Korvettenkapitän Wolfram
Kiel: Korvettenkapitän Rogalla von Bieberstein
Nest Bremen: Leiter: Kapitänleutnant Dr Pfeiffer
Kapitänleutnant Bendixen

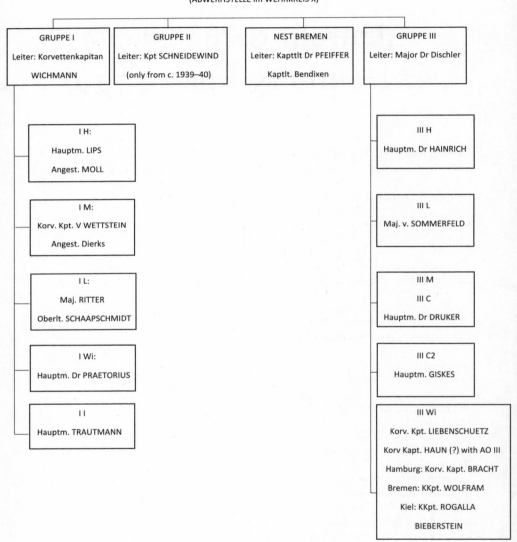

German Ranks Mentioned in the Text

Germany Navy (Kriegsmarine)	Royal Navy
Kapitän zur See	Captain
Freegattenkapitän	Commander
Korvettenkapitän	Lieutenant Commander
Kapitänleutnant	Lieutenant
Oberleutnant zur See	Lieutenant (Junior Grade)/Sub Lieutenant
Leutenant zur See	Ensign/Acting Sub Lieutenant
Oberfähnrich zur See	Midshipman (Senior Grade)
Fähnrich zur See	Cadet/Midshipman (Junior Grade)
Oberfeldwebel/Oberbootsman	Chief Petty Officer
Heer (Army)	**British Army or British equivalent**
Oberst	Colonel
Major	Major
Hauptmann	Captain
Oberleutnant	Senior Lieutenant/1st Lieutenant
Sonderführer	Specialist Leader
SS Schutzstaffeln	
Gruppenführer	Major General
Obersturmbannführer	Lieutenant Colonel
Sturmbannführer	Major
Other	
Leiter	Leader
Angestellter	Civil Servant

APPENDIX 6

Definitions of a Spy

The *Encyclopedia Britannica*, 1771:

> A person hired to watch the actions, motions, etc. of another; particularly of what passes in a camp. When a spy is discovered, he is hanged immediately.[1]

The Hague Convention 1899:

> An individual can only be considered a spy if, acting clandestinely or on false pretenses, he obtains, or seeks to obtain, information in the zone of operations of a belligerent with the intention of communicating it to a hostile party.[2]

The *Hague Convention 1907*:

> CHAPTER II
> Spies
> Art. 29. A person can only be considered a spy when, acting clandestinely or on false pretenses, he obtains or endeavours to obtain information in the zone of operations of a belligerent, with the intention of communicating it to the hostile party. Thus, soldiers not wearing a disguise who have penetrated into the zone of operations of the hostile army, for the purpose of obtaining information, are not considered spies. Similarly, the following are not considered spies: Soldiers and civilians, carrying out their mission openly, entrusted with the delivery of despatches intended either for their own army or for the enemy's army. To this class belong likewise persons sent in balloons for the purpose of carrying despatches and, generally, of maintaining communications between the different parts of an army or a territory.[3]

MI5's official website:

> Espionage (or spying) concerns those who intend to help an enemy and deliberately harm the security of the nation. The Official Secrets Acts of 1911 and 1920 still provide the main legal protection in the UK against espionage. Official information is further protected by the Official Secrets Act 1989 [*This latter is obviously not applicable in the Dronkers case*].

First page of the Official Secrets Act 1911
Under the 1911 Act, a person commits the offence of 'spying' if he, for any purpose prejudicial to the safety or interests of the State:

(a) approaches, inspects, passes over or is in the neighbourhood of, or enters any prohibited place,
(b) makes any sketch, plan, model, or note which is calculated to be or might be or is intended to be directly or indirectly useful to an enemy; or
(c) obtains, collects, records, or publishes, or communicates to any other person any secret official code word, or pass word, or any sketch, plan, model, article, or note, or other document which is calculated to be or might be or is intended to be directly or indirectly useful to an enemy.

The 1920 Act creates further offences of doing any "act preparatory" to spying, or of soliciting, inciting, seeking to persuade, or aiding and abetting any other person to commit spying.[4]

Other definitions:

1. a person employed by a government to obtain secret information or intelligence about another, usually hostile, country, especially with reference to military or naval affairs.
2. a person who keeps close and secret watch on the actions and words of another or others.
3. a person who seeks to obtain confidential information about the activities, plans, methods, etc., of an organisation or person, especially one who is employed for this purpose by a competitor: an industrial spy.[5]

Inventory from *Joppe* and Dronkers' Personal Possessions

3 Coils wire
3 Funnels?
1 canvas cover
1 Electric lamp holder
1 pr. Socks
1 Boiling tin
1 Electric Lead
1 Winch handle
2 Light shade boards
1 Seat cushion
1 Water canister
1 Electric bulb
1 Esso pennant
2 Tea cups
1 Egg cup
1 Salt pourer
1 Fork
1 Tea spoon
1 Table spoon
1 Water bottle
1 Strap
2 Stretchin[g] screws
4 Shackles
1 Table knife
1 Nail brush
1 tablet soap
1 Bottle
1 Electric light with lead
1 Swab
1 Compass with lid. No. M.478

1 Mirror fixed on door
1 Galvanised bucket
1 Water bottle in wicker basket
1 Mop
1 Hand brush
2 6-volt batteries
1 Life belt
1 Starting handle
1 Anchor and chain
1 Boat hook
1 Tiller handle
1 Main sail
1 Fore sail
1 Dish pan
1 4-fold rule
1 rotary pump - fixed
1 Fiat engine – fixed

Property for examination and return
[NOTE: Items highlighted in bold removed for examination; items highlighted in *italics* tested to destruction. A second document bears the hand-written note: 'Received the above 29.6.42. H.L. Smith.']
Sandbag, marked Dronkers 4A containing:
1 Jar Shaving Cream
1 Tube Tooth Paste
1 Pkt. Containing 9 Powders
3 Pieces Washing Soap
1 Tablet Toilet Soap
1 Piece (?) Alum, in soap Box
1 Bottle Ink
1 Shaving Brush
1 Tube Face Cream (practically empty)
1 Pkt. Carters Little Liver Pills
1 Bottle   -do-   -do-
1 Bottle
1 Fountain Pen
2 Lead Pencils
1 Tube Cream
1 Bottle Vick Vaporus (practically empty)
1 Cigarette Lighter
1 Safety Razor, in lined case
1 pr, Leather Sandals
1 Mouth Organ
1 Hank Rope
1 Tin Shoe Polish
1 Tooth Brush
1 Piece Pink Paper
2 Pieces paper, with cotton round them
1 Small card Darning Wool
1 Small Leather Wallet (lined)
1 Gold watch (inside above wallet)
1 Larger Leather Wallet (lined)

1 Pkt. 8 Winchester Cigarettes
1 Cigarette rolling apparatus, containing 1 pkt. Cig. Papers
1 *Hat Brush*
1 Pencil case, containing piece of lead pencil
1 Key Ring, holding 2 keys
1 Tin Box Tobacco
5 Cigarettes in envelope
1/4 Camp 020:
MB
24.6.42

Items received from John Day, B1b to D. Sinclair   5.12.42
1 comb
1 snapshot
1 pot crème de Savon
5 handkerchiefs
1 shirt
1 pr. woolen pants

Items from Camp 020 to Insp. Bridges, Scotland Yard,
Special Branch   3rd November 1942
8/2d (eight shillings and twopence)
3 10-Guilder Notes (Dutch)
1 2.5-Guilder Notes (Dutch)
3 1-Guilder Notes (Dutch)
1 Silver Cigarette Case
3 Foreign Stamps (Aden)
1 Fountain Pen
2 Gold Rings (one minus stone)
Envelope containing
Photographs
Personal papers
Clothing contained in Gladstone Bag

A document dated 16 June 1942 when Dronkers arrived at Camp 020 from
Camp 001 also lists as being in the Gladstone bag the following items:

9 Handkerchiefs
1 pr. Woolen Stockings
1 Shoe Cleaning Duster
1 Dressing Comb
1 Tooth Comb
1 Shoe Horn
1 Box Matches
3 Collars
1 Cigar Box containing:
2 Hanks brown wool
3 Reels Cotton
2 Pkts. Needles
1 Thimble
1Pr. Scissors
Odd Buttons
1 Small Tin Box containing:

1 Reel Cotton
1 Tin box containing buttons and pins
1 Coat Hook
Miscellaneous buttons, studs, nail file
1 Pencil sharpener
1 Tea Caddy containing:
3 Cards Darning Cotton
2 Penknives
3 Clothes Pegs
1 pr. Scissors
1 Piece Eraser
1 Leather Purse (unlined) containing 2 Keys and pr. Tweezers
1 Suit Pyjamas (Mark: C. Busch der Hague)
1 pr. Shorts (Mark: Novana)
1 Flannel Shirt
1 Collar (Mark: Gerzon)
2 Collars (Mark: Trubenijs)
1 Made-up Tie
1 Silk Tie (Mark: Tootal Ties)
1 Unlined Leather Wallet
1 Pocket Comb, in unlined case
1 Pocket Mirror
1 pr. Folding Scissors
1 Metal Nail File
2 Pocket Knives
1 pkt. Razor Blades
1 Amber Cigarette Holder
1 Sponge
1 Box Swan Matches
1 Pr. Shoe Socks
1 Pr. Blue Socks
1 Pr. Suspenders
1 Pr. Glasses, in case

as well as

1 pr Black Leather Shoes containing pair heel protectors
8 Razor Blades

The sandbag marked "Dronkers II" contained:

1 Flannel Shirt
1 cotton Shirt (Mark: Holland)
2 prs. Woollen socks
2 Woollen Vests
1 pr. " Pants
1 Sleevless woollen Pullover
1 Waterproof

The sandbag marked "Dronkers III" contained:

1 Blue Suit (jacket, waistcoat, trousers)
1 pr. Braces

On 30 December 1942 Dronkers compiled a list of his belongings which he expected to be forwarded to his wife, mentioning that his suitcase (Gladstone bag?) had gone missing between Bow Street Court and Brixton Prison. He lists the fountain pen as a Waterman.

NOTE: Nowhere in any of the inventories are any navigational aids listed, such as maps and charts, only a compass; nor any food.

<u>Property belonging to de Langen</u>   18th June 1942
1 Identity Card V38 002414
1 Tram Season Ticket No.30358
1 Covering tram card No.23985
1 Travel Permit, dated 30.3.1942
1 Piece of paper with times of trains etc.
1 small note pad
Envelope containing 7 photographs

APPENDIX 8

Mulder's Organisation

NOTE: Unfortunately, some of the documents in Mulder's file (KV2/47) containing information about his so-called organisation and other individuals have been obscured by being laminated between tissue as a result of conservation treatment, thus obscuring parts of the text. Consequently, some information is illegible. Mulder is referred to as 'the Source' in the documents.

According to Mulder while at the RVPS the *Vrij Nederland* organisation's only activity was 'the gathering of information as well as the collecting of arms and the distribution of the anti-German propaganda paper'. The only one of Mulder's organisation known to him was:

KLATT, Henk ex-Army officer now working in one of the distribution offices at The Hague, living at Snelliusstraat The Hague; tall; heavy build; dark brown hair; dark [comp]lexion; dark brown eyes; about 27 years of age. 'Source knows that this man was in direct contact with [*illegible*] by radio.'

The De Geuzen Organisation, an amateur resistance group set up by Bernard IJzerdraat in May 1940, had only two members known to him:

VAN [*illegible*]
VAN BLENKOM
... it is said that both the above-mentioned considered the traitor Hugo de [Bap?] who betrayed the De Geuzen Organisation (see report KEN/68
    NAUTA, Felix Ruurd Dutch, born 21.11.1917, Bandoeng, Dutch East Indies; student in aeronautical engineering; address: Kievitalaan 23, Wassenaar.)
    Source's [own?] Organisation generally was to provide people with a means of escape and preparing for armed resistance to the British in the event of of an invasion of Britain and her Allies.
    Two brothers KAYA of the Dutch East Indies. Both living in [*illegible*] straat 166 The Hague. (a) 25 years of age; small; normal build; dark brown eyes; black hair; dark complexion; (b) 21 years of age; normal build and height; grey eyes; black hair; dark complexion.
    Boy B[RUINING] Indian ex-Army officer; now clerk in one of the traffic departments in The Hague, about 24 years of age; short; strong build; dark

hair; dark brown eyes; dark complexion; address: living in a side street off Laan van Meerdervoort following the Goudenregenstraat, no.155.

Leecky VAN LEER Dutch Indian; ex-2nd Lieutenant, Dutch army; unemployed; about 24 years of age; normal build; normal height; dark brown hair; dark brown eyes; dark complexion; address: unknown.

Nono LAPRE Dutch Indian; originally a student of economics; now working in one of the distribution offices in The Hague; about 23 years of age; short; strong build; very dark complexion; dark brown eyes; wears glasses; lives at Goudenregenstraat, no.155. Has a friend at Roosendaal who has information of the whereabouts of a secret store of weapons. Lapre lives at 155, Goudenregenstraat.

Commander NORTH Dutch; ex-Commander, Dutch navy and formerly Dutch military attaché (unknown where), now employed in a bank; can be reached at the café "Brestagi"; aged about 40; small; slim; brown eyes; brown/black hair; dark complexion; wears glasses.

Dr. A. DE WEERT Dutch; living in village of Zundert near the Belgian border; medical doctor; about 55 years of age; 173 cm tall, thin; grey hair; grey eyes. Endeavouring to form sub-organisation in south Holland.

JANSEN Dutch; Customs official in village of Wernhout; about 24 years of age; 172 cm tall; strong build; brown hair; grey eyes.

There are several two more of his collea[gues] both Customs officials who have as[sisted?] Source on his escape to Belgium; the [...] however, are unknown.

Jacques VAN RYS (or RIJS) Dutch Jew. Address: Scheldestraat 32, The Hague. Formerly steward aboard an American liner; now in the forwarding agent's firm of his brother; about 24 years of age; 168 cm tall; normal build; black hair; dark brown eyes.

This man was instructed to form a secret organisation, and eventually, in the event of an invasion by the British and her Allies to cover vital points near the H.S.S. Station [in] The Hague.

Raden SADELL Dutch East Indian; ex-Army officer; now clerk in the office of a gas works company at The Hague. His parents live at Mrs Stumpff [*address illegible*] The Hague; about 24 years of age; 172 cm tall; thin; black hair; dark brown eyes.

Abdul RACHMAN(?) Dutch Indian; ex-Army officer; family living at Sweelinkstraat 11, The Hague; now hidden somewhere in Amsterdam; about 22 years of age; 172 cm tall; heavy build; black hair; dark brown eyes.

Jan LE HEUX Army officer; living c/o Susanna Hennie (girlfriend of source); address 84, Van der Aastraat, The Hague; about 27 years of age; 173 cm tall; normal build; light blond hair; blue eyes; his parents live at [*illegible*]; at Waalsdorp there are still some stables, and 100 soldiers under a captain and a lieutenant (Le Heux) have taken over some of the stables and horses. He was to organise these men and to carry out sabotage and fight against the Germans in the event of an invasion from the British side.

MEEUWSEN One of the directors of the café "Brastagi", living above it. Also owns a broker's shop at the same address, Kneuterdijk 6, The Hague. Very tall; heavy build; fair hair; blue eyes.

KUCHLIN Dutch. Address: 283 Waalsdorperweg, The Hague; ex-Army officer; unemployed; 36 years of age; very tall; heavy build; corpulent; brown hair; light brown eyes. Has 100 grenades and 2 machine guns, but a limited quantity of ammunition. Is also trying to form a sub-organisation.

Organisation address: The address which could be used for this organisation was that of Van Meerwijk, No.4, Lepelstraat, 's Hertogenbosch. (fiancée of Source)

Mr NAVIS Dutch. Ex-Army officer. Living at The Hague, address unknown; about 25 years of age; tall; strong build; dark brown hair and eyes. This man is probably one of the officers shot by the Germans.

APPENDIX 9

Intelligence Obtained from Mulder

RVPS 21/21.5.1942
Pass: With regard to the pass received from Verkuyl mentioned in the report, Source [Mulder] thinks that Dronkers bought it from a maré-Chaussée [sic]. The pass, Source understands, was used by someone else, who was merchant, and travelled in the protected area, and, upon finishing his business, had to hand the pass in again. Apparently the maré-Chaussée sold the pass and gave it to Dronkers or Verkuyl. Source understands that both Dronkers and Verkuyl are working for a secret organisation. The telephone number is known to Source, 77541 The Hague.

Arrests in Holland: By the time that Source left Holland 2200 ex officers were arrested by the Germans, and put into prison at Scheveningen and Amersfoort. Further were arrested about 466 prominent Dutchmen, such as priests, Burger masters, etc. who were put into camps near the villages of [illegible] and [illegible]. Among the officers, who have been shot lately are known to Source,
2nd Lieutenant [illegible]
Cadet sergeant [illegible]
Journalist and reserve lieutenant DE BEAUPORT
2nd Lieutenant [illegible]
and probably also NAVIS mentioned in secret or orgnaisation list.

Distribution of arms: Source reports that explosives and fire arms are secretly distributed. It is not known by Mulder, however, who are in possession of arms,etc. and where these come from.

The Police: The police, according to Source at The Hague, cannot be trusted, as many NSB members have been drawn into the Police Force.

B.B.C.: People listen still to the B.B.C. and punishments such as fines and even death punishment, are given. Other broadcasts listened to are Radio Oranje and Braederie. One does not listen to Radio Oranje so much, however, so the broadcasts are lately said to be of no great interest.

Secret senders: Secret senders known to Source are [*illegible*] which, however, are not heard so much lately, and further Source knows of a Belgian secret broadcast announced as the [*illegible*].

Sabotage: Sabotage known to Source is the cutting of telephone wires and electric cables, the smashing of windows and German cars, and last summer the main telephone line of communications between a place somewhere in Waassenaar and Berlin direct was destroyed.

Parachutists: Source knows that parachutists are dropped by British planes, but does not know where. He understands that these parachutists are agents sent out from England.

Ration cards: People in Holland now-a-days have a stammkaart. Also the [stammkaart] (ration book) valid for one month. A Textilekaart (textile card). On the stammkart is mentioned what sort of cards one receives and what coupons are taken off. For meals in hotels, etc., coupons have to be given.

Identity cards: Source's identity card was never controlled, and he believes that only now and then do the police control this document.

Morale: People in Holland still hate the Germans and hope that an attack from Britain and her Allies will begin very soon. They certainly expect an attack this summer, and source points out to me that, if this does not happen, the population of Holland, in feeling another winter, probably will give in to the Germans, to have at least a little rest, and probably a little more comfort. The sarcastic feeling towards the British and her Allies, certainly after Singapore and the loss of the Dutch East Indies, is growing day by day, and it cannot be sufficiently pointed out here in England that something has to be done this summer.

Propaganda: According to Source, more propaganda should be made by the British in the form of leaflets dropped over towns, and the British should be very careful in broadcasting results of raids on Holland because many times Dutchmen heard from the B.B.C. of how factories, etc. were destroyed and when the Dutch investigated, they found that only minor damage was done. This is wrong propaganda, because people now do not know what to believe, knowing that they cannot belive the Germans. This again gave food for growing concern, which is very profitable for the Germans. The persecution of the Dutch and arrests of ex officers and prominent Dutchmen was a smack in the face of the population. Source reports, however, that, before he left, no reprisals in the form of sabotage, etc. were taken by the Dutch yet, which may be a sign of tiredness. The Dutch are losing their confidence and hope of an attack from the British and her Allies, and in view of the hard fighting of the Russians, one thinks it necessary for the British to attack the Germans in Western Europe in order to relieve the Russians.

Morale of German soldiers: The morale of the German soldiers in Holland is not very high, although, according to instructions from the German High Command to be polite and kind, etc. the situation has lately noticeably improved.

R.A.F. attacks: These have not been too successful.

Restricted areas: Restricted areas known to Source are the whole coast from the Hook of Holland to Den Helder, and over a distance of about 2 kilometres inland, the Zuiderzee Islands as well as some of the province of Zeeland.

Invasion: The Germans seem to expect an invasion from England from the British and her Allies in the north part of Holland. A very nervous feeling is noticeable and there is a rumour that the coast line district till 5 miles inland will be evacuated, and strong holds are set up in some parts on the coast.

Details of interest to the R.A.F. and Military as well as the Naval Departments have been given by Source to the interrogators concerned.

Arrests: Just before they left about 2200 Dutch ex army officers were arrested and imprisoned in Amersfoort and Scheveningen prison. About 460 prominent Dutchmen such as priests, burger masters, etc. were arrested and taken into concentration camps. Reasons for the arrests they thought in Holland were:-

(a) Eventually to be used as hostages.
(b) To prevent these people in the event of an invasion from England siding with the British and Dutch against the Germans.
(c) As reprisals against the mentioned existing secret organisations, which are said mostly to be organised in ex army officials circles.

Source knows of arrest of Domino Van der Bosch and Domino Itterson, both from The Hague.

Gas Attacks: The Germans make propaganda in Holland about the British supplying gas to the Russians for the use against the Germans. At the same time, the Dutch are told that they need not be surprised if the British use gas in the vent of an invasion from England.

Genealogies of Seignette and Dronkers Families

Seignette Family

Generation I
I. Petrus Franciscus Seignette, physician, married to Allegonda Johanna Koene. From this marriage:

1. Benjamin Egbertus Cornelius, born at Heemskerk on 29 December 1857, follows II.

Generation II
II. Benjamin Egbertus Cornelius Seignette (son of Petrus Franciscus Seignette), born at Heemskerk on 29 December 1857, Kandidaat-notaris; died at Haarlem on 19 June 1915; married at Heemskerk on 6 October 1885 to Elisabeth Koorn, born at Alkmaar on 27 December 1860; died at Rotterdam on 29 October 1928. From this marriage:

1. Frans Theodoor Carel, born at Den Helder on 17 August 1886, director of a stage company; married Anna Catharina Hooft.
2. Maria Theodora, born at Den Helder on 10 September 1887; married Frederik Hendrik Schoemaker, born Batavia (Dutch East Indies); age 33; profession: employee PTT possibly in Dutch East Indies.
3. Elise Benjamin Henri, born at Den Helder on 23 January 1889; died at Leiden on 10 March 1951 [male]. Shows up in military registers in 1909.
4. Johan Bernard Gustaaf, born at Den Helder on 14 April 1890, stockbroker; married Catharina Henriëtte Maria Everts.
5. Elise Antoinette Eleonora, born at Den Helder on 26 May 1891; died at Den Helder on 15 February 1892.
6. Elise Antoinette Eleonora, born at Den Helder on 15 January 1893; married at Velsen on 10 June 1926 to Johannes Marinus Dronkers, son of Marinus

Dronkers and Jannetje Moor; born at Nigtevecht on 3 April 1896, clerk in 1926; executed Wandsworth (UK) on 31 December 1942.

7. Eleonora Antoinette Elise, born at Haarlem *c.* 1895; married at Haarlem on 21 September 1920 Gerard Jozeph Marie Moussault.

8. Stillborn son, born at Haarlem on 18 June 1896.

9. Hermine Louise, born at Haarlem *c.* 1898; married at Rotterdam on 26 May 1932 to Cornelis Johannes Klever, office manager, travelling salesman, broker, son of Johannes Klever and Maria van Kats, born at Benschop on 12 September 1894.

10. Herman Anton Frits, born at Haarlem *c.* 1903; died at Haarlem on 12 May 1923.

Dronkers Family

Generation I

I. Marinus Dronkers, born 1874, died 1938; married Jannetje Moor, born 1874. From this marriage:

1. Johanna Jacoba, born 26 May 1893; married Hendrik Jan Morren, a carpenter (born 17 January 1893), 14 August 1919 in Velsen; died 29 March 1979. From this marriage: Harri (or Harry) Marius Morren, born Enschede, 11 December 1918, died 15 February 1990.

2. Johannes Marinus, son of Marinus Dronkers and Jannetje Moor, born at Nigtevecht on 3 April 1896, clerk in 1926; executed Wandsworth (UK) on 31 December 1942; married Elise Antoinette Eleonora Seignette, born at Den Helder on 15 January 1893, at Velsen on 10 June 1926.

3. Elisabeth Cornelia, born 15 February 1895; married Pieter Cornelis Pieterse, 1 August 1918; died 5 November 1995. Buried Vredenoord cemetery, Arnhem.

4. Maria Martina, born 1898; died 1899.

NOTE: Harri actually appears to be the son of Maria Gezina Morren (born 5 September 1891, died 24 January 1965), married to Johan Euverman (1893–1977).

Bibliography

Primary Sources

The National Archives (TNA):
Boeckel: KV2/1333; *BRUTUS*: KV2/72; KV2/73; *Dronkers*: KV2/43; KV2/44; KV2/45; KV2/46; PCOM 9/969 (redacted) Prison Commission and Home Office, Prison Department; HO 45/25605 1942 Registered Papers; CRIM 1/1454 Central Criminal Court Depositions; *Erasmus brothers*: KV2/1931;*Eriksen*: KV2/14; *Giskes*: KV2/961; *Grobben*: KV2/1150; *Kramer*: KV2/1742; *Kratzer*: KV2/2133; *Meissteuffen*: KV2/742-746; *Morel*: KV2/1151; *Mulder*: KV2/47; *O'Neill*: KV2/1155; *Pfeiffer*: KV2/267; *Pons*: KV2/13; KV2/1452; KV2/1700; HO1442-21472; KV2/1699: KV2/1700; *Protze*: KV2/1740; *Ritter*: KV2/85-88; *Salzinger*: KV2/2135; *Schipper:*KV2/2736; *Schroeder*: KV2/399; *Schuchmann*: KV2/1491; *Schütz*: KV2/1297-1302; KV2/2736; *Simon*: KV2/1293; *Unland*: KV2/1295; *Van Koutrik*: KV2/3643; *Van Wijk*: KV2/1145; *Wichmann*: KV2/103.

Secondary sources

Andrew, Christopher, *Defence of the Realm* (Toronto: Viking Canada, 2009)

Batey, Mavis, *Dilly: The Man Who Broke Enigmas* (London: Biteback Publishing, 2010), paperback edition

Bower, Tom, *The Perfect English Spy: Sir Dick White and the Secret War 1935–90* (London: Heinemann, 1995)

Crowdy, Terry, *Deceiving Hitler: Double Cross and Deception in WWII* (Oxford: Osprey, 2008)

Curry, John, *The Security Service 1908 – 1945: The Official History* (London: Public Record Office, 1999)

Foot, M. R. D., *SOE in the Low Countries* (London: St Ermin's Press, 2001)

Hayward, James, *Double Agent Snow* (London: Simon & Schuster, 2014), paperback edition

Hennessey, Thomas and Claire Thomas, *Spooks: The Unofficial History of MI5 from Agent Zigzag to the D-Day Deception, 1939–45* (Stroud: Amberley, 2010), paperback edition

Hinsley, F. H. and Anthony Simkins, *British Intelligence in the Second World War Volume 4: Security and Counterintelligence* (London: HMSO, 1990)

Hinsley, F. H. and Michael Howard, *British Intelligence in the Second World War Volume 5: Strategic Deception* (London: HMSO, 1990)

Holt, Thaddeus, *The Deceivers: Allied Military Deception in the Second World War* (London: Weidenfeld & Nicolson, 2004)

Kahn, David, *Hitler's Spies: German Military Intelligence in World War II* (Boston: DaCapo Press, 1978), paperback edition

Masterman, J. C., *The Double–Cross System* (New Haven: Yale University Press, 1972), 3rd printing; Vintage Books, paperback edition, 2013

Milne, Tim, *Kim Philby: The Unknown Story of the KGB's Master Spy* (London: Biteback Publishing, 2014)

Morton, James, *Spies of the First World War* (London: The National Archives, 2010)

Paine, Lauran, *German Military Intelligence in World War II* (New York: Military Heritage Press, 1988)

Pinto, Oreste, *Spycatcher* (London: Werner Laurie, 1953), 6th impression

Smith, Michael and Ralph Erskine (eds), *Action This Day* (London: Transworld/Random House, 2002), paperback edition

Smith, Michael, *Station X: The Codebreakers of Bletchley Park* (London: Channel 4 Books, 1998)

Stephens, Robin; Oliver Hoare (ed.), *Camp 020. MI5 and the Nazi Spies* (London: Public Record Office, 2000)

Trevor-Roper, Hugh; Edward Harrison (ed.), *The Secret World. Behind the Curtain of British Intelligence in World War Two and the Cold War* (London: I.B. Tauris, 2014)

West, Nigel, *MI5: British Security Service Operations 1909–1945* (London: Bodley Head, 1981)

West, Nigel, *Unreliable Witness: Espionage Myths of the Second World War* (London: Weidenfeld & Nicolson, 1984)

West, Nigel and Oleg Tsarev, *The Crown Jewels: The British Secrets at the Heart of the KGB Archive* (London: Harper Collins, 1998)

West, Nigel, *Historical Dictionary of British Intelligence* (Lanham, MD: Scarecrow Press, 2005), 1st edition

West, Nigel (ed), *The Guy Liddell Diaries, Vol. 1, 1939–1942* (London: Routledge, 2005)

West, Nigel (ed), *The Guy Liddell Diaries, Vol. 2, 1942–1945* (London: Routledge, 2005)

West, Nigel and Oleg Tsarev (eds), *Triplex: Secrets from the Cambridge Spies* (New Haven & London: Yale University Press, 2009)

West, Nigel and Madoc Roberts, *Snow: The Double Life of a World War Two Spy* (London: Biteback, 2011)

West, Nigel (ed.), *MI5 in the Great War* (London: Biteback Publishing, 2014)

West, Rebecca, *The New Meaning of Treason* (New York: Viking Press, 1948)

Articles and websites

John (Jan) Bruno de Langen: http://translate.google.ca/translate?hl=en&sl=nl&u=http://nl.wikipedia.org/wiki/Jan_Bruno_de_Langen&prev=search

Johannes Marinus Dronkers: http://pondes.nl/detail/indetail%20ENG.php?inum=1469035161

http://pondes.nl/detail/sfinfo.php?sour=2252173679&naam=

Janetje Moor: http://www.pondes.nl/detail/i_d_ENG.php?inum=793957405

Elise Antoinette Eleonora Seignette: http://pondes.nl/detail/indetail%20ENG.
   php?inum=1469035162

http://www.stephen-stratford.co.uk/treachery.htm

http://www.british executions.co.uk/execution-content.php?key=648

Davies, D. Seaborne, 'The Treachery Act, 1940', in: *Modern Law Review*,
   January 1941, pp. 217–220

Kluiters, F. A. C. and E. Verhoeyen, *An International Spymaster and Mystery
   Man: Abwehr Officer Hilmar G. J. Dierks (1889–1940) and his Agents*

Simpson, A. W. Brian, 'Trials in camera in security cases', in: *Domestic and
   international trials, 1700–2000. The trial in history, Vol.2*, R. A. Melikan (ed)
   (Manchester: Manchester University Press), 2003, Ch. 5, pp. 75–106

After the Battle Magazine, Issue 11, pp. 13; 30

Supplement to London Gazette, 22 December 1939, p. 8,541

Notes

Preface

1. As a result of my research further documents (PCOM 6/969) were released on 10 March 2015 under the Freedom of Information Act (FOIA), albeit redacted.
2. Lander, Sir Stephen, opening address to Public Records Office conference, 'The Missing Dimension', 21 June 2001.
3. Pinto, Oreste, *Spycatcher* (London: Werner Laurie, 1953), 6th impression, Ch. 6. 'Patience is a virtue', pp.80–93.
4. *TIME* magazine, 29 September 1961.
5. Liddell, Guy; Nigel West (ed), *The Guy Liddell Diaries, Vol. 1, 1939–1942* (London: Routledge, 2005), p. 205. There were apparently some dealings with fraudulent company promoting.
6. West, Nigel, *MI5. British Security Service Operations 1909–1945* (London: Bodley Head, 1981), pp. 264; 270.
7. See: Jackson, Sophie, *Churchill's Unexpected Guests: Prisoners of War in Britain in World War II* (Stroud: History Press, 2010/2013), and Thomas, Roger J. C., *Prisoner of War Camps (1939–1948)*. Twentieth Century Military Recording Project, Project report for English Heritage, 2003: https://content.historicengland.org.uk/...camps/prisoner-of-war-camps.pdf
8. Stephens, Robin; Oliver Hoare (ed), *Camp 020. MI5 and the Nazi Spies* (London: Public Record Office, 2000), pp. 191–192.
9. Liddell; West, *The Guy Liddell Diaries, Vol. 1*, p. 278: 'The Royal Victoria Patriotic School has turned up a spy in the person of a Dutchman called Johannes Dronkers. This man arrived in England nearly a month ago in company with a half-caste and another man, who like himself was an employee of the Posts & Telegraph. Dronkers was interrogated by a Dutch intelligence officer who by his knowledge of certain associates and contacts was able to prove that Dronkers had a brother-in-law who was a well-known Quisling called Klaever. Dronkers eventually confessed that he was Karel van Dongen, an ISOS character known to us for some time. His cover address is the same as that of FATHER, and Meissteuffen, and was brought over in the pages of a dictionary. He also tried to get a broadcast message of his arrival sent in the name of Karel.'

Prologue

1. Motor ship. Launched on 15 September 1924 by Cook, Welton.
2. Bryans Knights. Personal communication; the Navy List for September 1940 shows Cannon as being a Probationary Temporary Lieutenant.
3. The *Navy List Corrected to 18th September 1942*, p. 1,284.

4. The house was demolished in 1972 and in its place stands the Hotel Continental at 28–29 Marine Parade.

5. Most likely Inter-Services Research Bureau (cover name for SOE).

6. The MI5 B1 registry 'trace' of 8 May 1942 had turned up a Karel van Dongen who was a seaman; another, a shipbuilder of the same name, who was pro-German; a Karel or Martin van Dongen, a seaman who had deserted in Durban; and another who had deserted from the MV *Djambi* at Batavia in Java. None of these men are relevant to this story.

7. Herbert Lionel Adolphus Hart (1907–92), later Professor of Jurisprudence at Oxford University and Principal of Brasenose College (Curry, p. 28, note 90). Hart was at that time working at MI5's St James's Street office and responsible for receiving ISOS decrypts from Bletchley Park and passing them on to officers in B1b and B1a (West, *MI5*, pp. 162; 170; 273). Nigel West describes him as a left-wing barrister. Hart also later confirmed that Jan Willen Ter Braak, another Dutchman, whose body had been found in a Cambridge air raid shelter on 1 April 1941, had been a spy.

8. TNA KV2/43.

9. Appears to be the code name for the *Abwehrstelle* in The Hague (unconfirmed). *Kaeserei* (*Käserei*) means dairy in German.

10. TNA K2/44.

11. TNA KV2/43.

12. Ronald 'Ronnie' Haylor, Commandant, London Reception Centre (LRC), Wandsworth Common. It is interesting to note that some documents in the files are signed E. V. Haylor, also a major, which tends to confuse the issue but they appear to be one and the same person.

13. TNA KV 2/43.

14. TNA KV 2/43.

15. A quick check of Google Maps reveals it to be Alameda de recalde, not far from the Guggenheim Museum, Bilbao. Google StreetView shows what appears to be an apartment building next to a florist's and a shop selling artists' materials, La Trasteria da Goya.

16. Milne, Tim, *Kim Philby. The Unknown Story of the KGB's Master Spy* (London: Biteback Publishing, 2014). Milne confirms that there was an Abwehr station in Bilbao (p. 89), as does Kim Philby in *My Silent War* (New York: The Modern Library, 2002), p. 50, in regard to the Leopold Hirsch and Gilinski affair; Liddell; West, vol. 2, 1942–1945) p. 71; Holt, p. 106: 'Bilbao was a centre for courier traffic via Spanish merchant ships'; Desmond Bristow adds that the Iberian sub-section of MI6's Section V covered Bilbao, San Sebastián, Vigo, Zaragosa and Seville (Bristow, Desmond, with Bill Bristow, *A Game of Moles* (London: Little, Brown & Co., 1993), p. 27).

17. TNA KV2/2736.

1: By Interceptions Which They Know Not Of

1. See: 'Box 25. The RSS from 1939–1946.' www.zamboodle.demon.co.uk/rss_old/box25his.pdf

2. Trevor-Roper, Hugh; Edward Harrison (ed), *The Secret World. Behind the Curtain of British Intelligence in World War Two and the Cold War* (London: I.B. Tauris, 2014), p. 37.

3. Hastings, Max, *The Secret War. Spies, Codes and Guerrillas 1939–1945* (London: William Collins, 2015), p. 59.

4. Hastings, *The Secret War*, p. 59.

5. Trevor-Roper; Harrison, *The Secret World*, p. 7.

6. For a full description of this see: Trevor-Roper; Harrison, ibid., pp. 2–3.

7. Trevor-Roper; Harrison, ibid., p. 3; see also Hinsley, F. H. and Anthony Simkins, *British Intelligence in the Second World War Volume 4: Security and Counterintelligence* (London: HMSO, 1990), pp. 88–89.

8. West, Nigel and Oleg Tsarev, *The Crown Jewels: The British Secrets at the Heart of the KGB Archive* (London: Harper Collins, 1998), pp. 146–147.

2: Treachery, the Practice of Fools

1. The Act is discussed in some detail by Jennings, W. Ivor, 'Statutes. The Emergency Powers (Defence) (No.2) Act, 1940' in: *Modern Law Review*, October 1940, pp. 132–136.
2. Sir Edward Coke (1552–1634), barrister, judge and politician, considered the greatest jurist during the Elizabethan and Jacobean eras. Coke, Sir Edward, *The Third Part of the Institutes of the Law of England Concerning High Treason and Other Pleas of the Crown and Criminal Causes* (London: W. Clarke & Sons), 1817, Ch. 1, p. 11. '*Centra ligeantium suam debitam*' – 'His allegiance is due to the centre'.
3. West, Rebecca, *The New Meaning of Treason* (New York: Viking Press, 1947), p. 13.
4. *British Military and Criminal History 1900–1999*: http://stephen-stratford.co.uk/spying. htm
5. War treason is a term used to categorise 'the commission of hostile acts, except armed resistance and possibly espionage, by persons other than members of the armed forces properly identified as such'. (Baxter, Richard (2013), 'The Duty of Obedience to the Belligerent Occupant', in: *Humanizing the Laws of War: Selected Writings of Richard Baxter*, Oxford University Press, p. 16). According to the 1914 edition of the *British Manual of Military Law*, espionage could be considered war treason if it was committed by people acting openly outside the zone of military operations. It defined war treason widely as including 'obtaining, supplying and carrying of information to the enemy' or attempting to do so. http://en.wikipedia.org/wiki/War_treason
6. Morton, James, *Spies of the First World War* (London: The National Archives, 2010), pp. 107–110. Interestingly, MI5's official account *MI5 in the Great War* edited by Nigel West states in Appendix 1, 'German espionage suspects investigated by MI5', that Lody committed suicide in November 1914 although on page 187 it states that he was indeed shot in the Tower on 6 November.
7. Simpson, A. W. Brian, 'Trials in camera in security cases', in: *Domestic and international trials, 1700–2000. The trial in history, Vol. 2*, R. A. Melikan (ed) (Manchester: Manchester University Press, 2003), Ch. 5, pp. 75–106; p. 80, cites G. A. R. Fitzgerald (ed), *Manual of Military Law*, 3rd edition (London: HMSO), paragraph 41, and Emer de Vattel (1714–67), Swiss philosopher, author of *The Law of Nations, Or The Principles of Natural Law*, 1758. 'Spies are generally condemned to capital punishment, and with great justice, since we have scarcely any other means of guarding against the mischief they may do us.' (1797 edition, *The Law of Nations, Or Principles of the Law of Nature, Book III, Of War*, Chapter X: 'Of Faith Between Enemies – Of Stratagems, Artifices in War, Spies, And Some Other Practices', p. 380) Online edition: http://oll.libertyfund.org/title/2246.
8. Treason Acts had been passed in 1351, 1495, 1695, 1702, 1708, 1814, 1842, and 1848.
9. Sir John Anderson, *Hansard*, HC Deb. 22 May 1940, vol. 361 cc185–95; Order for Second Reading.
10. Viscount Simon, quoted in 'The Treachery Act 1940' in *Modern Law Review*, January 1941, p. 218.
11. Davies, D. Seaborne, 'The Treachery Act, 1940', in: *Modern Law Review*, January 1941, pp. 217–220. David Richard Seaborne Davies (1904–84), Welsh law teacher and former Liberal MP for Caernarvon Burroughs (1945–46) after David Lloyd George; Chair of Common Law, University of Liverpool; member of the Criminal Law Revision Committee; High Sherriff of Caernarvonshire (1967–68), etc.
12. Davies, 'The Treachery Act 1940', p. 219.
13. *Hansard*, HC Deb. 22 May 1940 vol. 361 cc185–95, Order for Second Reading.
14. Defence Regulation 2A stated that 'If, with intent to assist the enemy, any person does any act which is likely to assist the enemy or to prejudice the public safety, the defence of the realm or the efficient prosecution of the war, he shall be liable to penal servitude for life.' Defence Regulation 2B carried a prison sentence of penal servitude not exceeding 14 years, a fine not exceeding £500, or both. (Cited in *Hansard*, HC Deb. 22 May 1940 vol. 361 cc185–95, Order for Second Reading)
15. USA Patriot Act, passed 26 October 2001; UK Anti-terrorism, Crime and Security Act, passed 19 November 2001; Canada Anti-terrorism Act (Bill C-36), passed 18 December 2001.
16. See: Knowles, Julian B., QC, *The Abolition of the Death Penalty in the United Kingdom. How it Happened and Why it Still Matters*, The Death Penalty Project, 2015, p. 18.

17. Lord Williams of Mostyn, *Hansard*, 31 March 1998, Column 219: 'It may be of interest that the Treachery Act 1940 was passed specifically to provide the death penalty for treacherous acts committed during the Second World War, but it applied only to that period of emergency.'
18. Wikipedia: http://en.wikipedia.org/wiki/Treachery_Act_1940?oldformat= true#Suspension_and_repeal
19. Wikipedia: http://en.wikipedia.org/wiki/Capital_punishment_in_the_ United_Kingdom
20. In the House of Commons debate of 1 February 1965, Sir Richard Glyn asked the Secretary of State for the Home Department how many persons have been executed in the United Kingdom for offences other than murder in the 25 years to the last convenient date. Sir Frank Soskice replied that 'In the years 1940–1964 17 persons were executed in Great Britain after conviction by a civil court of an offence other than murder. Two had been convicted of treason, and 15 of an offence under the Treachery Act, 1940. There was also one execution in Great Britain of a person convicted by court martial of an offence under the Treachery Act.' (*Hansard*, HC Deb. 01 February 1965 vol. 705 c219W). The discrepancy in the number lies in the fact that fourteen were from Camp 020.
21. McKinstry, Leo, *Operation Sealion* (London: John Murray, 2014), pp. 220–225; trade paperback edition. See also Searle, Adrian, *The Woman Beside the Sea: The Extraordinary Wartime Story of Dorothy O'Grady* (Stroud: History Press, 2012), pp. 11; 49–50; 52–54; 60; 65–68; 71; 80–82;107–108; 129–131; 137 (on court proceedings).

3: Double Cross

1. Curry, John, *The Security Service 1908–1945. The Official History* (London: Public Record Office, 1999), p. 253.
2. Masterman, John C., *The Double-Cross System* (New Haven: Yale University Press, 1972), 3rd printing, p. xii; pp. 8–9 for a more detailed explanation.
3. Lily Sergueiew (1912–50). See: mi5.gov.uk and http://www.nationalarchives.gov.uk/spies/ spies/treasure/default.htm and http://www.nationalarchives.gov.uk/spies/spies/treasure/ tr3.htm
4. Curry, *The Security Service*, pp. 248–249.
5. Bower, Tom, *The Perfect English Spy* (London: Heinemann, 1995), p. 43; also cited in Hinsley & Simkins, *British Intelligence in the Second World War Volume 4*, p. 97.
6. The Security Intelligence Centre was set up on 10 June 1940 as a larger staff of the Security Executive, whose task it was to supervise those departments investigating Fifth Column activities. CAB 93/2, HD(S) E and Hinsley, p. 65.
7. Philip Cunliffe-Lister (1884–1972), Viscount Swinton (1935–1955); 1st Earl of Swinton (1955–1972).
8. Hinsley & Simkins, *British Intelligence in the Second World War Volume 4*, p. 96.
9. *Ibid*. p. 97.
10. *Ibid*. pp. 97–98.
11. Masterman, *The Double-Cross System*, Vintage Books paperback edition, 2013, pp. xxvii–xxix.

4: A Most Unlikely Enemy Agent

1. It now houses a restaurant, Hudson.
2. Koninklijke Nederlandsche Stoomboot Maatschappij/Royal Netherlands Steamship Company.
3. The SS *Hector* was in service with KNSM 1912–1928.
4. This is the third ship named SS *Medea* belonging to the KNSM, which was in service in 1916. The second SS *Medea* was sunk by a U-boat (*U-28*) on 25 March 1915 off Beachy Head, Sussex, near the Royal Sovereign light vessel. The third *Medea* was also sunk by a U-boat (*U-658*) in the Caribbean on 12 August 1942. See: http://www.wrecksite.eu/wreck. aspx?132106 and http://www.theshipslist.com/ships/lines/knsm.shtml.
5. Schorr, Daniel. *Staying Tuned* (NY: Pocket Books/Simon & Schuster), 2001, p. 11, '... who was establishing, in the Associated Press building on Rockefeller Plaza, a bureau of

ANETA, the news agency for the Netherlands East Indies (today Indonesia)' in 1941. In fact, Vas Dias became its managing director. He is mentioned in an article published in *The Evening Citizen* (Ottawa), 15 January 1943, as coming to Canada to cover the birth of 'a possible heir to the Dutch throne to Princess Juliana of the Netherlands and Prince Bernhard'. He is described in the article as 'Very Dutch-looking and distinguished by his copious grey-black Vandyke beard' (p. 4). An article he wrote about the forthcoming birth for the Canadian Press agency was included in *The Evening Citizen* (Ottawa), for 14 January 1943 (p. 17). Abraham Arnold 'Nol' Vas Dias was born in Amsterdam on 17 July 1890, died Sarasota, Florida, 21 February 1966.

6. 20 Copthal Avenue, London EC2, just south of London Wall and close to Moorgate station, where a modern Japanese sushi restaurant, K10, is now located.

7. A Nelly Basey was born in East Ham, Essex, in 1895 to Robert and Mary Basey; however it is unconfirmed whether she is the same one who was later Dronkers' landlady.

8. The records I have been able to find go back to 1755, but there is no reference to anything French in the family.

9. Born *c.* 1891 in Velsen; married to Neeltje Kolijn, 21 November 1917 in Haarlem. There is also someone of the same name listed as a soldier in 1915 and 1916.

10. Post & Telegraph Service.

11. There are two possibilities for C. J. Klever: Cornelis Johannes Klever, b. 12 September 1882 in Benschop; or Cornelis Jacobus Klever, d. 11 March 1956.

12. There was a Willem van Baalen, born Maassluis 19 November 1885, died Maassluis 21 November 1962, married to Catharina van der Velden (1891–1959) on 14 June 1916 in Schiedam who might possibly fit the bill. They had a child, Wilhelmina Geertuida van Baalen, who died *c.* 1937/8. Given the proximity to the area covered in the story, it is a likely possibility, but as yet unconfirmed.

There was also a Willem van Baalen, born 1 November 1893 in Rotterdam, who married Eleonora Theodora Landheer (1897–1972). The couple divorced on 3 January 1928. Van Baalen died in Ermelo, Gelderland, on 15 August 1972. He was listed as a clerk. However, to date, there is no evidence that he is the same man associated with Dronkers.

13. Population registers for The Hague show that as of 9 March 1932 Dronkers and his wife were living at Bentinckstraat, 10; 25 July 1932 at Slinglandstraat, 156; and 18 January 1939 at Valeriusstraat 55.

14. TNA KV2/43.

15. TNA KV2/43.

16. TNA KV2/43.

17. TNA KV2/72; TNA KV2/73.

18. *Who's Who in Nazi Germany* (4th edition, dated May 1944, declassified by the CIA in 2001 and 2007). http://www.foia.cia.gov/sites/default/files/document_conversions/1705143/WHO'S%20WHO%20IN%20NAZI%20GERMANY%201944_0001.pdf

19. George C. Gerolimatas, 'The Politics of Irresponsibility and Anti-Semitism of the Rural People's Movement in Schleswig-Holstein 1928 – 1930'. Thesis submitted to University of North Carolina at Chapel Hill, 2010. https://cdr.lib.unc.edu/.../uuid:8383eb82-b023-471f-8507-b5918975ad0.

20. Hans Johan Franz Oskar von Meiss-Teuffen (1911–84), a Swiss agent recruited by the Abwehr. See: Stephens, *Camp 020*, pp. 189–191; and TNA KV2/742-746. Interestingly, a report from H. L. A. Hart of B1b to H. A. R. 'Kim' Philby of VD (MI6 Section VD) states that Meissteuffen's wife Eirka [*sic*] Landsberg was formerly married to R. H. S. Crossman, then of SOE. This is Richard Howard Stafford Crossman (1907–74), who was a Cabinet minister in Harold Wilson's government and famous for the Crossman Diaries. Crossman is listed as heading the German propaganda section of the Political Warfare Executive (PWE) under Robert Bruce Lockhart, later becoming Assistant Chief of the Psychological Warfare Division of SHAEF. Erika Susannah Glück (*née* Landsberg) (1906–79) was married to Crossman in 1932; divorced 1934. Meissteuffen married her in 1937 in Ndola, Northern Rhodesia.

21. Heinrich Schuchmann, alias Schroeder, Abwehr officer in charge of naval intelligence-gathering operations in Le Havre and in Holland after the invasion. See: CIA file from Deputy Director of Plans (Desmond FitzGerald) to Director of Naval Intelligence,

Department of the Navy, dated 1966: www.foia.cia.gov/sites/.../SCHUCHMANN,%20 HEINRICH_0016.pdf. See also: TNA KV2/1491.

22. Kahn, David, *Hitler's Spies. German Military Intelligence in World War II* (Boston: DaCapo Press, 1978), paperback edition, pp. 90; 322.
23. TNA KV2/742.
24. TNA KV2/1491.
25. TNA KV2/2749.
26. TNA KV2/743.
27. Dr Marinus Hendrikus Damme (1876–1966); appointed Postmaster-General in 1925 or 1939. http://www.encyclopedia.com/doc/1G2-2840900110.html. Minister of Social Affairs, 25 July – 10 August 1939.
28. TNA KV2/45.
29. The café now appears to be called Bites n' Booze.
30. Most likely Normaal Amsterdams Peil or Amsterdam Ordnance Datum, established *c.* 1818.
31. TNA KV2/43.
32. TNA KV2/43. In fact Dronkers had given his wife 1,000 guilders, plus money she had already saved from his dealings on the black market and a further 2,000 guilders as a result of a forthcoming deal to sell railway shares.
33. Lucian Zion Willem van der Vegte, born Valkenburg, South Holland, 7 June 1895, died Pretoria, South Africa, 5 May 1982. Also Minister of Transport (1943–45). http:// nl.wikipedia.org/wiki/Willem_van_der_Vegte.

5: Mission Impossible

1. TNA KV2/43.
2. Stephens, *Camp 020*, p. 192.
3. The Christian Historical Party was a conservative Reformed Party (1903–08). http://en.wikipedia.org/wiki/Christian_Historical_Party.
4. TNA KV2/47.
5. TNA KV2/43.
6. Alexander Verkuyl. http://translate.google.ca/translate?hl=en&sl=nl&u= http://nl.wikipedia.org/wiki/Jan_Martinus_Dronkers&prev=search. Other possibilities are Arie Verkuijl, born Haarlemmermeer, 2 May 1906, or Matthius Nicholas Verkuijl, born 19 February 1919, both of whom served in the German Army, although their membership in the NSB is unconfirmed.

   He should not be confused with Colonel J. A. Verkuyl, a cryptologist who worked for a time in the Japanese Army section of the US Army Signals Intelligence Service at Arlington Hall *c.* 1941 and later became head of Marid 6, later WKC, the communications intelligence centre in Amsterdam (Aid, Matthew M. & Cees Wiebes (eds), *Secrets of Signals Intelligence During the Cold War and Beyond* (Abingdon & New York: Frank Cass), 2001, p. 291; see also, West, Nigel, *Historical Dictionary of Signals Intelligence* (Lanham, MD: Scarecrow Press), 2012, p. 168), who was linked to Joseph S. Petersen, an NSA employee convicted of passing secrets on the Dutch Hagelin B-211 cypher system in 1954.
7. TNA KV2/43.
8. TNA KV2/43.
9. Inspector Ir. D. Noordhof, *Politiek Opsporingsregister*, No. 5, Spring 1945, marked 'Geheim' (Secret). 'This was the Bureau of Political Investigation. Its purpose was to arrest and bring to court all those who had collaborated with the Germans during the war. All in all this Bureau and its successor investigated some 100,000 Dutch nationals. In September 1945 the Zaandam branch of the Bureau issued a register showing the names, addresses and birth dates of all people arrested up to that date … The register itself contains the data of close to 15,000 people.' Personal communication from Peter Miebies.
10. TNA KV2/45.
11. TNA KV2/43.
12. Kahn, David, *Hitler's Spies*, p. 306. See also: Delattre, Lucas, *A Spy at the Heart of the Third Reich: The Extraordinary Story of Fritz Kolbe, America's Most Important Spy in World War II* (New York: Grove Press, 2005), English translation from the French, p. 129;

Kahn, David, 'Intelligence in World War II: A Summary', in: *Journal of Intelligence History*, Hamburg, 2001, pp. 1–20; Horst Boog, 'German Air Intelligence in the Second World War', in: Michael Handel (ed). *Intelligence and Military Operations* (London: Routledge/Frank Cass), 1990, pp. 350–424, and Note 146. Also published in *Intelligence and National Security* (Taylor & Francis), vol. 5, issue 2, 1990.

An entry in Guy Liddell's post-war diaries for 12 January 1946 (p. 59 of the original manuscript online) states that Kraemer also used the codename 'Siegfried' and refers to him as the Assistant Press Attaché in Stockholm: 'His information on British air power was said to be derived from a member of the Swedish delegation in London who passed it to a member of the Swedish FO in London. Kraemer said that he obtained the information from this FO member in return for a fairly considerable sum of money paid monthly.' (KV4/467)

13. Hayward, James, *Double Agent Snow* (London: Simon & Schuster, 2014), p. 88, paperback edition.

14. TNA KV2/1333. Major Julius Boekel @ Bruhns (or Bruns), Beyer (or Beier), Dr Ernesto Werner, Abwehr, Amt I Luft or *Ast* Hamburg. His file states that he was 'Reported in Hamburg where he was concerned with the training of agents and their dispatch to the UK (Sept '40 – Feb '42).'

15. TNA KV2/46.

16. TNA KV2/1150.

17. TNA KV2/1931.

18. Verhoeyen, Etienne, *Spionnen aan de achterdeur: de Duitse Abwehr in België 1936–1945* (Antwerp & Apeldoorn: Makla & Verhoeyen), 2011, p. 48, and TNA KV2/103. Hauptmann Werner Ritter von Raffay, Leiter II/I Organisation, cars, petrol, photography, inks. Abt.Ig dealt with secret inks and writing; experimented with photostats and used duffs (counterfeits). Shown in organisational chart for the Kommando Meldgebeit Hamburg, 1945, as being in Leiter II/1, Organisation, headed by Major Dr Kiesselbach.

19. TNA KV2/103.

20. TNA KV2/46.

21. Alias Ludovico von Karstoff. See: West, Nigel, *The Historical Dictionary of World War II Intelligence* (Lanham, MD: Scarecrow Press, 2007), p. 15; and note 119 (p. 197). Fritz Kramer, alias Cramer, can be found in TNA KV2/1742.

22. West, Nigel, *Historical Dictionary*, p. 139. Schroeder also used the alias Enzmann or Pollmann. See: TNA KV2/399.

23. Campbell, John P., *Dieppe Revisited: A Documentary Investigation* (London: Frank Cass/Routledge, 1993), p. 6. Robert Bruce Lockhart (1887–1970), who had been a spy for MI6 in Russia during the Revolution and afterwards, was Director General of the Political Warfare Executive, the government's propaganda arm during the Second World War.

24. Villa, Brian Loring, *Unauthorized Action. Mountbatten and the Dieppe Raid* (Toronto: Oxford University Press, 1990), paperback edition, 2nd printing, p. 204. Referring to Austrian investigative journalist Günther Peis, who made the allegations.

25. Peis, Gunther, *The Mirror of Deception* (London: Weidenfeld & Nicolson, 1977), quoted in West, *Unreliable Witness*.

26. West, Nigel, *Unreliable Witness. Espionage Myths of the Second World War* (London: Weidenfeld & Nicolson, 1984), Chapter 6, 'Jubilee or Betrayal?' pp. 85–98.

27. Cook, Tim, *The Necessary War. Volume One. Canadians Fighting the Second World War 1939–1943* (Toronto: Allen Lane, 2014), p. 282.

28. Neillands, Robin, *The Dieppe Raid: The Story of the Disastrous 1942 Expedition* (Lodon: Aurum Press, 2006), paperback edition, pp. 99–100.

29. Lovell, Stanley P., *Of Spies and Stratagems* (New York: Prentice-Hall, 1963).

30. Bonsall, Arthur, 'Bletchley Park and the RAF Y Service. Some Recollections', 2008. www.nuffield.ox.ac.uk/Research/OIG/Documents/bonsallpaperfinal.pdf

31. TNA KV2/43.

32. A Belgian Air Force pilot, Captain Henri Arents, active June 1941 – June 1943. See: West, *MI5*, pp. 237; 242; West, *Historical Dictionary of World War II Intelligence*, p. 76; Crowdy, *Deceiving Hitler*, p. 157; Holt, *The Deceivers*, p. 410.

33. The MI5 file on Major Julius Boeckel, aliases Bruhns, Dr Beyer/Beier, Werner, who served in *Ast* Hamburg from June 1940 and Berlin 1941–43, and later again in Hamburg, mentions two cover addresses: one, a girl in Lisbon, the other LUNDT in Stockholm.

However, these only became known to MI5 in 1945 when Boeckel was interrogated at CSDIC (KV2/1333).

34. Possibly Nigh & Van Ditmar, publishing house founded in 1837, still in existence. http://en.wikipedia.org/wiki/Nijgh_%26_Van_Ditmar. Attempts to contact the publisher have been met with silence.
35. TNA KV2/43.
36. A raid took place on the Frisian Islands and Heligoland on the night of 17/18 May 1942 involving thirty-two Stirling bombers and twenty-eight Wellington bombers of 3 Group. It may have been one of these bombers which spotted the *Joppe*. See: Middlebrook, Martin and Chris Everitt, *The Bomber Command War Diaries. An Operational Reference Book 1939–1945* (Surrey: Midland, imprint of Ian Allan, 2011), p. 266.

6: Escape

1. Middlebrook, *Bomber Command War Diaries* pp. 259; 263. According to *The Bomber Command War Diaries* a raid by twenty-four Boston medium bombers took place on 24 April 1942 and on 30 April when twenty-four Bostons bombed Le Havre and Flushing docks.
2. TNA KV2/43.
3. TNA KV2/43.
4. TNA KV2/43.
5. TNA KV2/43.
6. TNA KV2/43.
7. TNA KV2/45.
8. Bixley, William, *The Guilty and the Innocent* (New York: Philosophical Society), 1957, Ch. 6 'Trials for Espionage and Treachery', p. 83.
9. TNA KV2/46.
10. TNA KV2/43.
11. TNA KV2/43.
12. TNA KV2/43.
13. Flying Officer Rudolf 'Rudy' Frans Burgwal (1917–44) of 322 (Dutch) Squadron, RAF, shot down while escorting Lancasters over Orléans on 12 August 1944. Neil, Tom, *The Silver Spitfire* (London: Weidenfeld & Nicolson, 2013), p. 275: 'Two Dutch pilots, Flying Officers Burgwal and Jonker, took off on 12 August in two of the old Mark 9s [Spitfires] (one of which was 3W-K) presumably to fly over, or seek targets in, the more northerly British and Canadian operational areas of France and Belgium … At this point Burgwal disappeared and was pronounced missing.' Burgwal's aircraft was 3W-F.
    Burgwal was responsible for shooting down twenty-four V1s, five in one day, and awarded the Bronze Cross, 6 November 1941. There is a note in Mulder's file (KV2/47) indicating that according to E1a (D), as of 23 July 1942 Burgwal was in Canada. A Wikipedia entry, translated from the Dutch, states that after 21 June 1942 Burgwal had travelled from New York to Canada for flying training and aerobatics, including in Spitfires. https://nl.wikipedia.org/wiki/Rudy_Burgwal.
    An entry for the NIOD *Instituut voor Orlogs* mentions Burgwal being in Moncton, New Brunswick, and Calgary, Alberta, for six months' training.
    Another entry states that he joined 322 (Dutch) Squadron RAF on 22 July 1943 and credits him with nineteen V1s and five shared. http://www.europeanaf.org/history/322.htm
    In May 1941 Burgwal had helped Sieste Rienksma and Kees Waardenburg in a failed attempt to sail to England; on 3 September the trip was repeated successfully. They were first sheltered at the headquarters of the Dutch Intelligence Service at 82 Eaton Square, London, where they were questioned by François van't Sant, then head of the service, as well as Queen Wilhelmina, about conditions in the Netherlands. Burgwal passed through Camp 020 on 9 September 1941. Mulder had been introduced to Burgwal by Henk Klatt.
14. Stumpff passed through Camp 020 on 9 September 1941.
15. Stephens, *Camp 020*, p. 192.
16. TNA KV2/43.
17. TNA KV2/43.
18. TNA KV2/43.

19. TNA KV2/43.
20. TNA KV2/45.
21. TNA KV2/43.

7: The Radio Oranje Episode

1. TNA KV2/43.
2. TNA KV2/43.
3. Bixley, *The Guilty and the Innocent*, Ch. 6, pp. 83-84.
4. *Ibid.*, p. 83.
5. E. H. Cookridge (aka Edward Spiro), 'The Spy in the BBC' in: TNA KV2/44.
6. Hayward, *Double Agent Snow*, p. 37. Lily was Lily Sophia Bade, described as a twenty-seven-year-old 'shapely blonde seamstress', 'blue-eyed and curvaceously sexy', with whom SNOW had fallen in love.

8: Who Was 'Dr Schneider'?

1. Hayward, *Double Agent Snow*, pp. 219; 251.
2. In the MI5 Wichmann file, TNA KV2/103, there is a chart of *Abt.* Hamburg with Ritter shown as being in charge of 1L [1 Luft] under Wichmann. In a Top Secret Ultra communication from Wichmann, Ritter is recorded as being on his way to Libya as of 22 March 1941; he is also shown as being in Libya on 24 April 1941.

   See also: deZeng IV, Henry L. and Douglas G. Stankey. Lutwaffe Officer Career Summaries L–R, Version 01 April 2014 *ww2.dk/Lw%20Offz%20-%20L-R%20-%20 Apr%202014.pdf*:

   RITTER, Nikolaus. (DOB: 08.01.99). 16.04.42 Maj. (Erg.O.), trf from Stab/X. Armeekorps to Ob.d.L. pool and assigned temporary duty to Stab/Lg.Kdo. XI. 01.11.42 promo to Obstlt. (Wm.). 13.11.42 trf from Res.Flak-Abt. 247 (previously in RLM pool) to Division "Hermann Goring". 11.42 appt Kdr. Nachschub-Rgt. "Hermann Goring" (to 16.08.43). 16.08.43 trf to Lw.-Befh. Mitte for further assignment. c.08.44 appt (acting?) Kdr. Flak-Rgt. 63 (to c.24.11.44). 24.11.44 Obstlt., appt provisional Kdr. Flak-Rgt. 60. 17.03.45 appt permanent Kdr. Flak-Rgt. 60 (to 04.45).
3. Hennessey, Thomas and Claire Thomas, *Spooks. The Unofficial History of MI5 from Agent Zigzag to the D-Day Deception, 1939–45* (Stroud: Amberley, 2010), paperback edition, pp. 9; 12; 25.
4. From MacKay, C. G., *Information to Intrigue: Studies in Secret Service Based on the Swedish Experience 1939–1945* (London: Frank Cass, 1993). 'Bureau Wagner takes shape', pp. 160–161.
5. TNA KV 2/2135.
6. Matthews, Peter, *SIGINT. The Secret History of Signals Intelligence, 1914–45* (Stroud: The History Press, 2013), pp.134–135. 7/VI was part of the *Oberkommando der Wehrmacht Chiffrierabteilung* (OKW/Chi), formed in 1920; in 1942 7/VI became one of three sections of the OKW/Chi, analysing traffic of the USA, Britain, Italy and the Balkans. It was based at Bendlerstrasse, Berlin, and bombed by the RAF in November 1943. In 1944 it split from OKW/Chi and became the *Oberkommando ders Heers/General der Nachrichten Autklaerung* (OKH/GdNA), serving the army.
7. http://chris-intel-corner.blogspot.ca/2014/07/case-wicher-information-from-war-diary. html. See also: Meyer, Joseph A., 'Der Fall Wicher. German Knowledge of Polish Success on Enigma' in an NSA technical journal originally classified Top Secret UMBRA. https:// www.nsa.gov/public_info/_files/tech_journals/Der_Fall_Wicher.pdf.
8. Pietsch is listed as the head of the mathematical section of Inspectorate 7/VI (In 7VI), the Signal Intelligence Agency of the Army High Command (OKH/G d NA) in *European Axis Signal Intelligence in World War II as revealed by "TICOM" Investigations and by other Prisoner of War Interrogations and Captured Material, Principally German. Volume 2 – Notes on German High Level Cryptography and Cryptanalysis.* Army Security Agency, 1 May 1946, pp. 10; 93. Originally classified TOP SECRET CREAM; declassified by the NSA, 11 August 2012. https://www.nsa.gov/ public_info/_.../volume_2_notes_on_german.pdf

9. Paine, Lauran, *German Military Intelligence in World War II. The Abwehr* (NY: Military Heritage Press, 1984), p. 130.

10. CIA report from Chief of Base, Pullach, to Chief, EE [Eastern Europe?], Subject: Operational/ SYMBOLIZER, Specific: Interview with Joseph Schreieder, 27 July 1955, originally marked SECRET. Declassified 2006.

11. Evertsen, who was Dutch, and Krag, a Nazi fanatic from Schleswig-Holstein, were aboard the M/V *Josephine* whose captain was Evertsen which put into Fishguard in November 1940, claiming that they were all refugees from France. All were taken to Camp 020. Robles was a Cuban who, along with fellow Cubans Pedro Hechevaria and Nicolas Pazos-Diaz, was recruited by German intelligence in Paris 1940. See: TNA KV2/546.

12. *Korvettenkapitän* Schneiderwind is listed as being *Leiter* Gruppe II *Nest* Brest in 1940. Referent in Abt. Ausland III October 1942. Born 1900. Also known as 'Dr Schneider'. See: Central Intelligence Agency, Organization of Kreigsmarine: http://www.foia.cia.gov/documen t/519cd81e993294098d5166ef.

13. TNA KV2/103.

14. 21 AGp/DIC/D/CI/20 *n.d.*

15. KV2/87.

16. TNA KV2/103.

17. Kluiters, F. A. C. and E. Verhoeyen, *An International Spymaster and Mystery Man: Abwehr Officer Hilmar G.J. Dierks (1889–1940) and his Agents.*

18. For more information on this episode see: Day, Peter, *Klop. Britain's Most Ingenius Secret Agent* (London: Biteback, 2014), Ch. 10, pp. 139–56, and Kluiters and Verhoeyen, *An International Spymaster and Mystery Man.* Her files in the National Archives are heavily redacted.

19. TNA KV4/486.

20. TNA KV2/14 Vera Eriksen.

21. It is unknown whether this was Louis Tas, Freudian psychiatrist (1920–2011). While a medical student he was imprisoned in Bergen-Belsen (known to have been there in March 1944). Published *Diary of a Camp*, about his experiences, under the name Loden Vogel (Göttingen, 2000).

22. TNA KV2/43.

23. TNA KV2/103.

24. TNA KV2/267.

25. TNA KV2/267.

26. TNA KV2/267.

27. Siedentopf, Monika, *Unternehmen Seelöwe. Widerstand im deutschen Geheimdienst* (München: DTV Deutscher Taschenbuch, 2014) (in German only). English translation: *Operation Sea Lion: Resistance Inside the Secret Service.*

28. This is possibly Erich Windels (1899–1966), German Consul-General to Ottawa, 1936–39; Consul-General to Philadelphia, 1939–41. It was noted in a telegram written by Godfrey Haggard, the British Consul-General in New York, on 21 March 1940 to the Chancery at the British Embassy, Washington, commenting on an article which appeared in *Staatszeitung* that 'his loyalty to the German government is under suspicion ... a correct and conscientious Foreign Office official of the old school. He was reticent on the subject of Nazism.' Sir Godfrey Digby Napier Haggard, KCMG, CVO, OBE (1884–1969) was Consul-General in New York City 1938–44).

29. Bergemeyer is not listed in the list of officers in Abwehr HQ Berlin in Boeckel's MI5 file [KV2/1333]; however, Berlin also had an Abwehrstelle (*Ast* Berlin) which operated independently of HQ (Army District III). Nor is he listed in Wichmann's list of contacts and friends in his file, KV2/103.

30. TNA KV2/103. GLASS was Ann Glass (later Elwell) (1922–96); STAWITZKI was SS-Sturmbahnführer Kurt Stawitzki (1900–59), *Kriminalrat* and head of Section 4 (Gestapo) in Lemberg/Lvov. Member of the Special Commission investigating the 20 July Plot to assassinate Hitler.

31. Oberstleutnant Raydt, *Ast* Hamburg, listed by Boeckel in TNA KV2/1333.

32. TNA KV2/1333. Major Julius Boeckel.

33. Wichmann is recorded as having sciatica as early as 20 June 1941. His file (TNA KV2/103) also records that in his Health Book (part of the inventory of his personal

property) according to his doctor, Dr Stolly, he 'has been under medical treatment since 1941 and requires careful attention'.

34. Josef Jakob Johannes Starziczny, code named LUCAS by SIS and organiser of a major Nazi spy ring and radio transmissions to Hamburg from Brazil intercepted by the Allies. See: West, Nigel, *Historical Dictionary of International Intelligence* (Lanham, MD: Scarecrow Press, 2006) 1st ed., p. 238.

35. Wikipedia gives the location as Thorn/Toruń, Poland.

36. James Cromwell O'Neill, alias Andreas Moreca Russell, a ship's carpenter captured by the Germans in the South Atlantic. According to his MI5 file (TNA KV2/1155) he only agreed to cooperate with the Germans to effect his escape.

37. Lt Werner von Janowski. See: Rose, R. S. and Gordon D. Scott, *Johnny. A Spy's Life* (University Park, PA: Pennsylvania State University Press, 2013), p. 325.

38. TNA KV2/103.

39. This could be Ebbe Theodor Wijkander, MBA (b. 6 December 1912; d. 23 March 1996) of Gothenburg, Sweden. Married to Monica Bratt (b. 1913; d. 1961). Chairman of the Board, Väsa Götaland, employer Botanical Garden.

40. Bijl, Nick van der, *Sharing the Secret. A History of the Intelligence Corps 1940–2010* (Barnsley: Pen & Sword, 2013), p. 167. Peter Witte and Stephen Tyas refer to Camp 031 as a 'Civilian Interrogation Camp [*Kolhagen near Barnstedt*]' in *Himmler's Diary 1945. A Calendar of Events Leading to Suicide* (Stroud: Fonthill Media, 2014), no pagination in online version viewed.

41. TNA KV2/2750.

42. Karl-Heinz Moehle (1910–96), spelled Mohle in Nuremburg Trials testimony; also Möhle. U-boat ace responsible for sinking twenty-one ships, implicated in the sinking of the *Laconia*. Captured June 1945; sentenced in 1946 to five years' imprisonment.

43. M.A. Karl Reber (b. 1902).

44. TNA KV2/103.

45. TNA KV2/103.

46. TNA KV2/103. Herman Walter SIMON, also known as Karl Anderson, landed on 12 June 1940 in Eire. All were interned in Eire. SIMON is mentioned in WRC1/c report for 22 August 1945. The MI5 file on Herman SIMON (b. 1881) in the National Archives (KV2/1293) states that he 'had been drawn to Security Service notice in 1937 when he was caught making notes of British air defence dispositions, for which he was imprisoned and then deported. He reappeared in June 1940 having landed by small boat near Dingle in south-west Ireland. He aroused the suspicions of the Irish authorities during a train journey from Tralee to Dublin, and was arrested. Simon subsequently admitted to landing illegally, to hiding a transmitter on the beach where he landed, and to having been sent to Ireland to transmit weather reports to Germany. He was sentenced to three years' penal servitude - in Mountjoy prison, Dublin, and then in Athlone. After the war he remained in Ireland until January 1947, when he returned to Germany and was again imprisoned.'

'Wichmann knows that H.W.SIMON was operated by Hauptmann RITTER I.L before the war and by DIERKS early in the war up to the time when he was arrested in Eire. He has no knowledge of details.' [KV2/103]

The weeded file on Werner UNLAND (b. 1892) (KV2/1295) 'covers 1939–1949, and begins when the Irish authorities alerted the Security Service to suspicious correspondence between Unland, who was based in Dublin, and the 'Dansk Import & Export Co' in Copenhagen. The letters were seemingly written in plain language code (there are copies on the file), and the Irish Department of Defence kept a close watch on Unland's activities, informing the Security Service of all developments. Unland was eventually detained in 1941. After the war, he was permitted to remain in Ireland because it was feared that he and his (English) wife would commit suicide rather than be deported to Germany. The file contains much correspondence between the Irish official Colonel Liam Archer of the Department of Defence and his opposites in London (chiefly Guy Liddell), a lengthy case summary and a photograph of Unland.'

The files on Günter SCHÜTZ (b. 1912) (KV2/1297–1302) state that he was 'a German agent whose cover was that of a commercial traveller in heavy chemicals, in which guise he first came to the attention of the Security Service in June 1938 when he entered the UK. A member of the public, Mr H. Westbury Preston, reported that Schütz was a suspicious character, and initial investigations were made before he left for Belgium shortly before the outbreak of the war. Schütz soon emerged in Barcelona, where the German agent Walter Unland wrote to him in plain language code. It emerged that Schütz had asked a female Jewish friend to photograph plans for him before the war, and it became clear that he was a German agent (and he later admitted to espionage activity in Belgium before the war as well).'

'Schütz was parachuted into County Wexford, south east Ireland, in March 1941, using the alias Hans Marchner with false South African papers, and a plan to rendezvous with Unland. He was, however, quickly picked up by the Irish local defence forces, in possession of his wireless transmitter, and was interned in Mountjoy prison, Dublin. Schütz escaped in February 1942 and was at liberty in Dublin for 74 days before being recaptured, and eventually moved to Athlone barracks. After the war he was paroled to get married in May 1947, and soon thereafter was deported to Germany. It is believed that his mission was to report economic intelligence on conditions in Britain back to Germany.'

See also: Martin, Brian D., 'The Role of Irish Military Intelligence During World War Two', MA Thesis, St Patrick's College, Maynooth, August 1994 eprints. maynoothuniversity.ie/.../Brian_D_Martin_20140620160904.pdf.

47. Cave Brown, Anthony, *Bodyguard of Lies* (Toronto: Fitzhenry & Whiteside, 1975), p. 234. It was also alleged by William B. Breuer that it had been Kim Philby who had passed the report to Wichmann, although this has never been corroborated. (Breuer, William, *The Spy who Spent the War in Bed and Other Bizarre Tales from World War II* (New Jersey: John Wiley, 2003), p. 81.)
48. West, Nigel & Oleg Tsarev (eds), *Triplex. Secrets from the Cambridge Spies* (New Haven & London: Yale University Press, 2009), p. 106.
49. Hayward, James, *Myths and Legends of the Second World War* (London: History Press, 2010). No pagination in online edition viewed.
50. Campbell, John P., *Dieppe Revisited: A Documentary Investigation* (Routledge, 1993), pp. 50–52.
51. François Malbrant, captain of the SS *Yser*, who came to England in September 1944 and had been in contact with the German Secret Service since 1940 (TNA KV2/1491).
52. Reederei Schuchmann, or the Schuchmann Shipping Company of Bremen.
53. TNA KV2/1491.
54. TNA KV2/1491.
55. TNA KV2/47.

9: 'Playing with the Souls of Innocent Men'

1. TNA KV2/47.
2. Gerth van Wijk had been in Tangier at least up until 20 March 1941. See: Kersten, A. E. & Manning, A. F., *Documenten Betrefende Buitenlandse Politiek van Nederland 1919–1945. Periode C 1940–1945.* Deel II, 1 November 1940 – 31 Mei 1941, pp. XIII; LVIII; also Deel VI, 16 December 1942 – 30 Juni 1943. He was still reporting from Tangier on 20 May 1943 (p. LXX), so he must have been released. At Camp 020 Van Wijk revealed that Russian ballerina Marina Lie, b. 1902 (aka Lee, Goubonina, Alexevna, Louise Lohmann), a tall, blonde, beautiful Nazi spy, had infiltrated the BEF's HQ in Tromsø in 1940. She leaked plans of Auchinleck's failed attack on Narvik in May 1940. Van Wijk revealed that German General Eduard Dietl was contemplating defeat, but reversed his plans on the information received from Lie. See: Jörgensen, Christer, *Spying for the Führer. Hitler's Espionage Machine. The True Story Behind One of the World's Most Ruthless Spy Networks* (Guildford, CT: Lyons Press, 2004), p. 61. Van Wijk was 'turned' as a British spy.
3. Don Pablo Lopez Canterro, German agent in the Villa Cisneros in the Spanish Colony of Rio de Oro. Quoted from an Interim Report on Hans Karl Scharf, German agent captured by French authorities in North Africa in Schuchmann file, TN KV2/1491.
4. A possible contender for Kuchlin is Joseph Kochling, official of I.M. *Ast* The Hague. Recruited BAYOT (arrested) and other agents who went through a training period at Bischoff's school in the Wacht Strasse, Bremen [see MI5 file on Bischoff, J.W., TNA KV2/2749]. There is also a Karl August Karl Küchlin (1906–79), who married Elizabeth Anne Auguste (*née* Grimm; b. 23 November 1909) and had seven children. However, no connection can be made at this point with the Kuchlin who recruited Mulder. Koechling

met Bischoff in Biarritz and was also known to Korvettenkapitän Humpert in Berlin. Koechling had also recruited an agent, THOMPSON, for training in W/T in *c.* late 1944. A note in the Bischoff file states: 'Thompson, Gottfried Heinrich. In December 44 he was at Griesendam [*or Giessendam? Copy is illegible*] awaiting transfer to Nest Bremen. [*illegible*] at Ast Antwerp.'

5. TNA KV2/47.
6. TNA KV2/47.
7. KV2/43. The files on Dronkers are KV2/43, KV2/44, KV2/45 and KV2/46; the file on Mulder is KV2/47.

10: Mulder's Story

1. The Martherus website lists a total of seven children: Theodorus Anton John, b. 16 June 1913–?; John Alphonsus, b. 24 September 1915–?; Paulina Jacoba, b. 24 January 1917–?; Alex Avith, b. 16 June 1919, spouse A. C. Kerkoff, child, A. Mulder; M. Mulder; R. Mulder (Rudi); K. P. Mulder (Paul?). See: http://www.martherus.com/genealogy/familygroup. php?familyID=F277&tree=martherus Attempts to contact the Martherus family in the USA have been unsuccessful.
2. TNA KV2/47. An Albert John Mulder is shown as holding an Aviator's Certificate from the Royal Aero Club, 1910–50.
3. *Kasima Maru*, sometimes written as *Kashima Maru*, belonging to NYK Line (Nippon Yusen Kaisha). Its sailings between March 1938 and March 1939 are listed as: Yokohama, Nagoya, Osaka, Kobe, Mozi, Keelung, Shanghai, Hong Kong, Singapore, Penang, Colombo, Aden, Suez, Port Said, Naples, Marseilles, Gibraltar, London. Aden, Penang, Mozi, Osaka and Nagoya were omitted on return voyages. Mulder would likely have embarked at Penang. The ship, which had become a Japanese Army transport vessel, was torpedoed by the US submarine *Bonefish* (SS-223) and sunk on 27 September 1943 off Cape Padaran, French Indochina, 10°10' N, 109°40' E.
4. The Brastagi café was located at Kneuterdijk 6 in the Johan de Witt House, built in 1652. It only became a restaurant in the late 1930s. It is now a national monument.
5. *Vrij Nederland* started out as an underground magazine on 31 August 1940 but has since morphed into a left-wing intellectual magazine. It had a London address at 7 Old Park Lane, W1.
6. Henk Klatt does not appear to be connected with Klatt, an Austrian Abwehr officer (alias Richard Kauder) who ran the Klatt network in Vienna, and later Sofia and Bucharest, providing intelligence on British and Soviet forces in the Eastern European theatre of war.
7. This is possibly Witjze Bisschop (b. Amsterdam 28 April 1918; d. The Hague, 1 November 2006), listed as an SOE agent and sabotage instructor. See: *www.nisa-intelligence.nl/ PDF-bestanden/KluitersDAGversie2.pdf* and Foot, M. R. D., *SOE in the Low Countries* (London: St Ermin's Press, 2001), p. 285. Annoyingly, the reference in the Index to Foot (p. 420) does not exist. Witjze Sietze Bisschop, listed in Frans Kluiters, *Dutch Agents 1940–1945*, as an agent codenamed ARARAT; the mission was codenamed HOWL; HENDRIKSEN; sent into Hilversum, Holland on 11/12 April 1945 (listed in Kluiters as Lekkerkerk, Zuid-Holland). The network was overrun in May 1945. The file in the National Archives (HS 9/157/9) is closed until 2019. The file entry lists his aliases as HENDRIKSEN, ROLF and HOWL. He is also listed in *The Most Secret List of SOE Agents*, compiled by Elijah Meyer, published 11 October 2015: https://archive.org/details/ TheMostSecretListSOE.

   'HOWL's training name was HENDRIKSEN (Wijtze Sietze Bisschop). He would be known in the field as ROLF.

   In view of the important operational tasks which they had undertaken, the resistance forces in Rotterdam and Zuid-Holland had urgent need of instructors who had been trained in the use of arms and of reception committees. SCREAM and HOWL would be sent to act as instructors under the orders of VICTOR, the commander of the KP in Rotterdam, or any such other person he might appoint. They had received special training in sabotage, weapons and reception committee work and they would advise and instruct on these matters. SCREAM and HOWL were dropped in the Rotterdam area on the night of April 11th. They remained until liberated in May.' (See: http://www.weggum.com/ April_1945_Part_1.html, 'SOE War Diaries, April 1945 Part 1'.)

Not to be confused with Sonderführer, later Hauptmann, Johannes Bischoff who worked in *Nest* Bremen, the Abwehr sub-station. In 1939–40 he is shown as being an assistant to Freegatten Kapitän Dr Erich Pfeiffer, also Ip2, the Press section; in February 1941 he was in IM and Ig; in December 1944 in Ii as a Hauptmann (Captain). See: Central Intelligence Agency, *German Intelligence Service, Volume III, Counterintelligence War Room London, Liquidation Report 206A, Aussenstellen Bremen.* https://www.google. ca/?gws_rd=ssl#q=ast+hamburg+ww2&start=20.

8. This may have been the Oede Buisse Hoeve in Actmaal, a famous smuggler's café close to the Belgian border.
9. See: http://wwii-netherlands-escape-lines.com/airmen-helped/members-of-the-smit-van-der-heijden-line/civilians-in-the-line/
   http://www.nmkampvught.nl/biografieen/weert-jacobus-j-de/
   NIOD Institute for War, Holocaust and Genocide Studies.
   http://www.oorlogsdodennijmegen.nl/persoon/weert/70f4e621-d993-448c-82ad-30d71933e781

   However, the same Dutch website ('World War II Netherlands Escape Lines') mentions a report by Karst (probably Boele Karst) in 1945 as saying, 'Jacques de Weert, pseudonym of Gemert, son of a doctor in Zundert, for the time being still sick: in the vicinity of Hamburg.' http://wwii-netherlands-escape-lines.com/airmen-helped/aid-given-to-people-in-need/aid-to-dutch-families/

   The website lists an A. de Weert at Tongeren 52, Boxtel in the South Netherlands, Brabant region.

11: Mulder's Later Activities

1. The Wikipedia entry states that Burgwal had come to England with Rienksma and Waardenburg and that Strumpff [*sic*] had arrived earlier with Bebe Daniels, Ter Beek and François van 't Sant. https://translate.google.ca/translate?hl=en&sl=nl&u=https:// nl.wikipedia.org/wiki/Rudy_Burgwal&prev=search.
2. Wibo Peekema was the author of 'Colonization of Javanese in the Outer Provinces of the Netherlands East Indies' in the *Royal Geographical Society Journal*, No. 101, April 1943, pp. 145–153. In *The London Gazette* for 16 February 1945 in the list of the 'Official Staffs [*sic*] of the Members of the Government' he is listed as being under the direction of the Minister for the Colonies. In 1953 he is listed as Legal Advisor to the Standard-Vaccum Oil Company in The Hague (Source: *Britannica Book of the Year 1953*, Contributors, p. xvi. Encyclopædia Britannica Ltd, London, Chicago, Toronto.).
3. Protze = Kapitän zur See Traugott Andreas Richard Protze, alias Paarman, former naval officer and *Leiter* (Head) of Abwehr IIIF. From 1938 when he retired as head of Abwehr counter-intelligence he ran Stelle 'P', an independent Abwehr bureau in Holland and reported directly to Canaris in Berlin. (TNA KV2/1740.) Involved in the Venlo Incident and the Putlitz case.
4. P. M. C. J. (Peter) Hamer, Commissioner of Police for The Hague, 1940–43. Dismissed by SS-Brigadeführer Hanns Albin Rauter in 1943 for alcoholism and had his NSB membership terminated. After the war he was sentenced to fifteen years' imprisonment.
5. Rudolf or Karl Adolf Kratzer, alias Wilhelm Krandell, Lamarr, Krugger, agent-runner as Leiter I *Ast* Brussels, later Wiesbaden, who sent agents to the Balkans, Spain and Portugal, the UK and one to Canada in a submarine. See TNA KV2/2133.
6. Sonderführer Richard Crone who was in Gruppe III C, *Ast* Niederlande from 1942.
7. TNA KV2/1740.
8. Liddell; West, *The Guy Liddell Diaries*, Vol. II, 1942–45, p.102.
9. TNA KV2/2133.
10. TNA KV2/2133. Confidential report by Captain Leroy Vogel, Headquarters United States Forces European Theater Military Intelligence Service Center APO 757, 17 December 1945.
11. TNA KV2/2133.
12. TNA KV2/2133. Interview between Major Karl Kräzer, formerly *Leiter* I *Ast* Brussels, and Major D. M. Besley, RE HQ Intelligence Corps (Field), BAOR, at Camp 74 Ludwigsburg, 26 February 1946.
13. Annex I Personality List report APO 757 in TNA KV2/2133.

14. TNA KV2/2279; KOLP is possibly Hans KOSP, a Polish Abwehr wireless instructor in Brussels.
15. TNA KV2/2279.
16. PF66115 noted against the name 'Dolly', now KV2/2279.
17. TNA KV2/2133. Appendix II to an extract of a Camp 020 interim report on Julius Hagerman, dated 29 May 1945.
18. Boer, Gerard, 'Damsel Dolly Dibbets: Traitor, Spy and Mistress of Seyss-Inquart' (published as 'Jonkrouv Dolly Dibbets: Verraadster, Spionn en Mâitresse van Seyss-Inquart'), 24 October 2005: https://gerard1945.wordpress.com/tag/peekema/.
19. Tomas Ross (Pieter Willem Hogendoorn), 2005.
20. TNA KV2/47.
21. TNA KV2/47.

12: The Further Adventures of Mulder

1. TNA KV2/47.
2. TNA KV2/47.
3. TNA KV2/47.
4. Probably Sgt Cor Sipkes, Air Defence Detachment, Royal Netherlands Air Force, a Dutch flying instructor who became an RAF pilot. See: Stenman, Kari, and Peter de Jong, *Fokker D.XXI Aces of World War 2* (Oxford: Osprey, 2013), pp. 14; 15; 63. Sipkes introduced Dorothy 'Dodie' Sherston's (1912–2011) aunt, Ethel 'Outoo' Dugdale, to 'Oranjehaven', the house in Bayswater which was a refuge for *Engelandvaarders* (23 Hyde Park Place, Paddington, W2). Dodie, later known as Door de Graaf, married Kas de Graaf, the second-in-command of SOE's N Section, and helped to run it.

13: The Case of Mulder and de Langen

1. TNA KV2/43.
2. TNA KV2/43.
3. TNA KV2/43.
4. TNA KV2/47.
5. TNA KV2/43.
6. TNA KV2/43.
7. TNA KV2/45.
8. TNA KV2/47.

14: Mulder's Future

1. TNA KV2/47.
2. TNA KV2/47.
3. There is now a company named Mono Containers, a member of the British Plastics Federation, in Durham.
4. An undated note in the file mentions that the original plan to send him to Dutch Guiana had proved impracticable owing to 'shipping difficulties'.
5. TNA KV2/47.
6. Willem Hendrik Fokkink, aged thirty (1912–73?), who served as Fifth Engineer Officer on the steamship *Zaanland* when it was sunk in the North Atlantic (position 50° 38'N 34° 46'W) by U-boat *U-758* commanded by Kapitänleutnant Helmut Manseck, part of the *Raubgraf* ('Robber Baron') patrol, on 17 March 1943. The crew of fifty-three survived. The ship was part of convoy HX-299 out of New York via Halifax, Nova Scotia, en route to Liverpool carrying a cargo of wheat, zinc and meat.
7. TNA KV2/47.
8. TNA KV2/47.
9. TNA KV2/47.
10. There is a listing for an S. E. Opperman of Elstree, Hertfordshire, which was making a Unicar from 1956 to 1959; and another company, Carl Opperman Electric Carriage

Company Ltd, which was making electric cars from 1898 to 1907, although the dates do not fit the company Mulder was supposed to work for.
11. TNA KV2/47.
12. unitedkingdom.nlembassy.org/binaries/...in.../en-8-nov.pdf
13. TNA KV2/46.

15: 'As Sordid a Tale As Any We Have Had'

1. TNA KV2/46.
2. TNA KV2/43.
3. TNA KV2/43.
4. Stephens, *Camp 020*, p. 9.
5. In the *Edinbugh Gazette* of 1941 Derksema is listed as Mr Robert Derksema 'Under the direction of the Minister of Justice'; likewise in the *London Gazette*, 10 September 1943.
6. TNA KV2/43.
7. Hooper had been dismissed by SIS in September 1936 over the scandal caused by the suicide of Maj. H. E. Dalton, SIS Head of Station in The Hague, and his embezzlement of funds. Hooper then offered his services to the NKVD as well as the Abwehr, for whom he worked 1938–39. He was re-engaged by SIS in 1939 after exposing a Soviet spy in the Foreign Office Communications Department. Upon escaping to Britain with van Koutrik, he was employed by MI5 as an agent-runner. (See Andrew: *The Defence of the Realm*, p. 246.)

   This is also mentioned in an entry in Guy Liddell's diary for 18 June 1945: 'The only outstanding event during my absence was the discovery from a German P/W that W.J. Hooper of B1L had just before the war been working for the G.I.S. [German Intelligence Service]. He had sold them information about the Russian agent Hans Christian PIECK and he had sold them further information for which he received on one occasion £50 and on another £80 through Feldman of the Abwehr in Colog[ne.] The most sinister aspect relates to an agen[t] called Dr. Kruger who was employed by S.I.S. The P/W [prisoner-of-war] whose name is GISKIS or GESKIS [Giskes], says that this agent's name was given to the Germans by Hooper and that he was subsequently liquidated.'[TNA KV4/466]
8. TNA KV2/3643.
9. TNA KV2/3643.
10. Major, later Lieutenant Colonel, Montague Reany Chidson, MBE. Van Koutrik says it was in 1937 in a letter dated 13 August 1941 to an unknown addressee, but likely MI5. He mentions being employed by Vrinten.
11. Guy Liddell's post-war diaries state in an entry for 23 May 1946 that 'Vesey [Captain/later Major Desmond] has discovered that Koutrick [*sic*] was for a short period in B24 but that we got rid of him in 1941. I do not think there is the least likelihood that he would have been working for the Germans then. Had he wished to do so he would probably have remained where he was. He subsequently worked for S.I.S but where he is now I do not know. We shall have to find out.' [KV4/467]
12. John Nicholas Rede Elliott (1916–94): Honorary Attaché, The Hague 1938–40; Acting Lieutenant, Intelligence Corps 1940–45; Head of Station, Secret Intelligence Service, Berne 1945–53, Vienna 1953–56, London 1956–60, Beirut 1960–62; friend of Kim Philby.
13. TNA KV2/3643.
14. Andrew, *The Defence of the Realm*, pp. 244–47. See also: Richard Norton-Taylor, 'Britain's MI5's Penetration by WWII German Agent', *The Guardian*, 16 February 2012. Also TNA KV2/3643.
15. TNA KV2/43.
16. TNA KV2/43.
17. Cannon had been sent to America to take delivery of a new BYMS, a wooden-built minesweeper under construction by the Wheeler Shipbuilding Corp. at Whitestone, Long Island, New York. His nephew, Bryans Knights, reports that Cannon was delayed in New York because of delays in construction and the ship being unable to make the Atlantic crossing in winter. The vessel was finally launched on 21 December 1942 and commissioned on 22 January 1943 as HMS BYMS 2065 (none of the ships were given a name). Email from Bryans Knights to author.

16: The Trial, Day One

1. TNA CRIM1/1454, p. 26.
2. TNA KV2/45.
3. TNA HO45/25605.

17: The Trial, Day Two

1. TNA KV2/46.

18: The Trial, Day Three

All trial transcripts are taken from TNA KV2/45.

19: The End of the Affair?

1. TNA KV2/46.
2. The agent's name was redacted in 2015; however, it appears as Verkuyl in a handwritten copy of this document in KV2/45, a file which had been declassified without the redaction in 1998.
3. TNA HO45/25605.
4. TNA KV2/46.
5. TNA CRIM1/1454.
6. TNA HO45/25605.

20: Judgement Day

1. TNA HO45/25605.

21: The Death of a Spy

1. TNA HO45/25605.
2. It is unknown who Annie and Henk, Bets and Piet, or Marie were; however, Henk is likely Hendrik Jan Morren, his sister Johanna's husband; Piet is possibly Pieter Cornelis Pieterse, his sister Elisabeth's husband; Bets could be a shortened version of Elisabeth; Marie could be Maria Seignette, Elise's sister; Annie could be Anna Catherine Hooft, the wife of Elise's brother Frans.
3. TNA PCOM9/969.
4. Lefebure, Molly, *Murder on the Home Front* (New York; Boston: Grand Central Publishing, 2013), paperback edition, p. 93.
5. For a detailed study of the process and pathology of hanging see: Rao, Dr Dinesh, 'Hanging', in: *Dr. Dinesh Rao's Forensic Pathology*, http://www.forensicpathologyonline. com/e-book/asphyxia/hanging.
6. TNA PCOM9/969.
7. TNA KV2/45.

22: Fall-out and the Media

1. *Vrij Nederland*, 9 January 1943, p. 760.
2. TNA KV2/45.
3. Büttner was the secretary of Julius Streicher (1885–1945), a prominent Nazi and *Gauleiter* of Franconia executed by the Dutch after the Second World War for crimes against humanity. Maud Elizabeth Buttner, b. 24 July 1886 had gone to Paris in the spring of 1938. In the Home Office file HO396/12 she is listed as a Female Enemy Alien – Exemption from Internment – Non-Refugee, dated 16 November 1939. No reason is given for the exemption.
4. GRUBE is probably Willy Grube of the German Signals Corps (see below); LUDOVICO is most likely Major Ludovico von Karsthoff, Leiter Gruppe III, Abwehr counter-intelligence, Lisbon, real name Kremer von Auerode; in 1939/40 he was listed as Gruppe

I Luft in *Nest* Köln; THEODOR is Obersturmbahnführer Theodor Paeffgen (1910–69), of the SD Berlin and the Stapo Stellen, Tilsit; David Kahn's book *Hitler's Spies* names him as head of RHSA VI's Group D, responsible for spying on the USA and UK; he lists him as an Obersturmbahnführer in January 1945 (see: Kahn: pp.7, 10–11, 262, 264, 266, 327, 339–340); MARCEL is Marcel Zschunke of the SD. KERSTEN unlikely to be Felix Kersten (1898–1960). The others have yet to be identified.

Colonel Willy Grube, Chief of the Telecommunications of the German OKW (see: *Extracts of SHAEF Interrogations of the Following German Communications Personnel.* TICOM I-17, 27 June 1945; and *Detailed Interrogation report. The German Signals Corps.* 6824 DIC (MIS)/1185 26 June 1945. TICOM 11F-I15).

BRUNO could be Generalmajor Walter BRUNS, Lisbon from April 1942, formerly Col., MA Deutschegesandtschaft Portugal up to 5 June 1942. (See: *Notes on OKW/CHI and Intercept Organisation under KO Spain*, TICOM I-49, 30 July 1945.)

5. Corporal Alan Tooth, 50 FSS, Intelligence Corps. See: Van der Bijl, Nick, *Sharing the Secret*, p.40. 50 FSS (Field Security Section) is listed as UK 1940–44; NW Europe (Lines of Communication), 1944–45. See: Clayton, Anthony, *Forearmed. A History of the Intelligence Corps* (London: Brassey's, 1993), p. 266. According to Ben McIntyre, Tooth remained a senior NCO in the Field Security Service after the war.
6. Booth, Nicholas, *Zigzag. The Incredible Wartime Exploits of Double Agent Eddie Chapman* (New York: Arcade Publishing, 2007), trade paperback edition, pp. 156–157.
7. TNA KV2/44.
8. TNA KV2/44. Section V of SIS dealt with foreign counter-espionage under Col. Valentine Vivian and Maj. Felix Cowgill.
9. TNA KV2/44.
10. United States Department of Justice, Federal Bureau of Investigation, Bureau Bulletin no. 15, Second Series 1943, 24 March 1943, marked 'Strictly Confidential'.
11. TNA KV2/44.
12. TNA KV2/44.
13. TNA KV2/44.
14. HO45/25605.
15. TNA KV2/1452.

23: 'The Kent Spies', 1940

1. Earl Jowitt, 'My Secret War Trials. The Four Men Who Landed in Kent', *Evening Standard*, 11 May 1954, p. 13.
2. TNA KV2/1452.
3. The Rising Sun no longer exists as a pub and is now two houses.
4. TNA KV2/1452.
5. The fighters were probably from JG26, JG27 or JG54; JG=Jagdgeswader (fighter squadron) http://www.battleofbritain1940.net/document-43.html.
6. Bishop, Patrick, *Battle of Britain. A Day-by-Day Chronicle* (London: Quercus, 2009), p. 298.
7. There were a number of battalions of the Somerset Light Infantry serving in the UK at that time; whichever unit was in Kent was possibly based at Shorncliffe: The 7th Battalion, 135 Infantry Brigade, was in the UK from September 1939 to September 1942; the 2nd Battalion, 160 Infantry Brigade, in the UK from September 1939 to June 1944; the 3rd Battalion, 159 Infantry Brigade, in the UK from September 1939 to June 1944; and the 4th Battalion, 113 Infantry Brigade, 43rd (Wessex) Infantry Division, in the UK from September 1939 to September 1942. Source: Bellis, Malcolm A., *British Armoured & Infantry Regiments 1939–45* (Crewe, Cheshire, privately published, no date). The 43rd (Wessex) Infantry Division was based in Kent and known as 'The Kent Home Guard'. Nigel West states that 2nd Lt. E. A. Batten, involved in the Kieboom arrest, was in the 6th Bn, also Pte Tollervy ('D' Company); Pte Chappell (16th Platoon), and Cpl. Goody (10th Platoon) were in the 5th and 6th Bns. (West, *MI5*, pp. 244–245).
8. TNA KV2/1491.
9. TNA KV2/1491.
10. Ministry of Economic Warfare. Transcript of shorthand notes of A. Giles, HM Treasury, of interview with Samuel Stewart on 10 June 1941, extracted on 16 September 1944. Stewart

had been working for Schuchmann since approximately the early 1930s as a shipping agent. Information in the Schuchmann file, TNA KV2/1491.

11. TNA KV2/742. See also Chapter 8, note 26, and Chapter 15, note 2.
12. TNA KV2/742.
13. There is an announcement in *The Daily Banner of Greencastle*, Indiana, dated Monday January 8 1940 which states: 'Miss Margaret Moseley returned to Bloomington Saturday to resume her studies at Indiana University after spending the holidays with her parents Mr and Mrs W.H. Moseley, 608 Ridge Avenue.' An announcement in *The Daily Banner of Greencastle*, Indiana, dated Tuesday September 3 1946, states that: 'Mr and Mrs William Henry J. Moseley of Santa Barbara, California, announce the marriage of their daughter Margaret, to Harry Joseph Krade at Cleveland, Ohio on Saturday, August 25th. The Moseley family formerly resided in Greencastle and Margaret is a graduate of DePauw University and a member of Kappa Alpha Theta. After September 5th the couple will be at home at 1505 Alameda Padre Serra, Santa Barbara, Cal.' The address of 608 Ridge Avenue is the same address to which Meier's letters were sent. There is also a Margaret Moseley of Springfield, IL, listed on p. 187 of the *Mirage Yearbook*, Class of 1935.
14. R. H. Blundell was the author, with R. E. Seaton, of 'The Trial of Jean Pierre Vaquier' in: *The Howard Journal of Crime and Justice*, vol. 3, issue 1, pp. 92–117, September 1930, and an editor of the pamphlet *Notable British Trials and War Crimes Trials* (Edinburgh: William Hodge & Co. Ltd, 1954).

24: 'The Kent Spies' on Trial

1. Sir (William) Bentley Purchase (1890–1961), Coroner for St Pancras district, would later feature in *Operation Mincemeat*, obtaining a body to pose as 'Major William Martin'.
2. TNA KV2/1452.
3. At that time he was living at 58 Suttons Road [*sic*], Maidstone. The *London Gazette* for 30 October 1953 has a Horace Rendal Mansfield, general and precision engineer of Rendal Engineering Co., as living at 92 Haydons Road, Wimbledon, London SW19, and owing the sum of 20s (£1) to the Official Receiver's Office.
4. Humphreys had written a thorough report on the radios dated 5 September 1940. The report lists him as Inspector, RSS, which is taken to mean Radio Security Service.
5. Major Seymour Bingham (b. 1898–?), later Head of N (Dutch) Section, SOE, March 1943.
6. TNA KV2/1452 applies to all preceding references to the code book.
7. TNA KV2/1452.
8. Robert Churchill (1886–1958). Owner of a firearms company of the same name in London; also associated with Sir Bernard Spillsbury. Regarded as Home Office firearms expert. Author of *Game Shooting* (1955).
9. *R v. Meyrick and Ribuffi*, 1929, *Criminal Appeal Reports*, volume 21, p. 102: Conspiracy is 'a difficult branch of the law, difficult in itself, and sometimes even more difficult in its application to particular facts or allegations' and it is: ' … necessary that the prosecution should establish, not indeed that the individuals were in direct communication with each other, or directly consulting together, but that they entered into an agreement with a common design. Such agreements may be made in various ways.' [Court: CCA; Date: 01-Jan-1929; Judges: Lord Hewart CJ; References: (1929) 21 Cr App R 94, (1929) 45 TLR 421] http://swarb.co.uk/rex-v-meyrick-and-ribuffi-cca-1929/
   This case is cited by Williams, J. E. Hall, 'Blanket Charges of Conspiracy in the Criminal Law' in: *Modern Law Review*, vol. 23, No. 4 (July 1960), pp. 432–34.
10. Levine, Joshua, 'The Unlikely Story of the German Invasion Spies', https://levinehistory.wordpress.com/2014/06/
11. It was suggested in an article in *Prison Service News* that Pons had turned 'queen's evidence' [*sic*]! Not only is this unsubstantiated, and there is no record in the official transcripts of the trial that he did so, but it was King George VI who was on the throne, so it would have been king's evidence. http://archive.is/Nijq5. This allegation is also included in 'German Spies in Britain', *After the Battle* magazine, 1976, p. 16.
12. Levine, Joshua, 'The Unlikely Story of the German Invasion Spies'.
13. TNA KV2/1452.
14. TNA KV2/1452.

15. Bliss's long article for the *Sunday Express* – catchline 'The Kent Spies' – is in Pons's file, KV2/1452.
16. TNA KV2/1452.
17. TNA KV2/1452.
18. TNA KV2/1452.
19. TNA KV2/13.
20. TNA KV2/13.
21. The obligation to affix a notice to the prison doors of an intended execution is statutory and arises from the Criminal Punishment Amendment Act, 1868. In 1902 the Home Secretary made a rule that the notice must be affixed to the doors of the prison not less than twelve hours before any execution takes place, and must remain there until the inquest on the executed person has been completed. (Taken from an MI5 document dated 28 November 1940.)
22. TNA HO144/21472.
23. TNA KV2/1699.
24. There were numerous internment camps established on the Isle of Man: Douglas – Hutchinson Camp (July 1940 – March 1944); Ramsey Camp (Mooragh) (May 1940 – September 1945); Knockaloe (1939 – 1945); Onchan Camp; Douglas – Central Camp; Douglas – Metropole; Douglas – Regent; Douglas – Granville; Douglas – Palace; Douglas – Sefton Camp; Port Erin, Port St Mary – Rushen Camp; Peel – Peveril Camp; No. 171 Prisoner-of-War Camp (disbanded March 1945). It is not known to which camp Maxwell was referring. However, the Liddell Diaries, vol. 1 refer to The Old Parsonage at Hinxton, Cambridgeshire, as 'The Home for Incurables' (p. xv). Lingfield was in operation 1940–1945. Hinsley (vol. 4, 221n) notes that Camp WX was used for detainees at Camp 020; however, it was only in operation from 1941 to September 1942 when it was moved to Dartmoor.
    Source: http://www.airfieldinformationexchange.org/community/show thread.php?6891-WWII-Internment-Camps-in-the-Isle-of-Man and: www. manxnationalheritage.im/wp-content/.../CG4-Internment_Web.pdf.
25. Levine, 'The Unlikely Story of the German Invasion Spies'.
26. Wing Commander J. A. Dixon; on 28 March 1939 he was listed as Air Attaché. See: *Air Force List* (London: HMSO) June 1940, p. 71.

25: The Self-Confessed Agent

1. TNA KV2/1145, citing FO File C.19377.
2. Frederick Gerth van Wijk's sister Selina (1913–1985) had married Lord Rhidian Crichton-Stuart (1917–1969), younger son of the 4th Marquess of Bute, on 20 July 1939 at St James's Church, Spanish Place, London. A wedding announcement in the *Glasgow Herald* for 14 July 1939 gives Selina's age as twenty-six. All documentation relating to Selina Crichton-Stuart in van Wijk's MI5 file was destroyed by MI5 on 6 February 2002.
3. TNA KV2/1145.
4. TNA KV2/1145.
5. TNA KV2/1145.
6. TNA KV2/1145.
7. TNA KV2/1145.
8. The M/V *Taanevik* had arrived in Wick, Scotland, on a spying mission from Norway on 27 April 1941 with Bjarne Hansen, Hans Hansen, Henry Torgersen and Johan Strandmoen, sent by Carl Andersen; all of them were sent to Camp 020. See: Stephens, *Camp 020*, pp. 162–163.
9. TNA KV2/1145.
10. TNA KV2/1145.
11. TNA KV2/1145.
12. TNA KV2/43.
13. TNA KV2/43.
14. TNA KV2/43.
15. TNA KV2/43.
16. TNA KV2/1145.
17. TNA KV2/1145.

18. Robin W. Pay, Arthur Pay's grandson, wrote that his grandfather had travelled to Holland and played with such jazz 'greats' as saxophonists 'Kid Dynamite', real name Ludewijk Arthur Parisius (1911–63), and Coleman Hawkins (1904–69), although being dark-skinned he had a problem being allowed to play. His father, also named Arthur, was a mining engineer who had discovered bauxite in Surinam in 1915, and his mother was of African and Indian descent. Source: http://sussexhistoryforum.co.uk/index. php?topic=2741.0;wap2 (link now not accessible).

26: Three Men in a Boat

1. A report by Col. Robin Stephens, Commandant of Camp 020, known as a 'Yellow Peril' because of its colour and dated 25 April 1942, cites an MI6 CX report, 12650/9142 V.B.4, dated 24 April 1942 that identifies Japs [*sic*] as Schulz.
2. TNA KV2/2736.
3. TNA KV2/2736 does not include a list of these personnel.
4. TNA KV2/2736.
5. Owned by Schipper, August 1952; formerly owned by the Java-Sumatra Handel Maatschappij, NV (1942) and John P. Mast (1946). He also owned the *Cinderella* (August 1952).

27: 'The Greatest Living Expert on Security'

1. West, *Historical Dictionary of British Intelligence*, 1st ed., p. 423.
2. Nash, J. Robert, *Spies: A Narrative Encyclopedia of Dirty Tricks and Double Dealing from Biblical Times to Today* (New York: Evans & Company, 1997), p. 191.
3. *Ibid.*, p. 193.
4. *After the Battle* magazine, Issue 11, 1976, p. 14.
5. Foot, M. R. D., *SOE in the Low Countries* (London: St Ermin's Press, 2001), pp. 398–399.
6. Moran, Christopher, *Classified. Secrecy and the State in Modern Britain* (Cambridge: Cambridge University Press, 2013), Ch. 3, p. 117.
7. Pinto, Oreste, *Spycatcher* (London: Werner Laurie, 1953), 6th impression, p. 81.
8. The quote was attributed originally to Edmund Burke in 1796: 'Falsehood and delusion are allowed in no case whatever: but, as in the exercise of all the virtues, there is an economy of truth.'
9. Nash, *Spies*, p. 193.
10. See: https://www.justice.gov.uk/.../psi_2010_51_dealing_with_evidence.doc as an example guide.
11. TNA KV2/44, Dronkers file. I have not been able to confirm the origin of the article.
12. Lieutenant-General of Infantry Kurt Oskar Heinrich Ludwig Wilhelm von Tippleskirch (1891–1957).
13. Obergruppenführer Johan Baptist Albin Rauter (1895–1949). Generalkommissar für das Sicherheitswesen (State secretary for security forces) and Höherer SS-und Polizeiführer (Highest SS and Police leader). Executed by the Dutch.
14. According to an article by Ladislas Farago in the *St Petersburg Times* (Florida) on 4 February 1953 about the American spy William G. Sebold, Nicholas Ritter was the head of the spy school. The same article also appeared in the 28 January 1955 edition of the *Daily Sentinel* (Rome, New York). This article also mentions that it was extracted from Farago's book *A War of Wits. The Anatomy of Espionage and Intelligence* (New York: Funk & Wagnall, 1954). Sebold was part of the thirty-three-member Dusquesne Spy Ring.
15. Farago, Ladislas, *Burn After Reading. The Espionage History of World War II* (New York: Walker & Co., 1961), p. 55.
16. Breuer, William B., *Deceptions of World War II* (New York: John Wiley & Sons Inc., 2001), p. 7.
17. Breuer, William B., *Daring Missions of World War II* (Castle Books, 2005). (No pagination in the version accessed online).

Postscript

1. Anna Wolkoff (1870–1954) was a White Russian and member of the Right Club who was opposed to the war against Germany and conspired with Tyler Kent (1911–88), a cypher clerk at the American embassy in London, to subvert the course of the war by supplying Germany with secrets obtained from Kent and Right Club members. Also implicated was Sir Archibald Maul Ramsay, MP (1894–1955). See: Clough, Bryan, *State Secrets. The Kent-Wolkoff Affair* (Hove: Hideaway Publications, 2005).
2. Seaborne Davies, D., 'The Treachery Act, 1940', p. 218.
3. 'German Spies in Britain', *After the Battle* magazine, Issue 11, 1976, p. 12.
4. There are two mentions of Dijkstra/Dykstra at the beginning of the MI5 file on Schipper (KV2/2736); unfortunately, neither document now exists, having been destroyed at some unknown date. These were a telephone message from Camp 020, dated 14 September 1942, regarding the identification of Dykstra by Schipper, and a message from Camp 020, dated 15 September 1942, regarding information on Grootveld and Dykstra. Guy Liddell reported in his diary: 'The Royal Victoria Patriotic School reports two spies, Dykstra and Grootveld, who arrived in a party of twelve Dutch escapees. Pieter Schipper ... has recognized these people as German agents from Ymuiden. Grootveld appears to have communicated with one of the ISOS trawlers which has recently been operating in Skategatt.' (Liddell, Vol. 1, p. 300) It was reported that Pieter Grootveld (1888–1986), skipper of the trawler (spy ship) KW 110 (Katwijk 110), and Dijkstra came across to England on 29 August 1942 aboard the ship and landed in West Hartlepool. Dijkstra was a *V-Mann* (name also given as Johannes A). Along with Grootveld and Schipper, he was interned at a camp on the Isle of Man for the duration of the war.
5. TNA KV2/43.
6. TNA KV2/1150.
7. TNA KV2/1931.
8. TNA KV2/1931.
9. Johannes A. Dykstra, deported back to Holland on 2 July 1945.
10. TNA KV2/1931.
11. See Appendix One; also: http://www.josefjakobs.info/2015/04/tl-winn-dentist-and-interrogator-at.html.
12. TNA KV2/1931.
13. TNA KV2/1931.
14. TNA KV2/1931.
15. TNA KV2/1931.
16. TNA KV2/1931.
17. TNA KV2/1931.
18. TNA KV2/1931.
19. Friedland, Martin L., *Cases and Materials on Criminal Law and Procedure* (Toronto: University of Toronto Press, 1978), 5th edition, reprinted 1980, pp. 387–388, citing Kennedy, John de Navarre, *Aids to Jury Charges: Criminal*, 2nd edition, 1975.
20. *Ibid.*, p. 388.

Appendix 2

1. Andrew, *Defence of the Realm*, p. 117.
2. Curry. *The Security Service*, pp. 203–205.
3. *Ibid.*, pp. 215–217.
4. *Ibid.*, p. 321; further details are included on pp. 321–323.
5. Clayton, Anthony, *Forearmed. A History of the Intelligence Corps* (London: Brassey's, 1993), 1st English edition, reprinted 1996, p. 268.
6. Unpublished manuscript by Alan F. Judge, Senior Researcher, Intelligence Corps Museum, Chicksands.

Appendix 3

1. TNA KV2/46.

2. *The Medical World*, vol. 7, p. 432; *Canadian Practitioner*, 1890, vol. 15, p. 11 (formerly *The Canadian Journal of Medical Science*).

3. Dr Peter Magirr. Personal communication.

4. Wikipedia: http://en.wikipedia.org/wiki/Phenolphthalein. This is confirmed in: Mackrakis, Kristie, *Prisoners, Lovers and Spies: The Story of Invisible Ink from Herodotus to al-Qaeda* (New Haven, CT: Yale University Press, 2014), p. 196: 'When he [J. W. McGee, a chemist at the FBI's technical laboratory in Washington] placed the handkerchief over the ammonium hydroxide, like magic, red writing began to appear before the eyes of the jury and the attorney general. The red color and developer meant that the chemical substance was phenolphthalein, an ingredient still used in laxatives.' [Military commission held 8–31 July 1942]

5. www.paperlessarchives.com/FreeTitles/GermanSaboteursMI5Files.pdf

Appendix 6

1. *Encyclopedia Britannica*, 1771.

2. *Convention (II) with Respect to the Laws and Customs of War on Land and its annex: Regulations Concerning the Laws and Customs of War on Land.* The Hague. 29 July 1899. Ch. II, Article 29. www.opbw.org/int_inst/sec_docs/1899HC-TEXT.pdf.

3. *Convention (IV) respecting the Laws and Customs of War on Land and its Annex: Regulations concerning the Laws and Customs of War on Land*, Section II, Hostilities, Chapter II, Article 29, Spies.

4. https://www.mi5.gov.uk/home/about-us/what-we-do/the-threats/espionage/espionage-and-the-law.html.

5. Dictionary.com.

Index

Abwehr:
  Ast Berlin 296
  HQ Berlin 296
  Abwehrstelle:
    Ast Niederlande 75, 301
    Hamburg 4, 50, 74, 76, 78-81, 83, 87,
      181, 263, 291-292, 296
    Paris 222
  Nebenstelle:
    Huelva 19
    Mellila1 9
    San Sebastian 19
    Tetuan 19
  Nest Bremen 41, 87, 263, 299-300
  see also German Intelligence Services
Acts of Parliament (UK):
  Aliens Order 1920, The 126, 158, 200,
    220, 225
  Allied Powers (War Service) Act 1942,
    The 122
  Anti-terrorism, Crime and Security Act
    2001, The 287
  Capital Punishment (Amendment) Act
    1868, The 74
  Crime and Disorder Act 1998, The 30
  Criminal Appeal Act 1907, The 166
  Criminal Justice Act 1967, The, 23, 30
  Defence Regulation 18B 23
  Emergency Powers (Defence) Act 1939,
    The 23, 25
  Emergency Powers (Defence) Act 1940,
    The 23, 286
  Human Rights Act 1998, The 31
  Official Secrets Act 1911, 1920 and
    1939 236
  Poor Prisoners Defence Act 1930,
    The 131
  Treachery Act 1940, The 24, 26-7, 30-1,
    111-12, 127, 129-130, 133, 144, 167,
    174, 198-9, 205, 210-11, 215-7, 223,
    234-6, 240, 243, 283, 387, 310
  Treachery Act (End of Emergency) Order
    1946, The 30
  Treason Acts 1351, 1495, 1695, 1702,
    1708, 1814, 1842, and 1848, The
    25, 287

Adam, Lieutenant Colonel John H. 54, 249,
  257, 258
Adams, Thérèse 225
Allchin, Detective Sergeant William 196
Amsterdam see Netherlands, The
Anderson, Sir John 25-7, 236, 287, 297
Andrew, Christopher 126-7, 227, 281,
  303, 311
Anti-terrorism Act (Canada) 2001 287
Archer, Lord, of Sandwell 30
Arents, Captain Henri, see FATHER 292
Asquith, Mr. Justice 166-7,174
Atkinson, Major Sir Edward Hale Tindal 35,
  210, 253

Baisey, Mrs Nelly, see Basey
Barr, Rev. James, 28
Basey, Mrs Nelly, see Baisey 37, 289
Batten, 2nd Lieutenant Eric Arnold 189,
  192, 306
Battle of Britain, The 89,186, 235, 306
Becker, SS-Obersturmbahnnführer August,
  see also Bucking 41, 222, 238-9
Beekema, Dolly, see Peekema Dibbets, Dora
Beekema, Willy 110
Belgium:
  Antwerp 96, 98-9, 105, 109, 114,127-8,
    216, 291, 299
  Brussels 14, 96, 98-9,101-4, 109, 189,
    196, 301
  Customs 97-100,104
  Liege 54
  Mons 96-8
  Polygom, 98-9,105
  Wernhout 97, 99-101,106,109, 274
  West Wezel 97
  Zundert, 97,100, 274, 300
Benson, George 27
Bergemeyer, Hoib 83, 296
Bevan, Colonel John 32
Bieber, Lulu,
  married to Herbert Wichmann 79
Bilbao 19, 53, 83, 222, 285
Bingham, Miss L 88, 249
Bingham, Seymour 193, 208, 249, 256, 307
Bischoff, Johannes W. 87, 296, 298-9

Bisschop, Witzje 96-101, 299-300
Black, Edgar 30
Black Market 42-5, 47, 67-8, 95,101,106,
    114-15,134,137,140-1,145,148-
    49,157,168,173,215, 230-1, 245
Bletchley Park, see Government Code &
    Cypher School
Bliss, William Kerr 204, 307
Blitz, The 188, 235
Blundell, Mr. 192, 306
Blunt, (Sir) Anthony 22,126
Bornheim, Dr. Ernst 40-2
Bonsall, Arthur 52, 292
Börressen, Jörgen 84
Breuer, William 233, 298, 310
Bridges, Inspector Frank 116,
    123,129,139,144,189,196, 201,204,
    252, 270
Briscoe, Henry Vincent Aird 253
British Army:
    Intelligence Corps 5-6, 8,17,61-2,
        85,130,133,136-7,156, 214,
        247, 249-52, 258, 296, 301, 303,
        305, 311
        123 Field Security Section (FSS) 5-6,17
        138 Field Security Section (HPSS), 258
    Royal Engineers 192, 251
    Somerset Light Infantry 189,192, 306
British Intelligence, see GC&CS, MI5,
    MI6, SIS
Brixton Prison 11,120, 204-6, 272
Brooke-Booth, Captain Septimus Paul 117-8,
    249, 258
Brookes, Ann
    wife of Pinto 226
Bruining, Boy
    and Mulder 96,101,105,110
BRUTUS (Garby-Czerniawski, Roman)
    39-40, 281
Bucking, see Becker, 222
Bundesnachtrichtendienst (BND) see
    German Intelligence Service, 76
Bunstone, George Frederick 193
Burgess, Guy Francis de Moncy 22
Burgwal, Rudy 64,101,106,110, 293, 300
Burt, Superintendent Leonard 13,120, 227,
    256-7
Buswell, Detective Sergeant Stanley 196
Bute, 4th Marquess of 208, 308
Butler, Colonel R. 21,131, 249
Büttner, Elisabeth 181, 304
Byrne, (Sir) Lawrence A. 132-6,138-
    141,144-5,148-56, 166, 192-4, 253

Café Atlanta 45, 57, 226
Café Brastagi 95,101,104,106-7,110,
    275, 299
Café Mayer 59, 67-8
Café Prinses 42
Caldecote, Viscount, (Thomas Inskip) of
    Bristol, see Lord Chief Justice 166-7, 253
Camp 020, see Latchmere House

Canaris, Admiral Wilhelm 21, 82, 88,
    232, 301
Cannon, T/Lieutenant Clifford Kennard 5,
    17, 61,130-1,133,136, 232, 252, 285, 303
Canterro, Don Lopez Pablo, see PABLO
Caroli, Goesta, see SUMMER
CELERY, see Dicketts, Walter 48, 81
Central Criminal Court, see Old Bailey
Central Intelligence Agency (CIA) 7, 76,
    295, 300
Chapman, David 30
Chapman, Eddie, see ZIGZAG 13,182, 305
Chappell, Private Arthur Richard 306
Cheney, Christopher Robert 249, 258
Chenhalls, Joan (MI5) 185, 225, 249
Chidson, Major Montague 'Monty' Reany
    125, 303
Cholmondeley, Flight Lieutenant Charles 47,
    229, 249
Churchill, Robert, 197, 307
Churchill, Winston 23, 25, 35,131,186,199,
    230, 234-5, 255, 258, 284
Clayton, G.F. 204, 206
Clegg, M.H. 249
Clevers 240
Cohen, Mr 37
Coke, Sir Edward 23, 286
Cole, Mabel 188
Cologne 39-42, 69, 190
Combined Services Detailed Interrogation
    Centre (CSDIC) 7-8, 85, 292
Cookridge, E.H. (Edward Spiro) 73,
    231-3, 294
Cooper, Alfred Duff 128, 216, 253
Corin, Captain Edward John Ronald 121-2,
    126, 184, 249
Cowgill, Colonel Felix Craig Christopher 21,
    249, 305
Crichton-Stuart, Lord Rhidian, 208, 308
Crichton-Stuart, Selina (*née* Van Wijk) 308
Cruickshank, Lt. James Ian 130, 136, 252
Crusader tank 47
CSDIC (see Combined Services Detailed
    Interrogation Centre, MI19) 7-8, 85, 292
Curry, John 32, 227, 255-6, 281, 285-6, 311
Cussen, Major (later Lieutenant Colonel)
    Edward James Patrick 69, 76, 129,
    223, 249

Davids, David 19, 31, 220, 222, 225, 237
Davidson, M. 249
Davies, David Seaborne 26, 234, 236, 283,
    287, 310
Day, 2nd Lieutenant J.P. de C. (John Day)
    112-13, 124, 223-4, 242, 245, 250,
    260, 270
Dearden, Dr. Harold Goldsmith 65, 250
Defence Regulation 18B, see Acts of
    Parliament 23, 312
de Laeren, J.W. 67
de Langen, Bruno Jan
    father of de Langen, Jan Bruno 17

de Langen, Jan Bruno:
  arrest 17
  birth of 17, 115
  death of 248
  and Dronkers 55, 57
  Engelandvaarders 247
  joins Prinse Irene Brigade 116
  and Radio Oranje broadcast 70-2, 115,
    230
  release 114
Derksema, Captain Robert Pieter Jan 117-
  19, 125, 173, 252, 302
Deutsch, Arnold 22
Deuxième Bureau
De Vries, Major Reginald 'Rex' Fallows 5-6,
  54, 56, 61, 116, 130-1, 133-4, 136-7,
  148-9, 156, 159, 165, 167-8, 172, 220,
  246, 250, 258
de Weert, Dr. A. 100-1, 274, 300
Dicketts, Walter, see CELERY 48, 81
Dieppe 51-2, 88, 116, 292, 298
Dierks, Hilmar 80-1, 263, 283, 295, 297
Dijkstra, Johannes Jacobus 238, 310
Director of Public Prosecutions (DPP) 8, 35,
  112, 129, 175, 205, 207, 209, 212-15,
  224, 238, 247, 253
Dittel, Dr. Paul 85
Donovan, William 'Wild Bill' 182
Double-Cross Committee, see Twenty
  Committee 9, 32, 239
Dr. Becker, see Becker,
  SS-Obersturmbahnnführer August, and
  Bucking 41, 222, 238-9
'Dr. Hamkens', see 'Dr. Hampkus' 39-40, 42
'Dr. Hampkus', see 'Dr. Hamkens' 39-40, 42,
  69, 81
'Dr. Korrell' 222
Dr. Pietsch 75, 295
Dr. Rantzau, see Ritter, Nikolaus 74, 80, 87
'Dr. Schneider' 45-6, 48-9, 53, 64, 68, 74-8,
  80, 84, 89, 123, 135, 140-1, 145, 147-8,
  150-1, 153-5, 159, 168-9, 218, 230,
  294-5
'Dr. Schneiderwind' 76
Dronkers, Johannes 12
Dronkers, Johannes Marinus
  appeal of verdict 162-171
  arrest 17, 19
  birth of 36
  and black market 42-5, 67-8, 134, 137,
    140-1, 145, 148-9, 168, 173, 215, 230-
    1, 245, 290
  confession of 69, 90, 97, 113, 125, 135,
    154, 156-7, 170, 173
  and Dr. Hampkus 39
  and 'Dr. Schneider' 45-9, 53, 64, 68, 80,
    123-4, 135, 140-1, 145, 147-151, 153-
    5, 159-60, 166, 169, 172-3, 218, 230
  employment 36-8, 42
  escape from Netherlands 54-62
  execution 173-4, 177-8

family tree 280
  in London 36-7
  interrogations by MI5 37, 45, 53, 58, 62, 67,
    80, 89, 124, 127, 141, 183, 185, 213, 243
  marriage to Seignette, Elise Antoinette
    Eleonora 37
  parents 36
  post-mortem 178
  and Radio Oranje broadcast 70-3, 134,
    138, 141, 150, 159, 175, 181, 226, 230
  recruitment 44
  and SIS Trace 37
  trial at Old Bailey 131-161
  and van Dongen, Karel (Carel) 18, 50, 69,
    72, 80-1, 284
  and Vas Dias 36-7
Dronkers, Marinus
  father of Dronkers, J.M. 36
Drücke, Theodore 80
Dutch East Indies (Java)
  Bandoeng 94
  Macassar 95
  Solo Seerakarta 17, 94
Dutch Intelligence:
  Bureau Nationale Veiligheid (Office of
    National Security (BNV)) 7, 227
  Centrale Inlichten Dienst (CID - WW2
    Dutch intelligence service) 7, 259
  Politiebuitendienst (Police Field Service) 227

Eisenhower, General Dwight D. 13
Erasmus, Abraham Janni 49, 238,
  240-2, 262
Erasmus, Jacobus Cornelis 49, 238,
  240-2, 262
European Convention on Human Rights
  (ECHR) 1953:
  6th Protocol (1983), Restriction of death
    penalty 30
  13th Protocol (2002), abolition of the
    death penalty in all circumstances 31
Evertsen, Cornelius 76-7, 295

'Fairhaven', see Harwich 5, 18, 258
Farago, Ladislas 232-3, 309-10
FATHER, see Captain Henri Arents 53, 284
Federal Bureau of Investigation (FBI) 8, 18,
  78-9, 182-4, 254, 259, 305, 311
Fidrmuc, Paul Georg, see OSTRO 52
Firmin, Sergeant 252
Fokkink, William H. 119-120, 302
Foot, M.R.D. 228, 281, 299, 309
Focke, Oberstleutnant Albrecht 40
Freeman, Miss G. 244, 311
Friedland, M.L. 132
Fuchs, Klaus 13-14, 33

GARBO, see Garcia, Juan Pujol 13-14, 33
Garbutt, J.L. 204
Garby-Czerniawski, Roman, see BRUTUS
  39-40, 281

Garcia, Juan Pujol, see GARBO 13-14, 33
Gedge, H.N. 174, 177, 253
German Intelligence Services:
  Abteilung Fremde Heere Ost (FHO), see
    Gehlen Organisation 76
  Abwehr 9-11, 18-22, 33-4, 39-41, 45, 48,
    51-4, 74-5, 79, 81-4, 87-9, 102-4, 123,
    125-7, 143, 148, 189, 220-1, 224, 232,
    236, 238-9, 242-3, 246, 250-1, 256,
    263, 283, 285, 289-91, 295-96, 299-
    301, 303, 305
  Bundesnachtrichtendienst (BND) 76
  Gehlen Organisation 76
  Gestapo (Geheime Staatspolitzei) 57, 73,
    76, 82-4, 101-2, 105-6, 110, 134, 137,
    140-3, 146-7, 160, 164, 168, 172-3,
    191-2, 195, 200-1, 209, 222, 230, 232,
    245, 296
  Reichssicherheitshauptampt (Reich Main
    Security Office, RHSA) 8, 85, 305
  Schutzstaffel (SS) 6, 9, 84-5, 116, 143,
    221-2, 225, 232
  Sipo (Sicherheitspolitzei, or Security
    Police) 9, 56
  Staatssicherheistsdienst (SD) 9, 50, 76, 85,
    143, 256, 305
Gibbs, Reginald D. 18-19, 182-3, 250
Gill, E.W.B. (Ernest) 20-1
Giskes, Hermann 75-6, 263, 281, 303
Glass, Ann Catherine (later Elwell) 82-3, 296
Glover, Robert Lawrence 252
Glyn, Sir Ralph, Bt. 27, 287
Goddard, Rayner, Lord 244
Godfrey, Vice-Admiral John 57, 252
Goodacre, Captain Eric Brereton 77, 250
Goody, Lance Corporal Reginald 192, 306
Government Code & Cypher School, see
  Bletchley Park 8, 20-1, 33, 52, 143, 250-1
Grew, Major B.D. 173-4, 177, 253
Griffiths, George 174, 179
Griffiths, Captain H.P. 131
Grobben, Jacobus Johannes 49, 238-9, 242,
  262, 281
Grogan, Alan 19, 250, 257
Gwyer, Major John 78-9, 250

hanging 30, 132, 172, 177-8, 238, 304
Harker, Brigadier Oswald Allen 'Jasper' 24,
  127-9, 131, 205, 215-16, 238, 250, 255
Hart, Herbert Lionel Adolphus 18-19, 250,
  256-7, 285
Harris, Detective Sergeant Bertram 116, 123,
  131, 139, 252
Harvey, Thomas Edmond 28-30, 243
Harwich: 14, 17, 54-8, 60-2, 71, 130, 133,
  136-7, 140, 143, 148, 158, 167-8, 214,
  229, 232, 250-2, 254, 258-9
  Dovercourt 4, 18
  'Fairhaven' 5, 18, 258
  HMS *Badger* 17
  Parkeston Quay 14, 17, 61, 130

history of 14
Hayles, Denis Henry 193
Haylor, Major E.R. or H.V. "Ronnie 18-19,
  44, 56, 63, 80, 125, 250, 257, 285
Hayward, James 48, 88, 281, 291, 294, 298
Head, C.B.V. 129, 131-2, 162, 165, 253
Hechevarria, Pedro 77
Hedger, Reginald Ernest 129, 138, 253
HEKTOR, see Krämer, Dr. Karl-Heinz 48
Hendon Airport 86, 206, 219, 225
Henny or Hennie, Susannah
  girlfriend of Mulder 72, 106, 274
Herrewyn, Sergeant Robert Henry Charles
  62, 130, 250
Hill, Bernard A. 185
Hilliard, Basil 176-7
Hinchley-Cooke, Lieutenant Colonel
  William Edward 46, 116, 123, 127, 129,
  131-3, 135, 138-41, 143-4, 160, 165-6,
  170-1, 173-5, 179-80, 184-5, 193-7, 204-
  6, 210, 212-13, 225-6, 258
Hindmarsh, Captain 119
Holt-Wilson, Sir Eric 24, 255
Home Defence (Security) Executive 9, 35,
  128, 254
Home Office:
  Aliens Department 111-12, 38, 119, 223,
    225, 242, 253
Home Port Security Section (HPSS) 8, 258
Hooper, Herbert 113, 124, 126, 173, 184, 204
Hooper, William John 125, 302-3
Horsfall, St.John Ratcliffe Stewart 'Jock'
Howard, Stephen Gerald 192, 198
Hughes, Captain 85, 257
Humphreys, Leonard William 193, 307
Humphreys, Travers Christmas 132, 166,
  174, 192, 195-6, 198, 201, 205, 236, 253

Inskip, Thomas, see Lord Chief Justice 166,
  253
Inter-Services Research Bureau, see Special
  Operations Executive 8, 18-19, 250, 285
Inter-Services Security Board (ISSB) 8, 51
'Invasion spies', see Kieboom, Meier, Pons,
  Waldberg
Invisible ink 49, 123, 129, 138, 149, 169,
  181, 260, 262
IRB 8, 18
ISK 8, 11, 18, 22, 143, 181, 246
Isle of Man:
  internment camps 187, 205-6, 308, 310
ISOS 8, 11, 21-22, 33, 102, 251, 256, 284-5

Jackson, F. 40, 42, 44-5, 57-8, 62-4, 66-7,
  70-1, 11, 123, 134-5, 141, 149, 159, 172-
  3, 218, 230-1, 250, 284
Jacobs, Jakob 31, 35, 296
'Jan' 42, 45, 56-9, 62-4, 68-9, 133, 137, 140-
  1, 148, 168, 184, 230, 243
Jansen, H. 37, 98, 100
Janson, Auk Hendrik 37

Jeffery, Lieutenant 85
Jeffreys, M.E. 250
Jones, R.L. 225
Johns, Commander Phillip 252
JOSEFINE, see Oxenstierna, Count Johann Gabriel 48
Jowitt, Sir William, see Earl Jowitt 187, 192, 197, 199-201, 253, 305
Joyce, William ('Lord Haw-Haw') execution 24, 131-3, 253

Kaya brothers 96, 273
Keitel, Field Marshal 88
Kendal, Sir Norman 201
Kieboom, Charles Albert van den execution 206 trial 192-201
Kielema, Jan 239, 241
Klatt, Henk 64, 95-6, 101, 107-8, 293, 299
Klever 37, 38-9, 44-7, 67, 135, 144, 151, 159, 240, 246, 280, 289
Klever, Cornelis Johannes, see Klever, J.C. 37-8, 280, 289
Klever, J.C., see Klever, Cornelis Johannes 37-8, 280, 289
Knock, Police Constable John Albert 130, 137-8, 149, 253
Knox, Alfred Dillwyn 'Dilly' 8, 22, 250
Koechling, Joseph 298
Koninklijke Marechaussee (KMar) 8, 67, 99
Koorn, Elisabeth mother of Seignette, E.A.E. 37, 279
Koppers 97-100, 104-5
Krag, Peter Marcussen 76-8, 295
Krämer, Dr. Karl-Heinz, see HEKTOR 48
Kratzer, Major 101-4, 281, 301
Kreigsmarine 8-9, 295
Kuchlin 91, 101, 107, 110, 114, 191, 298

Lacy, Montague 181
Landers, John Joseph 177, 253
Langdon, Major 204-5
Lapre, Nono and Mulder 274
Latchmere House, see Camp 020 7, 11, 18, 255-7
Lee, Mrs. K.G. 242, 253
Lefubure, Molly 177
Le Heux, Lieutenant Jan and Mulder 274
Lever, Mavis 22
Liddell, Captain Guy 13, 15, 22, 32, 80, 91, 102, 119, 127-8, 215-6, 227, 250-1, 256-7, 282, 284-5, 291, 297, 301, 303, 308, 310
Lindemanns, Christiaan ('King Kong') 228
Lisbon 50, 52-3, 91, 104, 123, 135, 139, 148-9, 181, 190, 208-10, 214, 221-2, 231, 236, 240, 292, 305
Lody, Carl-Hans 24, 286

'London Cage', see Combined Services Detailed Interrogation Centre (CSDIC) 7, 85-6
London Reception Centre (LRC) 8-9, 18, 56, 62, 116, 138, 153, 175, 224, 257, 285
Lord Chief Justice, see Caldecote, Thomas Inskip, Viscount of Bristol and Dronkers appeal 166, 174, 219, 244, 253

Macalister, Lieutenant 250
Macdonald, Miss 19, 250
Maclean, Donald Duart 22
McCarron, Patrick 30
McDonnell, Private James 192
McGrowther, Mrs. A. 205-6
McKinnell, Captain 72, 92, 108, 110, 112, 250
Maltby, Lieutenant Colonel E.F. (Ted) 21
Mansfield, Horace Rendel 188, 193, 204, 307
Marriott, John 32
Marseille, Captain 88, 95
Martherus, Lucia Geertruida Jansje: mother of Mulder, John Alphonsus 17, 94
Masterman, (Sir) John Cecil and Double Cross (Twenty) Committee 11, 32-3, 35, 239, 250, 282, 288
Maxwell, Sir Alexander 24, 201-3, 206, 308
Maxwell, Michael 129, 131-2, 136-8, 141, 143-5, 152, 154-8, 166, 170, 215, 235, 245, 253
Mayor, Tess 250-1
Meeuwsen 275
Meier, Carl Heinrich 53, 132, 186-9, 191-3, 196, 198, 200-6, 219, 228, 306
MEISSTEUFFEN, see Meiss-Teuffen, Hans von 40-1, 53, 190, 281, 284, 289-90
Meiss-Teuffen, Hans von, see MEISSTEUFFEN 50, 289
Milmo, Helenus Padraic Seosamh "Buster" 38-9, 47, 53, 80, 85-6, 92, 111-17, 119, 121-2, 126, 173, 184, 209, 216-7, 223-4, 236, 239, 242, 250
MI5, see Security Service 8-10, 13, 20, 32, 102, 113, 118, 121-2, 131, 134, 173, 185, 197, 202-3, 210, 227, 239, 255, 281-2, 284, 288, 297, 305, 307, 311
MI6, see Secret Intelligence Service 7, 9, 21, 255, 259, 303
Section V, Counter-espionage 21, 88, 183, 249, 285, 289, 305
MI8c, see Radio Security Service 8-9, 20, 251
MI19, see CSDIC (Combined Services Detailed Interrogation Centre) 7-8, 85
Moe, John, see MUTT 12, 34, 85
Mohle, Korvettenkapitän 296
Moor, Jannetje 36, 280, 283
Morren, Hendrik Jan 36, 280, 304

Morrison, Herbert 126, 172, 237, 253
Moseley, Margaret S. 191, 306
Mosley, Leonard 88
Mosley, Sir Oswald 234
Moussault, Gerard Jozeph Marie 37, 280
Muff, George 29
Mulder, Alex Avith:
　brother of Mulder, John Alphonsus 94, 299
Mulder, Johan Alphonsus:
　father of Mulder, John Alphonsus 17,
　94-5
Mulder, John Alphonsus:
　arrest in Belgium 97-8
　and black market 95, 101
　and Rudy Burgwal 64, 101
　and Hennie or Henny, Susannah 106
　and Henk Klatt 64, 95-6, 101, 107-8, 293
　and imprisonment 117-122
　and intelligence 276-278
　and North, Commander 101, 106-7, 141
　and Radio Oranje broadcast 70-72
　and secret organization 100, 104, 273-5
　and van Meerwijk, Stannie 72, 106, 108
Mulder, Mary:
　sister of Mulder, John Alphonsus 94
Mulder, Paul:
　brother of Mulder, John Alphonsus 94
Mulder, Rudi:
　brother of Mulder, John Alphonsus 94
Munter, Mrs 42
Mussert, Adriaan 227, 232
MUTT, see John Moe 12, 34

Nash, J. Robert 227, 230, 309
National Socialistische Beweging (NSB), see
　Nazi Party in The Netherlands 8, 43-4,
　46, 67, 143, 196, 227, 239, 246, 276,
　290, 301
Nauta, Felix Ruurd 273
Naval Intelligence Division (NID) 8, 62, 251
Navis, Mr. 275-6
Nazi Party in The Netherlands, see National
　Socialistische Beweging (NSB) 8, 43-4, 46,
　67, 143, 196, 227, 239, 246, 276,
　290, 301
Netherlands, The:
　Amsterdam 36-7, 42, 68, 75, 100, 185-6,
　220-2, 225-6, 248, 274, 289-290, 299
　Breda 96-7, 105
　The Hague (Den Hague) 17-18, 36, 38-9,
　42, 45, 54, 59, 62, 95-102, 106, 108-9,
　114, 125, 127, 139, 141, 148-9, 168,
　176, 181, 220-2, 232, 238-9, 241,
　247-8, 252, 266, 273-6, 278, 285, 289,
　298-303, 311
　Helder (Den Helder) 37, 278-80
　Hellevoetsluis 53-7, 59-60, 68, 140
　invasion of 48
　Leiden 38, 71, 95, 248, 279
　Nieuwe Sluis 57, 59, 68
　Nigtevecht 36, 174, 280

Rotterdam 37-8, 43, 45, 53, 55, 57-9, 81,
　96, 108, 115, 163-4, 184, 225, 238,
　279-80, 289, 300
Velsen 37, 279-80, 289
Voornsche Canal 54, 57, 62
Ymuiden (Ijmuiden) 36, 53, 163-4, 184,
　220-2, 310
Netherlands Shipping and Trading Company
　8, 120, 288
Newsam, (Sir) Frank Aubrey 114, 172, 175,
　237, 254
Nigh, Hendricus, see Nygh 292
Nol, Hans 105-6, 110
Noltes, J.M. 67
North, Lance Corporal Robert Henry
　192-3, 201
North, Commander
　and Mulder 101, 106-7, 110, 141
Nygh Hendricus, see Nigh 53-5, 57, 62-4,
　133, 140, 184-5, 230

O'Grady, Dorothy 31, 237, 288
O'Neill, James Cromwell 84, 296
Old Bailey, see Central Criminal Court 46,
　72, 131-2, 157, 192, 218, 238, 246, 259
Operation:
　Jubilee 51
　Lena 82
　Rutter 51
　Sea Lion 56, 81-2, 186, 295
Oratory Schools, see London Reception
　Centre 119, 208, 219, 224
Osborne, Mr. 119, 121, 250
OSTRO, see Fidrmuc, Paul Georg 52
Owens, Arthur, see SNOW 13, 20, 74
Oxenstierna, Count Johan Gabriel, see
　JOSEFINE 48

PABLO, see Canterro, Don Lopez Pablo 91,
　207-8
Paris 81-2, 88, 96, 98-9, 101, 109, 114, 181,
　222, 226, 295, 304
Passport Control Office (PCO) 8, 125, 252
Patriot Act (USA) 2001 287
Pay, Arthur 19, 31, 125, 220, 223, 225,
　237, 308
Payne Best, Captain Sigismund 125
Peake, Osbert 29, 254
Peekema Dibbets, Dora, see Beekema, Dolly
　101-4, 248 Peekema, Wibo Godfried 101,
　104, 300
Pentonville Prison 192, 200, 204-5
Petrie, Brigadier Sir David 127-8, 131, 175,
　216, 238-9, 251, 255
Pfeiffer, Erich 81-2, 189-90, 263, 281
Philby, Harold Adrian Russell (Kim) 22, 40,
　88, 126, 250, 282, 285, 289, 298, 303
Pierrepoint, Albert 177, 181, 254
Pieterse, Pieter Cornelius 36, 280, 304
Pinto, Lieutenant Colonel Oreste 13-14, 69, 75,
　80, 118, 218, 226-31, 252, 282, 284, 309

Pons, Sjoerd
Trial 132, 192-203
Popov, Dušan, see TRICYCLE 13
Praetorius 81, 87, 263
Prince Bernhardt 222, 288
Princess Juliana, 288
Protze, Kapitän Sur Zee Traugott Andreas Richard 102, 125, 281, 301
Purchase, Bentley 192, 306
Purser, Charles Richard 131, 254
Queen Wilhelmina 101, 116, 230, 293
Quin, Mrs. D.M. 126, 185, 225, 251, 262
Quisling, Vidkun 56

R v. Meyrick and Ribuffi 199, 307
Rachman, Abdul
and Mulder 274
Radio Oranje 64, 70-3, 108, 115, 134, 138, 141, 150, 159, 175, 180-1, 226, 230, 276, 294
Radio Security Service, see MI8c 8-9, 307
Ramsbotham, Peter Edward, 3rd Viscount Soulbury 182-3, 251, 258
Rathbone, Eleanor 26
Reber, Kapitänleutnant 85, 296
Richter, Karel 35
Riddell, J.A. 44, 67, 251
Ritter, Hauptman Nikolaus, see 'Dr. Rantzau' 48, 73-4, 78-81, 87, 232, 263, 281, 291, 294, 309
Robertson, Sergeant Frank George 193
Robertson, T.A. (Tommy) 20, 32, 223, 256-7
Robles, Silvio Ruiz 76-8, 295
Rogers, Rear Admiral Hugh Hext 17, 57, 62, 252
Roozemboom, Annette Abigael 226
Rothschild, Victor, Lord 250-1, 256-7
RAF (Royal Air Force) 47-8, 85, 89, 132, 163, 186, 188, 229, 235, 249, 292-4, 301
Royal Navy:
Director of Naval Intelligence (DNI) 33, 57, 62, 252, 290
HMS *Badger* 17
HMS *Icarus* 239
HMT *Corena* 17, 58, 61-2, 133, 136, 159, 252
Home Waters Fleet 17
Minesweeping & Patrol Group 4 17
Naval Intelligence Division (NID) 8, 63, 251
Nore Command 17
Royal Navy Reserve (RNR) 9, 17, 252
Royal Navy Volunteer Reserve (RNVR) 9, 62, 85, 131, 136, 251-2
Staff Officer (Intelligence) (SO(I)) 62
Royal Naval vessels:
HMS *Badger* 17
HMS *Gipsy* 14
HMS *Icarus* 239
HMT *Corena* 17, 58, 61-2, 133, 136, 159, 252

Royal Victoria Patriotic School (RVPS) 8-9, 18, 40, 42, 44, 57, 62, 71-2, 80-1, 90, 95-9, 101, 106-8, 111-13, 124-6, 141, 143, 149-51, 165, 175, 208, 218, 225, 227, 250-2, 257, 273, 276, 284
RSS, see Radio Security Service (MI8c) 8-9, 20-21, 257, 285, 307
Ryder, Lieutenant Colonel C.F. 119, 251

Sadell, Raden
and Mulder 101, 274
Saint-Quentin 96, 98
Salzedo, Samuel Lopez 138, 144, 254
Salzinger, Major Hans, see Major Hans Wagner 75, 281
Sampson, Major George F. 37, 251
Sands, 2nd Lieutenant R.S. 63-4, 71, 251, 255
Schellenburg, Walter 125
Schipper, Pieter Jan 19, 31, 49, 75, 185-6, 219-225, 235-9, 243, 246, 281, 309-10
Schmidt, Wulf, see TATE
Schneider, Dr 45-9, 53, 64, 68, 74-81, 83-5, 87-9, 123-4, 135, 140-1, 145, 147-8, 150-1, 153-5, 159-60, 168-9, 172-3, 218, 230, 263, 294-5
Schneider, Major Hans, see Major Hans Wagner 75
Schreckenberg, Josef 232
Schreieder, SS-Obersturmbahnführer Joseph 76, 101-2, 295
Schroeder, Erich Emil 50, 88, 189-91, 281, 290, 292
Schuchmann, Heinrich 40, 88, 189-91, 281, 290, 298, 306
Schule 231
Schumacher, Captain 223
Schutz, Gunther 87
Scotland Yard 46, 61, 91, 116, 123, 139, 185, 189, 196, 252, 256, 270
Special Branch 13, 116, 122, 139, 144, 189, 197, 201, 204, 252, 270
Scott, Police Constable Cecil Luke 137, 253
Secret Intelligence Service (SIS), see MI6 7, 9, 21, 255, 259, 303
Security Control Officer, Harwich (SCO) 62
Security Service, see MI5:
A Division:
Registry 258
B Division:
ADB1 7, 117, 126, 256-7
ADB2 256-7
ADB3 256-7
B1 Espionage 7, 117, 250, 256-7, 285
B1a Special Agents 7, 32, 47, 78, 85, 257, 242
B1b Espionage, Special Sources 7, 18, 53, 88, 118-19, 122, 124, 126, 190, 204, 223-4, 238, 249-51, 255-7, 270, 289
B1c Sabotage & Espionage, Inventions & Technical: Lord Rothschild 256-7

B1d Special Examiners 126, 193, 249, 251
B1e Latchmere House (Camp 020) 255, 257
B3d Censorship Liaison 7, 19, 250, 256-7
C Division:
    C2b 122, 251
    C4a 7, 225, 249
D Division:
    ADD4 256-7
    D4 7, 54, 249, 255-8
E Division:
    ADE 7, 126, 173, 180-1, 249, 252, 258, 274
    E1a 113, 117-18, 122, 124, 173, 184, 204, 249-51, 255, 258, 293
    E1b 8, 121, 184, 249, 255, 258
    E1c 126
    E4 119, 250-1
Legal section:
    SLA 258
    SLB 9, 126, 129, 131, 185, 249-51, 258
Security Branch (IB or I(B)) 7-8
Seignette, Benjamin Egbertus Cornelius father of Elise Antoinette Eleonora 37
Seignette, Elise Antoinette Eleonora (1) 37, 279-80
Seignette, Elise Antoinette Eleonora (2) (wife of Dronkers, Johannes Marinus)
    birth of 37
    death of 248
    family tree 279-80
    inheritance 38
    marriage to Dronkers, Johannes Marinus 37
Seignette, Hermine Louise
    sister of Elise Antoinette Eleonora 37
    wife of Klever, C.J. 37
Senter, Commander (Sir) John Watt 63, 126, 251
Serguieiw, Lily, see TREASURE 33
Seyss-Inquart, Arthur 43, 102, 301
Shepherd, N. 124, 251
Ships:
    'Joppe', yacht 17, 45, 53-4, 56-7, 59, 61-2, 68, 84, 89, 114-5, 124, 133, 136, 140-1, 174, 184, 231, 268-9, 271, 292
    S.S. *Brussels* 14
    S.S. *Hector* 36, 288
    S.S. *Kasima Maroe* 95
    S.S. *Medea* 36, 288
    S.S. *Zaanland* 302
    Sursum Corda, fishing boat 221-2
Sicherheitsdienst (SD), see German Intelligence Services 9, 50, 76, 85, 143, 305
Silverman, Samuel Sydney 28
Simon, Viscount 25, 287
Simon, Walter 87, 281, 297
Sinclair, D.H. 131, 251, 270

Sipkes, Sergeant Cor 111, 301
SIS, see MI6, Secret Intelligence Service 6-9, 21, 35, 37, 46, 52, 67, 94-5, 125-6, 131, 182-4, 194, 225, 249, 252, 255, 296, 302-3, 305
Smink, Gerrit 36
Smith, H.L. 120-1, 251-2, 254, 269
Smith, Reginald Charles 17, 130, 137-8, 149
Smith-Gordon, Lieutenant Sir Lionel Eldred Pottinger, Bt. 62, 252
SNOW, see Arthur Owens 13, 20, 33, 48, 74, 81, 294
Society of Engelandvaarders 247
Somervell, Sir Donald Bradley 29, 35, 129, 243, 253
Special Operations Executive (SOE), see Inter-Services Research Bureau 8-9, 34, 63-4, 75-6, 101, 126, 182, 228, 249-51, 259, 281, 285, 289, 299, 300-1, 307, 309
Speirs, Sergeant Robert Brown 61, 137, 251
Spies, definitions of 266-7
Stamp, Edward Blanchard 88, 119-21, 251, 270
Stanowsky, A. 185
Starziczny, Josef 84, 296
Stein, Hauptmann (Dr. Hille) 221
Stevens, Major Richard 125
Stephens, Colonel Robin William George 'Tin-Eye' 15, 44, 53, 64, 85-6, 90-3, 112, 116-7, 119, 124, 126, 128-9, 182, 208-9, 218-9, 224, 239-40, 245, 251, 256-7, 260, 282, 284, 289-90, 293, 302, 308-9
Stephenson, Sir William 182
Stewart, Sir Findlater 32, 86, 131, 306
Stimson, Major Douglas Bernard 'Stimmy' 72, 85-6, 119, 251, 260
Stockholm 48, 50, 53, 75, 123, 135, 149, 231, 291-2
Strachey, Oliver 8, 21-2, 251
Strauch, Kapitänleutnant Friederich Carl 75, 220-2, 230
Stumpff, Frederick 64, 101, 110, 293
Stumpff, Mrs 96-7, 106, 274
SUMMER, see Goesta Caroli 35
Suurmondt, barman at Café Brastagi 101, 106
Swinton, Lord 35, 123, 128, 202-3, 205-6, 254, 256, 288

Tas, Louis 295
TATE, see Schmidt, Wulf 12-13, 48, 52
Thomson, Rear Admiral Gordon Pirie 180, 254
Thurston, Arthur M.
and FBI 18, 182-4, 238, 254
Tielman & Dros 38
Tollervy, Private Sidney Charles 306
Treachery Act 1940, The, see Acts of Parliament
Treason Acts, see Acts of Parliament